Foxfire Reconsidered

JOHN L. PUCKETT

Foxfire
Reconsidered

A Twenty-Year Experiment in
Progressive Education

University of Illinois Press
Urbana and Chicago

For Louise

Publication of this work was supported in part by a grant from the Andrew W. Mellon Foundation.

This book is printed on acid-free paper.

Library of Congress Cataloging-in-Publication Data

Puckett, John L., 1947–
    Foxfire reconsidered : a twenty-year experiment in progressive education / John L. Puckett.
        p. cm.
    Includes index.
    ISBN 0-252-01574-6 (alk. paper)
        1. Appalachian Mountains, Southern—Social life and customs—Study and teaching (Secondary)—Georgia—Rabun Gap.   2. Folklore—Appalachian Mountains, Southern—Study and teaching (Secondary)—Georgia—Rabun Gap.   3. Progressive education—Georgia—Rabun Gap.   4. Journalism, School—Georgia—Rabun Gap.   I. Title.
F217.A65P83   1989
370′.9758′123—dc19   88-17106
                                                                                CIP

Contents

Acknowledgments

During the five years of research and writing required to bring this book to fruition, I have been assisted by hundreds of helpful people who shared my interest in Foxfire. Needless to say, this work would have been impossible without the cooperation of Eliot Wigginton and his Foxfire staff, who tolerated having me in their midst for a full year. Similarly, I would have made little headway without the support of the administration and faculty of Rabun County High School. I am deeply indebted to the many former Foxfire students who enthusiastically participated in the study, particularly Jan Brown Bonner, Paul Gillespie, Andrea Burrell Potts, Phyllis Carver Ramey, Rhonda Black Waters, and Barbara Taylor Woodall. I am also grateful to the Appalachian elders who invited me into their homes and shared with me their special perspectives on Foxfire.

I gratefully acknowledge the indispensable financial support provided for my research by the Mary Reynolds Babcock Foundation, the Graduate School of the University of North Carolina at Chapel Hill, and the Appalachian Center at Berea College, Kentucky. I also wish to thank Appalachian Research and Education Associates in Crossville, Tennessee, the nonprofit organization under whose aegis I conducted the research.

I owe an immeasurable debt of gratitude to Jonathan P. Sher of Rural Education and Development, Inc., for his indispensable advice and superb editorial assistance. Such was Jonathan's enthusiasm for the study that he wrote letters in my behalf to private foundations, shared with me his abundant insights about rural education and development, patiently counseled me at critical points in the field-work, and commented skillfully on various drafts of the manuscript.

Guy Larkins of the University of Georgia was of great assistance with the fieldwork, helping me to develop sampling strategies and interview questionnaires. Pete Schinkel provided an invaluable service by arranging my access to Eliot Wigginton's papers at the Georgia Department of Archives and History. For their competent and gracious assistance, I am also indebted to the librarians at the University of North Carolina at Chapel Hill and the University of Georgia.

I am especially grateful to Roberta Woolever, Samuel Holton, Wallace Hannum, and William Burke, all of the University of North Carolina at Chapel Hill, whose competent advice benefited my synthesis of the fieldwork and library research. Professor Holton also guided my analysis of John Dewey, directed me to the works of Erik Erikson, and provided a useful sounding board for my interpretations of Foxfire. The final version of the manuscript profited from a thorough review and critique by Alan DeYoung of the University of Kentucky and Loyal Jones of Berea College, both of whom enlightened me about Appalachian education. Of the many scholars and representatives of private and public agencies who shared useful information with me, I am particularly indebted to John P. Hill of Virginia Commonwealth University; John Gaventa of the University of Tennessee; Richard Coop of the University of North Carolina at Chapel Hill; Karl Mathiasen III of the Management Assistance Group; and Rita Spivey of the Appalachian Regional Commission.

Special thanks go to Judith McCulloh and Harriet Stockanes of the University of Illinois Press for all their help on editorial and legal matters related to the book. I wish to thank Carol Bolton Betts, my copy editor, for her careful scrutiny and adroit handling of the manuscript. I am grateful to Ruth Ebert of the University of Pennsylvania for donating her proofreading skills and for her unflagging good humor in the final stages.

For their superb and long-suffering assistance in helping me find information in the Foxfire files and locate former Foxfire students, I wish to thank Joyce Colburn and Ann Moore. The administration at Rabun Gap–Nacoochee School also lent timely support by allowing me to interview former Foxfire students at the school's annual homecoming.

For raising my spirits in the dark hours of the study, I express my gratitude to my close friends Kate Cathy, Jamie May, and Denise Layfield. Finally, I am especially grateful for the unstinted personal support and encouragement provided by my wife, Karin Schaller.

ONE

Introduction

Since its inception twenty years ago, Foxfire has become a popular and respected vehicle for the preservation and dissemination of southern Appalachian traditions and folk wisdom. Its thriving quarterly magazine and nine *Foxfire* books (with combined sales in excess of 6.7 million copies) attest to its role as the vehicle through which the larger society has learned about and come to appreciate native Appalachians—people whose lives belie the media image of the dumb, lazy hillbilly. Over the years, Foxfire has inspired over two hundred similar projects in schools across the United States and overseas, as well as a Broadway play bearing its name. Foxfire itself has grown from a tiny magazine project into a fully staffed, nonprofit organization providing a variety of educational services to high school students in the Georgia highlands.

Undergirding the production of Foxfire's anthologies of Appalachian folk culture is an educational process that embodies the pedagogy advocated by John Dewey early in the twentieth century. Under the tutelage of Eliot Wigginton, a high school English teacher, hundreds of young people in Rabun County, Georgia, have been engaged in "cultural journalism," a term for the collection and publication of local history and culture. In theory, the Foxfire educational program not only links the school life of students to their out-of-school experience in a meaningful way, but also gives them vital academic and personal growth skills. The assumption is that the interest in having their work come to fruition as published articles suffuses every phase of the students' endeavors (from collecting the information to compiling and editing manuscripts) with both a desire to learn and a willingness to work hard to produce quality publications on a regular basis.

The fact that rural mountain youngsters have played a significant role in the creation of a sizable publishing empire has been compelling enough to inspire hundreds of articles in newspapers, magazines, books, and educational journals—not to mention three dissertations. And yet, the striking feature of this burgeoning literature is its noncritical—indeed, "testimonial"—nature. Foxfire has been canonized by its many admirers who for years have lauded it with such accolades as "the light that lit up learning." Sweeping claims have been made about the virtues of "the Foxfire glow," but these claims have not been based upon a systematic consideration of Foxfire's day-to-day operations.

Originally *foxfire* was the Appalachian appellation for a luminescent fungus that grows in the damp forest undergrowth in this region. Twenty years ago, students at the Rabun Gap School adopted it as the name of the magazine that had originated in Eliot Wigginton's tenth-grade English classes. Subsequently, it became the name of Wigginton's learning concept, the name of his nonprofit educational fund, and a generic name for cultural journalism carried out at the secondary-school level.

Previous observers have capitalized upon the association of light and learning implicit in the name *Foxfire*. In the process of extolling Foxfire's "glow," these admiring chroniclers have created a legend that obscures as much as it reveals about the reality of Foxfire. Even the academics helping to write the "Foxfire story" have not bothered to examine carefully how Wigginton's ideas have actually translated into practice—either in Rabun County or elsewhere.

Being a Southerner interested in both the history of the region and the broad topic of educational reform, I was drawn to what Foxfire appeared to represent. My intent was not only to fill the vacuum that existed in terms of a serious consideration of Foxfire's strengths and weaknesses, but also to satisfy my own curiosity about the extent to which Foxfire could live up to its own extraordinary reputation.

Between November 1982 and June 1983, I negotiated with Eliot Wigginton to undertake a yearlong field study of Foxfire. It made sense, I argued, not to attempt to adjudicate Foxfire's success as a pedagogy but rather to specify precisely its theoretical underpinnings and program processes. I wanted to know how Foxfire worked, both as the embodiment of a learning concept and as an organization. Moreover, I wanted to know who its beneficiaries were and how they had benefited.

It made further sense to view the project in the context of education writ large. The story of Foxfire, as refracted through my own observations, my reading of the historical record, the voices of the participants themselves, and the more distant voices of John Dewey, Erik Erikson, Anna Freud, and other theorists, promised to be an intriguing endeavor. It certainly seemed more rewarding than designing an instrument to measure the extent to which Foxfire's cultural journalism activities improve students' writing skills. In short, I proposed to create a realistic *portrait* of Foxfire—rather than the kind of caricature that typifies the existing literature about this long-standing educational innovation.

Wigginton agreed with the propositions I had set forth. Public infatuation with the *Foxfire* books had run its course and sales were on the downturn. Without the royalties that had been its economic lifeblood, the organization would require a bolstering of its endowment. From Wigginton's perspective, an evaluation study might provide the evidence needed to convince private foundations that Foxfire was worthy of their financial support. In any case, my careful scrutiny would give the organization an outsider's appraisal of where it stood after twenty years of operation. Accordingly, I was the first researcher to be granted fully open access to Wigginton's staff, students, community contacts, and organizational documents. The study was born.

In the literature on how to conduct field research, ethnographers and other experts tout the virtues of "triangulation"—research that integrates an analysis of primary and secondary documents, systematic observations, and field interviews. The basic idea is that each component will serve as a check on the validity of the other two. Yet, this ideal is rarely emulated in practice. For all that one hears and reads about the dire necessity of triangulation in field research, the fact remains that precious few serious studies have ever been attempted in this genre. A notable exception to the rule of lip service to triangulation (and a model for my own research) is John Gaventa's remarkable book, *Power and Powerlessness* (University of Illinois Press, 1980), a scholarly (and provocative) sociological treatise on power relations in an Appalachian coal-mining valley. Gaventa conducted hundreds of interviews and synthesized this information with a plethora of documentary and observational evidence. My goal was to follow a research methodology similar to Gaventa's, which not only triangulated sources of information but also attended to Foxfire's historical, social, and economic contexts.

I began the field research on 4 January 1984. During the first phase of the study, I conducted five months' worth of observations at Rabun County High School, where Foxfire has been located since 1977. I also interviewed Foxfire staff, Foxfire students, other students and faculty at the high school, local school administrators, and guidance counselors. During the second phase, I spent two and a half months examining Foxfire's extensive records, perusing manuscripts, organizational correspondence, business and legal documents, plans for community development projects, funding proposals, and investment portfolios. I also investigated Foxfire documents at the Georgia Department of Archives and History. During the third phase I spent four and a half months identifying, tracking down, and interviewing young adults who had participated in Foxfire as high school students; Appalachian elders who had contributed information to the *Foxfire* publications; and political, business, and industrial leaders in the county. Throughout the entire year I also attended weekly Foxfire meetings as well as special organizational activities and community events. (Details of the methodology are explained in Appendix B.)

Like all research endeavors, mine has its share of flaws—not the least of which has been an unavoidable lag between the time I conducted the field study and the time I completed the final draft of the manuscript. Readers are reminded that my present-tense descriptions of Foxfire, unless otherwise indicated, are based on field notes taken in 1984. Unless otherwise documented, all quotations are from these notes.

I have entitled the study *Foxfire Reconsidered* because it is the first major attempt to dig beneath the hill of "hype" built over the twenty-year period during which Foxfire became a household word in the United States. It is also the first systematic attempt to explore its theoretical underpinnings and to link the theory and practice of Foxfire to a set of global issues and concerns in American education.

The study is divided into three parts. In the first part, I trace Foxfire's history from its origins to the present, focusing primarily on the evolution of its educational programs, with brief attention paid to its contributions to folkloric preservation. In the second part, I examine the issues and effects of Foxfire's operation at the level of the student, school, and community. In the final part, I have integrated the findings and conclusions of the previous two sections with relevant literature in educational history and philosophy, Freudian and other schools of developmental psychology, Appalachian studies, and educational reform. Here my intent has been to define Foxfire's place in American education and to determine its implications for educational theory, practice, and reform.

Any analysis compares whatever (or whoever) is being studied to either an explicit or an implicit standard. To answer the question, "What has Foxfire achieved?" I had to ask, "Compared to what?" My decision was to assess this innovation in terms of two exacting standards: (1) its own ideals, intentions, and potential; and (2) its national reputation as a model educational program. Had I chosen to evaluate Foxfire against the standard of conventional school practice in the United States, my report would have been entirely different—and far more effusive in its praise.

However, the more interesting question is whether Foxfire measures up to its own higher standards and lofty reputation. Is Foxfire's "success" a fluke—a happy accident of being in the right place at the right time—or is it the predictable result of an educational model others could, and should, emulate? Similarly, can Foxfire be dismissed as one of those innovations that can succeed only when implemented by unusually gifted and charismatic teachers (and therefore one that remains beyond the reach of more "ordinary" teachers in "ordinary" circumstances)?

Readers of my analysis of Foxfire, which might be called an "ethnohistory" (building on ethnographic and historiographic sources of information), should bear in mind that Eliot Wigginton and his staff allowed me to subject them and their organization to rather relentless scrutiny for a full year. My daily presence in their classes was not always easy for them, and at any time they could have requested that I pack my bags and leave Rabun County. Thus, my study was always vulnerable to being cut off before it was completed.

Yet the Foxfire staff was in a vulnerable position as well. They were taking a stranger into their midst—and, more important, into their confidence—with no real guarantee that the resulting study would be fair, accurate—or favorable. Given that Foxfire was at a major transition point in its history during the year I lived on-site, the situation was particularly delicate. Just as I was risking my study, so, too, they were risking exposing themselves to a potentially disruptive force at a critical juncture—as well as risking the possibility of an assessment that might diminish their prospects for attracting much-needed new sources of outside funding.

Happily for all concerned, this negative scenario did not come to pass. Although an appropriate distance was assiduously maintained (I did not end up, as the anthropologists say, "going native"), a good working relationship developed. Thus, while less ego-boosting than the rousing testimonials to which the Foxfire staff have become accustomed, my hope is that the following pages will yield a deeper understanding and a more realistic portrait of this important twenty-year-old educational experiment.

PART ONE

The Historical Context

TWO

The Rabun Gap Era: Origins and Early Growth

Throughout his childhood, Eliot Wigginton accompanied his father on weekend trips to the Betty's Creek Valley in Rabun County, Georgia. Eliot's father, Brooks Wigginton, a renowned landscape architect, was a close friend of Mary Hambidge, founder and spiritual leader of the Jay Hambidge Art Foundation, a sprawling 710-acre estate that encompassed forested hillsides and fertile bottomlands in the narrow, winding valley. The younger Wigginton spent much of his time on these outings exploring the woods and fields along Betty's Creek and getting to know the mountain people who worked for Mary Hambidge. His friendships with the last generation of southern Appalachians to have a firsthand knowledge of the traditional mountain culture provided both a touchstone and impetus for the educational experiment that Wigginton, as a twenty-four-year-old novice schoolteacher, embarked upon in 1966 at the Rabun Gap–Nacoochee School, just four miles southeast of the Hambidge Foundation.

Born in Wheeling, West Virginia, in 1942, Wigginton moved with his widowed father to Athens, Georgia, where the elder Wigginton had accepted a professorship in landscape architecture at the state university. Eliot excelled in the schools of Clarke County, Georgia, which he attended through the ninth grade. "I don't think we ever realized he wasn't anything but an excellent student as long as he was in Athens," his father has remarked. "We always thought he was very good."

This impression changed, however, after Brooks Wigginton sent his son north to attend (on scholarship) the Hill School in Pottstown,

Pennsylvania. Discovering that Eliot's educational skills were deficient, Hill School officials required him to repeat the ninth grade. According to his father, "He didn't realize until he got there and had to come up to Hill School standards that his education to this point really had some shortfalls."

Thus, Eliot Wigginton, in the fall of 1956, was ensconced in a prestigious private school whose graduates routinely gained admission to Ivy League universities. Yet he did not aspire to academic excellence. Humiliated by the administration's decision to enroll him as a freshman, he resented the school, floundered in his studies, and by the end of his sophomore year, lost his scholarship.

According to Wigginton, a single event catalyzed by an empathic teacher turned around his disappointing performance, motivated him to a high level of academic achievement at Hill, and added another experience that would guide his conceptualization of Foxfire: "Jack Tyrer, an English teacher whom I've never forgotten, was enthusiastic about a composition I had written for his class. He helped me polish it for submission to our school's literary magazine, and it was accepted and published. I think I watched every day for that magazine to appear, and when it finally did, I can still remember taking a copy to my room and sitting there alone, holding it, for what must have been an hour. . . . That single event—more than any other—changed my school career and had an indelible imprint on my life."[1]

By the time of his graduation from Hill, Wigginton had served as the chief editor of the literary magazine and news editor for the school newspaper; he had even written an extensive independent study on the principles of artistic design discovered by Jay Hambidge.[2]

Wigginton enrolled at Cornell University in the fall of 1960 as a premedical major; by the fall of 1963, however, he had changed his career plans, leaving the premedical program for the English department. Following his graduation from Cornell and a summer of travel and work at odd jobs in 1964, that fall Wigginton enrolled in Cornell's Master of Arts in Teaching (MAT) program in English, intent on becoming both a writer and a high school teacher. A journal entry from that era suggests Wigginton's ambivalence about his career plans: "At this point, all I know is that I *think* I want to teach either in the New York City or San Francisco area. Boston would also be nice. Something keeps saying Georgia (as always, it seems), but at this point, that remains an outside chance. If I'm going to write, I now know I can't split it with teaching. And since it looks like I'm going to teach, I might as well go whole hog teaching for several years, then write a book and quit. God knows."[3]

Wigginton graduated as the top intern in the MAT program, circumvented the military (and Vietnam) with a 1-Y draft status, and decided to seek a teaching position in Rabun County, Georgia. "I wanted to live in Rabun Gap," he has written. "That's all. No great sense of mission or purpose as far as a school and its students were concerned. No scheme playing like a symphony . . . in my mind. I wanted to live in that part of the country, and teaching was a legitimate way to get there and support myself."[4]

At the time Wigginton applied to the Rabun County Schools, there were no positions available for an English teacher at Rabun County High School. The superintendent, however, gave Wigginton's name to Morris Brown, the principal at the Rabun Gap–Nacoochee School—a private institution, with nearly one hundred boarding students, that also served as a public school for about one hundred forty day students from the rural communities in the northern section of Rabun County. Brown hired Wigginton sight unseen, having elicited favorable recommendations from the community people who had known him over the years. "He was the only teacher we ever employed without an interview," Brown recalls.

The Rabun Gap–Nacoochee School, a cluster of administrative, classroom, dormitory, and farm buildings, straddles several hillsides along the northern periphery of Wolffork Valley, traditionally a farming community. The school overlooks Highway 441, a four-lane thoroughfare that traverses the sprawling mountain gap for which the unincorporated area is named. Its view to the north includes Betty's Creek Valley, the diminutive town of Dillard, Georgia, and the mountains of Macon County, North Carolina.

Andrew Ritchie had founded the Rabun Gap Industrial School in 1905. A Rabun County native with a Harvard education, Ritchie had the enlightened idea of using the school as a vehicle for community economic development. With the help of Harvard president Charles W. Eliot, Ritchie located funding sources for the purchase and maintenance of approximately 1,800 acres of property on which to build his facility. When the school opened, it served as a day school for local Rabun Gap students and as a boarding school for county students who lived outside the Gap.[5]

In 1917 Ritchie instituted at Rabun Gap School the Farm Family Program, arguably the first example of a school-based economic development enterprise in the United States. Ritchie invited area tenant farmers to settle on the thirty or more farms that he marked out on the school property. With the help of school employees, the farmers built their own houses, barns, and outbuildings; Ritchie provided the building materials, livestock, implements, and seed. The farmers were allowed to keep all proceeds from their work, and their children were educated, with no tuition charges, at Rabun Gap School.

In exchange for the school's largess to the farm families, Ritchie required the farmers to attend night classes at which progressive farming techniques were taught by a Smith-Hughes Act agricultural expert. Rabun Gap School itself was self-supporting; the school raised its own crops, beef and dairy cattle, providing wage labor for the men and larger boys when their work was not required on their own boundaries.[6]

Each family was allowed to remain at the school for a period of five to six years. Unfortunately, there is no extant data to indicate how many of these farm families were able to maintain independent farms after their tenure at Rabun Gap School had ended. Suffice it to say that Ritchie's institution, far ahead of its time, became a model and demonstration site for international rural education and development.

In 1928, Rabun Gap School merged with the Nacoochee School, a Presbyterian-supported boarding facility near Cleveland, Georgia. During the Depression years the Farm Family Program thrived, and the school added a junior college, with an emphasis on teacher training.[7] The subsequent years witnessed several major changes in the operation of Rabun Gap–Nacoochee. In 1945, the school dropped its junior college and joined its boarding school with the small community school in Dillard, drawing the eighth and ninth graders from that school, thereby creating a program of grades eight through eleven for boarding *and* community students. The twelfth grade was added in 1948–49.[8] By the early 1950s, the coming of industry to Rabun County provided an attractive alternative to bone-weary small farmers for whom agriculture had become unprofitable; this, in turn, forced the Farm Family Program to cease operations.[9]

When Eliot Wigginton arrived to teach at Rabun Gap–Nacoochee in 1966, the school had several characteristic features that would contribute to the nurturance and growth of Foxfire. First, it had a conservative, church-oriented administration that enforced behavioral conformity with a rigid system of rules and regulations. Second, the school had a work-study program that required all students to defray at least part of their tuition costs by working daily on the school grounds. Boys worked on the school's farm; girls worked in the dining hall and dormitories. This meant that students' time outside class was circumscribed. Third, Rabun Gap–Nacoochee, despite being privately operated, was a genuine "community" school—a gathering place, rallying point, and source of pride to the people living in the northern tier of Rabun County.

Rabun Gap–Nacoochee (also still called Rabun Gap School) had a unique administrative arrangement with the Rabun County school board. For a dollar per year, the county leased the school's two-story classroom building as a public school facility from 8:00 A.M. to 3:30 P.M. daily. This contract resolved in a relatively inexpensive way the problem of overcrowding at the central high school in Clayton.[10] In exchange, the school received free teachers for its boarding students, textbooks, and other county/state services. After 3:30 the school reverted to a private status, fully within the purview of the boarding school administration and governed by rules and regulations that were not applicable to community students.

The school allowed Wigginton to rent a small apartment on the campus for fifty dollars per month. His contract assigned him to teach five classes of ninth- and tenth-grade English and one of ninth-grade geography. In addition to his teaching salary, Wigginton received a small supplement for working as an assistant dormitory parent (primarily a weekend responsibility). This assignment exposed him to the disparities in treatment accorded the dormitory students by the boarding school administration and staff. Unlike their peers outside the school, the dormitory students had relatively few opportunities to leave campus, could not date without chaperones, and had no access to automobiles. The situation was exacerbated by the fact that the community students had these freedoms (and many more).

In a letter to a Cornell friend, Wigginton observed: "The dorm students spend half their time trying to figure out ingenious ways of getting together with each other. Last night, for example, four boys left the dormitory (they dropped out of the second-floor windows onto the ground) and skirted briefly around the girls' dorm during the study hall. Really crazed—had they been caught it would have been curtains. The other day four girls came up missing—they had pulled the same stunt but after lights—they were all caught and sent home the next day."[11]

As described by Wigginton in his semiautobiographical *Sometimes a Shining Moment* (1985) and confirmed by numerous interviews with former Rabun Gap–Nacoochee students and administrators, a distinctive feature of the school's judicial code was its system of so-called major and minor infractions. The system's logic dictated that three minors equaled a major, which put the student on a week's restriction from recreational activities. Each dormitory issued a weekly misconduct report, announcing the issuance of minors for such relatively innocuous offenses as "left a window open," "talking to waitress during breakfast," "bathing suit left in the bathroom two days," "carrying a soft drink into living room," or "too amorous." Majors were meted out for such offenses as "foul mouth," "skipped breakfast and hid," "reading magazine late at night," "disturbing others doing a war dance at 11:45," and "extremely dirty room repeatedly."[12]

Undergirding these strictures on behavior was a Calvinistic world view which emphasized evangelism (one community member described it as "Baptist Presbyterianism"). A member of the boarding school administration during the Foxfire era explained the school's philosophy as follows:

> It is our belief that coming to know Jesus Christ as Savior is a stepping-stone to a more effective life. A case in point is a young person who feels no one loves him. Young people who have accepted Christ know that even if others haven't accepted them, God does. And it gives them a goal and a purpose in life. We were men and women who had accepted these things and wanted to share with others the Lord Jesus Christ. And these other things I'm talking about are a part of it.
>
> Thus, Christianity is a relationship of an individual with Jesus Christ; it's not just rules and regulations. We had the Christian emphasis that the young person have a relationship with Jesus Christ. The relationship was necessary in and of itself because . . . without Christ, you're lost.
>
> The starting point of this process is the problem of sin—John 3:16—that's the starting point. Our targeted Christian emphasis was that young people would come to have a relation with Jesus Christ and handle the problem of sin that divided them from God. The young person was lost without the love of Jesus Christ—that's where we were. The realization that someone loves you, the recognition of a goal or purpose in life—God's plan for our lives—these are two things that become helpful in one's life.
>
> But we don't have the Christian emphasis for this purpose. The purpose is the establishment of a relationship with Christ that solves the individual's problems for eternity. These other things flow from that. It's an evangelistic purpose. We're saying the same thing as Billy Graham about Jesus Christ—you're lost without Jesus Christ. We agree, but we're also saying that other things grow from that. We provided the environment and the individual had to make the choice.
>
> We did not try to throw anybody into the Kingdom of God by the scruff of the neck. We carried it out by endeavoring to select Christian men and women [as teachers]. As it related to the school when we were public, all we could do was select a person who indicated he was a member of a church. . . . In the privately hired staff, it was an expectation that those we selected were born-again Christians. . . .
>
> This was the first time some young people had heard there was a need for God in their lives. Here the people lived Christianity in the dormitories

and the work program. There were those who were accepted on the academic faculty [including Wigginton] who would not have considered themselves born-again Christians. [Requiring the public school teachers to avow being Christians would have been a violation of the First Amendment's establishment clause.]

Numerous former students from Foxfire's Rabun Gap era, boarding and community, recall that the school was too severe in its governance of the boarding students. Perhaps the most onerous strictures for these young people were the taboos concerning physical contact between the sexes. A 1974 boarding school graduate recalled, "You didn't date. If you went out with a boy to a movie on campus then you were walked back to the dorm, by [a] chaperone, as a group. You were allowed to hold hands. Then you got to the porch. At the porch you hid behind a column, and you were allowed to kiss goodnight, with the chaperone watching."

Apparently the chaperones at Rabun Gap shared a modicum of empathy with these young people. Kissing was anathema to the administration, which believed it had sound reasons for forbidding such contact. As one administrator put it:

When you're dealing with adolescents, the young persons need to know as clearly as possible the parameters in which they can function in group life; they need to know the boundaries. It's so much easier when they know what is to be expected of them.

Social life was restricted to certain time blocks. A case in point—after school was typically a work time; so it wasn't a time for a guy and a gal to get together. After supper was the time guys and gals got together. For example, in that era, we had Tuesday night Rec Center, when they could get together. On Saturday nights, there was normally a movie or an activity kids could participate in. What's important to know in this is that since they were together in the class buildings and since they saw one another before and after meals, the boys and girls had quite a bit of time with each other. Outside of the school, there weren't as many kids with cars and that sort of thing. The fact that our guys and gals didn't get together very much at that time wasn't as out of step as it seems looking back from 1984. They wouldn't have been together much had they been at home.

We did not go for . . . intense emotional involvement. You sometimes have to say no to some things that might be acceptable if Mom and Pop were around. Boarding life is different from family [life]. We used adults as escorts for Tuesday nights, Saturday nights, basketball games, and similar large group activities. On Sunday afternoons and [at] times immediately after supper when boys and girls could get together outside of a building, seldom did we have appointed escorts. But the meetings were at such places we considered public; that took care of most of the supervision.

> In that era we limited hand holding to when they were going back and forth to the auditorium, or to a basketball game, for example. The kids used to call us "Rabun Gap–No Smoochee." Some things which we felt were appropriate in a family context were inappropriate in a boarding school community. In that era we did not have kissing. We had too many problems to work out a system where a goodnight kiss could work appropriately. So we didn't allow that.

Certainly there is truth in the administration's argument that the school's *in loco parentis* role necessitated rules that might differ from those governing a student's own home. And there is also truth in the argument that the conservative school represented the mores of the surrounding Rabun County community. Yet the tenor of the interviews conducted with former dormitory students and fragments of documentary evidence suggest that the school, however well-intended, fettered its charges with unrealistic and, in some cases, bizarre restrictions. A case in point is an undated letter to parents signed by the boarding school administration, describing measures to be taken against violators of the school's prohibition against smoking:

> The first time a boarding student is found smoking, an on-campus punishment will be meted out. For boys it will mean that they will have to dig a grave, five feet deep, four feet across, and six feet long. [They] will be on dorm restriction until the hole is dug and filled back. For the girls it will mean a room restriction in the dormitory. This means that the girl attends classes, takes care of her work responsibilities, attends meals and of course worship activities, but at all other times she is to be in her room. She is not to visit others and she is not to be visited. We have a room, comfortable, but spartan, without radio or record player, to which the girl will move during the ten day period.
>
> The second time the student is found smoking, he or she will be dismissed.

The testimony of former students confirms that the grave-digging punishment was indeed enforced; as one woman, a 1975 day school graduate, stated: "I remember the guys having to dig a six-foot grave and having to bury a package of cigarettes."

Such was the school culture that Wigginton negotiated in his eleven years at Rabun Gap–Nacoochee. Previous journalistic and scholarly accounts of Foxfire have ignored the role this culture played, both positively and negatively, in the birth and growth of the Foxfire phenomenon. (See Appendix A for citations.) These accounts have placed far too heavy an emphasis on the role of Foxfire's community students in the organization's early literary and financial success. Indeed, the composite impression drawn from the existing literature on Foxfire is that of cohorts of Appalachian youngsters, armed with tape recorders and cameras, venturing forth to explore their common ancestry and heritage. With respect to Foxfire's origins and the majority of its history, the picture is a distortion.

Like most novice teachers, Wigginton was overworked and underpaid, saddled with six classes totaling 146 students and no planning period, laboring on a state salary of less than $400 per month.[13] To make matters worse, he was confronted with hostile, bored, and rambunctious students, who made his life a misery. "Our class was pretty bad," recalled Linda Garland Page, a native of Wolffork Valley and now director of the Foxfire Press. "Some of the kids were real mean. [Their attitude was] 'We'll get this guy!' I felt bad for him."

Tommy Wilson, also a Rabun County native, has stated: "Because he was bent to intellectual pursuits, a big element of the students decided he was wimpy. Anybody not belonging to the 'good ol' boy' clique was subject to ridicule or physical abuse, at worst."

Wigginton's personal correspondence from the fall of 1966 suggests that the community students were the source of most of his classroom problems. He described one particularly troublesome English class as follows:

> It has about four "A" dorm students and twenty-four rearing community ones who can't pass a thing they are taking. They enter my class, turn off their ears, turn on their mouths, and settle down for a period of socializing. Everytime I think I've gotten through to some of them, one of two things happens—either someone belches and breaks the spell, or the period ends and they are out in the free world again where the last fifty minutes evaporate like the mist from dry ice. They really do *not* see why they should have English, and in a sudden revelation several days ago I suddenly realized that I couldn't see why they should have it either. Lots of them will never leave this area of the country except perhaps to go to war—they will never learn to read and write—they will help with a gas station and love it— that's all they need. All the disciplines and beauties are as foreign to them as an opera and that's the way they want it.[14]

When the discipline in his classroom had broken down, Wigginton first retaliated against the students by sending them to the principal's office, which only increased their resentment. His personal letters contain such passages as "Always, in the back of my mind, is the unreality of the demand that I make it through the year,"[15] and "The hope of moving to other things besides teaching keeps me alive."[16]

In his frequently cited introduction to *The Foxfire Book*, Wigginton suggests that one evening he "surveyed the wreckage," hit upon the idea of a student-produced magazine, and the next day promptly jettisoned the literature texts in favor of a product-focused curriculum.[17] What actually happened, as interviews with former Rabun Gap students confirm, is that Wigginton infused his courses with the lyrical poetry of songs by the Beatles, Simon and Garfunkel, and Peter, Paul, and Mary; orchestrated a "wall-long bulletin board" (designed by students according to themes selected by a class vote); and initiated a dialogue with his students to elicit their ideas about enriching the study of English.

In their brainstorming sessions, Wigginton promoted the idea of a literary magazine, one of twenty-one activities that were under group discussion. Charles Childs, a former boarding school student who was present at the creation of *Foxfire,* recalled: "I think he [Wigginton] had an idea in the back of his mind of what he wanted to do. . . . I felt like he was already biased toward [the magazine], and he was directing it. What better way than to hide the carrot rather than pick it out himself—having the students pry it out for themselves."

From the ensuing discussions across Wigginton's classes came a series of decisions about the thematic focus of the magazine. It would be a literary journal and would include, first, creative writing and art submitted by Rabun Gap students, students at other Georgia high schools, and practicing writers and poets; second, articles based on materials drawn from the local community, e.g., superstitions, home remedies, folk expressions, and weather signs.[18]

While school administrators gave their approval for the project, they declined to provide any funds. Like the school annual, the quarterly magazine would have to finance itself. "In a very real sense, *Foxfire* stood on its own feet," an administrator recounted. "That was done intentionally. Our role was to help in finding additional funds." Clearly, the administration was not willing to take any risks on the fledgling journal. The school's bookkeeper would maintain a separate account for the project, and Wigginton agreed to accept full personal liability for any debts. The school required that Wigginton use the magazine as an adjunct to, not a substitute for, the standard curriculum. Moreover, no students would be allowed to leave class on magazine business.[19]

After they had written letters to various high schools requesting materials for the new magazine, Wigginton's students voted from a list of names they had compiled to call it *Foxfire.* Fund-raising for the project began in January 1967. Wigginton and his students unleashed a door-to-door subscription campaign, soliciting funds from local merchants and residents. "I remember walking around the valley getting subscriptions," Linda Page recalled. "There was a contest as to who could get the most subscriptions to the magazine, and I won the prize. I think explaining the magazine to the people and what we were trying to do with it and getting the money for it was memorable."

Foxfire was an instant sensation in Rabun County—the first six hundred copies sold out within a week, and a second printing was ordered. Of particular interest was the transcription of a taped interview conducted by Wigginton and several students with Luther Rickman, a retired Rabun County sheriff. An amiable raconteur, Rickman described in amusing detail the 1935 robbery of the Bank of Clayton and his pursuit and capture of the Zade Springel Gang.[20] Wigginton's friends Mary Hambidge and Marguerite Stedman advised him that articles such as the Rickman piece would prove of greater interest to local readers than poetry.[21] While *Foxfire* retained a poetry section, its primary focus after the first issue shifted to the indigenous mountain culture.

Its local popularity notwithstanding, the magazine was plagued from the beginning with financial problems. Over the next few years, Wigginton and his student editors routinely found themselves having to generate new subscriptions and gifts to pay for an outstanding printing bill. Occasionally, they debated the feasibility of continuing the project. Paul Gillespie, a 1971 Rabun Gap graduate, recalled those times: "I remember a lot of times talking about folding up. We had a long conversation one night about just folding up because we didn't have any money. The printer was real good about letting it slide. We'd get behind several hundred dollars [and] Wig would always scrounge some money . . . out of one of his fraternity brothers, or somebody. [Wig] spent a lot of his own money on the project. We spent a lot of our own money, too. We knew he was and he knew we were."

In 1969, Wigginton described the beleaguered project in the following terms: "Every issue we have printed so far has lost money. At times we were as much as $800 in debt. But each time newsstand sales, new subscriptions, grants and gifts have pulled us out of the hole and given us a little working capital with which to go to the printer again."[22]

An early bugbear was that the magazine, which sold for $.50 per issue, actually cost $.65 to produce. When a copy had to be mailed to a subscriber, its production cost soared to $.80. "This is not a paying proposition," Wigginton wrote, "if I want to keep the price at $.50 (and I do)."[23] Yet, by March 1968, the regular subscription rate had increased to $3.00 ($.75 per issue);[24] the 1969–70 rate would be $4.00 ($1.00 per issue).

In the spring of 1967 magazine finances were not Wigginton's only problem. His ninth-grade students still had not settled down. Wigginton has written that two actions on his part mitigated this difficulty. First, he persuaded the tenth-graders to create a junior board of editors and to enlist the younger students in collecting information for the next issue of *Foxfire*. Second, he agreed to hunt ginseng with one of the ninth-graders—a disorderly community student. Wigginton states that he was astounded that the youth had so much to teach him about the arcane subject of "sang digging" and its lore. His willingness to assume the role of a learner, he asserts, ended his discipline problems with this student and his friends.[25]

Despite his reservations about the boarding school administration, Wigginton signed a contract for the 1967–68 academic year. As he had requested, the school allowed him to take a salary cut in order to teach fewer classes and to devote more time to *Foxfire*. He also received the school's blessing to move off campus to a cabin on the Hambidge Foundation property. He spent the summer restoring the cabin, assisted by dormitory students who needed an occasional respite from Rabun Gap summer school.

Wigginton began his second year of teaching with a "determination to single-handedly salvage the careers of those students who were unhappy." Freed from a regular classload, Wigginton taught supplementary units for other English and social studies teachers. He also supervised the construction of a student coffee house in the basement of the gymnasium and founded a school newspaper, for which he served as advisor. Beyond these activities, Wigginton directed *Foxfire*, which published four issues and involved approximately fifty students in various stages of production.[26]

In its eleven-year tenure at Rabun Gap, the Foxfire program had an energy and verve not evident today. That dynamism was a function of several factors: the sociology of a small, religiously orthodox community/boarding school, the sheer novelty of Foxfire, the sense of ownership students felt for the project, and a *zeitgeist* that encouraged and rewarded efforts to preserve distinctive cultures.

At a tiny school in which the only serious sports were basketball and tennis, Foxfire became a magnet for community students with time on their hands. As a student from that era observed: "There wasn't much else to do except being in Foxfire and playing basketball. I mean if you didn't do that, you just watched TV." Moreover, the community itself had few recreational outlets for students. "All we had was the drive-in [movie theater] in Tiger [a community in the southern section of the county]," recalled Rhonda Waters, a Foxfire student in the early 1970s. Other former students mentioned hunting and fishing, "cruising" Dillard, and Saturday night visits to the Raco Drive-In, a fast-food restaurant outside the county seat of Clayton. "Man, on Saturday night, you couldn't get in the parking lot," said Mickey Justice, a 1970 graduate. Paul Gillespie, a 1971 graduate, recalled the ennui of rural life from an adolescent's perspective: "There wasn't a whole lot to do in Rabun Gap. I did a lot of Foxfire stuff on weekends—I mean tons of it. And summers. Mike [Cook] and I worked two summers just out of boredom. That was back when the organization didn't have any money at all. They didn't pay us or anything."

Foxfire's community students invested heavily of their free time in the magazine. Glenda Voiles, a 1970 graduate, described the late-night magazine sessions in the offices the school had set aside for the project: "I remember staying late on many nights working on the layouts. . . . When we worked late, it was fun. And our parents weren't concerned about our being out late because we were at Foxfire." For Linda Page, a 1969 graduate: "It was so different, so new an activity for kids to be involved in. . . . It was exciting. . . . We would work after school, on weekends, [and] late at night on something we felt was very valuable, something we really wanted to do, not just for a grade—because we didn't get a grade for it."

Cleverly or unwittingly, Eliot Wigginton had turned to advantage a liability of small rural schools and communities—their paucity of meaningful and engaging things to do. He had done it, in large part, by making rurality itself—its traditional practitioners, folk patterns, and survival arts—a source of adolescent activity and interest.

The testimony of former students, documentary evidence, and Wigginton's own recollections support the point that Foxfire, for the dormitory students, was a psychological haven and respite from the asylum-like confines of the boarding school. As a boarding school graduate remarked: "[Foxfire] gave the dorm students a freedom they didn't get in the structured environment of the school. Foxfire was their outlet. I think it's why the dorm kids gravitated toward [it]. That was their one light at the end of the tunnel. It was the one thing they could get in and work [in] with some kind of freedom. If they got an article published, it was something they had done on their own. It was *their* article. It didn't really belong to the school."

The testimony of these and other Rabun Gap School graduates is persuasive because their statements are not those of "bellyaching" adolescents but of young adults who have a special perspective on the ambience that gave rise to and nurtured Foxfire's infancy.

Wigginton has privately acknowledged the school's restrictions as a source of Foxfire's drawing power among the dormitory students; he maintains, however, that the program's *holding* power was attributable to other reasons as well. The testimony of two 1974 boarding school graduates supports this conclusion:

> I took [Foxfire] to get out . . . because I was confined in the dorm. Girls couldn't do anything. But after I got into it, I had a different reason. The enjoyment of working with the elderly and learning about animals and the people of the mountains and understanding the beginning of my life [this student's ancestors were Appalachian natives], getting to know myself—they're a different set of reasons for being in Foxfire. (Student A)
>
> I was mainly hunting for something to do when I got involved in Foxfire. The school didn't offer much as extracurricular stuff. I was looking for a little freedom also. We weren't allowed to go off campus. Foxfire offered a chance to get into the community. It was a more relaxed atmosphere. They gave us more of a freedom to make our own choices. They treated us more like adults than the school did. Their trust was one reason I got more and more involved with the project. At first I was not interested in Appalachian culture, but the more I did, the more I realized how important everything was. (Student B)

A careful scrutiny of the culture of the Rabun Gap School reveals far more than a simplistic "punitive parent" model of schooling. Indeed, the school had some benign features that were indispensable to Foxfire's growth. For example, the boarding school president could have vetoed Foxfire at the outset but did not do so. Instead, he allowed Wigginton to go forward with the magazine project, and when the time came, even to incorporate it as an *independent* educational fund within the school. Although the administration refused to provide any money for the project, its refusal applied to the school annual as well.

A teacher at Rabun Gap during the Foxfire era has stated: "I don't know a school anywhere that would have allowed Wig as much freedom and cooperation as he had here. When a kid showed up late [from an interview], the teachers understood because Wig was nice enough to write us a note or he came by sometimes and he'd say, 'We're a little late 'cause we got stuck.' If we knew the kid would be gone two or three days, [Wig] would make the arrangements. And this helped the kid. He'd study a little harder to get to go."

In *Sometimes a Shining Moment,* Wigginton recalls the support given by Morris Brown, the day school principal, whom he describes as "an extraordinary man to work for."[27] Although he is generally critical of the boarding school administration, Wigginton remains objective enough to acknowledge its contribution to the project. For example, he refers to the administrator who "took magazine editors with him to speak to various Rabun Gap–Nacoochee Guild groups, who normally raised money for the school, but who were encouraged on these occasions to donate money directly to *Foxfire*."[28]

Certainly, the school derived publicity value from the project's presence on its campus, yet the tenor of the interviews with these administrators and surviving memoranda suggest that more than self-interest was involved. For example, a boarding school administrator sent the following note to Wigginton: "Thanks for the role you played in helping some of these seniors who graduated yesterday. Giving them opportunities to travel with you and to write, photograph and see their work in finished form is a real assistance in their growth" (31 May 1976).

These administrators claim that they supported Wigginton despite their occasional differences with him over the treatment of students: "We looked on this as something that kids were benefiting from. . . . I saw it to be a worthwhile learning experience for those youngsters that wanted to be involved in it. As an administrator, I thought let's see what I can do to keep it going. If as an administrator you don't think it works, then you get rid of it. . . . There was a general consensus [that] it was a worthwhile project."

The private-school setting itself was a salient factor in Foxfire's early growth. Dormitory students who did not have study hall obligations were allowed to work, with adult supervision, at night in the Foxfire offices on campus. For community students, the transportation and security problems posed by a large and distant consolidated high school did not exist. Not only did they have easy access to a community school in close proximity to their homes, but they were also assured that if they came on campus at night there would be at least one hundred dormitory students and a cadre of adults (dormitory staff residents) within shouting distance. Much of Foxfire's work was undertaken after school (and after dark) at the Rabun Gap School.[29]

Wigginton received considerable logistical support from his friends in the community. For example, E. O. Mellinger taught Wigginton how to use the darkroom in his home on Boggs Mountain; Wigginton, in turn, taught his students, and they worked together printing the pictures they had taken with an old Leica that had belonged to Wigginton's uncle.[30] Mellinger's wife, Marie, a prominent naturalist, worked closely with the project for several years, contributing and editing materials on herbs and edible plants. "I started originally because I wanted to help Eliot," she explained. "I was very taken with him. He had this dream and vision. I also knew from past experience how very important it was to preserve culture. I think it was his personal magnetism and his dream that inspired everybody else to want to be in on it and to want to help him."

Strong community support, however, did not remedy the magazine's financial dilemma. "The mag[azine] is broke and I am broke," lamented Wigginton after the release of the second issue, which highlighted the mountain custom of planting by the signs of the zodiac.[31]

Early in 1968, events finally began to move in Wigginton's favor. Acting on the advice of a Cornell fraternity brother, John Dyson, whom he was visiting in New York, Wigginton took steps to get the magazine project incorporated as a 501(c)(3), nonprofit educational fund. His reasons were twofold. First, the nonprofit status would be an enticement to individual donors who could get a tax write-off for a contribution. Second, and most important, the status would make the project eligible for private funding available only for nonprofit organizations. Dyson's lawyers drew up the legal papers, and the project became the Southern Highlands Literary Fund, Inc. Dyson also personally donated $1,000, a gift that proved a harbinger of the magazine's shifting fortunes.[32]

En route to Rabun County, Wigginton spent a few days in Washington, D.C., where he made several fortuitous acquaintances. At the Library of Congress he discussed *Foxfire* with James Dickey, the Library's poet-in-residence, who recommended Wigginton to the Coordinating Council of Literary Magazines;[33] a visit there resulted in a $500 grant. Another propitious visit was with officials at the Smithsonian Institution, where Wigginton learned that "an enormous amount of collecting of music, folklore and crafts had been done in the Southern Appalachians, but very little in the north Georgia section where we were working. As such, we were a part of a long tradition with a definite role to play and a huge contribution to make—a contribution made even more significant by the fact that virtually none of the previous collecting had been done by people actually from the region—and absolutely none had been done by its teenagers. Most had been done by academic professionals from the outside."[34]

Wigginton's contact at the Smithsonian's Department of Performing Arts, Ralph Rinzler, proved instrumental in securing a $500 donation from the Newport Folk Foundation. By the end of the school year, with $2,000 flowing from private tills, Wigginton was buoyed.[35]

At the age of twenty-six, however, Wigginton was uncertain that he wanted to remain a high school teacher. Consequently, he decided to take a year's leave of absence to pursue a master's degree in English at Johns Hopkins University in Baltimore. Before leaving Rabun Gap School in the summer of 1968, Wigginton drew up a set of instructions for his magazine editors and made the necessary administrative arrangements to ensure that the magazine would continue in his absence. For example, he obtained the principal's assurance that the students could hold regular meetings during school hours to discuss magazine business.

Wigginton has written that his students exercised the lion's share of responsibility in putting out *Foxfire* during his year at Johns Hopkins; they handled all aspects of the magazine production, he asserts, "with the exception of preparing the final page proofs."[36] The key student editors from 1968–69 recall that they did indeed have a great deal of responsibility in Wigginton's absence: arranging and taping interviews, handling subscriptions and correspondence, and attending to the other details that could only be handled at Rabun Gap. Jan Brown Bonner, a 1969 editor, describes that role: "I remember Judy [Brown] and I handled all the circulation and most of the record keeping. I remember our dining room being filled with circulation material and mail. I can't remember that much about the actual articles. I know we were working on some and went out and did interviews at that time."

Judy Brown, the former editor in chief, recalls that she sent the tapes to Wigginton, who transcribed the material and assembled the articles at Hopkins: "We would get the tapes together and take pictures and different things. At that point we didn't have a lot of journalistic skill. It came out right as far as [being] the final product. He [Wigginton] certainly had the majority part in that. It was amazing to see what he got accomplished."

Wigginton's decision to resume teaching at Rabun Gap was attributable, in large part, to his devotion to his students and to a desire to have the magazine succeed. His weekly correspondence with the students and his editing and layout of articles—duties he assumed in addition to being enrolled as a full-time graduate student and to teaching a freshman English course—support this observation. A factor that also influenced, if not heavily, his decision seems to have been an antipathy to the internecine strife he witnessed at Johns Hopkins: "Expecting a tone of genuinely provocative informative dialogue and give and take, I found instead a level of paranoia and backstabbing and jealousy and open hostility for which I was totally unprepared."[37]

During the spring Wigginton revisited Washington and continued his lobbying in Foxfire's behalf. His visits resulted in the appointment of a prestigious national advisory board, including officials of the National Geographic Society, the Library of Congress, and the Smithsonian Institution. The board was then, and continues to be, a *technical board*, providing expertise in areas of interest to Foxfire. (A community advisory board would be appointed in 1973, its purpose being to apprise Wigginton of local opinion about Foxfire.)

Wigginton had vested legal responsibility for the Southern Highlands Literary Fund in a board of directors (legal board), which convened its first meeting in Baltimore on 27 February 1969. At this meeting, the legal board (which included John Dyson) appointed Wigginton president of the Fund.[38] On 16 May 1969, the Internal Revenue Service notified the Fund that its tax-exempt status had been approved. In 1973, the Southern Highlands Literary Fund would change its name to the Foxfire Fund, Inc.

After Wigginton's return to Rabun County, he and three community students spent the summer of 1969 assembling an entire issue of the magazine devoted to log cabin building. The end product was a collaborative effort on the part of Wigginton, the students, and community old-timers Harley Thomas, Hillard Green, and Bill Lamb. Paul Gillespie, now an attorney, describes how Wigginton got him involved in the project: "I remember the . . . summer I worked on the log cabin issue. I was on the lawn mower, and I'd finished mowing. And [Wig] came by in his Bronco and picked me up and said, 'Let's go see this guy [who] knows how to do a dove-tailed notch and a saddle notch. Here's a camera. Let's you and me go up there and see what he's got to say.' So we went to see Harley Thomas. That was the very first interview I ever did. Wig showed me how to use the camera, and he made me draw some diagrams. I never had done that before. And then he made me ask [Harley] some questions. And Harley Thomas was a good one to interview."

Wigginton and the boys worked together on the layout of the issue, sometimes late at night at his cabin. What was particularly memorable, Gillespie notes, was getting the materials to the printer: "[Wig] left and made us finish it up and take it to the printer. And I had the jeep, and we were coming from his house and one of the photographs flew out of the jeep. And we couldn't find it. And back then we didn't have a darkroom we could just run to. It was a real complicated process. You had to borrow somebody's darkroom. So we got a flashlight, and I remember Mike [Cook] hung out of the jeep. And David Wilson, who was blind as a bat. We were going up and down Betty's Creek at two o'clock in the morning hunting for a photograph. And David, who had the worse eyes in the bunch, found it. Then we took the magazine to the printer the next day."

Wigginton has described 1969–70 as a "watershed" year for Foxfire. The epithet is accurate on two counts. First, Foxfire was on the verge of breaking even financially; that is, not having to rely on new subscribers to keep the next issue afloat. Second, influential people in Washington, D.C., took a strong interest in the project, believing that it would prove a replicable model in other culturally distinctive regions of the nation.

When the year began, Wigginton was still running the magazine from a table in the back of his classroom. He had a full teaching load of five courses, including a journalism course explicitly for *Foxfire* magazine, as well as the student newspaper.[39] Because so many students wanted to be involved with the magazine, Wigginton allowed students who were not enrolled in the class to participate during study halls and after school hours.

During the school year, the project was the beneficiary of an administrative decision to allow Wigginton to use several rooms as magazine offices in a new administration building located behind the classroom building. Because Foxfire's circulation had grown too large for the local printer to handle efficiently, the students voted to send their layouts to Williams Printing Company in Atlanta. Another not inconsequential change was the addition of an adult advisor to the project, former VISTA worker Suzanne Angier, whose salary was funded partially out of Wigginton's own pocket.

By degrees *Foxfire* magazine had extricated itself from the financial red. Publicity in such periodicals as *Saturday Review, Christian Science Monitor,* and *National Geographic School Bulletin* helped to expand its national circulation to approximately four thousand by the end of 1969. And another challenge grant from the Coordinating Council of Literary Magazines—this time in the amount of $750, against which Wigginton and the students raised $1,700—thrust the project toward the break-even point. Yet even in the black, Foxfire did not have the necessary funds for badly needed new equipment.[40] At this point, Wigginton's door pounding in Washington paid a large dividend.

On one of his spring visits in 1969, Wigginton had dropped in on Junius Eddy at the U.S. Office of Education. Eddy was sufficiently impressed (and remains a staunch supporter) to arrange a meeting later in the summer between Wigginton and Herb McArthur at the newly founded National Endowment for the Humanities. At that meeting McArthur encouraged Wigginton to apply for an NEH grant.[41] NEH was sufficiently impressed with Wigginton's proposal to award the so-called Foxfire Folklife Training and Research Program, conducted by the Southern Highlands Literary Fund, Inc., $9,953 for darkroom equipment, a video camera and recorder, a single-lens reflex camera, supplies, travel expenditures, and summer salaries (for the first time) for four students.[42]

Previous observers have correctly assessed the importance of seren-dipity in Foxfire's emerging national prominence.[43] Certainly, Wiggin-ton had no idea he would land in Herb McArthur's office at NEH when he arrived in Washington in search of helpful agencies. Yet these descriptions miss the point that Wigginton had established some very useful connections *before* he moved to Rabun County, Georgia. A case in point was Mike Kinney, one of Wigginton's Cornell fraternity brothers, who happened to be an editor for the Doubleday publishing house's paperback division in 1969–70.

Wigginton had first broached the idea of compiling an anthology of *Foxfire* articles in a Christmas letter to his friends. Mike Kinney enthu-siastically responded to this letter, averring that the huge success of the recently published *Whole Earth Catalogue* had unveiled a national audi-ence that would be ripe for a *Foxfire* compendium.[44] Kinney's faith in Wigginton resulted in a contract whereby Doubleday gave him a $1,500 advance, with another $1,500 payable upon receipt of the manuscript.[45]

Enthusiasm for the forthcoming book reached a fever pitch at Doubleday. For example, Ronnie Shushan, a Doubleday editor, told Wigginton: "I've gone through the manuscripts and Paul's doing the same now. It's only *the* most exciting thing around. By the time I got to faith healing and then old Hillard Green peelin' 'maters . . . I was out of my mind with excitement! It's all such incredibly fine stuff, and I think the proportions of instruction and folklore are good."[46]

Wigginton's creative entrepreneurship resulted not only in the bur-geoning financial prospects of the Southern Highlands Literary Fund, but also in the eventual widespread dissemination of his learning concept. In the summer of 1969, Sam Stanley at the Smithsonian Center for the Study of Man had shown his copies of *Foxfire* to Brian Beun and Ann Vick of the Institutional Development and Economic Affairs Service, Inc. (IDEAS), a Washington-based, nonprofit "think tank" that identified new ideas and located people and money to "assist the disadvantaged to find for themselves a clearer civic, social and cultural identity."[47]

Intrigued with Foxfire's potential for improving education and cul-tural pride among ethnic minorities, Beun and Vick scheduled a meeting with Wigginton, to be held several months later. En route to that meeting Wigginton ran a stop sign and was ticketed by a police-man, who impounded his car, the school station wagon, at the local precinct station. Unable to muster the necessary cash to pay the fine, an embarrassed Wigginton called Beun and Vick, who rushed to the station, paid the ticket, and secured the release of the vehicle.

Wigginton and IDEAS came up with a plan for spreading the Foxfire concept. "Our agreement," Wigginton has written, "was to begin actively looking for other locations to which *Foxfire* could be transplanted. IDEAS would bear primary responsibility for finding locations and start-up funding, and our students would provide such consulting and training as was requested by the pilot sites."[48]

Full-scale dissemination of the idea was under way by the fall of 1970. Using the NEH money, Wigginton was able to create a student exchange between his journalism students and Diane Churchill's Fourth Street i, a magazine project on Manhattan's Lower East Side. The exchange sent Foxfire students to New York, and New York Hispanic students to Rabun County.

By this time IDEAS had located willing partners among the Oglala Sioux on the reservation near Pine Ridge, South Dakota. Published in 1971, *Hoyekiya,* a magazine compiled by Sioux Indian students and dropouts, became the first IDEAS-sponsored Foxfire descendant.[49] Other culturally distinctive groups (in such places as Maryland's Eastern Shore; Flathead Indian Reservation, Montana; Sea Islands, South Carolina; and Craig and Bethel, Alaska) solicited IDEAS's technical assistance and support in establishing Foxfire-like projects in their schools.[50]

Hiring Suzanne Angier relieved Wigginton of many of the burdens of running the magazine and helping IDEAS disseminate his learning concept. Angier, for example, arranged the exchange with Fourth Street i, and she accompanied Wigginton's students on their trip. The problem of her salary, until the late winter of 1971 funded personally by Wigginton and the Doubleday advance, was resolved by the announcement that NEH had awarded the Southern Highlands Literary Fund a new grant of $9,400, effective 1 March 1971. Angier's annual salary of $5,000 was covered by the award.[51]

If for no other reason, the school year 1970–71 was significant in Foxfire's history because three of Wigginton's journalism students—Andrea Burrell, Paul Gillespie, and Mike Cook—discovered "Aunt Arie" Carpenter, a wizened mountain woman who lived high on a ridge in nearby Macon County, N.C. The students were so charmed with Aunt Arie that they convinced Wigginton to drop by for a visit. The transcription of that interview, parts of which appeared in the first chapter of *The Foxfire Book,* included a humorous scene in which a queasy Wigginton pried out the eyes of a severed hog's head Arie was preparing for souse meat. In 1983, Wigginton reminisced about Arie: "Of all the people my high school students, my staff members, and I have documented and shared with the outside world since 1966, none has been more warmly embraced than Arie Carpenter. Though she has been dead for years, wherever I go with my students on speaking engagements—be it Alaska, Oklahoma, California, Maine, or wherever—someone will surely come up to one of us and inquire about her health. She is the only person we ever wrote about whose personality was so strong and whose face was so compelling that she literally walked off the pages of *The Foxfire Book* and into the lives of the millions who read it."[52]

NOTES

1. Eliot Wigginton, *Sometimes a Shining Moment: The Foxfire Experience* (Garden City, N.Y.: Anchor Press/Doubleday, 1985), 38. This 400-page volume contains numerous letters, journal entries, and memoranda; its historical focus is Foxfire's Rabun Gap era, 1966–77.

2. Ibid., 41.

3. This entry appeared in a draft of *Sometimes a Shining Moment,* which Wigginton completed in 1984–85. The entry was excluded from the published version.

4. Wigginton, *Shining Moment,* 9.

5. Andrew J. Ritchie, *Sketches of Rabun County History* (Published by the author, 1948), 465–503. Esco Pitts, a school employee during the Ritchie era, provided further information in an interview with the author, 10 September 1974.

6. Ibid. See also Patsy Wilson, *A Time to Sow, A Time for Planting: A 75-Year History of the Rabun Gap School* (Clayton, Ga.: n.p., 1978), 37–57.

7. Wilson, *A Time to Sow,* 58–71.

8. A former Rabun Gap School administrator provided this information in an interview with the author, 9 July 1984.

9. Wilson, *A Time to Sow,* 58–71.

10. Wigginton, *Shining Moment,* 12.

11. Eliot Wigginton to Howard Senzel, 4 October 1966, in ibid., 20.

12. Wigginton, ibid., 21–25.

13. Ibid., 14–15.

14. Wigginton to Senzel, 29 October 1966, in ibid., 26.

15. Ibid.

16. Wigginton to Senzel, 3 December 1966, in ibid., 30.

17. Eliot Wigginton, ed., *The Foxfire Book* (Garden City, N.Y.: Anchor Press/Doubleday, 1972), 9–10.

18. Wigginton, *Shining Moment,* 47–48.

19. Ibid., 48–49.

20. *Foxfire,* March 1967, 8–12.

21. Wigginton, *Shining Moment,* 52–53. Mary Nikas, director of the Hambidge Center (formerly called the Hambidge Foundation), recalled this discussion in an interview with the author, 14 November 1984.

22. Eliot Wigginton, "Doing Real English," *Media and Methods* 5, no. 5 (1969): 39.

23. Wigginton to Senzel, 8 April 1967, in *Shining Moment*, 64.

24. In the Fall/Winter 1968 issue, Wigginton included the following admonition to readers: "Without a constant flow of new subscribers, we're dead."

25. Wigginton, *Shining Moment*, 69–72.

26. Ibid., 82–90.

27. Ibid., 48.

28. Ibid., 105.

29. According to a Foxfire staff member from the Rabun Gap era: "The school was a community. [And] the community revolved around Rabun Gap–Nacoochee School for many activities. Parents didn't object to their children going over there; they felt they were safe. At Rabun Gap, [boarding school] kids had to work in the afternoon, and in the evenings they worked on the magazine. . . . Day students would come over to the magazine after basketball practice. For [them] it wasn't a dead building. The campus was movement."

30. Wigginton, *Shining Moment*, 93. There is a slight discrepancy between Wigginton's account and that of Mellinger, who recalls that Wigginton already had these processing skills when he began using Mellinger's darkroom.

31. Wigginton to Senzel, 8 October 1967, in ibid., 91.

32. Ibid., 94–95.

33. Ironically, five years later, Wigginton would excoriate James Dickey's novel *Deliverance*, charging that the poet/novelist, for all his literary talents, had unfairly stereotyped Rabun County lifestyles and mores as barbarous and amoral.

34. Wigginton, *Shining Moment*, 96.

35. Ibid., 98–99.

36. Wigginton, "Doing Real English," 38–39.

37. This statement, which appears in an early draft of *Sometimes a Shining Moment*, was excluded from the published version.

38. Minutes, Board of Directors, Southern Highlands Literary Fund, Inc., 27 February 1969. Beyond its right to appoint or replace Foxfire's president, the legal board is responsible for the financial and legal health of the organization; its powers also include the right to dissolve the corporation.

39. Wigginton, *Shining Moment*, 119.

40. Ibid., 120–22, 130–31.

41. Ibid., 117.

42. Final report on NEH Grant #EO-98-70-4208, submitted by the Foxfire Folklife Training and Research Program for the period 1 March 1970 to 1 March 1971.

43. For example, Gail Parks, "Foxfire: Experiential Education in America," in *Rural Education in Urbanized Nations: Issues and Innovations*, ed. Jonathan P. Sher (Boulder, Colo.: Westview Press, 1981), 281.

44. Wigginton, *Shining Moment*, 122–25.

45. Publishing agreement between Doubleday & Co., Inc., and Eliot Wigginton, 7 August 1970.

46. Ronnie Shushan to Eliot Wigginton, 24 March 1971.

47. IDEAS, Inc., "Spring Report," 1972.

48. Wigginton, *Shining Moment*, 133–34.

49. IDEAS, Inc., "Spring Report."

50. For extended discussion of the dissemination of the Foxfire learning concept by IDEAS and generalizations about various projects, see Thad Sitton, "The Foxfire-Concept Publications: A First Appraisal" (Ph.D. diss., University of Texas, 1978).

51. Final Report on NEH Grant #EO-5072-71-115, submitted by the Foxfire Folklife and Research Program for the period 1 March 1971 to 29 February 1972.

52. Linda Garland Page and Eliot Wigginton, eds., *Aunt Arie: A Foxfire Portrait* (New York: E. P. Dutton/Foxfire Press, 1983), xiii.

THREE

The Rabun Gap Era: National Celebrity

The financial success of *The Foxfire Book*, released in March 1972, astounded the publishing industry. Within a month of its publication, *The Foxfire Book* was already in its third printing; first-month sales totaled one hundred thousand, vaulting the book toward the top of the *New York Times* bestseller list.[1] And over the next decade, Doubleday would sell over two million copies. Mike Kinney's hunch had proved right: the national mood favored publication of an anthology filled with articles about "hog dressing, log cabin building, mountain crafts and foods, planting by the signs, snake lore, hunting tales, faith healing, moonshining, and other affairs of plain living."

The Foxfire Book (as well as the project) was favorably reviewed in scores of national newspapers, magazines, and journals. For example, David Shapiro, in a critique for *Saturday Review,* hailed the volume as "a fine example of Emersonian self-reliance and compassionate anthropology that would have charmed James Agee and Oscar Lewis."[2]

Yet criticism from some academic folklorists was not long in coming. What raised their ire, it seems, was the $196,000 grant awarded to IDEAS by the Ford Foundation in the wake of the huge success of *The Foxfire Book*. The leading critic was Richard Dorson, a professor at the Folklore Institute, Indiana University, who fired off a letter to Brian Beun, project director for IDEAS. "For high school students and for a director untrained in folklore," wrote Dorson, "the *Foxfire* magazine and book are not bad. But they are not good. This project which the Ford Foundation is supporting to the tune of $196,000 is actually a project in mis-education." Dorson vigorously objected to allowing students untutored in collecting and archiving to engage in fieldwork and to publish their findings.[3]

The tone of Dorson's letter conveys both professional concern and jealousy. Yet taken at face value, his explicit criticism missed the point that Foxfire was, at heart, an educational project for *adolescents*. Nancy Dennis, a Ford Foundation spokesperson, remonstrated with Dorson in the following terms:

> As I understand your criticism of both the original *Foxfire* project in Rabun Gap and spinoffs from it being developed through technical assistance from IDEAS staff, these amateur high school student research endeavors fail to measure up to professional standards of inquiry and documentation known to serious folklorists. I, and very likely Eliot Wigginton and IDEAS staff, would certainly be prepared to concede your objections. At the same time, however, we would counter that the purpose of these student projects is not primarily the production of sophisticated ethnologic research. Neither *Foxfire* nor its variants aspires to rival scholarly investigation. From the outset and still, its reason for being lies in the utilization of a focus on cultural heritage as a motivational force for learning basic skills. Experience so far has indicated that student initiative and collaboration in the planning and production of a marketable publication featuring documentation of local folkways can have substantial payoff in re-engaging alienated students in learning and also in adapting schools' programs toward more interdisciplinary and relevant teaching. That this kind of student writing may succeed in attracting wide public interest further boosts students' sense of identity and accomplishment. For the Foundation, the appeal of this activity lies foremost in its educational value.[4]

For all its putative flaws as folklore, *The Foxfire Book* made the Southern Highlands Literary Fund wealthy. The organization's records indicate that royalties from its sales amounted to nearly $100,000 annually for the next five years. And Doubleday had contracted with Wigginton for an entire series of books. The future was rosy.

The Doubleday royalties, Wigginton decided, would be invested in the project. Splitting it among students and contacts, he adjudged (and it is still his argument), was unfeasible because it would be virtually impossible to determine the value of an individual's contribution, student or contact, to the project. It is the "can of worms" argument. Moreover, returning the money to the Fund meant that the project could be expanded, to the benefit of students and community alike.

It is a measure of both his integrity and commitment to students that Wigginton did not use the royalties for personal profit. The money he has derived from Foxfire has been voted to him by the

Fund's legal board. He has not, despite local speculation to the contrary, "made hay while the sun shines."

In April 1973, the board voted a $500 monthly salary to Wigginton.[5] A year later, Foxfire's New York attorney, John Viener, wrote Wigginton: "I believe your salary should be raised no matter how much you receive from third-party organizations (IDEAS). The services which you render for Foxfire are worth many times the salary which it is paying to you, and I do not believe you should contribute your time for nothing."[6]

Embarrassed by Wigginton's modest salary, the legal board awarded him a $22,000 bonus in 1975.[7] Evidently, this action did not satisfy Viener, who continued to describe Wigginton's salary as "a pittance . . . [that] does not begin to reflect the enormous value of your contributions."[8]

Since 1972, Doubleday has published eight books in its *Foxfire* series, each based on *Foxfire* magazine articles as well as some original materials. *Foxfire 2* through *Foxfire 6* (published between 1973 and 1980) are stylistic replicas of *The Foxfire Book*, each with a potpourri of fresh topics drawn from the "affairs of plain living." *Foxfire 7* (1982) broke the pattern of the previous volumes, focusing exclusively on a single theme: mountain religions. *Foxfire 8* (1984), even with a three-hundred-page section on Southern folk pottery, resembled the pre-*Foxfire 7* books with its diversified focus on blacks in Appalachia, mule swapping, and chicken fighting. *Foxfire 9* appeared in 1986.

Thad Sitton has presented an excellent analysis of the form and function of *Foxfire* articles. Building upon an informal typology that Wigginton described in a speech to oral historians, Sitton classifies the articles into three categories: "The 'personality interview,' focused upon the personality of a single individual; the 'weather signs type,' featuring a compendium of limited cultural information collected from a large number of informants; and the 'topic-personality article,' collected from what a limited number of people think or feel about a certain topic."[9]

Most of the articles fit the topic-personality category, which comprises two subcategories: "Topic-anecdotal description" and "process analysis." The former, a term Sitton did not use but which is appropriate in the context of his discussion, includes articles on hunting, snake lore, and ghost stories; the latter includes "how-to-do-it" features on log cabin building, hog slaughtering, banjo construction, gun making, and moonshining.

The technological process article, replete with numerous photographs and meticulous diagrams, has distinguished *Foxfire*'s brand of cultural preservation from that of other oral historians and folklorists. In an insightful passage, Sitton explains the significance of its treatment of this particular genre: "It is in these technological process articles that *Foxfire* reaches its highest levels of sophistication in the analysis of cultural data and the descriptive account of 'how to do it.' There is a clear and sustained attempt to get down to the 'user's level' of culture and to describe the process under study not only in the actors' terminology for the process but with the actors' specificity of detail. This is 'salvage ethnography' of the old mountain culture, but . . . one that seems committed to a *functional* [emphasis added] and not just informational preservation."[10]

The following is a sampler of the personalities and folkways anthologized in the Doubleday *Foxfire* books:

"Slaughtering Hogs" (technical process)
Meanwhile the hog was killed (either by a sharp blow on the head with a rock or ax head, or by shooting it in the back of the head or between the eyes), and its jugular vein (on the left side of the throat about three inches back from the jawbone) pierced immediately. . . . When the bleeding slowed, the hog was dragged to the "scalding place" and dipped in the hot water and rolled over to loosen the hair (by pulling or scraping), hauled out and scraped with a not-too-sharp knife, immersed again immediately, and the procedure repeated until most of the hair was off the hide." (*The Foxfire Book*, 1972, 190)

"Home Remedies" (weather-signs type)
Some of the remedies undoubtedly worked; some of them were probably useless; some of them—and for this reason we advise you to experiment with extreme care—were perhaps even fatal (taking large quantities of whiskey for snake bites for example). . . . For a baby [with croup] pour a mixture of turpentine and white whiskey into a saucer and set it afire. Hold the baby over the smoke until he breathes it deeply. This loosens him up. . . . [For a sore throat] make a poultice of kerosene, turpentine, and pure lard (to prevent blistering), and place this on your neck. In five minutes you will be able to taste the kerosene in your throat, and the cure will have begun. Then take two or three drops of kerosene oil in a spoon with a pinch of sugar and swallow this to complete the treatment. (*The Foxfire Book*, 230, 237, 244)

"Maude Shope" (personality interview)
"I never did try t'drive a car. My mule is th'way I got around. Used t'ride him t'Otto [North Carolina] t'get groceries. I've drove him all th'way t'Franklin and back years ago. 'Course you couldn't do it now. There's too many cars on th'road. I've had him since he'uz eighteen months old. He'll be thirty-two in February. You can drag wood with him—anything y'want

t'do. He'll do any kind of work you want done. Yes, sir. He's something." (*Foxfire 2*, 1973, 19)

"Old-Time Burials" (topic-anecdotal description)

We soon became curious about just what it was the family or friends would do when they laid a body out. Aunt Arie said that it was essential to work fast or the body would stiffen up and swell. She talked about hearing arms break "in there" after the body had stiffened. They would massage the person's cheeks to get the eyes closed and then put a silver coin over each eye to keep them shut since, "lot a'times with homemade fixin' and th'jos-tlin', they'd come open." Silver was preferred because copper might turn the skin green. In one of the most touching moments that took place in our interviews, she revealed that when she washed her husband, Ulysses, before his "buryin'," she found a birthmark that she had never known was there. (*Foxfire 2*, 1973, 309)

"Simmie Free" (personality interview)

"I bought me a half gallon a'liquor up yonder. It cost me $6.00, and then it about cost my life. I didn't bother him; never did say a word about it because I wasn't able to. I was about dead. And I'll tell you how he made his liquor. He had four-foot-square boxes—vats and worked the beer off with them. Then when he got ready to run it, he had a bloomin' old thing—I don't know what it was, I never saw it. But I used some of the liquor. I give him $6.00 for a half gallon. . . . Boy, like to have killed me. Doc Turner sent some to Atlanta and they tested it, and they said they was enough lead in that little bottle to kill six men. Damn it didn't get me but it like to. . . . I had kidney trouble for a long time after that. Cost me $487.00 in doctor bills. Doc Turner said I was dead. Grover—that's my oldest boy—said I was dead. Another one of them said I was dead. But I wasn't. I ain't quite dead yet, that's th'truth." (*Foxfire 3*, 1975, 29)

"The People Who Take Up Serpents" (topic-anecdotal description)

The Church [of God] we visited—the location of which, at the request of the preacher, must remain nameless—was founded in 1931. Two years after its founding, the members began to handle serpents. . . .

Dexter [a church member] is far from casual about his attitude toward serpents as his wife's brother-in-law was bitten and died, and he himself has been bitten twelve times—three of those in one night. He admits that he was "laid up" as a result of two of those bites, but claims that he wasn't affected at all by the other ten. Several times he was "in the spirit" when he first took them up, but the spirit left him while he was holding them. At other times, there were bad feelings in the room that ruined the effect of the blessing, and caused the serpents to strike. He remembers that when he was bitten by a copperhead, it felt like he had put his whole hand in fire. (*Foxfire 7*, 1982, 374, 400)

Since the outset its focus on folk culture has distinguished Foxfire from other high school journalism projects. In his eloquent introduc-

tion to *The Foxfire Book,* Wigginton described the unique contribution
to be made by young people in the service of cultural preservation.
"Daily our grandparents are moving out of our lives," he wrote,
"taking with them, irreparably, the kind of information contained in
this book." Wigginton asserted that the "logical researchers" for saving
the copious yet disappearing oral legacy of this generation were "the
grandchildren, not university researchers from the outside"; the benefit to these young people would be "an invaluable, unique knowledge
about their own roots, heritage, and culture."[11]

Despite the academic criticisms of Foxfire, Wigginton's statement
made sense for two reasons. First, the grandchildren of southern
Appalachian traditionalists had an easy and natural rapport with their
elders, who were typically reticent with strangers. Second, if the
grandchildren did not collect the oral history and traditions, who else
would? For all their criticisms of Foxfire, academic folklorists and
historians had largely ignored the north Georgia mountains in their
collection efforts.

However, the passage obscures the role of the Rabun Gap boarding
school students *qua* boarding school students in the collection of
Foxfire materials. Myra Queen Jones, a 1975 day school graduate,
highlighted this special role, describing the enthusiasm of these students: "When I went into Foxfire, it didn't seem to faze me as much as
the dorm kids. When we had people like Harry Brown making a chair
bottom out of cornhusks . . . , the dorm kids went wild. They got there
around him—interested and asking questions. I was taking notes, but
I'd seen stuff like that all my life."

For Linda Page, the enthusiasm of the dormitory students helped to
give the Appalachian elderly a new and special credibility: "The fact
that they got so excited got us excited. We'd say, 'Hey, that lady who's
been living next door all these years—she's pretty neat after all.'"

Paralleling the huge success of *The Foxfire Book* and subsequent
volumes was the widespread dissemination of the learning concept
that had midwifed these anthologies. Sponsored by IDEAS, the first
large-scale Foxfire workshop was held at Rabun Gap in the summer of
1972, attended by students and teacher project advisors from South
Dakota, New Mexico, South Carolina, Montana, Maryland, Alaska,
and California. Foxfire students served as peer tutors, helping to teach
every component of magazine production, from interviewing techniques to darkroom procedures to layout and printing; they also
accompanied their visitors on daily interviews in the Rabun Gap
community. Jan Brown Bonner, a former Foxfire student editor, describes a memorable scene from the multiethnic workshop:

Probably the most exciting part of the whole workshop was the afternoon we spent watching a hog chase. Cameras and tape recorders in hand, the whole group gathered around a barbed wire fence and listened to Eldon Miller explain what would happen. The *Foxfire* staff was preparing an article on the hog chase, so quite a number of brave students were wandering around inside the fence to get a better view of things. At that time the boar just stood passively and watched. But as soon as the dogs were unleashed, it was complete bedlam. Amid barking dogs, a shrieking snorting boar, and screaming students, no one knew which way to go. The boar brushed against the legs of one visiting student and there was a mad scramble for the fence. Soon after everyone was pulled across the barbed wire and into the weeds on the other side, the dogs came through and cornered the wild boar right in front of the fence so everyone there could see. Later a number of kids admitted, "My knees are still knocking from that hog chase."[12]

Bonner also recalls "the friendly bond" that developed among these diverse cultural groups, one that enhanced her understanding "that there *can* be communication between races and *within* races."

Following this workshop, IDEAS sponsored three Rabun Gap School graduates as consultants ("Foxfire associates") to help the staff of new projects learn the nuances of cultural journalism. Jan Brown traveled to the Flathead Reservation in Ronan, Mont. (Dovetail); Laurie Brunson, to Johns Island, S.C.(Angel Oak); Mike Cook, to the Navajo Reservation in Ramah, N.M. (Tsa'Aszi').[13] Cook, then a nineteen-year-old college student, describes his experience:

It was my first time really a long way from home. I was living in a bilingual society, working with a small group of kids. Probably, I learned more about *me* than anything else. It was another one of those things that turned into a confidence builder. I knew from that experience that I could go on and just about do whatever I wanted to do. There I was at nineteen and running a project [practically] by myself. And I wasn't getting a whole lot of support from the school administration. The Navajo had some real trepidation about my being another white guy with another project. When the first issue came out, it made us all feel pretty good. It was what Wig's always talking about in stretching people. It stretched me a long way. It had a lasting impact.

In 1973, IDEAS began publication of its Foxfire network newsletter, *Exchange,* a vehicle for sharing information among the various projects; issues featured technical and funding advice, letters, essays, and editorials. In March and June, IDEAS sponsored two further student/ teacher workshops. The latter included participants from eleven school districts in the United States and Caribbean countries. Following this workshop, three Foxfire associates took to the field, each a 1973 Rabun Gap graduate: Claude Rickman, to the Navajo Reservation, Johns Island, and Kennebunk, Maine (Salt); Gary Warfield, to Neshoba County, Mississippi (Nanih Wayah); and Stan Echols, to Haiti (Kric Krac) and Jamaica (Peenie Wallie).[14]

Claude Rickman, a community student, also spent the summer of 1974 as a consultant to projects in the' Virgin Islands, Haiti, and Hawaii. Rickman remembers the vigor of some projects, the lassitude of others. Particularly striking was the acute poverty of Haiti, where Rickman spent three frustrating weeks in a school in Port-au-Prince. "If you got two hours a day out of them," he recalls, "you were exceptional. I let them slide."

Now a twenty-nine-year-old building contractor, Rickman describes these experiences as formative: "Foxfire provided the chance and the transportation for me to see the world at a good time in my life—as an eighteen-year-old with as bright eyes as anybody could have. You weren't eighteen but once and things just didn't come along like that very often. Sometimes my mind just drifts back to those times."

IDEAS provided not only free consulting to a sponsored project in its incipiency, but free cameras, darkroom equipment, and photographic supplies as well. A project was allowed to keep the equipment permanently once it had published the third issue of its magazine.[15] In the period covered by the Ford Foundation grant, IDEAS reported that it "directly supported the initiation of fourteen Foxfire Learning Concept projects," twelve of which were located in the United States and two in the Caribbean. Moreover, IDEAS claimed another fourteen projects that had "indirectly evolved from the program undertaken within the Foundation's grant," representing "the second generation of extensions from FOXFIRE."[16]

In the final year of the funding period, IDEAS staff members shifted their focus from direct sponsorship and skills training to "the development of teacher training and instructional materials intended to further strengthen each project's available continuing resources as well as provide prospective new projects with concise distillation of the total Foxfire experience."[17] The resulting materials were *Moments,* Wigginton's philosophical/pedagogical testament, and *You and Aunt Arie: A Guide to Cultural Journalism,* by Pam Wood, advisor to Salt, the Foxfire descendant in Kennebunk, Maine. These books and the *Foxfire* film produced by IDEAS in 1973 composed what Thad Sitton has described as the "core curriculum" of the Foxfire descendant projects.

Between 1971 and 1977, the years of its affiliation with Wigginton and Foxfire, IDEAS employed at least three dissemination strategies.

The initial strategy (1971–73) was to identify suitable project sites within culturally distinctive, typically rural areas and to recruit teachers within those sites as project advisors. As previously stated, IDEAS and Foxfire sponsored a series of Rabun Gap workshops for new advisors and student editors. The strategy was successful in initiating twelve Foxfire descendants. The success of *The Foxfire Book*, however, dictated a change in the strategy, relieving IDEAS of the time and expense of locating new project sites. Teachers who had read the book were now soliciting Wigginton and IDEAS for assistance in establishing new projects. Thus began the "second wave" of Foxfire-descendant projects. Late in 1973 Beun and Wigginton decided that IDEAS, in the future, would locate its workshops at the sites of selected projects and employ teachers and students from the first-generation projects as trainers. By 1975 this strategy had been replaced by a self-help approach whereby IDEAS, strapped by funding limitations, helped fledgling projects locate funding sources, typically state departments of education, arts councils, and historical societies.[18]

In 1978, Sitton reported the results of his survey of thirty-five Foxfire descendants (he had mailed questionnaires to fifty-three projects). The study is significant because it documented a "grass-roots" movement of teacher-initiated, Foxfire-like projects in predominately rural, but including urban and suburban, locales. Sitton concluded that "the projects derive from (in most cases) common origins, and share a common body of literature and some sense of common purpose." The author also speculated that by 1977 (Foxfire's last year at Rabun Gap School), there were at least 80 Foxfire descendants.[19]

The five years that linked the appearance of *The Foxfire Book* and Wigginton's decision to leave Rabun Gap School witnessed the expansion of the Foxfire organization within its own school and community and a shift in the project's thematic focus. Wigginton's aspirations for his students and his genuine concern for the welfare of the indigenous mountain people made this growth inevitable.

The impetus behind Wigginton's decision to buy land for the expansion of Foxfire was the vision of a community museum he had nurtured as early as 1970. "The material we've gotten in the area *belongs* in this area, and I'd like to see it stay here where it can be used and enjoyed," he told the Foxfire boards. "If I were to insist on anything, it would be that the museum truly be a community enterprise, with some of the old-timers in the area acting as foremen for this log work, students doing the labor, etc."[20]

The first step toward the realization of Wigginton's dream, unwittingly, was his purchase of a tract of fifty-nine acres of mountain land, on which he planned to build his own log home. Wigginton bought the property with a bank loan of $32,400, countersigned by his father on 20 January 1972, the date he received his first advance copy of *The Foxfire Book*.[21] One factor that prompted, or at least coincided with, Wigginton's decision to buy his own property was a personality conflict with the Hambidge Foundation board of trustees. When it had become evident that the aging Mary Hambidge had grown quite frail and increasingly senile, her board of trustees and other friends began to haggle over the disposition of the Foundation property. For reasons that are not clear, Wigginton had nettled these individuals and was apparently targeted for eviction from his cabin if he was not out by the time of Mrs. Hambidge's death. Had he chosen to remain on the premises he would likely have been embroiled in a legal battle with the Hambidge board.[22]

Wigginton began work almost immediately on his new home, enlisting the physical labor and companionship of his students. His close, filial relationships with adolescents, corroborated by interviews with scores of former students, dispel the accusation that Wigginton exploited the labor of these young people; he was no Tom Sawyer conniving others to whitewash his fence.

Wigginton has cast the experience in the following terms: "It was an experience that became simply one more massive chunk of evidence to buttress my conviction not only that young people are often starved for opportunities to be engaged—heart, body and mind—in positive action, but also that they can be counted on to carry their share of the load when the project truly interests them. Without those fourteen and fifteen year olds, I could never have built that house. They were with me from the first day, and they never gave up. And they never expected a dime in payment."[23]

Wigginton's new cabin stood high on a ridge on the eastern slope of Black Rock Mountain, overlooking the tiny community of Mountain City, several miles south of Rabun Gap School. Wigginton decided that the property immediately adjacent and below his own would make a suitable site for a community museum as well as Foxfire's expanding offices. What he had in mind by now was a large-scale reconstruction project that would salvage and reassemble, log by log, old and decaying yet venerable structures in the northeast Georgia counties. Apparently his inspiration had been an old grist mill that he and the students had found rotting in the undergrowth near Aunt Arie Carpenter's cabin in Macon County, N.C. After a vote, they purchased the old mill for $2,000 and reconstructed it on Wigginton's property.[24]

Wigginton consulted his journalism students before moving to purchase for Foxfire the fifty-one acres adjacent to his own property. Phyllis Carver Ramey, a former Foxfire student, recalled how the issue was decided: "At the beginning of class, he talked about the possibility of purchasing the land. Were we in agreement? Yes—at least the majority. Then he wanted to know what we wanted to do about the future of the land. We told him we didn't want to see it as a tourist attraction. We had discussed reconstructing log cabins, and we felt it should be preserved. It shouldn't be open territory."

In April 1973 Wigginton's board of directors approved the expenditure of $36,000 for the property.[25] The Foxfire Center was born. Over the next four years, local carpenters and students employed by Foxfire converged at sites across northeast Georgia to disassemble log structures, painstakingly numbering each salvageable log for reassembly on "the land" (the local appellation for the Foxfire Center). Throughout these years, a long, flatbed lumbering truck filled with log beams made countless trips up the largely unpaved, bone-rattling county road that winds by the Blue Heights Baptist Church, past wood frame houses and trailer homes and mongrel dogs, to the old lumbering track that leads onto the Foxfire property.

When the center was completed in 1977, it comprised twenty-four historic and traditional design log structures, including a grist mill, blacksmith shop, wagon shed, hog-scalding shed, mule barn, woodworking cabin, museum cabin (furnished with nineteenth-century artifacts), chapel, storage cabin (housing Foxfire's loom collection), and cabins for Foxfire offices and staff housing. A split rail fence paralleled a steep, narrow road through the property.

Several of the houses were antebellum structures, named for the mountain families that had occupied them for generations. For example, the Carnesville House, used for staff offices, had been built in the 1850s in Franklin County, Ga. The Moore House, from the community of Shooting Creek, N.C., dated from approximately the mid-1830s. Other houses bore the names of their communities of origin. For example, the Savannah House, built between 1830 and 1840, had fronted the Tennessee-Georgia road in the Savannah community of Jackson County, N.C.

During Foxfire's Rabun Gap era, Wigginton and some of his students became increasingly interested in social, economic, and environmental issues that impinged upon and threatened the sense of community, cultural identity, and self-reliance that were hallmarks of the traditional mountain culture. Evidence of this interest appears in issues of *Foxfire* magazine, albeit sporadically, from the late-1960s to the mid-1970s. For example, in 1969, the editors printed an article by an outside scholar on the plight of coal miners in Pikeville, Kentucky. In the same issue, naturalist Marie Mellinger contributed an essay that examined the mindless pillage of mountain wildflowers. In his introduction to the issue, Wigginton, still on sabbatical at Johns Hopkins University, noted that "the [Mellinger] article will be reprinted, and copies will be given free to the people who visit our mountains. They will be distributed through motels, restaurants, gift shops, state parks, and Chambers of Commerce as a public service of FOXFIRE. We can't really afford it—we don't even have enough money in the bank to pay for this issue—but neither can we afford to sit idly by and watch our forests spoiled."[26]

The first significant investigation of social and economic problems by Foxfire students coincided with the publication of *Foxfire 2* in 1973. In a letter to his advisory boards, Wigginton described the "new direction" that some of his students had taken in the journalism class. Foxfire had hired three recent graduates—Mary Thomas, Barbara Taylor, and Laurie Brunson—to work for a full year investigating community problems and issues.[27] In support of what became known as the "MARBARLA" project, IDEAS had secured a grant from the Office of Environmental Education, and it sent Pat Peterson, a staff member, to Rabun Gap to assist the young women in their research and writing.

MARBARLA's work resulted in two articles for *Foxfire* magazine. The first piece, printed on colored-stock paper as a center selection in the magazine, focused on changes in Rabun County wrought by the film "Deliverance," whose leading actor, the Chattooga River, forms the county's eastern boundary with South Carolina. The most pressing issue, the authors surmised, was the increased canoe and backpacking traffic on the river and the attendant environmental pollution: discarded beer cans, punctured rubber rafts, and assorted garbage. Wigginton expressed his own disquietude about the film, placing the blame squarely on James Dickey's book. Wigginton complained that Dickey had "obviously" set the novel in north Georgia and peopled it with "men more animal . . . than human." While he applauded Dickey's literary gifts, he objected to his use of mountain people as a foil for civilized society: "It powerfully reinforces a stereotype we have been fighting with Foxfire for eight years: that of the hick with his liquor still, ignorant, depraved, stupid—sometimes laughable—his only concession to the 'finer' things being an occasional crude 'dulcimore' or banjo hanging on the wall of his battered, filthy shack."[28]

The second MARBARLA project was of a larger scope than the

"Deliverance" centerpiece—a five-month research effort reached fruition as an entire issue of *Foxfire* magazine. MARBARLA focused exclusively on the nearby Betty's Creek Valley, presenting a "cold, sobering look at what pressing change and terrific increases in the pace of life can wreak on such a community."[29] The forces of change examined by MARBARLA included the paving of the Betty's Creek Road in 1958 and the subsequent influx of visitors, tourists, and second-home residents into the valley; the former students also traced the interplay of these forces and their effects on the county at large. They concluded that growth in Rabun County was being neither adequately planned nor restricted by zoning ordinances. Here they foresaw the overdevelopment and misuse of land that plagues Rabun County even today.

Wigginton assessed the pedagogical value of the Betty's Creek study in the following terms: "If our students are to walk out of the doors of our high schools both anxious to and prepared to take some responsible role inside our communities of the future, then examination of the type represented by this issue of *Foxfire* is perhaps a part of the work they should be about during their school years."[30] The reality behind this forceful rhetoric, however, has been, with a few exceptions, a retreat from efforts such as the "Betty's Creek Issue." Subsequent Foxfire students have never matched the sustained involvement in current social issues of the MARBARLA group.

A perusal of issues of *Foxfire* magazine from the Rabun Gap era reveals that it remained a literary, as opposed to exclusively cultural, journal until 1974. In 1970, Wigginton had defended *Foxfire*'s colored-stock poetry section on several counts. First, it provided a medium for promising young poets; second, it gave his students the opportunity to adjudicate the merits of individual poems; and finally, it gave them the opportunity to experiment with creative layout designs.[31]

Reader sentiment against the special center-section gradually pressured Wigginton and the students to abandon it. A letter from reader Louise Fonda typified the growing antipathy to the counterculture pieces that often appeared in the magazine:

Although I was *enchanted* with FOXFIRE and still am dedicated to the idea of preserving priceless mountain lore, I am actually offended by the so-called poetry offerings. Several people with whom I have discussed the magazine agree that they are interested in the SOUTHERN HIGH-LANDS. We are not fascinated by the hippie influence and couldn't care less who has a thing going with some kook at a Brooklyn water hydrant or a wild and dreamy affair in some field one night. It's EITHER-OR. And if I have to take the indoctrination of a culture I find offensive, then I suppose

I'll just skip the one I love deeply. So don't renew the subscription *when* it expires. I can't imagine my mother-in-law enjoying the other side of the magazine enough to compensate for the "poetry."[32]

Another shift in the magazine occurred early in 1975 with the creation of Foxfire Press, a vehicle for books of local and regional interest. The first publication of this new entity (which only existed on paper) was a compilation of newspaper columns written by Harvey Miller, who lived near Spruce Pine, N.C. According to Wigginton, he and his students had rescued Miller's articles from an unethical newspaper editor who planned to publish them without negotiating the copyright or royalties with Miller; the threat of a lawsuit forced the editor to relinquish the columns. Foxfire's quid pro quo with Miller allowed the Fund to publish "a compilation of twenty-five years' worth of columns as an issue of *Foxfire*" in exchange for allowing Miller to market 1,500 free copies under a different cover, to keep the copyright for himself, and to order reprints whenever he liked, at his own expense.[33] Miller made over $2,000 from the first printing alone.[34]

In 1976 the Foxfire Press published its first book, *Memories of a Mountain Shortline: The Story of the Tallulah Falls Railroad*. Edited by students Myra Queen and Kaye Carver, this 115-page oral history recounted the life and times of the fifty-eight-mile railroad that had run north from Cornelia, Georgia (1882), through the Tallulah Gorge to Clayton (1904), and finally to Franklin, North Carolina (1907). The twelve students who worked on the project interviewed fifty-four former railroad employees and area residents, collecting stories about hewing crossties, building roadbeds and wooden trestles, driving spikes, and running the trains. Enriching their portrait of the old railway, which was finally bankrupted and demolished in 1961–62, were tales of "derailments, wrecks, going to the station to meet the train, hearing the whistle blow at a certain time of day . . . riding the train for the first time, hitching free rides, etc."[35]

Of greater significance, the book assayed the social and economic role of the railroad in the mountain counties of Habersham, Rabun, and Macon: "The TF belonged to the people it served; it gave them jobs, bought things from them, took them places, brought people to see them, shipped out their farm produce, brought in things they couldn't raise or make, provided depots to gather in, kept them company, provided excitement, and even forecast the weather by the sound of the whistle. It seems there was hardly a facet of life which the railroad did not touch upon."[36]

Given that the Tallulah Falls Railroad and other rural shortlines are only a memory, this book—like its counterparts in the Doubleday

Foxfire series—recaptures an essentially agrarian past and its values. Yet in the spirit of the Betty's Creek study, the students and their advisors, Pat Rogers and Suzanne Angier, also examined an existing shortline in the North Carolina mountains that ran from Topton, in Graham County, to Robbinsville. "By observing Graham County's operation, and finding out how the line adjusted and stayed solvent, we felt we could more accurately project what *might* have happened with the TF."[37] Ironically, shortly after the students completed their interviews, the seventy-year-old Graham County railroad ceased operation. Perhaps this explains why the editors chose *not* to speculate how the Georgia shortline might have escaped bankruptcy or what the implications of its continued operation might have been. At all events, the volume ended by serving the static function of cultural preservation, not by addressing an explicit social problem or issue. This is not to criticize Foxfire or its students, but rather to suggest that despite Wigginton's rhetoric about "a new direction," Foxfire was playing, with some variations, an old and familiar tune.

As Wigginton had expected, the "TF" book had only marginal sales. It was, however, the beginning of an enterprise that would become the only operating division of Foxfire's community development project in the early 1980s, as well as the recipient of a $400,000 publishing contract with E. P. Dutton.

Ironically, the forces of modernization being tentatively examined by Foxfire students during the 1970s inexorably changed Foxfire itself by impelling the consolidation of Rabun County's secondary schools. In March 1974, Rabun County citizens voted in a referendum to build a new, countywide high school, which would include grades seven through twelve. The old county high school in Clayton was partially burned and had grown dilapidated; it was an embarrassment to county politicians. To the chagrin of the majority of voters in the county's northern end, the referendum ended the school board's affiliation with Rabun Gap School; Rabun Gap community students were to be bused to the new school scheduled to open in the fall of 1977. Presented in the next chapter are the details of Foxfire's tenure at Rabun County High School, beginning with Wigginton's decision to leave Rabun Gap School.

NOTES

1. Sitton, "The Foxfire-Concept Publications," 18.

2. David Shapiro, "Discovering a Sense of Past & Place," *Saturday Review,* 29 April 1972, 36–38. See also Peggy Thompson, "Old Timers Tell All to Foxfire," *Smithsonian,* December 1971, 46–51; David W. Hacker, "The Joy of

Learning, *National Observer,* 4 March 1972; David Johnson, "They Learned & Loved It," *New York Times,* Education Section, 9 April 1972; John Pennington, "A Mountain Success Story," *Atlanta Journal and Constitution Magazine,* 9 April 1972, 8–9, 23–28; Peggy Thompson, "In the Footsteps of 'Foxfire,'" *American Education* 8 (1972): 4–10; "Foxfire," *Senior Scholastic,* 18 September 1972, 16–17; Arthur Gordon, "The Magic Glow of Foxfire," *Reader's Digest,* November 1973, 67–72; Patricia Peterson, "The Foxfire Concept," *Media and Methods* 10, no. 3 (1973): 16–18; Daniel Mack, "The Foxfire Experience Reviewed," *Harvard Educational Review* 46 (1976): 477–80.

3. Richard Dorson to Brian Beun, 5 March 1973.

4. Nancy Dennis to Richard Dorson, 9 March 1973, Ford Foundation Archives, PA 730-0084. In a "Report to the [Foxfire] Boards," 18 April 1973, Wigginton himself responded to Dorson's criticism: "My reactions to blasts of this sort run the gamut from rage to sympathy. . . . As we have always maintained, our work is not—and never was—an attempt primarily to collect in professional fashion a body of folklore. My primary focus was always on what happened to a kid's head and his concept of himself and education in general if we could get him out of the classroom and into the community and turned on to something of value during those high school years."

Dorson and Wigginton debated their views in issues of the *North Carolina Journal of Folklore* 21, no. 4 (1973): 157–59; 22, no. 2 (1974): 35–36, 39–41. They finally reached a rapprochement, as discussed in 26, no. 1 (1978): 3–17. Dorson acknowledged that high school students were capable of folkloric inquiry, and Wigginton stipulated "that students [should] have a working knowledge of what folklore as a discipline . . . is all about: folklore versus fakelore" (p. 14). Dorson accepted Wigginton's invitation to write an "afterward" to *Foxfire 4* (Garden City, N.Y.: Anchor Press/Doubleday, 1977), 482–85.

5. Minutes, Board of Directors, Southern Highlands Literary Fund, Inc., 14 April 1973.

6. John Viener to Eliot Wigginton, 10 May 1974.

7. Minutes, Board of Directors, Foxfire Fund, Inc., 14 August 1975.

8. Viener to Wigginton, 19 September 1975. Viener has told me that the bonus was a one-time compensation to Wigginton for seven years of service to Foxfire, a sum that raised his average annual compensation for the period to approximately $4,000.

9. Sitton, "The Foxfire-Concept Publications," 53.

10. Ibid., 55.

11. Wigginton, ed., *The Foxfire Book,* 12–13.

12. Jan Brown Bonner, unpublished memoir quoted with her permission.

13. *Exchange* 1, no. 2 (1973): 7.

14. Ibid., 8; 1, no. 3 (1973): 8–19.

15. *Exchange* 1, no. 3 (1973): 10–11.

16. Final Report on the Foxfire Program, Ford Foundation Grant No. 730-0084, submitted by IDEAS, Inc., for the 1 October 1972–30 September 1974.

17. Ibid.

18. Sitton, "The Foxfire-Concept Publications," 63–69.

19. Ibid., 74–77.

20. Wigginton, "Report to the Boards," March 1971.

21. Wigginton, *Shining Moment,* 14–15.

22. One of the sources of this information was a close associate of Mary Hambidge. See also Wigginton's elegy for Mary Crovatt Hambidge, *Foxfire,* Fall 1973, 209–24, 254–55. An amusing, albeit unscholarly, account of the strife within the Hambidge Foundation after Mrs. Hambidge's death is Nathan James, "What Did Mary Say?," *Brown's Guide to Georgia,* October 1982, 50–55, 82–88.

23. Wigginton, *Shining Moment,* 154.

24. Ibid., 157.

25. Ibid., 158. The price of the property was listed in a manuscript version of this book.

26. *Foxfire,* Spring 1969, Introduction.

27. Wigginton, "Report to the Boards," 25 December 1973.

28. *Foxfire,* Winter 1973, 259.

29. "Betty's Creek Issue," *Foxfire,* Spring 1975, 2–3.

30. Ibid., Note, 2.

31. *Foxfire,* Winter 1970, 194.

32. *Foxfire,* Fall 1970, 178. Wigginton announced in his introduction to *Foxfire,* Spring 1974: "From now on that center section will be devoted to articles . . . that deal with topics of a more social nature that affect all of us in this part of the mountains" (2–3).

33. *Foxfire,* Winter 1974, Foreword. This issue was titled, "News from Pigeon Roost."

34. Eliot Wigginton, *Moments: The Foxfire Experience* (Washington, D.C.: IDEAS, 1975), 83–84.

35. Kaye Carver and Myra Queen, eds., *Memories of a Mountain Shortline: The Story of the Tallulah Falls Railroad* (Rabun Gap, Ga.: Foxfire Press, 1976), 50.

36. Ibid., 101.

37. Ibid., 68.

FOUR

The Rabun County High School Years

Wigginton has asserted that he moved Foxfire to Rabun County High School because he believed "that the *real* beneficiaries of the program *should* be community students—students who needed to know their community and their roots well if they were ever to take some responsible guidance over its future." He has also stated: "The fact that we could easily become divorced from a community we had long since made up our minds to serve was a disturbing, and potentially fatal, reality."[1]

Whether Wigginton wanted to leave Rabun Gap School because of his sustained dislike of the boarding school administration is immaterial. Given his strong ties to the local community and his own expansionist vision for the organization, he really had no other choice. When the new high school opened in 1977, if an arrangement could be made with the school board, Foxfire would move there.

After Wigginton learned that the schools would be consolidated, he notified Leland Dishman, the principal at Rabun County High School, that he was interested in establishing Foxfire at the new high school. Later Dishman invited Wigginton to teach a "test" course at the old high school in Clayton during 1976–77, the year prior to consolidation.[2]

Wigginton began to hire new staff in 1975. Heretofore, he had employed three adult staff members. Suzanne Angier, the VISTA worker, had joined Foxfire in 1970. In 1972, Wigginton hired Pat Rogers, a former community student, and Margie Bennett, a former medical technician and wife of the Rabun Gap School farm manager. Rogers, the organization's vice president, left Foxfire in 1975 to work full-time with IDEAS. Until the fall of 1975, Foxfire staff had worked exclusively with the journalism class at Rabun Gap, advising both *Foxfire* magazine and the school newspaper, *Talon*. The hiring of Paul Gillespie and Mike Cook, former Foxfire community students, signaled the creation of new departments within the organization. Cook, a journalism major at the University of Georgia, was hired to teach video and television production; Gillespie, a graduate of the University of Virginia (who would later attend law school), was assigned to teach photography as well as other components of magazine production. New departments (Wigginton called them "divisions") did not fully crystalize while the organization remained at Rabun Gap, but they were being planned for the program at the new high school.

Acting on the advice of musician Guy Carawan, a member of Foxfire's national advisory board, Wigginton hired George Reynolds, a talented Appalachian musician who was completing a master's degree in folklore at Western Kentucky University. In a letter to his boards in March 1976, Wigginton announced that Reynolds had been "hired by us to do research with our kids in traditional mountain music, to get some music happening here at the school and at the [Foxfire] Center, and to look at the possibilities for Foxfire starting a record company which would produce albums by local musicians and songwriters like Varney Watson [a local musician]."[3]

Local critics of Foxfire have charged that Wigginton hired "outsiders" for jobs that rightfully belonged to Rabun County natives. The criticism rests on the assumption that Foxfire has an obligation to hire directly from the local community, which provides the interview "contacts" for its magazine and books—a tacit quid pro quo. The historical record indicates that Wigginton has honored, in large part, his side of this assumed and unstated bargain, hiring from the local community when it has been feasible. Through the years, he has hired four former students from the local community to his full-time teaching staff and at least nine to various administrative and clerical positions. He has also employed approximately thirty community men to work on various Foxfire construction and maintenance projects.

In some cases, however, a local person has not been available or suited for the position. For example, when Wigginton needed an environmentalist, he had two choices among Rabun County natives: a forestry school graduate and a high school science teacher. The former, who had worked on Foxfire's reconstruction project, recalls:

> They weren't ready for the position when I left, but Wig talked to me and gave me the impression that the position would be available for me when they got it. Yeah, he really wanted me to stay. I could have had that position

had I decided to stay on. It was a combination of things that prompted my leaving. [The foreman] was an aggravation. I really decided also that I didn't want to teach. I had already applied with the forest service before I went up there to work at Foxfire.

You talk about the staff positions. I really think he tried to fill them locally. [But] it's hard to find qualified individuals locally.

The science teacher states that Wigginton knew better than to offer him the position: "I wanted to continue what I'm doing now. There would have been teaching in it, but not five periods a day. My relationship with Wig was such that he would not have offered me the job because he knew I was interested in [full-time] teaching."

Wigginton eventually hired an "outsider," Bob Bennett, the Rabun Gap School farm manager—also a conservationist and wilderness enthusiast. Bennett joined the staff in the summer of 1977 to head Foxfire's environmental/outdoor education programs.

During the school year 1976–77, Wigginton taught an English class of twenty-three tenth-graders at the old Clayton high school, introducing them to all phases of magazine production and arranging interviews with old-timers such as Kenny Runion and Amanda Turpin.[4] The administration and school board were sufficiently impressed with Wigginton's performance and student enthusiasm for Foxfire that they invited him to bring the entire program to the new high school. In the summer, Wigginton enthusiastically informed his legal and advisory boards that "during pre-registration last May for the upcoming September quarter, the ten fully accredited courses we were able to offer were all filled completely half way through the *second* of four registration periods." Wigginton also added that every one of his twenty-three English students in Clayton had registered for a Foxfire course.[5]

The year prior to consolidation witnessed a large-scale expansion of the Foxfire program at Rabun Gap School. Foxfire staff taught individual courses to approximately one hundred students (over 40 percent of the student body) in magazine production, creative photography, video and cable television production, and Appalachian music and folklore. George Reynolds directed the production of Foxfire's first record album, *The North Georgia Mountains,* a collection of traditional Appalachian music that featured folksinger Joyce Brookshire. Reynolds's wife, Sherrod, began archiving the six hundred cassettes and reel-to-reel tapes and 30,000 photographs in Foxfire's collection.[6]

Early in June 1977, Wigginton's staff moved into offices and residences at the Foxfire Center. The second floor of the Bennett residence, situated on a ridge overlooking the other cabins, included dormitory housing for visitors; the "dogtrot" cabin assigned to the Reynoldses included four bedrooms upstairs and was licensed as a group home for runaways and other troubled adolescents. Each staff teacher maintained a separate office and production studio on the property.[7]

For Wigginton, the summer of 1977 was auspicious for more reasons than the move to the Foxfire Center. Playwright Susan Cooper and distinguished actor Hume Cronyn had decided to coauthor a play based on materials in the first three *Foxfire* books, and they had written Wigginton for permission to the dramatic rights. Foxfire staff and students requested that Cooper and Cronyn visit Rabun County to present their ideas for the play. Cronyn describes the meeting that took place at the Foxfire Center:

> It [the play] wasn't taken for granted by them. They were very questioning. They didn't want a reproduction of L'il Abner or the Beverly Hillbillies and that was as far away from what we had in mind as anything could be. Anyway, Susan and I went down and we were ushered into Wig's office. And there were about a dozen students there and two or three of the staff, and they all sat on the floor, and Susan and I occupied the only two chairs. And they started asking questions: What was it about, the books that we'd enjoyed, what interested us, what sort of a play [would it be], where was it going to be done? We answered all sorts of questions. They obviously were puzzled as to just what we were up to. And did they want to risk the association of the Foxfire name with something that might or might not end up in the New York theater and might be good or might be absolutely horrible? After I suppose twenty minutes of questioning, they excused us, and we went out and walked around the hillside, waiting for them to make up their minds as to whether or not we were to have the rights or not. And finally a sixteen- or seventeen-year-old boy came out and he said [Cronyn affects a southern drawl], "I guess you all can come in now." And I could not resist it—I said, "How'd we do?" And he said, "Well, I guess we think you're all right." And then we went in and sat down, and they asked us some more questions and then they gave us their blessing. The only thing that they requested was that they see a final draft of the script, and we agreed to this on the understanding that once they had approved the direction in which we were moving, . . . they wouldn't have approval of every single rewrite because that would have just been impractical.[8]

The *Foxfire* play first opened in 1980 at the Avon Theater of the Stratford Festival, Ontario, with Cronyn's wife, Jessica Tandy, in the lead role of Annie Nations and Cronyn in the role of Annie's husband, Hector. Annie and Hector are characters whose life histories and idiosyncrasies are based on a composite of characters from the *Foxfire* books. The Foxfire "contact" whose presence is most strongly felt is Aunt Arie Carpenter. A conspicuous example is a scene in which Annie cajoles the land developer Prinz Carpenter to cut out the eyeballs of a hog's head that she plans to cook for souse meat—recalling Wigginton's first encounter with Aunt Arie. Less conspicuous is the funeral scene in which Annie confesses to the doctor that as she was washing Hector's body, she found a scar she had never noticed before—a memory poignantly described by Aunt Arie for the article "Old-Time Burials," published in *Foxfire 2.*

Described by one critic as "a hillbilly 'Our Town,'" the play sensitively examines the generational conflict between Appalachian traditionalists and their children, who have been acculturated into the mainstream American culture. As the play opens, Hector Nations has been dead for five years, buried up in the apple orchard on his mountain farm. Hector's ghost (or a figment of Annie's imagination) converses with Annie throughout the play, recalling scenes of their marriage, family life, and Hector's death—all dramatized as flashbacks on stage. He is particularly troubled that his son Dillard, a country music singer, wants her to sell the homeplace and return with him to Atlanta. A major focus of the play is the struggle between father and son that culminated in Dillard's decision to leave home (and, symbolically, the traditions it represented). At play's end, Annie leaves with Dillard, having sold her property to the land developer, and Hector returns to the orchard.[9]

After successful runs in Minneapolis, Baltimore, and Boston, the critically acclaimed *Foxfire* opened on Broadway on 11 November 1982 at the Barrymore Theater. The play lasted ten months, and Jessica Tandy won a Tony Award as best dramatic actress for her elegant portrayal of Annie Nations. By the summer of 1984, numerous theatrical groups had scheduled performances, and several sent actors to Rabun County to visit Foxfire "contacts."[10]

The late 1970s were a halcyon, free-spending era for Foxfire, which used its burgeoning royalties not only to provide free educational services to the local community, but also to underwrite the costs of an annual summer jobs program for students, to maintain the Foxfire Center property and reconstruction project, to support an expanded college scholarship program (begun at Rabun Gap School in 1975), to initiate an ambitious community development project, and to build what has become a $1.8 million endowment.

In the decade 1973–82, Doubleday royalty checks from the sales of *The Foxfire Book* and six subsequent volumes in the *Foxfire* series averaged nearly $310,000 per year, with a highwater mark of $454,000 (on the strength of volumes 1–5) in 1978. By 1983, however, the boom was over, the national audience evidently satiated with the formulaic *Foxfire* compilations. Royalties plummeted from $299,000 in 1982 to $152,000 in 1983; and the downward trend continued into 1984. Wigginton and Doubleday announced that they would discontinue the series after the publication of *Foxfire 9* in 1986.[11]

Wigginton's stated goal in bringing Foxfire to Rabun County High School was "eventually, to integrate one (at least) good, solid experiential component into every department in the high school."[12] At the outset of Foxfire's tenure at the new school, Wigginton's goal seemed within reach. In a newsletter article, magazine advisor Margie Bennett described Foxfire's educational program as a wheel. The hub was *Foxfire* magazine, with a circulation of approximately 4,500 (a surprisingly low figure, given the huge popularity of the *Foxfire* books). The other divisions, variant applications of the Foxfire pedagogy (in theory, at least), were the spokes. "The magazine," Bennett wrote, "was the initial impetus for the organization and continues to be the mainstay of the organization."[13]

Although Foxfire had the status of a department, students in its programs received credit through the traditional departments: English, fine arts, social studies, science, and media. Wigginton and Margie Bennett taught beginning and advanced levels of magazine production. George Reynolds taught courses in Appalachian folklore, music, and record production. "The students in the record production class," Bennett stated, "help find local traditional musicians and original artists, coordinate the schedule for the recording studio [in Franklin, N.C.], design the record copies and inserts, and market the records."[14] Mike Cook taught video as a medium for the Foxfire interview, but his focus was modern Rabun County, its people and lifestyles. Bob Bennett, the environmentalist, taught a course in environmental awareness that featured a study of water pollution in Rabun County and clear-cutting in the Chattahoochee National Forest.

Foxfire's move to Rabun County High School coincided with the retrenchment of IDEAS from active support of Foxfire descendant projects. Given that IDEAS had successfully demonstrated the replicability of the Foxfire concept in a diversity of cultural settings, private foundations were reluctant to continue funding for an idea they considered "old hat."[15]

An early indication of the withdrawal of IDEAS from the Foxfire arena was its abandonment of the *Exchange* newsletter at the end of 1976. Wigginton agreed to publish the defunct newsletter at Foxfire expense, with Sherrod Reynolds as coordinator. The first issue of the *Nameless Newsletter* appeared in the late fall of 1977. Murray Durst, of the Commission of National Resources for Youth, stated that approximately one hundred projects existed at this time.[16]

In the four years she worked with Foxfire, Sherrod Reynolds edited *Hands On* (the name given the *Nameless Newsletter* in 1979), served as liaison to the descendant projects, and systematized Foxfire's archive collection. Reynolds had a knack for attracting private foundation grants to support her projects. For example, she raised $13,740 in matched funds from the National Historic Preservation and Records Commission and the Rockefeller Foundation to defray Foxfire's archiving expenses.[17] Reynolds also played a leading role in organizing the National Workshop for Cultural Journalism, held in St. Louis in the summer of 1979.[18]

Although Wigginton continued to travel after 1977 (often in the company of students), to speak to teachers and myriad educational organizations, he did not invest heavily his organization's time or resources in curriculum dissemination. For example, a notice in the *Nameless Newsletter* in 1978 announced that henceforth subscribers would have to pay an annual $3.00 fee. Foxfire had provided the first six issues of the newsletter free of charge to the descendant projects.[19]

Foxfire's growing insularity featured a renewed concern with local community issues and affairs that had implications for education in other corners of rural America. In the late 1970s Wigginton struggled to formulate a workable community development plan that would enlist his pedagogy in the resolution of pressing social and economic issues in Rabun County. He directed his energies toward a tiny piece of highway frontage property in Mountain City, purchased by Foxfire in 1977.

Over the next six years, this 8½-acre tract in the town's business district (purchased at a cost of $85,000) would be the focus of a succession of Foxfire community development plans, none of which would come to fruition. These plans had a twofold purpose: first, the creation of businesses that would provide attractive career alternatives for Rabun County High School graduates; second, the linkage of these businesses to educational activities at the high school. Among the residual effects of these initiatives were the creation of a Foxfire Grants Management Office (to solicit seed funds for the businesses), the establishment of the Foxfire Press as a regional publishing firm, and the construction of two buildings on the property. (See Chapter 6 for extended discussion of Foxfire's Mountain City Project.)

In the fall of 1983, legal board members advised Wigginton to discontinue Foxfire's community development planning. The rapid and irreversible decline in Doubleday royalties had forced them to rethink Foxfire's mission, which they believed should be explicitly educational and directed to a national audience. Although Wigginton had consistently averred that the Mountain City Project was, *at heart,* educational and also a replicable model for rural development, he acquiesced in the decision.

The time had come, the legal board decreed, for Foxfire to quit frittering away its resources in the local arena and to begin a program of national curriculum dissemination. They argued that American education was in a deplorable condition; teachers, administrators, and policymakers desperately needed an infusion of new (and tested) ideas. Foxfire, they believed, had an obligation beyond the boundaries of Rabun County to contribute to this dialogue.

During the years of their involvement in planning for community development, Wigginton and his teaching staff devoted the overwhelming majority of their time to Foxfire's educational programs at Rabun County High School. As to be expected, the Foxfire curriculum changed; yet (as discussed in Chapter 8), the changes were not always in step with the philosophy that Wigginton had articulated in *Moments* (1975). In fact, by 1984–85, the pedagogy had veered from striking a balance between cognitive and affective learnings (the Deweyan "middle way") and was perilously close to becoming a "feel good" program that meted out rewards, good times, and "meaningful experiences" to students without demanding a solid academic performance in return.

The quarter system of credits at the new high school proved, in the long run, detrimental to Wigginton's *Foxfire* magazine program. Rabun Gap School had not succumbed to the cries for "relevancy" that heavily influenced curriculum planning in the early 1970s; under its Carnegie unit system, students were required to remain in a single course for a full year. Foxfire journalism students, for better or worse, worked on the magazine from autumn to spring. At Rabun County High School, where the school board had mandated a "shopping mall" curriculum tailored to real and imagined student needs, Wigginton struggled to maintain continuity in the magazine classes from quarter to quarter. The result was that many articles were left in a sort of suspended animation until a new crop of students or Wigginton himself finished them. The advantage of the quarter system (and this is what initially attracted Wigginton to the idea) was that it quickly weeded out students for whom the magazine was an inappropriate vehicle for learning. In 1984 the school board, fearful that its high school graduates lacked adequate skills in reading, writing, and numeracy, ordered the implementation of a semester credit system, beginning in the 1984–85 academic year. That experience is too recent for any conclusions to be drawn about its effects on Foxfire.

Foxfire magazine is now linked to the academic program as two courses: Foxfire I and Foxfire II. The first is an introductory course that offers academic credit through the English Department. Given that the nation's educational milieu is friendly only toward curricula that have an expressly intellectual content, Wigginton has created a writing course for students in grades nine through eleven that enlists each component of magazine production explicitly in the service of composition skills.

The idea behind Foxfire I differs more in degree than in kind from Foxfire II, the magazine production class. Unlike its progenitor, Foxfire I begins with an agenda of writing skills. The vehicle for addressing those skills is the traditional Appalachian culture, which provides the raw material for the weekly (on the average) themes. The compositions range from physical descriptions of the mountain elderly to imaginative essays about the life history of an artifact (written as a narrative monologue) to process analyses (e.g., describing how a cornstalk airplane is made).

In one imaginative exercise, Wigginton has the students create a culture "from scratch." First he helps them identify the elements of a culture, e.g., food, clothing, housing, customs, religion (Wigginton and the students come up with approximately thirty). Then he says, "We'll invent a creature. What does it look like?" Field notes from one class describe what happens next:

> The class becomes a whirling dervish. . . . Students shout out answers, such as "ten-feet tall," "pink," "eye in the center of forehead," "horns," etc. Wig's writing is pretty sloppy and crowded on the board by this time. Al yells, "zits!," to which Tammy responds, "That's gross! We want a clean monster!" There is an uproar of excitement as students shout out their ideas for the creature, which Wig selectively writes on the board. Jerry comes in, and the girls who sit near the door yell, "There's the monster!" Next Wig calls for choices for naming the creature. Hedy lobbies for her choice, the "hooky-mujical," but the "geek" wins out.

Following the specification of the creature and its habitat, Wigginton explains that each student must choose an element of culture as the focus of his or her essay. The students raise hands to show their preferences as Wigginton reads down the list and marks off the topics that have been chosen. Finally, he instructs them to write an inventive paper that describes the role of the specific cultural feature in the creature's life, given the limitations of its physical characteristics and habitat. After marking the papers, Wigginton incorporates each student's best paragraphs into a composite class paper that provides a complete description of the creature's culture.

One dramatic difference between the two Foxfire courses is the *style* of the student interviews with community elders. Wigginton has found it logistically unfeasible to take a class of twenty to twenty-five students on an interview to meet a Foxfire contact. The alternative has been to invite the contact to be interviewed in the Foxfire classroom. In the spring quarter of 1984, students interviewed four elderly mountain residents about their childhood toys and games. The interviews were the basis of compositions using the expository modes of description and process analysis. (For discussion of the role of the elderly as community teachers, see Chapter 5).

Although the goal of the introductory course is not the production of a publishable article, students in the class collect and transcribe interview materials, take photographs and print them in a darkroom, construct diagrams, and begin the layout of an article. In short, they learn the basic skills of doing magazine work. Students who advance to Foxfire II usually complete these articles for publication in the magazine, with credit given to the students who worked on them in Foxfire I.

Foxfire II is a lineal descendant of the journalism course that Wigginton taught at Rabun Gap School. Until 1984–85, with the transition to a semester system, the magazine was an elective which did not carry English credit. Despite the rhetoric that *Foxfire* magazine is a vehicle for teaching communications as well as vocational skills, these skills have not set the agenda for the course. Herein lies perhaps the major distinction between the two Foxfire courses.

In Foxfire I, Wigginton teaches writing in the various expository modes from a perspective that says, in effect: "Look, what we have to write is a descriptive paper. The way we're going to do that is to invite an old-timer to come here, and then while he sits and visits with us, you guys are going to take some notes about his physical features and his mannerisms and then later you're going to write a composition from those notes."

Usually a day before each interview or special class activity (e.g., proper use of a tape recorder), Wigginton introduces the paper and discusses with students the sorts of things they must observe and include in their writing; students write the papers on the day following the interview or activity. After he marks and grades each set of compositions, usually on the same day the papers are completed, Wigginton types up grammar and style sheets which highlight student writing errors. The next day he returns them to the students with the corrected compositions for group discussion.

In Foxfire II, neither writing nor any other communications or vocational skill receives such explicit attention. In fact, the entire agenda is determined by the requirements of the articles that compose each magazine. A subject is not chosen because it is appropriate for teaching a particular type of writing or vocational skill. It is chosen, either by Wigginton or the students themselves, because it serves the goal of cultural preservation or, at the pragmatic level, just looks interesting.

In addition to the Foxfire classes, Wigginton teaches a college preparatory English composition class for high school seniors that, in large part, is indistinguishable from a typical college freshman writing class. The impetus for creating the expository writing class at Rabun County High School was Wigginton's realization that some of his former Foxfire students were failing their introductory college English courses. In organizing the class, he has drawn upon the course guides and writing manuals of several nearby universities. Using the models in a college-level anthology, each student writes a draft of a weekly narrative or essay that Wigginton shepherds and critiques for revision; as in Foxfire I, he makes ample use of grammar and style sheets.

Wigginton's classroom provides a colorful and appropriate setting for his courses. Overlooking the rear parking lot of Rabun County High School, Room F201 was originally built as a business education classroom, but given to Foxfire when the school opened in 1977. Wigginton and his students worked around both the protruding floor plugs scattered about the green-carpeted room and the school rule that proscribed nailing or gluing anything to the walls. He has noted: "Since we were allowed to hang nothing from the cement block walls, the students lifted the ceiling tiles, attached wires to the girders above, and suspended bamboo poles horizontally against the ceiling from which we then hung quilts and other artifacts."[20] Foxfire staff and students also constructed a darkroom on one side of the large classroom and mounted bulletin boards on the exterior paneling.

Over the years, the Foxfire classroom has become a museum of Appalachian arts and crafts. A wooden man carved from a tree trunk by folk artist C. P. Ligon, painted in red, white, and blue and positioned with a replica "Don't Tread on Me" flag in his right hand, maintains a humorous vigil at the door of the room. Quilts of variegated colors and patterns, including three crafted by Aunt Arie Carpenter, hang along the spacious walls. Scattered along the walls and in odd corners are a wagon wheel built by John Conley, a broadaxe, a beam from an ancient log cabin, an urn filled with Kenny Runion's walking sticks, a horse collar, and an assortment of handcrafted tools. Crowded on cabinet tops are face and rooster jugs by Edwin and Lanier Meaders, primitive folk sculptures, a cornstalk airplane and a cornstalk horse, a dipper gourd by Lawton Brooks, and a miniature copper still by Buck Carver.[21]

Beyond the courses taught by Wigginton (with assistance from Margie Bennett), the Foxfire program has heavily emphasized the teaching of technical and personal growth skills. For example, in 1984, Mike Cook, Foxfire's video and photography specialist, taught two levels of video/television production that were manifestly manual skills courses. In September 1979, Cook had made arrangements with the Marchman family, owners of the cable television company in Clayton, to begin renovation of the second floor of their building as a "local origination" studio for Foxfire video productions. Cook had abandoned his original idea of building a broadcast studio on Foxfire's new property in Mountain City because the organization lacked the capital for such a venture. The Marchmans stipulated that if Cook would build the production studio at Foxfire's cost, they would lease it to the Fund at no additional charge. After nearly a year of work and an expenditure of $6,000, Cook and his students completed the Clayton studio, where they began producing color video tapes of interviews and community events. In the fall of 1984, however, they abandoned the Marchman building because of what Cook vaguely describes as "logistical and money problems" related to running the program off-campus.

In 1984 George Reynolds, the folklorist and bluegrass musician, taught music performance, folklore (a social studies credit), and Appalachian instrument building (a manual skills course). He directed three string bands and a choral group, which practiced daily in the music performance classes and frequently performed at local elementary schools, restaurants, and community fund-raising events. A group of former Foxfire music students (including a high school junior) formed the fourth band under Reynolds's direction; in fact, this was the original Foxfire string band, founded in 1979, called the Foxfire Boys—an ensemble that had played at the Knoxville World's Fair (1982) and on Roy Acuff's show at the Grand Ole Opry (1983).

From 1977 to 1984 Reynolds taught record production classes at the high school. In addition to the first album on the Foxfire label, *The North Georgia Mountains* (released in 1978), he has directed students in the production of five more tapes and albums, performed by Appalachian folk musicians, Christian Harmony singers, the Rabun County Singing Convention, and the Foxfire Boys.

In each of his classes in 1984, Reynolds, a native Appalachian from the Virginia coal fields, taught largely by preachment and example the values of cultural pride and regional identity. Yet, like Cook and Bob Bennett, he dealt only superficially with academic skills, e.g., reading and writing—even when they were required for mastery of a subject like folklore. Inexplicably, Reynolds did not use a single *Foxfire* book or magazine article in the twelve-week folklore course observed for the Foxfire evaluation.

Bob Bennett, Foxfire's environmentalist and outdoor educator for eight years, taught an introductory course to the Foxfire programs (exclusively for seventh graders), outdoor education, running (he was also the school's cross-country coach), and a special two-period environmental science/physical education course for a select group of ninth- and tenth-grade boys.

The students in Bennett's special course had classroom learning and behavioral difficulties but for various reasons had not been assigned to special education classes. Bennett's chief aim, however, was not to teach environmental science or physical education, but to instill in the handful of youths who enrolled with him every quarter a modicum of self-confidence and to teach them cooperative skills that would transfer to their other classes. Two instruments of this purpose were a ropes course (an assortment of "high wires" that students had to climb and traverse) and a partially completed log cabin, both situated on a ridge behind the Rabun County High School. Bennett and his students built the ropes course in 1979, with help from Project Adventure; in 1982, they enlisted master builder Peter Gott to help them begin construction on the log cabin that was expected to become Bennett's outdoor classroom. In 1984, Bennett used both facilities for cooperative work activities, e.g., building the cabin's chimney and working as teams on the ropes course. He also taught these students gardening and rudimentary conservation techniques at the Foxfire Center. In previous years, Bennett had included in the course additional activities such as apple tree grafting, beekeeping, nature trail construction, and the study of local fauna.

Since joining Foxfire in 1977, Bennett had taught several experimental courses in environmental science that focused on such topics as the effects of clear cutting in the federal forest preserves (with attendant water pollution studies) and solar heating devices. Yet these experimental courses never endured or jelled into a core environmental program—unlike the programs of the other Foxfire staff members.

To implement the legal board's 1983 mandate for national curriculum dissemination, Wigginton ordered his staff to begin a self-evaluation to determine what had worked well in their classrooms in the past that might be replicated by other teachers. Wigginton himself had just completed the final draft of *Sometimes a Shining Moment,* to which he had devoted several years of research and writing. Written explicitly for teachers, the lengthy manuscript included Foxfire's history (primarily at Rabun Gap School), Wigginton's educational philosophy, and a course outline and description of Foxfire I. Wigginton advised his board members that the book directed to teachers was part of an integrated staff effort to disseminate the best of Foxfire. "In preparation for the publication of the book and as a part of their evaluation of the effectiveness of their courses," he added, "Mike, George and Bob are all writing similar, extensive descriptions of the most academically relevant (and thus transferable) courses they have designed. By the time my book is published, these supplementary course descriptions should be finished, and if there is demand for them, Foxfire Press is in place to publish them and fill that demand. If the demand is not there, the staff members will still have the benefit of having had to scrutinize their own courses carefully. . . ."[22]

The philosophical bugbear in this passage was Wigginton's application of the term "academically relevant" to courses taught by his staff. The fact of the matter was that the staff did not teach *any* courses that were consciously academic, either by virtue of subject-matter content or intellectual skills addressed—at least, not as they were taught in 1984. It was also apparent that Wigginton previously had not given his staff a clear or firm mandate even to regard this as their agenda. Consequently, Foxfire's curriculum dissemination effort began as a rearguard action to reshape the entire program along lines that would make the acquisition and refinement of intellectual skills (defined in this context as reading, writing, and numeracy; general concepts and understandings) a primary goal for its own sake, as well as a support or reinforcement for the individual student's self-esteem and confidence. Wigginton demanded no less than allegiance to the educational philosophy he had formulated at Rabun Gap School.

As the 1984–85 school year opened, Foxfire staff members began restructuring their courses. Addressing his national advisory board in the fall of 1984, Wigginton presented an ambitious two-year plan for curriculum development and dissemination. In its late-summer planning sessions, he remarked, the entire staff had drawn up a comprehensive set of educational objectives, keyed to state competency requirements. Teaching-staff members were now busy designing instructional activities to address the appropriate competencies. Wigginton acknowledged that the magazine course—the "hub" of the Foxfire wheel—needed refurbishing: "Margie and I . . . are in the midst of revamping *Foxfire II,* complete with daily lesson plans which Margie is writing. Up until now, many of the instructional objectives Foxfire II can meet have been met only haphazardly as far as all the students in the class are concerned, and now we are attempting to create activities in association with the magazine's production that address these objectives directly, head on, and for all the students."

By the fall of 1985, Wigginton averred, each staff member would have on hand sets of daily lesson plans detailing competency-specific activities for each of his or her courses. Moreover, the staff was currently "designing or testing" *new* courses that were expected to be more effective than previous efforts in addressing intellectual skills. "Bob, for example, is testing a new science course now—one which hopefully will be a stronger science course than anything he has attempted thus far. Mike and George are both designing new courses which I hope we will be able to field test next semester. George and I are currently designing and field testing together, as peer teachers, a new course in Appalachian literature. With two semester's [*sic*] worth of experimentation and lesson plans, we should be able to put together a reasonably complete guide to that course that will include what worked, what failed, and the planned alteration."[23]

Wigginton anticipated that the course guides would be completed in the second year of the plan (1985–86). He also stated that he intended to revive the *Hands On* newsletter, dormant for two years, as a forum for responding to questions and comments raised by his new education book.

Throughout the fall of 1984, the Foxfire staff met weekly to discuss educational objectives and to critique lesson plans. Despite these good intentions, a critical flaw remained the lack of any real plan to measure the effectiveness of Foxfire courses. Exactly how these courses would be validated, if at all, was an open question at the end of 1984.

A second major decision, vigorously affirmed at the annual board meeting, was the launching of a national endowment campaign to raise at least $2 million to make Foxfire financially independent, even without ever selling another book. In December, a hopeful Wigginton told his boards: "Because your feelings on this were so strong, I have decided to take all of next summer and all of the Fall semester (a total of eight months) and devote this time entirely to the campaign."[24]

In 1984, Foxfire's endowment stood at $1.8 million, divided between investment portfolios in New York and Atlanta. Legal board member Leroy Sinclair, president of the New York Power Authority, estimated that the Fund could live entirely off the endowment at $203,000 per year for another twenty years; at its 1984 budget of $437,000, less than twelve years.[25] Given the demise of the Doubleday *Foxfire* series, coupled with the modest financial success of *Aunt Arie* and *The Foxfire Book of Appalachian Cookery* (a 1984 Foxfire Press release), it is evident the organization will require a bolstered endowment if it is to operate at even its *present* level of activity beyond the next decade.

Thus Wigginton has linked Foxfire's academic and financial future directly to the two-year plan for curriculum dissemination. Part of his strategy is to recruit a national chairperson for the campaign and to appeal personally to the foundations, arguing the case that Foxfire's educational mission is *national* in scope, aimed at the dissemination of "a project-centered curriculum that demands experiential [i.e., beyond the classroom], community-based linkages as the heart of the academic agenda."[26]

The second part of this study draws upon and amplifies the historical record presented in the first part. It should be evident to readers that the historical context is essential for an analysis of the specific issues and effects that pertain to Foxfire's role in the Rabun County community. This part, which relies heavily upon observational and interview data, is best described as an on-site evaluation that specifies precisely how the project works, who benefits (and the counterpoint, who does not benefit), and what the nature of the relationship between Foxfire and each category of its intended beneficiaries has been.

NOTES

1. Wigginton, *Shining Moment*, 166–67.
2. Eliot Wigginton provided this information in an interview with the author, 21 December 1984.
3. Wigginton, "Report to the Boards," 8 March 1976.
4. *Clayton Tribune,* 4 November 1976.
5. Wigginton, "Report to the Boards," 27 July 1977.
6. Wigginton, "Report to the Boards," 7 September 1976.
7. Wigginton, "Report to the Boards," 27 July 1977.

8. Transcription of *The Foxfire Glow* (New York: "Prime of Your Life," WNBC, 25 December 1982).

9. Susan Cooper and Hume Cronyn, *Foxfire* (New York: Samuel French, 1983).

10. For histories of the play, see Susan Cooper, "The Making of the Play," *Guthrie Theater Program Magazine*, 1981; and D. C. Denison, "How 'Foxfire' Journeyed to Broadway," *New York Times*, 7 November 1982, sec. 2.

11. "Schedule of Sales & Royalties," Foxfire Center financial records, 31 October 1972 to 31 October 1984.

12. Wigginton, "Report to the Boards," 5 March 1977.

13. *Nameless Newsletter* 1, no. 1/2 (1977): 6.

14. Ibid., 6–8.

15. This information was provided in a draft version of the manuscript of *Sometimes a Shining Moment*.

16. *Nameless Newsletter* 1, no. 1/2 (1977): 4–6.

17. *Nameless Newsletter* 1, no. 4 (1978): 12–13.

18. Wigginton, "Report to the Boards," 28 August 1979.

19. *Nameless Newsletter* 1, no. 6 (1978): 16.

20. Wigginton, *Shining Moment*, 328.

21. In addition to my own observations, a useful source for this information was Foxfire student Theresa Thurmond's account in the community newsletter, *Foxfire Reflections*, February 1984.

22. "Report to the Boards," 28 February 1984. Wigginton presented a timetable to his staff on 5 March. Interestingly, the document indicates that he initially expected the curriculum guides to be completed as early as the summer of 1985.

23. "Foxfire's Two-Year Plan." Also Minutes, Foxfire National Advisory Board Meeting, September 22–23, 1985.

24. Wigginton, "Report to the Boards," 5 December 1984.

25. Leroy Sinclair to Eliot Wigginton, 6 July 1984.

26. "Foxfire's Two-Year Plan."

PART TWO

Issues and Effects: The Local Context

FIVE

Educational Issues and Effects

Issues and effects related to Foxfire programs encompass four spheres of influence: student, school, community, and the Foxfire organization itself. This chapter highlights issues and effects that bear primarily on students and the school culture. Given the dominant role of cultural journalism in Foxfire's history and Wigginton's pedagogical theory, analysis at the level of students is restricted to educational processes that have attended the growth of *Foxfire* magazine and to the effects of this particular innovation from the perspective of young adults, high school graduates from 1969 to 1983, looking back on the Foxfire experience.

Student Issues and Effects

Authorship and Decision Making

In his heated letter of resignation from Foxfire's national advisory board in 1979, Herbert Kohl, a widely known radical educator and school critic, accused Wigginton of having drifted from his pedagogical moorings by putting the demands of a quality product ahead of the educational needs of his students. Kohl did not mince words in telling Wigginton he believed that Foxfire was a sham. Specifically, he raised two issues concerning Foxfire and the education of adolescents that have been routinely and consistently ignored by the Foxfire testimonial writers. The first was the issue of student authorship, which Kohl formulated in an accusatory rhetoric: "Who actually produces the Foxfire books? Are they the work of the students, who should then take pride of authorship, or are they reworked versions of materials students collected? Does the staff of Foxfire and the editorial staff of

Doubleday do the actual writing? If so, is there any misrepresentation of this fact? Is permission granted by the students to do the rewriting?" Kohl's second question raised the issue of decision making within the Foxfire organization. Clearly, he was incredulous about Wigginton's published claims that students had a genuine voice in the management of Foxfire affairs. Kohl asked, "Who makes the decisions at Foxfire anyway? I have had a number of talks with Wig about the problem and he assures me that students make the decisions, etc. I find myself then asking him over and over again who could make a decision to give away the endowment, to redistribute the wealth as it were, and get no answer to that one."[1]

The question of authorship is undeniably the thornier of the two issues raised in Kohl's letter to Foxfire. Kohl's phrasing, however, reduces a complex issue to an either-or proposition—a nonnegotiable item that has no middle ground for varying degrees of collaboration between teacher and student. Responsible scholarship demands that the issue of authorship be addressed, but not necessarily in Kohl's absolute terms. A more instructive approach is to delineate the various roles of students and adult staff in the production of *Foxfire* articles and to ascertain the pedagogical soundness of the processes that culminate in the publication of a magazine or book. This approach moves the issue beyond the level of playground discourse ("Is not!" "Is too!") to a more useful level that specifically addresses pedagogy.

The manuscripts of all the articles that have ever appeared in a *Foxfire* magazine or book are housed in files along the wall of a narrow alcove in Wigginton's office at the Foxfire Center. In many cases, attached to these manuscripts are drafts of the articles (dating as far back as 1967), which provide insights about staff editing procedures and the quality of unedited student writing. An examination of the materials accompanying more than seventy-five articles suggests the following groupings: Articles written exclusively by Wigginton from materials compiled by students and himself, articles compiled and written exclusively by students, and articles that are collaborative (compiled and written by Wigginton *and* students).

Belonging to the first category is one of the finest pieces ever to appear in the *Foxfire* publications: "The End of Moonshining as a Fine Art" (*Foxfire*, Winter/Fall 1968, 35–56, 90–130), a superb process analysis, replete with the anecdotes of local moonshiners and skillful diagrams, that describes how to build a still and make quality sour-mash whiskey. The draft of the article, which matches the printed version word for word, appears in Wigginton's handwriting. The confusion about authorship arises from the fact that Wigginton neither signed the piece himself nor attributed authorship to any student(s); in fact, the only attribution is an acknowledgment of two students "who were of special help."[2]

Wigginton explains tersely that he wrote this article when "the philosophy wasn't formulated and all of us were just sort of thrashing around." *Foxfire* magazine was in its incipiency at Rabun Gap School, still just an extracurricular activity, and students who were not expected to take a hand in the writing accompanied Wigginton on interviews. Wigginton says, "I remember ['The End of Moonshining as a Fine Art'] being largely something I put together. That's one of those examples in the really early days of the magazine where I took a far heavier hand in the creation of [the] articles than I would today, and where one of the main ideas operating was to get as many students to do as much as possible, and then to grab that data and go ahead and wrap it, but have enough stuff in there so that kids that were involved could see their hand in the thing."[3]

A major article of recent vintage is Wigginton's unsigned narrative history of the Rothell House, an antebellum log house reconstructed on the Foxfire property in Mountain City, which constitutes the text of an entire issue of *Foxfire* (Summer 1984). In this case, Wigginton argues persuasively that it made sense to intervene in the writing because the article had become too complex for his students: "On the log cabin thing I had students involved in every one of those visits to courthouses and dealing with data and stuff like that. But in the final analysis what happened was that the kids just plain damn got in over their heads and they couldn't make any sense out of it. At that point in time it turned into a situation that was just *damn* close to being educationally bankrupt in terms of the amount of energy and the amount of frustration that those guys would have encountered in trying to make *some* sense out of that thing."

This logic also seems to have applied to a sophisticated piece Wigginton wrote (again unsigned) as the historical overview for a 228-page article on gun making in *Foxfire 5*.[4] This kind of historical analysis and writing is beyond the ability of most of Wigginton's students. The manuscript file indicates that students conducted the interviews, did the photography, edited transcriptions, and wrote introductions, albeit with heavy editing by Wigginton, for the various sections of this lengthy article.

Pat Rogers, a staff member in the 1970s, has stated that Wigginton never finished an article when his intervention wasn't warranted: "There was a lot of talk about process versus product. He would definitely allow articles to be printed that could have been better. It was just the articles that had stalled [that Wigginton completed] because the kid or kids who were working on the article found that the subject matter had too much scope, or they couldn't handle it thoroughly and they got frustrated with it."

Wigginton or his staff occasionally will complete an article left by a student who graduates or fails to take the magazine class the next session. "In the sense of [a staff member] finishing up or cleaning up, there's a rationale behind it," explains a staff member. "You've got an article you're committed to a contact for and you don't have a kid to finish it." Wigginton remarks that the alternative, grudgingly invoked, is to "leave it and try to talk somebody into picking it up who wasn't involved with the article at all and probably doesn't want the damn thing."

It is a given that *Foxfire* articles are edited, or at least approved, by Wigginton or another staff member. What distinguishes a student-authored piece from a collaboration is the degree and intensity of the editing. These categories are not fixed in stone; distinctions between light and heavy editing become blurred. The manuscript files, as well as interviews with former Foxfire students and observations of *Foxfire* magazine classes, provide enough clear-cut examples within each category to support the conclusion that Wigginton and his staff edit in a fashion that is commensurate with what they believe is the upper limit of a student's capabilities and motivation. The work of talented, highly motivated students generally requires minimal editing.

A case in point is the article "Three Days Away from Home" (*Foxfire,* Fall 1971, 174–88), written by three girls at the Rabun Gap School who drove a jeep into the Great Smoky Mountains, camped out, and interviewed, by themselves, elderly Appalachians who were total strangers to them. The draft of this entertaining piece was written entirely by the girls, with virtually no editorial assistance from Wigginton or his staff.

Paul Gillespie recalled his role in the early *Foxfire* books, particularly in the production of "Aunt Arie" (*The Foxfire Book,* 17–30), one of the most famous Foxfire articles: "I had a lot of stuff in the first and second book. I'd say 98 percent of [it] was pretty much mine. I mean, I did it. I wrote the introduction to the Aunt Arie thing. . . . The interviews and transcriptions I did were mine. I worked on the hominy article and the article on log cabins. That stuff was mine. I labored and sweated over it."

The general rule is that students need help in organizing and editing transcriptions into articles and in writing introductions. The majority of the draft materials on file suggest as much. In some cases, the editing is heavy enough to change substantially both the content and style of a student's introduction and the ordering of textual materials. These articles are arguably more collaborative than the student-authored pieces.

An example of such a collaboration is the introduction to "Ernest Franklin" (*Foxfire*, Fall 1974, 181–82). A student wrote the first draft by hand; either the student or Wigginton typed the second draft on notebook paper. Wigginton's handwritten emendations appear on the latter draft, to which he has added three paragraphs of his own, as well as words and phrases elsewhere.

Another example is "J. F. Gray: A Forgotten Man" (*Foxfire*, Spring 1980, 32–40), a tribute to the man who financed and directed the construction of the road that winds to the top of Black Rock Mountain. Kim Wall, who conducted the interviews with Wigginton, wrote the introduction; his folksy, unpolished handwritten draft apparently required little final editing to get it into publishable form. On the other hand, Wigginton liberally edited the transcriptions that make up the text of the article—adding, deleting, and moving materials to make it readable.

Wall, now a highway department employee, described the assistance he received from Wigginton on the article: "He didn't write [the introduction] for me. He just gave me some ideas of things I should look at in writing it, and I formed it. He took a look at it and said, 'It's great.' He didn't take it and write it himself and say, 'Kim, take a look at this and see how it sounds.' He was there to help me but not do it for me. Wig helped me with all the organizing [of the transcriptions]. Again, he didn't do it for me. We worked together as a team."

In other cases, Wigginton or a staff member actually leads the student "by the hand" through each step of putting an article together. This latter style of editing is most prevalent with students who have marginal writing skills. Paul Gillespie, who was a *Foxfire* magazine advisor for several years, recounted the difficulties of working with students of low academic proficiency: "You run into that dilemma where you get a student that's not real good in writing. I remember [Wigginton] had one [group] and I guess the combined reading level of the four kids wasn't eighth grade. Bad shape. They did take the photographs. I remember he made them write the captions, and it was painful. I think they spent weeks on the captions. They were basically a bunch of hellions [who] had somehow gotten to the tenth or eleventh grade despite themselves. Good kids [though]."

A potentially troublesome document that begged an explanation was a piece written in 1981 by a student I knew to have extremely limited writing skills. Wigginton had not only written the draft of a readable introduction, but he had also signed the student's name to it. An interview with the student clarified the matter. First, he had been one of a select group of seventh graders that Wigginton had recruited to work with older students in Foxfire II. Second, his skills were so marginal that Wigginton had encouraged him to explain in his own words what should be included in the introduction: "I told Wig what to write and Wig wrote it out. And if I couldn't get the right words, he'd put it in the right words."

The varying degrees of collaboration raise a broader pedagogical concern than the issue of authorship. If adult editing is a necessary and desirable feature of magazine production, the issue *at heart* becomes a matter of the efficacy of the editing in teaching students language arts skills. The following questions must be addressed: How is the editing done? Is it consistent with current theories of teaching writing?

There is ample evidence that Wigginton and his staff edit the magazine with the knowledge and consent of the students. A full year's worth of observations in magazine classes confirmed that the editing is typically done with the student or presented afterwards, not as a *fait accompli*, but as a negotiable item subject to change if the student can make a defensible case. Both staff and students believe this to be the case. Margie Bennett, co-adviser to the magazine, described her editing as follows:

> The general policy for me is to get the student if I can and go over the material after school. And I will type as she looks over my shoulder or reads [the draft] to me. At that point she's done it to the best of her ability. I like to have [the student] by me for a lot of that. If I possibly can, I like to point out [the error or problem] to them. If [I think] it's wrong but she's convinced it should be a certain way [or] if she feels a certain section comes in front of [another] section [of the transcribed text], then she can convince me. If she feels really strongly about an opinion and it doesn't hurt a contact, then I'll change my judgment.

Foxfire student Allison Adams explained how Bennett edited her work:

> If there is a problem with the finished edited copy of the article for Margie to type, she will call me over as she types it. And as she comes across a mistake, she will say, "Maybe it would sound better if we did this rather than this." And so we discuss it and usually we come to something agreeable. When I did the "Praying Rock" article [*Foxfire*, Fall 1984], there was a big controversy on [an] entire section. It was good material but it was irrelevant to the rest of the article. And I didn't think it should be in there. But Margie

thought it should, and so we took it to Wig and he agreed with me. When you're editing, if Margie has called you over there and she's saying something like, "Maybe this section [on] the lady's childhood would sound better after the games she played as a youth rather than after arts and crafts"—that's an example of a change that might be needed. Sometimes it involves moving entire sections and paragraphs. No change is ever made without the student who writes the article knowing about it. Occasionally when we're rushed for time, if the change is obvious, Margie will make the change while she's typing and get with us later. If there's a controversy, then we can find another solution.

Foxfire articles generally have a twofold structure: first, a student-written introduction; and second, a text that is an edited transcription of one or more interviews with a single Foxfire contact (e.g., personality articles) or, of greater complexity, transcribed materials from interviews with several contacts that focus on a single theme (e.g., technical process articles). After they have transcribed their tapes, the students index, cut up, and sort the information by topic into folders. Next they order and edit (by culling redundancies) the information within each folder. Then they arrange the folders in a logical sequence and assemble the text, moving from folder to folder, adding bracketed explanatory and transitional phrasing to make it readable.

In an early formulation of his pedagogical creed, Wigginton opined that Foxfire was a sounder and more powerful approach to teaching English than textbook or lecture methods: "Is the subject, English, ignored in the process? Hardly. In fact, the opposite is true. English, in its simplest definition, is communication—reaching out and touching people with words, sounds, and visual images. We are in the business of improving students' prowess in these areas. . . . In their [magazine] work . . . they learn more about English than from any other curriculum I could devise."[5]

Yet the reality of Foxfire fails to support Wigginton's rhetoric. If students acquire or refine these English skills, particularly writing, they do it fortuitously rather than by design. Indeed, Foxfire's potential as a powerful writing curriculum is diminished by a style of staff editing and teaching that is geared more to publication deadlines than to the academic deficiencies of students. Editing, by its nature, tends to be didactic. It becomes a hazardous pedagogical strategy, however, when it is conducted in lieu of, rather than as a supplement to, other less didactic strategies that give students practice in remediating deficiencies in paragraph unity and coherence, grammar, syntax, and diction. Such has been the case with Foxfire II.

The following descriptions from field notes exemplify the *style* of much of the Foxfire editing, which tends to place the burden of remediation on the teacher rather than the student:

> Kelly and Allison huddle in the floor with the Carolyn Stradley materials. Kelly says that some of the pages are out of order. Kelly and Allison talk about the ordering of the material. Margie joins them after helping Rance. Allison points out where a transitional paragraph is needed. Margie pencils in "transitional paragraph." . . . Margie points out an "awkward" sentence and gets Allison's approval to move the elements around. The rhetorical question to which Allison assents is, "Would it sound better like this?" Next she reads through each sentence aloud in the pieces the girls are working with, pointing her finger to the page as she moves through the material. She suggests another change and gets Allison's approval. Margie then turns through the pages of the Carolyn Stradley article, checking the ordering of the material.
>
> (six days later)
>
> Margie has made changes in the written draft of the text. She walks Allison through the changes. Margie says of one sentence, "Now I know I've worked this around. 'The preacher's house' doesn't work." "Oh yeah," responds Allison. "All right, I see what you did. That's fine with me." "Yes," adds Kelly, looking on. "It's better."

The pitfalls of staff editing practices appeared in the work of a former Foxfire student who had been hired by the organization to assist in the preparation of manuscripts for the Foxfire Press. Molly [a pseudonym] had contributed several articles to the magazine during her student years with the organization and had even co-edited an entire issue of *Foxfire*. A staff member at the Press cited the following problems in Molly's work:

> Lack of grammatical skills, carelessness, being sloppy about her work, not checking to make sure that she's accurate when she's unsure of a spelling or a word . . . just being generally sloppy about transcribing word for word, not going back . . . later to it again in order to get it right. She typed maybe what she thought she heard without going back to check whether it made sense. When you . . . read the sentence, it made absolutely no sense. And I think the [Foxfire] practice is, once you've transcribed a tape you're supposed to go back and check what you've transcribed against the tape. . . . In several transcriptions that hadn't been done.
>
> So far Margie has worked [with Molly]. I don't think Wig has. I know that yesterday Molly was late, and that's because she was with Margie. I'm glad to see they're trying to give her a chance. She's a local person. She needs skills to be a professional rather than work in a factory. She was a Foxfire student, and they're trying to maintain a commitment to that. I don't think she would have been given all that leeway if she hadn't been a Foxfire student.

In his Foxfire I and College English courses Wigginton teaches English far more thoroughly and systematically than in the magazine course. First, students in the former courses submit numerous expository papers for a thorough critique. The only expository writing that most students do in the magazine class is a one- or two-page introduction to an article per quarter or semester. "In the magazine class you don't write," commented a Foxfire senior. "You rearrange what was said [in the interview transcription]."

Second, in Foxfire I and College English, Wigginton makes ample use of grammar and style sheets and other exercises to teach the fine points of sound composition. Foxfire II has been virtually devoid of such activities. This is not to suggest that the cultural journalism concept, as practiced at Foxfire, does not have the *potential* to become what the Foxfire rhetoric and the testimonial mythos proclaim it already to be. The point is rather that Wigginton and his staff have made a trade-off, perhaps unwittingly, that sacrifices this potential to the pressures of assembling a professional-quality magazine by quarterly printing and mailing deadlines; dilatoriness, they argue, would jeopardize their second-class mailing permit and the good faith of 3,000 subscribers.

The second issue raised by Kohl is decision making within the Foxfire organization. That adolescents can, and should, be entrusted to make meaningful decisions during their high school years is a cornerstone of Wigginton's philosophy. For example, in his critique of schooling in *Foxfire 2,* Wigginton challenged the conventional wisdom that adolescents are incapable of making responsible decisions traditionally the purview of adults: "We have ruled out the possibility of a student's being able to make competent decisions regarding his life, his environment, his conduct—even his bedtime—so we make those decisions for him. And we expect him to be able to walk out of our schools self-confident, ready to make competent decisions regarding his life, his environment, his conduct. . . ."[6] And in *Foxfire 6,* he stated: "Once a certain public-school mind set is overcome, it becomes increasingly difficult to identify issues and decisions in which . . . students should *not* be directly involved. . . . The fact is that students in possession of accurate information are far more skillful, responsible, creative, and moral in making and carrying out decisions than most adults are willing to admit."[7]

In the early years of Foxfire, students had a surfeit of responsibility for the magazine; in fact, the project would have floundered had students like Jan Brown and Judy Brown not run the organization responsibly and well during the year Wigginton spent at Johns Hopkins University. The evidence of testimony and observation, however, points to the conclusion that students exercised a much larger share of organizational power and responsibility during the tenure at Rabun Gap, where Foxfire remained exclusively a magazine project, than after the move to Rabun County High School, where its new divisions crystallized.

Several examples indicate that Foxfire's Rabun Gap students participated as equal partners with adults in decisions of real importance to the organization and community alike. One example is the decision that allowed the JFG Coffee Company to film a series of commercials using Foxfire interview contacts as subjects. "The plan was to make six commercials, each featuring a mountain person . . . demonstrating some skill," Wigginton has written. "At the end of the thirty-second scene, all the person had to say was something to the effect that, 'It takes a lot of skill and patience to do this.' Then the announcer would come in and say, 'Just as it takes this person time and patience to make butter, so, too, it takes JFG time and patience to make fine coffee.' Something like that." To save filming time, the company had solicited Foxfire's aid in locating subjects for the commercials. "It sounded unsavory at first, but we told them the kids might be willing to do it. They would simply have to come up and present their case and let the kids decide."[8]

The testimony of Bit Carver Kimball, a former Foxfire student who participated in recruiting local craftsmen for the commercials, supports Wigginton's contention that students shouldered the responsibility for approving the commercials and for establishing the protocols under which they would be filmed:

The staff didn't make the decision whether Foxfire would help JFG with the commercials. The kids did. JFG had to present its case to the students, and the students provided the stipulations under which they would assist the coffee company. One of the stipulations was that the contacts would not have to say, "I plant by the signs, but I also drink JFG coffee." In other words, they wouldn't have to endorse the product. And I think it bowled them [JFG] over. This big corporation having to present itself to a bunch of kids and the kids making the final decision about what will or will not be done. They had to bring their storyboards into the class and show their general ideas about what would be done in the commercial before we would approve it.

Wig left it up to us. He would bring out the good points and the bad points. [But] he never tried to influence the way a kid thought. He always left it up to each kid. It made the kids have a real sense of responsibility because they were making the decision, and they wanted it to be a good one for the community (or the people involved). The sense of responsibility was a very important thing I brought from Foxfire.

In another case, a commercial film company began negotiations with Foxfire for the right to produce a fictionalized account of a youth's experience in a Foxfire-type project. Pat Rogers, a former staff member, recounts how the students ran afoul of the company:

> [Tomorrow Entertainment, Inc.] sent a script writer with a rough draft script, and we spent a lot of time with them. The first draft was pretty rough—lots of cliches. We had a core of really strong students that had a handle on what was going on. The kids grilled the script writer in class. In terms of the decision, what it all boiled down to was that the kids felt it would be okay to do a movie and they would be a part of it, but they didn't want the name *Foxfire* to be used with it. The [film] company wouldn't agree [to the latter stipulation], and the scheme didn't come off. That decision did come from the kids.

Despite his own enthusiasm for the film, Wigginton did not contravene the students' decision, which, in his words, "was adhered to even though I personally thought (and told them I thought) that making the film might be a fine educational experience, might be a chance for us to provide an antidote to *Deliverance,* and might be a fine chance for us to help shape what could be a genuinely exciting television offering." He concluded that "the experience the students went through in the act of having to come to their decision was probably enough."[9]

A final example of student involvement in organizational affairs during Foxfire's Rabun Gap era is the discussion that preceded the decision to allow Hume Cronyn and Susan Cooper to write and produce a play about Foxfire. Debbie Thomas, now a television producer, was a Foxfire student who participated in that meeting in the summer of 1977. Thomas recalls that Wigginton asked the students to weigh several factors before making their decision: the authors' play-writing skills, their dedication to the project, and their commitment to authenticity. In her opinion, Wigginton did not attempt to sway the vote.

> My impression was that Wig definitely wanted to do it. He said we must be very careful about this, and he wanted to make sure that we weighed every aspect of it. I think it was obvious, but I don't think he tried to make it clear what he felt. He wanted to make sure that you didn't vote to please him, but that you voted your conscience. I'm positive that he was sincerely trying not to influence us. He is a human being, and I'm sure he was excited about the prospect. At first, he was not trying to show that he was positively in favor of it. As the discussion went on and it became clear that the atmosphere was positive toward selling the rights, then he let his opinion be known a little

more at that point. That day the atmosphere was not for Foxfire. Everybody at the meeting was concerned what this play would do for the people of the mountains.

Since Foxfire's move to Rabun County High School, the locus of organizational authority has shifted, by degrees, away from the students. In fact, student decision making is now almost solely restricted to the magazine—its story content, layout, cover design, and color. Organizational decisions that impinge on Foxfire's future or the quality of life in Rabun County no longer involve students. In 1984, students neither sought, nor were they encouraged to seek, a voice in the weekly staff meetings or periodic legal board meetings, where decisions of real import were adjudicated. Students did not attend any of these meetings.

In an article written in 1980, Wigginton indicated that students had an equal voice with adults in deciding "whether people who want to visit our classes may or may not come (will they and we really benefit from the visit or are they 'just curious'?)."[10] Yet, in 1984, students were *not* included in these decisions. Teachers and reporters routinely visited Foxfire—yet Wigginton and his staff did not consult students for their advice or consent.

These findings beg an explanation. Has there been a conscious divestiture of student power within the organization, given that Foxfire has become a burgeoning commercial enterprise (as compared to "the little magazine that could" at Rabun Gap School)? Have Wigginton and his staff succumbed to a "cult of efficiency" that militates against student decision making because it is a perilous and inefficient way to do business? Are there social and school cultural factors involved that have prompted the shift toward adult hegemony within the organization? Informed speculation suggests that all these factors have contributed to diminishing student participation in the governance of Foxfire.

The transition from a tiny community school to a consolidated, county-wide high school proved costly to Foxfire in terms of the *intensity* of student dedication to the project. The factors that made Rabun Gap School an institutional seedbed for Foxfire's vigorous early growth—a boarding student population, the proximity of school and community, and the paucity of recreational outlets for adolescents—were missing at Rabun County High School.

Other factors present at the new high school have exacerbated the psychological distancing of students from the project. The new school has been described by one journalist as "a fortress-like structure of poured concrete and brick that keeps vigil atop a hill outside Clayton."[11] The description is apt; the school is neither a hospitable nor a convenient place where students and staff can meet in the late afternoons or evenings to work on the magazine. In recent years the school property has been partially wrapped by a chain link fence, and a gatehouse (read *guardhouse*) stands at the entrance. For a short time, the guard even carried a revolver.[12] Moreover, the school is far removed from many of the students it serves. For example, students in the Satolah community, on the northeastern fringe of Rabun County, have to make a hair-raising trip of nearly twenty-five miles, much of it on winding country roads, to reach the school. Students from Dillard, who live in close proximity to Rabun Gap School, must now travel twelve to fifteen miles to school. In short, the uninviting physical ambience and relative remoteness of the school do not encourage the kind of "after-hours" commitment that was a hallmark of Foxfire at Rabun Gap School.

A factor of school structure impinges on the *time* students have to commit to Foxfire. The new high school offers a plethora of extracurricular outlets that were not available to students at Rabun Gap School, e.g., football (with off-season weight lifting), track, baseball, and band, each of which requires a major commitment of a student's after-school time. These activities divert and frequently exclude students from participation in Foxfire. At Rabun Gap, students who had after-school work and extracurricular commitments could work on the magazine in the evenings, given their proximity (particularly dormitory students) to Foxfire's on-campus offices. Evening work is no longer a viable option.

Another structural factor that has affected the nature of student participation in the magazine has been the scheduling system at the high school. In 1984, Wigginton taught two magazine classes (Foxfire II) each quarter. This bifurcation of the magazine project manifestly diminished group unity and continuity of effort. For example, when a decision had to be made about the magazine cover or color, Wigginton had to conduct separate votes in each class. Neither class was privy to the discussion that preceded the vote in the other. Only on rare occasions could Wigginton bring both groups together to discuss magazine business (the classes met at the second and fifth class periods during the day, so these meetings were difficult to arrange). By comparison, as one staff member observed: "You had almost a club at Rabun Gap. You had one class for the year. There were about thirty people in there, and your mission for the year was to put out four magazines. [And] you could vote on things as one class." In short, the new scheduling system has not fostered the kind of *esprit de corps* that characterized the magazine at Rabun Gap.

Underlying and weaving these factors into the tapestry of student withdrawal from organizational affairs is the reality that Foxfire is no longer a novelty. Students at Rabun Gap who were a part of the *building* of Foxfire had a commitment and sense of ownership that reasonably should not be expected of students a decade later when the project has become routine and predictable. A staff member expressed the point tersely: "We went down [to Rabun County High School] as an established fact. At Rabun Gap, [students] built the program. They felt like they owned it. It's like a town. If you build it, you own it. But if you come a hundred years later, you take it all for granted. [Students today] treat it as a classroom assignment: 'This is what I have to do to get a grade.' You didn't have that attitude at Rabun Gap—not primarily."[13]

Since coming to Rabun County High School, Foxfire has crystallized three new divisions: video, folklore/music, and outdoor education/ environmental science; it has also added the Foxfire Press and a grants management office. The day-to-day administration of these units and their budgets (in 1984, over $400,000) clearly require adult expertise and control. Weekly staff meetings are earmarked for discussion of administrative affairs. Yet many of the decisions that are made in these meetings (the question of who will visit Foxfire being a case in point) could be made readily and effectively by students, with teacher guidance. In the interest of efficiency, however, the adults have, by degrees, garnered to themselves what formerly belonged to the students.

During the school year 1980–81, Wigginton and his staff attempted to get students more involved in organizational affairs by holding the weekly meetings during class time at the high school. In his description of the experiment, Wigginton wrote: "We conduct Foxfire's business by consensus of all ten staff members and all the students in the Foxfire classes each quarter. This means that [we meet] one day every week during the quarter, every class period, first through sixth."[14]

Yet the plan was not feasible. "We realized it was taking up so much of our class time," a staff member recalls. "[Also] the homerooms, the intercom, and the changing of classes interfered with us. [Moreover] we had to give the kids involved an update on everything we discussed. It just wasn't very efficient. Now we have [the meetings] after school, and the students have other things to do."

This is not to say that students do not have a voice in Foxfire. They make decisions that affect every component of magazine production, including the subscription price. In 1984, Wigginton convened two in-school meetings at which students from each of the divisional programs discussed minor organizational business. On one occasion they voted on the allocation of Foxfire funds for community charities. Field notes show:

> The third-period students are voting on the disposition of the remaining $150 of the $500 earmarked in the budget for local charities. The Rabun County Rescue Squad and the local Boy Scout troop have requested donations. Standing at the board facing the students, Wigginton tells them, "We usually respond to requests like this in some way. I don't know how you feel about these things. But we need a sort of vote on these [and] a ballpark figure on how much—if we want to give." Scott says, "Give it to the rescue squad. If my dad was hurt, I'd rather have the rescue squad come after him than the Boy Scouts." (laughter) "Anybody suggest an amount?" asks Wigginton. Someone yells "ten dollars." "Ten dollars won't go very far," Wigginton remarks, "but it's an expression of support."
>
> This gets to be a noisy bidding war as other students shout their preferences, ranging from $20 to $50. When things quiet down, Brooks, who is active in the local Scout troop, says, "I really don't think the Scouts need very much. I think five dollars will be fine." When someone suggests that Foxfire give each organization $75, a chorus of "no's" peals from the left side of the room. Wigginton concludes the discussion by saying, "Okay, we're going to vote. Raise your hand when I ring your bell." Next he moves through the list of figures for each organization, counting the hands for each amount. After taking the poll, he tells the students that their votes will be added to the tallies of the other group meetings being held today.

At another meeting students decided how Foxfire would vote its 1,850 shares of Eastman Kodak stock at a forthcoming corporate board meeting. Suspecting that Kodak had signed contracts with the federal government to develop space weaponry, a group of irate stockholders had petitioned the board of directors for a full disclosure of the company's military dealings. In accordance with company by-laws, the directors put the matter to a vote of all Kodak stockholders. At a staff meeting, Wigginton had announced that he wanted the students to decide how Foxfire would vote its shares. The following week, students enrolled in Foxfire classes met as a group during each class period to discuss the issue and to vote for or against corporate disclosure (the final tally was forty-two to twenty-six for disclosure).[15]

In answer to Herbert Kohl's general question, "Who makes the decisions at Foxfire?," students are the lowest-level decision makers, their activity being limited primarily to the magazine. Budgetary and other administrative matters are the purview of the staff, which discusses and votes on these issues at its weekly meetings. Major organizational decisions, such as the shift in direction from community development to national curriculum dissemination or spending of the endowment, are made by the legal board, Foxfire's governing body. In recent years, given the instability of Foxfire's finances, the legal board has taken a far heavier hand in exercising its authority than previously, further distancing students from decisions of real importance to the organization's future.[16]

Foxfire-Related Life Skills

While the issues of authorship and decision making are useful and intriguing analytical tools for exploring the actualities of Foxfire, their adjudication is less critical from a pedagogical standpoint than a description and analysis of the project's effects in the lives of its former students, Kohl's accusatory rhetoric notwithstanding. Here the analytical focus shifts from what Foxfire *is* to what it *means* in the subjective experience of dozens of its participants from 1967 to 1984. The resulting information, woefully absent from previous studies, is indispensable for assessing Foxfire's specific strengths and weaknesses as a curriculum reform at the classroom level.

During the fall of 1984, I interviewed sixty-six former Foxfire students, scattered from Rabun County to Monterey, California. As discussed in the methods section of this report (Appendix B), I combined random sampling with more conventional case-study techniques to ensure a *systematic* coverage of the experience of students throughout Foxfire's history. The following questions were asked to elicit the perspectives of these young adults:

(1) What stands out as a memorable experience from your Foxfire days?
(2) What skills related to Foxfire have proved useful in your adult life?
(3) Do you think of yourself as a mountain person? How did Foxfire influence that identity?
(4) How did Foxfire influence your view of the elderly? How do you think the elderly benefited from the Foxfire experience?
(5) What changes would you have recommended in Foxfire?
(6) Would you recommend that your children take Foxfire? Why or why not?

These scheduled questions were merely the starting point for follow-up questions tailored to each former student's experience. The categories and percentages in Table 5.1 and Table 5.2 are based on an analysis of these interviews. Although these findings are not statistically representative, they are based on a sample of approximately 19 percent of all students who have contributed to the *Foxfire* books, and they are consistent with the observational and documentary evidence.

Personal Growth Skills and Influences

As the tables indicate, students report that they gain from Foxfire primarily affective/personal growth skills. The testimony of many of these young adults reveals that the experiences that nurtured these skills have become touchstones in their lives. In *Moments*, Wigginton predicted that his pedagogy would enable students "[to] go into life with a reservoir of good, solid experiences behind them."[17] The evidence presented in Table 5.1 tends to confirm his assessment.

Table 5.1   Affective/Personal Growth Skills Attributed to or Enhanced by Foxfire

Skill	% (*N* = 66)
Cultural Identity	74%*
Appreciation/Awareness of Elderly	71%
Self-Confidence	48%
Interpersonal Relations	56%

*Ten former Rabun Gap dormitory students and three non-Appalachian community students were excluded from the analysis of this item.

Psychologist Erik Erikson has observed that socially suppressed, exploited, or excluded ethnic or subcultural groups tend to accept "the evil image they are made to represent by those who are dominant."[18] Erikson's research on identity suggests that such a negative cultural identity, imposed by the stereotypes of the dominant culture, gives rise in the adult personality to phobias and compulsions—pathologies that symbolize the ego's attempt to live down the cultural past.

Certainly no subculture in America has continued to be more caricatured than Appalachia. The image of the moonshine-toting, illiterate, shiftless hillbilly is purveyed daily into the nation's consciousness by the likes of "The Beverly Hillbillies," "Snuffy Smith," and "L'il Abner." James Dickey added a more sinister element to the stereotype in his novel *Deliverance,* in which he convincingly portrayed mountain people as bereft of civilization and morally depraved. The Warner

Brothers film version of the book, released in 1972, projected even starker images of rural Appalachia as a hostile and backward region peopled by homosexual rapists and habitual practitioners of incest. Dickey set the novel in the north Georgia mountains on a river called the Cahulawassee, a thinly disguised pseudonym for the Chattooga, the white-water river that forms Rabun County's boundary with South Carolina. If anyone had any doubts about the location, Warner Brothers assuaged them by filming *Deliverance* in Rabun County and (ironically) hiring local people as extras.

There is a story about some skittish tourists who, after seeing the film, drove into Rabun County with their doors locked and windows up, straining to catch a glimpse of "a real-live mountain redneck." A Foxfire staff member avers that he heard a tourist ask a local if mountain men "really do that kind of thing." "Sure," replied the indignant local. "Bend over."

The *Deliverance* stereotype has not stymied tourism or second-home development; in fact, Rabun County is rapidly becoming a second-home and retirement community for wealthy Floridians and leisure-seeking urbanites throughout the Southeast. The antipathy of many Rabun County natives toward these newcomers is conveyed forcefully in their pejorative use of the term "Floridian," a generic referent for tourists and seasonal in-migrants. Expressed in their conversations about the changing social topography of the county are feelings of powerlessness and frustration that are reinforced by the deprecatory attitudes of outsiders toward the regional culture.

There is evidence that the "evil image" of Appalachia has been internalized by some young people in Rabun County. The testimony of a large majority of the native Appalachian young adults in the sample of former Foxfire students suggests that the Foxfire experience has been effective in building and reinforcing positive, counter-stereotypic cultural images that belie this malignant view.

> Wig made us aware of our heritage and made us look at ourselves, our families, and our community. He made us aware of the importance of the life we have here in this area. We started understanding that we *did* speak differently from the people in Atlanta and other cities. But we also became aware of the fact that the way we speak is a language. Just as northerners have an accent, we also have an accent. We became less inhibited when we were around people from other backgrounds—city slickers. [Our] understanding that there was nothing wrong with our language probably started with Foxfire. (Linda Page, 1969 graduate)
>
> Foxfire made me proud of being on the tip of the Appalachians. If someone [who] thinks of me as a mountain person has in mind the kind of people I

met in Foxfire, then I'm proud of that association. I [had] considered myself a hick person to a certain extent. [Meeting] these mountain folks in Foxfire gave me a different way of looking at who I was and where I was from. The things that were important to them are what should be important in a person's life. It was their basic values. They were plain, honest folks, and they didn't put on any airs. If that's what a hick was, then I was proud to be one. (Steve James, 1973 graduate)

[Foxfire] made me look on other families that I had previously thought of as different as being a part of one family that included mine. I had always known that my ancestry was from Appalachia, but when I looked at my line [for a *Foxfire* magazine article] and saw my family as typical of those that settled Appalachia, it became an awareness that the Appalachian heritage was a part of me. When you read something in a book, you don't necessarily think, "My family's a part of that." But when you then learn that's what *your* family did, that makes it solid. When I started studying my own family, I realized there was no longer a fine line between me and Appalachia. It was a part of me. (John Singleton, 1980 graduate)

One essential feature of Foxfire's strength as a vehicle for enriched personal growth—perhaps the key factor—has been the collaboration between the young people doing the interviewing and the old people being interviewed. The partnership and mutual respect that developed between these high school students in Rabun County and the elderly mountain folks who served as their subjects and informants is as unusual as it is laudable. Segregating old people is a common practice throughout American society, but nowhere is it more apparent than in our schools. The wisdom and experience the elderly have to offer is neither tapped by our schools nor even seen as being relevant to the education of the nation's youth. Consequently, most schooling reinforces the ignorance of young people about the value of the elders in their community and also encourages a feeling among older people that they are a useless burden to society.

By giving young people an intriguing *method* of eliciting the experience of old age, Foxfire has allowed students to appreciate who old people are and what they have to offer. "It opened my eyes to really hear what they were saying," stated Mike Cook. "That [listening] is the beginning of a road you start down that leads you to finding out that those folks who seem so different are people like you, who've seen a lot of things and done a lot of things that you haven't."

Over the years Foxfire students have interviewed hundreds of elderly mountain residents. Of these, Aunt Arie Carpenter has been the most celebrated, primarily because she demonstrated so well the positive influence of an old person who has lived "fully and well and long."[19] A widow who lived alone in an unchinked log cabin in a narrow mountain valley, Aunt Arie eschewed modern conveniences; her ingenuity and the rudiments of an early-twentieth-century life-style—woodstove, well, garden, fireplace, and privy—sufficed for most of her needs. She was a generous and loving woman who graciously shared the wisdom and beauty of her simple life with Eliot Wigginton's students, frequent visitors to her cabin from 1970 to 1974 (failing health forced Arie to abandon her mountain home and move in with relatives, in whose care she died, at age ninety-two, in 1978).

Throughout the years of their friendships with Arie Carpenter, Wigginton's students carried groceries up the winding dirt road to her cabin, dug potatoes in her garden, carried in the wood, helped out with the cooking, and listened to her sententious talk as she labored over the woodstove or as she sat by the fireplace popping corn in a tin box she had jury-rigged to a broom handle.[20]

In *Aunt Arie: A Foxfire Portrait*, Gary Warfield, now a veterinarian in Nashua, New Hampshire, recalled the lessons he had intuited as an adolescent from Arie's persona as an old person and the positive images she had inspired about growing old: "I'm sure she knew she fed me, shared her life experiences with me, and once gave me a place to sleep in a bed that was stacked one foot high with quilts. But I doubt that she knew that she renewed my faith in mankind and taught me what unselfish generosity was. No one could out-give Aunt Arie."[21]

From Aunt Arie, Andrea Burrell Potts, today a crafts store owner, learned about the special perspective that long years of experience bring to old age: "She lived alone, and she was partially crippled. She felt that whatever trials we have to go through in life are a growing experience. I think a majority of the older people felt that way. These impressions grow into the core of us as we grow older."

The Appalachian elders whom these Foxfire students interviewed have belied the distorted media image of native mountaineers. Arie Carpenter was no exception. Jan Brown Bonner, a former Foxfire student who is now a librarian, described in *Aunt Arie* how she had gained an appreciation of her cultural heritage from this very old woman: "Her greatest lesson to me . . . was her unashamed love of home. As a teenager it was sometimes difficult for me to acknowledge that I was born and raised in a small country town, naive and un-accustomed to big-city ways. Aunt Arie taught me that that didn't matter. After the summer I spent interviewing and visiting her, I returned to college with a new attitude about my heritage. I had learned through her camaraderie with the land just how important family, roots, and tradition are. They are lessons I'll never forget."[22]

For the most part, Aunt Arie and other elders taught the Foxfire students simple but important truths about life through the courage and dignity they brought to old age rather than through their preachments. For example, Rhonda Black Waters, now a licensed practical nurse, said that she "learned never to give up" from her interviews and friendship with Anna Howard, a frail, ninety-three-year-old woman. "She was in a homemade wheelchair, a little straight-back chair with wheels on it. She'd work her garden using that chair, rolling around in the garden. She'd roll around in the kitchen, cook, and do what she needed to do. I learned that if you're weak in an area, you can find a way to compensate with something else."

Foxfire has also proved effective in countering negative stereotypes about growing old. Some young people, for example, see old age as "a limbo of predeath and social nonexistence";[23] hence their belief that the denizens of this final stage of the life cycle are *ipso facto* decrepit and senile. "Working with Foxfire made me see that old mountain people were strong and useful people who weren't afraid of dying," observed Pat Arrowood Tolliver, a 1972 graduate. "Seeing that they still had useful lives helped me get over the fear of death that I had seen as the next step after getting old. That had been the only thing I had seen about being old, and it frightened me."

Growing up close to his grandparents in Rabun County and getting to know old-timer Leonard Webb taught Wesley Taylor, now a high school teacher, about the positive value of old people and gave the lie to myths about the ineptitude of old age. In the late 1970s, Taylor, fellow Foxfire student Mitch Whitmire, and Foxfire advisor Paul Gillespie interviewed Webb for an article on gourd banjos.

We went up there a bunch of times. We had to find a gourd and then we had to let it dry, which we did in the basement of his house. We found the [groundhog] hide and then we had to have the neck. So I found a piece of walnut in my great uncle's barn. Leonard worked on it when he felt like it. We took it in steps. And he'd have a little more done [each time]. We'd work with him an afternoon usually each time we went up. When he didn't feel like working or it was too cold, we'd sit with him by the woodstove, and he'd play the banjo and sing us old songs. He always did keep the house hot.

I tell you, I think Leonard really enjoyed us coming to see him. . . . He gave us a lot of good stuff on life. We'd ramble and let it go where it went. We'd just get to talking and sit three or four hours up there, just talking away. . . . We talked about power bills one time. And Leonard said, "If it goes any higher, I'll just turn it off and go without it." So I said, "Gosh!" He said, "I lived without it for forty years. Me and my wife could live without it [now]."

And that was an example that he and other old people learned the long, hard way. . . . The experience of being around old people, especially Leonard and my grandparents, taught me that they know valuable things and that there's a lot you can draw from their experience.

Not all the former students could say that their encounters with the elderly through Foxfire influenced their perceptions about old age. Some stated, in effect, "I had always liked and respected old people," or "I didn't have any stereotypes to begin with." On the other hand, a large majority (71 percent) did report a positive change in attitude or an increased awareness of the potentialities of old people.

One of Foxfire's most profound lessons has already been suggested by Jan Brown Bonner's experience with Arie Carpenter: the almost mystical realization that old age is "a source of continuity, linking the future with the past, death with life."[24] Myra Queen Jones, a Rabun County native looking back to her Foxfire years at Rabun Gap School, put it this way: "I never really ever knew what my heritage was until I got in Foxfire. Seems like I had a lot more in common with these old people than I had thought. It was like you've got a thumb here but you've never paid any attention to it. It was like something that's been there, but I never realized it was a part of me."

Throughout its history, Foxfire has mediated a dialogue between adolescents and the elderly. The testimony of former Foxfire students documents the salutary effects of this exchange. At one level, it has fostered a realization of the positive value of the elderly and has served to dispel adolescent stereotypes of growing old. At its highest level, however, it has helped a group of young people to discover and appreciate their cultural inheritance, while enabling young and old participants alike to understand the depth and variety of the contributions the elderly can make to the educational process.

Not surprisingly, the lines between enhanced cultural identity, positive images of the elderly, improved interpersonal relationships, and self-confidence often blurred in the recollections of former Foxfire students, most noticeably between the first two categories. Positive images of the elderly were also frequently associated with improved relations between the age groups; and in some cases, the Foxfire interviews reportedly boosted the self-confidence of shy or withdrawn students.

For Bit Carver Kimball, Foxfire offered a new perspective on her father, Buck Carver, a proud and genial mountain moonshiner who was one of Foxfire's favorite contacts until his death in the summer of

1985. Her statement indicates also a changed perspective on a craft that has been wrongfully maligned by media stereotypes: "We were poor. My daddy was a moonshiner. [Foxfire] made me see . . . that he was doing the moonshining for a reason. He did it to support his family, and that made me proud of him, and it made me proud of the moonshine he made. He made quality moonshine—not rotgut. He could have made rotgut and sold it just as easily as the good stuff, but he didn't."

During her high school years, Barbara Taylor Woodall wrote an article about Foxfire for *Seventeen* magazine, and that experience bolstered her self-pride and confidence: "When you were in that teenage stage and looking for identity, Foxfire made you feel like you were important. I got a lot of recognition—national recognition [and $400 for the article]. Foxfire made everything else fun because of the pedestal it put me on."

For Brenda Carpenter, a 1976 graduate, Foxfire offered a sense of achievement and increased self-confidence: "You really can't name a specific thing. It's just a total feeling. It was the working and knowing you did your best, that you'd done something you could be proud of. You knew it was interesting work [and] that other people would like it and thought you could achieve something. And it didn't come easy."

A 1977 graduate explained that her experience with the Foxfire staff enhanced her sense of self-esteem: "I always felt good about myself as an academic person. But as a real person, at a party or something like that, I felt mediocre—lukewarm. Of course, I wanted to be a 'hot' person—special. I think the people involved helped me to think of myself as important as anybody else in any situation."

Other former Foxfire students described the program's special contributions to their lives as young people growing up in rural America. Andrea Burrell Potts recalled her trip to the fledgling project Fourth Street i: "I got to go to New York—me, Laurie Brunson and Suzy Angier. You take a kid from here who's only been to Atlanta a few times and sit [her] down in the middle of New York City—that's a growing experience."

Doug James, a 1977 graduate, remembered a trip he had taken with Wigginton to a Foxfire-descendant project in Kodiak, Alaska, an experience that he called "the cream of the crop." Students from Cityscape (a Foxfire-type project in Washington, D.C.) and Pamela Wood's Salt project (Kennebunk, Maine) had also made the trip. "Going to Alaska," James recounted, "I met all kinds of people and got a whole chunk of how life is on that trip. After seeing people from Alaska and

D.C. and Maine, I realized that I was just as good as they were even though I was from Rabun County. And I saw they were just as interested in learning about me as I was about them."

Tommy Lamb, a 1975 graduate, now a Baptist minister, described the wide-eyed wonderment of a rural Holden Caulfield's first adventure in a large city, in this case New Orleans: "I had never been from home much to speak of. First time I'd ever flown. Scared to death. We rented a limousine—us and our blue jeans and boots. That was the first limousine I'd ever been in. Wig told us: 'Boys, you can go down on Bourbon Street and do what you want as long as you don't catch anything.' Me and Carleton spent a day and a night on Bourbon Street, and I'd never seen anything like it."

For Jimmy Enloe, now an insurance claims adjustor, Foxfire provided a constructive social outlet for youthful idealism: "In the late sixties and seventies, all we did was badmouth our parents. We wanted to change, but I don't think we knew what we wanted. I think Foxfire supplied a lot of kids a basis to use this radical-type energy; it gave us something to do with it. I think it was a need for social involvement. I don't think we knew that at the time."

Interestingly, two former Foxfire students interviewed for this study claimed that their experiences had given them an inflated self-confidence, a bubble that the rigors of a liberal arts college curriculum soon burst. For example, one stated: "I think it might have been a false confidence to a certain extent. I guess it overinflated me. I had a college professor in literature who told me I didn't know how to write at all. But I did improve. He gave me a C."

Interviews with the friends and relatives of some former Foxfire students indicate that they have not fared well in life, that they have, to quote Wigginton, "slipped through the cracks." Several have even gone to prison. One notable case is the Foxfire student who spoke to a Congressional subcommittee on behalf of an act for the creation of a center for folklore preservation within the Library of Congress. According to several knowledgeable sources, this student "fried his brains" on LSD and eventually landed in prison.

Mark, the pseudonym of a former Foxfire student who agreed to be interviewed in his home, left the house shortly before my arrival and did not return. His anguished mother related the following story that explained his reluctance to talk with an interviewer. Mark had not had steady employment since leaving the Army, she stated; he had quit after working three months for Rabun Mills. His pattern was to spend his days in bed and his nights on the town. Her son, a chain smoker (the cigarettes strewn about the living room were his), had become a drug user: "He can't get by a day without smoking some marijuana.

He's got a psychological addiction." Moreover, she had found cocaine paraphernalia in his bedroom. "The only thing he talks about is getting out of this place. He says when he gets to be forty-five, he'll be a millionaire. But he doesn't have enough money to buy cigarettes now."

In Arthur Miller's play *Death of a Salesman,* Willy Loman's son Biff reveals his adult identity crisis in the anguished statement: "I can't take hold, Mom. I just can't take hold of some kind of life."[25] The former Foxfire student Mark has a similar crisis. "I don't think anything was going on at Foxfire that would have been a negative influence," his mother concluded. "I feel like all that Mark did in Foxfire was a positive thing." The point is simply that Foxfire is not a panacea for resolving identity fragmentation or for salvaging psychically disturbed youth.

Cognitive/Intellectual Skills

As indicated by Table 5.2, cognitive/intellectual skills related to the Foxfire experience are not as salient in the perceptions of the former Foxfire students as affective/personal growth skills. The career patterns of these individuals provides a partial explanation. Only seventeen of the sixty-six interviewed subjects (26%) have completed, or are currently enrolled in, a four-year college-degree program. While many of the non-college graduates in the sample have escaped the career dead ends of the assembly line and lower-level office work, forging careers as developers, realtors, builders, small business owners, and middle-level managers, their life paths from high school to the present have not required refined writing skills; this observation applies equally to the lower-level blue collar and informational service

Table 5.2 Cognitive/Intellectual Skills Attributed to or Enhanced by Foxfire

Skill	% (N = 66)*
Writing and/or Information Gathering	42%**
Speaking	14%
Photography	23%
Graphics	17%
Bookkeeping/Office	11%
Practical Skills Related to Appalachian Culture	11%

*Two former students (non-college) were not asked Question #2 (or a variant of it): What skills related to Foxfire have proved useful in your adult life? This omission may account for a variation in each category of plus or minus 3%.
**Thirty-eight percent of the sample attributed gains in writing skills to Foxfire. Readers should compare this finding to the results of my analysis of *Foxfire* magazine production (pp. 69–77).

workers in the sample. Interestingly, the majority of the 38% who credited Foxfire as a vehicle for improving their writing skills were in the non-college category, a finding that may be explained by the fact that these students had more to learn than their college-bound peers.

The strongest statements about the efficacy of Foxfire in improving writing skills come from two college graduates in the sample:

> *Somehow* I learned to write more creatively as a result of Foxfire. I think it was a result of the whole experience. I just really have a strong feeling that I write so much better and express myself so much better because of Foxfire. And I don't think I can put my finger on it. It was the culmination of all I did in Foxfire, having to pick out a word or a phrase that would catch the reader's eye, listening to a tape you have to edit to make it readable, observing the environment, learning how to connect paragraphs and how to get from one paragraph to another and make the article flow. When you listened to a tape, you had to learn to use commas, exclamation marks, and [quotation marks] correctly, even spelling. I remember Paul Gillespie, Mike Cook, and [me] transcribing an interview about a turkey call and trying to figure out how to spell the words the man was using. I think all these things combined to help me be a better *communicator.* (Jan Brown Bonner, 1969 graduate)

> I learned a lot about going out and getting a mass of material and pooling it and getting some order into it. I learned a lot about organization—taking large amounts of material, going through it, and narrowing a whole spectrum of information into a cohesive system of thought. (John Singleton, 1980 graduate)

Of the seventeen graduates/current enrollees of four-year colleges in the sample, three have pursued journalism degrees as a result of their work in Foxfire, and three have returned to work for Foxfire as teaching staff members. Three other former students attribute their current employment directly to Foxfire's influence:

> Due to the fact that I had worked on Foxfire, I received my first job with a daily newspaper (*The Times,* in Gainesville, Georgia). I was told that since I had experience, I would be making more. I worked in the composing room doing paste-up and proofreading. I was then asked to do some feature stories and was later put in charge of the leisure section, a Friday supplement. I got a chance to work in sales, and after I found out I really liked it and could make some money, I stayed there for two years. I then went to work for WFOX radio station in Gainesville and WRFC in Athens as an account executive. I now have a good paying job and absolutely love what I am doing. If it had not been for my experiences with Foxfire, I honestly don't think I would have ever got my foot in the front door. (Glenda Arrowood Voiles, 1972 graduate)

In April of 1980, Sky Valley's (a resort village) entire housekeeping department walked out the door over a labor dispute with management. I was making $3.20 an hour. Some later went back, some took other maid jobs, and some went [to] work in local factories at minimum wage. I thought, "If I can remember what I learned in Foxfire about 'money,' such as the bookkeeping and accounting I had, I can start my own business." I was tired of taking orders from someone else (knowing how direct and hurtful some supervisors can be). In three weeks I went from working eight hours a day for $25.60 to working six hours a day for $100.00. I started a maid service, worked out independent contracts with people and continued to grow and employ until I had all the work I wanted to do. (Barbara Taylor Woodall, 1973 graduate)[26]

I feel that if I hadn't been involved in Foxfire, I wouldn't have the job I have today [with the Forsyth County Road Department]. When I was hired for the sign department, they wanted somebody that could spell and read good and take good directions, read a map and a tape. The experience that I had working with Foxfire during the summer on the construction crews, and all the classes I took, helped me get the job. [My employers] thought Foxfire was great and they wanted to hear everything I had done. [My boss] is always telling me how great it is to have me on the staff, with all my experiences. (Kim Wall, 1982 graduate)

School Issues and Effects

In his report to the Rabun County School Board for 1984, Wigginton listed nearly $336,000 expended by the Foxfire Fund, Inc., for services "directly related to work with students of Rabun County High School." This figure included expenditures for staff salaries; printing, record production, and copyrighting; general administration; and additional construction on the environmental cabin. Wigginton did not mention that more than $25,000 was allocated for the Foxfire Scholarship Program for 1984–85.[27]

From 1976 to 1984, Foxfire provided $119,202 in college or technical school scholarships to sixty-two Rabun County students. A committee of the Foxfire community advisory board selects students for these awards, based on the extent of their participation in Foxfire and their need. Each recipient is required to send periodic progress reports to his or her advisor on the scholarship committee. Extrapolations from Foxfire's records in 1984 indicated that 34 percent of the scholarship recipients had graduated from their programs, 31 percent had dropped out, and the remainder were still in attendance.

In his 1984 report, Wigginton also noted that since 1977, Foxfire had paid $169,313 in salaries to its summer student employees. In the summer of 1984, twenty students earned a combined total of $21,500. In a poor county where good summer jobs are scarce, the Foxfire jobs program is a windfall.[28] Each spring the staff meets to select the twenty to twenty-five students who will work for the various divisions and summer maintenance crew. Typically, these are the most highly motivated students across all the Foxfire classes, and they are paid for their skills in cultural journalism, record production, and community television.

Over the years of its tenure at Rabun County High School, Foxfire has sponsored student exchanges with the Network of Complementary Schools; the public schools of London, Ontario; and North Carolina Outward Bound. It has brought performing artists to Rabun County High School, hired Chicago artist John Weber to help students design a mural of Appalachian scenes for the school's commons area, sponsored a three-day schoolwide celebration of community resources, built playground equipment for local elementary schools, and sponsored an experimental writing program in the elementary schools.

Most important, Foxfire has provided for scores of its students free travel throughout the United States (including Alaska and Hawaii), Canada, and the Caribbean. In 1984, Wigginton accompanied Rabun County students on trips to New York; Washington, D.C.; Portland, Oregon; Tampa and West Palm Beach, Florida; Battle Creek, Michigan; Toronto, Canada; Providence, Rhode Island; and cities and towns throughout the Southeast. On one occasion several students attended Wigginton's meeting with Foxfire's national advisory board at the offices of *National Geographic Magazine* in Washington. These same students embarked to the Queen Anne School in Upper Marlboro, Maryland, for two days of workshops and informal discussions focused on educational uses of community resources. On another occasion three other students accompanied Wigginton to Berryville, Virginia, a trip described by Foxfire senior Tammy Blume:

> On March 15, Wig took me, Patsy Singleton and Richard Trusty to Virginia. We took Amtrak's Southern Crescent from Toccoa to Washington, D.C., where we met Loretta Barrett (Foxfire's editor) and one of Doubleday's representatives. From there we drove to Berryville, Virginia to visit one of Doubleday's plants where 100,000 copies of *Foxfire 8* were being bound, the covers attached, and packaged for shipment to bookstores. At 3:30, during the plant shift change, the employees gathered around a podium in the center of the plant to listen to short speeches that we each gave, expressing our appreciation of the work they do on our books. Upon leaving the plant, Doubleday presented each of us with a copy of *Foxfire 8*, just off the press.

That night, at Handley High School in Berryville, Doubleday sponsored us in a public presentation. Each of us spoke to the audience, which consisted of about 500 teachers, parents, and students. After the speeches, we autographed *Foxfire* books and were interviewed by the local radio station.[29]

Analysis of the transcripts of Rabun County High School students in the class of 1984 indicated that of the twelve seniors who had taken at least two *Foxfire* magazine classes, six were college preparatory and six were not. This particular class did not have a strong academic motivation, as suggested by the finding that only 37 percent (42/113) of the transcripts met the following college preparatory criteria beyond minimal graduation requirements: algebra I, algebra II or geometry, biology, and a cumulative average of eighty.[30] The terms "college preparatory" and "non–college preparatory" are heuristic devices, used here to show that Wigginton works in a school where the large majority of students do not pursue higher level academics. There is no denying, however, that some students identified as non–college preparatory will attend institutions of higher learning.[31]

The school culture in which Foxfire operated in 1984 was conservative and rule-bound. In 1982 the school board had a hired a law-and-order principal, giving him a mandate to restore discipline after a twelve-year era of what one school board member has described as loose governance at the high school. It was the board's impression that teachers were apathetic, that discipline was lax, and that drug dealers had infiltrated the campus. Prior to the arrival of the new principal, the board put up the fence and the gatehouse at the high school to keep the students in and the troublemakers out.

The new principal took his mandate seriously, creating what he described as "a controlled environment." Indicators of his success as a disciplinarian were the empty corridors during class periods, graffiti-free bathrooms, and an orderly lunchroom. "The halls were full when I came here," he stated. "The board wanted that stopped as well as lovemaking—kids pairing off in hidden corners and that sort of thing." He summarized his philosophy of discipline as follows: "I believe in prevention as opposed to reacting to situations. With hall passes every kid has a reason to be there. We don't give kids the opportunity to create problems. If you give people an opportunity to be bad, many will be bad. If you don't set up the opportunity for them to do bad things, they will channel their energies into positive things."

"I think he put a lot of people to work who weren't working before," posited a prominent school board member. "The students respect him, even though they may not like him. Speaking as a parent, I know I feel very comfortable about my kids being down there."

The administration meted out suspensions, detentions, and paddlings for a number of offenses. Smoking or chewing tobacco outside designated areas (and in the case of chewing tobacco, possession without a permit) warranted automatic three-day suspensions. After a third tardy to class, students were assigned a detention, or they could choose to be paddled in lieu of detention. One administrator occasionally patrolled the halls with a paddle in his back pocket.

Students leaving a class or homeroom had to carry a hall pass "signed by the teacher designating time, place and date." One Foxfire teacher used a metal plate embossed with the phrase, "Eat More Possum." "You've got to have a hall pass even if you step out of a door," complained one student. To ensure that students remained on campus unless they had parental authorization to leave, the administration enforced the following cumbersome procedure: "In order to check out of school, students must go to the office, have office officials call parents for permission to leave, take a checkout form to all teachers whose classes will be missed, return the signed checkout slip to the office and sign out on the signout sheet and pick up a gate pass. Students will not be allowed to check out to obtain items not brought to school."[32]

During lunch, students were not allowed to leave the cafeteria area without a hall pass. School officials gave seniors the exclusive privilege of occupying the ramp above the lunchroom; in warm weather, they allowed students to eat on picnic tables in the narrow outside corridor immediately adjacent to the cafeteria. After school, students were not allowed to remain in classrooms unsupervised by a teacher.

One student council leader charged that the administration did not take student ideas seriously: "The administration wants to supervise everything the students do instead of letting them have a feeling of being on their own. The administration is always talking about how we need to grow up and learn to be on our own, but they won't let us be on our own." A dissident teacher, an activist in the state teacher's association, supported this view: "The kids are not allowed to make their own decisions. They're not even allowed to make their own mistakes. There's no learning ground."

The school disciplinarians displayed contrasting authoritative styles in their dealings with students. One acted like a military drill instructor; his counterpart was the quintessential paternalist. A tornado warning at the high school in the early spring provided the occasion for me to observe these "Mutt and Jeff" styles in action. I noted:

During lunch, Administrator A (Mutt) runs along the ramp with arms spread in opposite directions, yelling that a tornado warning is in effect. "Get to the hallways!" he shouts. Next he announces the warning over the intercom. I go to F Hall, a thirty-five-yard-long corridor filled with approximately eighty students. The sit-in starts at 12:50 p.m. There is plenty of noise.

Administrator A comes into the hallway. He is soft-spoken and jocular, and the students kid with him. He explains in a calm, yet serious voice: "Boys and girls, there's been a tornado spotted in the northern end of the county." Next Administrator B (Jeff) enters the corridor through the double doors leading from the commons. Administrator A leaves. The noise level is up. In contrast to Administrator A, B is neither jocular nor friendly with the kids. His tone of voice even has me a bit intimidated. He bellows something like, "This is a tornado warning! I want everybody to get quiet right now!" I mutter, "Does he think they might not *hear* the tornado?" When he roars, the hall gets absolutely quiet. He leaves, but within five seconds, the noise reaches its crescendo again.

I notice that this is a restrained group—virtually all are seated—even though they are noisy. Each time the double doors open, the students lower the volume. When they see it's not Administrator B, they continue with their noisemaking. Next music floats in over the intercom, courtesy of WGHC in Clayton, whose DJ gives us tornado warning updates.

Administrator A comes into the hallway smiling, and the noise continues. He explains that the warning is still in effect: "Hush, hush! Boys and girls, we'll be in a tornado watch until 6:00. If there's still a warning, we're not going to be putting any of you on a bus." Shortly after this, Administrator A, who is standing at the far end of the hallway from where I'm sitting, says "Listen!" as the DJ advises the students to "sit tight." There is an uproar from the students. Administrator A is smiling. We've been here for a full hour. Finally, the warning is lifted, and those students who haven't finished eating go back to the lunchroom.

Initially, conservative school politics did not impinge heavily on Foxfire. The changes required by the administration were few and minor. For example, the new principal requested that Wigginton's staff submit to the school office the names of any visitors to Foxfire classes, explaining when and where they would be on campus. For the most part, however, he respected Foxfire's autonomy.

Unlike other teachers, Foxfire staff members were not required to sign in upon their arrival at school, nor were they required to notify the superintendent's office when leaving campus during school hours. Protected by Wigginton's mediation, they also were less vulnerable to administrative chastisements than other teachers, some of whom voiced harsh criticisms of the administration. One tenured teacher expressed her disaffection as follows: "It is very difficult to operate in a repressive atmosphere, which I feel we have here. Staff morale is very low. You are paranoid about following to the letter rules and regulations because you know if you don't, the resulting reprimand is likely to make you feel less worthy as a responsible adult. You can't fault the rules per se. It's not the rule[s] but the personality interaction—the way it's done."

When Wigginton moved Foxfire to Rabun County High School in 1977, county officials had chosen to ignore that he was the only Foxfire staff teacher who was certified in the subject he would be teaching. No contracts were signed, no documents were executed. Thus began an era of benign neglect during which Rabun County allowed Foxfire staff members, if they chose, to remain uncertified and without professional credentials. From 1977 to 1984, despite occasional complaints from parents, the county did not make certification of Foxfire teachers an issue; in fact, the high school administration did not list the organization or its teachers on its periodic accreditation reports to the Southern Association of Colleges and Schools and to the Georgia Accrediting Commission. The Georgia State Department of Education, which knew about Foxfire, did not challenge the county's autonomy in allowing the Fund to operate without certified teachers in one of its public schools.

On 6 November 1984, educational politics in Rabun County changed dramatically with the election of a new superintendent, a business education teacher in the high school, whose classroom had been situated across the hall from Wigginton's. The incumbency of the former teacher has resulted not only in the resignation of the principal at the high school, but also in the end of an era when county and state education officials tolerated the non-certification of Foxfire teachers.

On 14 May 1985, the principal tendered his resignation to the county school board. In March, the superintendent had first refused to offer the principal a contract renewal for the coming year, then two weeks later had changed his mind for reasons that are not clear. By this time, however, the principal's leadership and credibility had been undermined.

In a statement to a local newspaper, the principal charged that "the initial non-recommendation of me as principal was the implementation of a campaign promise." He further claimed that he had been unjustly pilloried by teachers and parents as a martinet, arguing that the school board had taken strong measures to control teacher and student behavior *prior* to his appointment: "I was blamed completely for the guard and I had nothing to do with it. . . . Another big issue was that if teachers left the school they were to call the county office. I did not make this rule, I had nothing to do with it."[33]

The principal further described himself as the enforcer of a school board mandate to restore discipline on the part of both teachers and students at the high school. Statements issued by school board members in the wake of the principal's resignation corroborated his testimony. "You would see some teachers in town during the school day," said the school board chairman (complaining about the behavior of non-Foxfire teachers). "We felt like they were hired to do a job and they should be at school as long as there were students at school. In fact, it was our understanding that some of the teachers were not even keeping complete records on the students, just giving grades from memory."[34] Yet, the school board reacted in a way that impugned the character of teachers, damaged their morale, and diminished their credibility.

Prior to taking office, the new superintendent disclosed that he planned to bring uncertified Foxfire staff into line with other teachers who had appropriate certification. His statement indicated that some vocational education teachers, who taught elective courses, resented having to compete for student enrollments with Foxfire teachers: "When you have a low number of students in your class, teachers say it's because of Foxfire. This is an area that a lot of teachers have difficulty with [about] Foxfire—competition. And they're not certified teachers. I've been certified a lot of years and I have to compete with them. A good many teachers feel this way."

This statement manifests more than professional concern with the competency of Foxfire staff teachers. At issue also is the fact that one group of teachers perceives another as unfairly privileged.

School officials indicated that they were not comfortable with the loose structure of the Foxfire classes, directing their remarks to the music, video, and environmental science/outdoor education divisions. "I've had a lot of problems with Foxfire staff [not] following procedure," one administrator stated. "The area of supervision is lax. As far as highly organized and highly disciplined teachers are concerned, the Foxfire staff *aren't*, with the exception of Wig. I think they'll tell you that."

These administrators also cited Foxfire's strengths and its numerous contributions to the high school. But the fact remained that they perceived the organization as a *mixed* blessing. Significantly, these conservative educators had high praise for Wigginton despite the huge disparities between their philosophy and his. They were less effusive in their praise of other staff members; in fact, one observed,

"Foxfire *is* Eliot Wigginton. If Wig left today, it would go under eventually."

The county's only college-educated school board member expressed a concern that Foxfire programs deflected students from more important academic pursuits: "As long as Foxfire is funding its own program, it's okay—but with non-certified teachers, strictly as an elective. But it's not ideal. I don't think studying log cabin building is a viable activity. I've had too many children working for me who spent time in media and Foxfire who can't read, write, and cipher. It's up to the powers that be to see that these children get the academic background they need."

By December 1984, Foxfire's dearth of properly accredited staff teachers had become a minor *cause célèbre* at the high school. Ostensibly, the administration had a legitimate complaint against the noncertified Foxfire staff. Reports had to be filed with accrediting agencies, and Foxfire's ambiguous status might threaten the school's certification. The administrator responsible for completing these forms stated that he had not listed Foxfire staff members, but he had misgivings about the omissions: "It seems to me to be a violation of state standards. It's really not right. [My] recommendation would be for these people to get off their butts and get a certificate."

Benign neglect of Foxfire officially ended in the spring of 1985, when the superintendent decreed that Foxfire staff members would either be certified or they would not be allowed to teach. His decision concurred with an opinion rendered by the regional educational compliance officer, whom the superintendent and principal had consulted. Other options, such as certifying the entire program as a special educational activity in a rural school, either were not explored or were disallowed. As a result, two staff members have begun taking the necessary university courses for certification, and a third has resigned from the staff.[35]

From 1977 to 1982, Foxfire had provided staff teachers free of charge to Rabun County, without executing a contract for their services. According to state regulations, a contract became mandatory when a Foxfire staff member began to coach one of the school's athletic teams. In the fall of 1982, Wigginton signed a formal agreement under the terms of which the Foxfire Fund, Inc., provided its teachers to the county in exchange for a $1.00 yearly salary; while this contract formalized a long-standing informal relationship, it did not impinge on Foxfire's autonomy.

With the incumbency of the new superintendent, Foxfire's contractual relationship with the county has again changed, but this time its autonomy has been circumscribed. Under the new contract, Foxfire staff members are paid by the county for the classes they teach at the high school. The department of education issues checks as well as W-2 tax forms to each Foxfire teacher. The Foxfire Fund makes up the difference between what it would have paid each teacher under the old system and what the county now pays, issuing another set of W-2 forms in each case.

The Catch-22 in these tortuous negotiations is that Foxfire provides the money to the department of education, a sort of *tertium quid* that pays Foxfire teachers. In theory, at least, these new rules make these individuals bona fide county employees, subject to the same encumbrances under which regular teachers labor, e.g., homeroom duty, hall monitoring, and dance chaperoning. Describing Foxfire's new relationship with county school officials, an irritated staff member quipped that Wigginton had surrendered his "quid" without eliciting a "quo" in return, e.g., "a reduction of harassment from [an unfriendly school administrator]." This criticism has merit, but it misses the point that Foxfire continues to receive a quid pro quo from the county by virtue of being allowed to run its programs inside a public high school. How much Wigginton will allow his autonomy to be restricted before leaving Rabun County High School is at present an open question.

If nothing else, this controversy has unearthed some rivalries and suspicions about Foxfire's worth as a total curriculum approach in an age of conservative school reform. The most serious criticisms challenge the application rather than the theory of Foxfire. For example, a well-respected and influential teacher spoke highly of the character of Foxfire staff members, but she also described some of their classes as dumping grounds for obstreperous and unmotivated students in search of easy courses. "The core—Foxfire I, Foxfire II—was solid," she opined. "But the other courses they've added are weaker. I'm not going to tell you they're totally bad."

Perhaps the greatest irony of the Foxfire experience has been the replication of its principles in hundreds of schools across America and the Western Hemisphere, but *not* within its own high school. Indeed, the responses of some teachers suggest that Foxfire is perceived as an alien (albeit benign) entity inside a traditional school culture. For example, one old-timer confided: "Foxfire's philosophy of education is too loose. For example, letting kids sit in the floor—is that the way to teach? I can't do it that way. That's too loose."

Teachers expressed less ambivalence about Foxfire than administrators. Typically they praised the efforts of Wigginton and his staff, particularly with problem students, applauded Foxfire's role in reducing the student-teacher ratio by providing five additional teachers, and voiced few serious complaints. Significantly, despite their avowed appreciation for Foxfire, they eschewed using the Foxfire concept or a related strategy in their own classrooms.

The sampling decision concerning which teachers to interview for the case study of Foxfire precluded vocational education teachers as a group because they had few dealings with Foxfire (see Appendix B for further discussion). One of their number who was interviewed, the superintendent-elect, suggested that some of his colleagues were disaffected, and he took action to remedy their putative complaints by mandating the certification of all Foxfire staff teachers.

Other complaints that teachers have voiced about Foxfire are more innocuous—predictable and less intriguing than the vocational education controversy. For example, two teachers complained that one student was routinely late for their classes because of his involvement in Foxfire community activities. In a paean familiar to all teachers who have detained students into the next class period, one of these remarked: "I don't like for kids to miss my class because they're late from a Foxfire class. I feel like my class is just as important as theirs."

Several teachers who arrived at the new high school with Foxfire in 1977 reported that the organization's unorthodox practices, e.g., taking students out of other classes for interviews or trips during the school day, caused jealousy and resentment among the faculty. "But I don't think that's much of a problem anymore," stated a physical education teacher. "Most teachers have adjusted to that."

Others commented that some teachers still have not adjusted, but suggested these are a minority. For example, a longtime social studies teacher observed: "They're [Foxfire staff] in a different world. I guess there is jealousy. I've heard several [teachers], but not many, make catty remarks. I don't want to create the impression that a majority of the teachers or personnel are bitter or jealous, because they're not."

Two department heads implied that in view of Foxfire's contributions to the high school, they had no objections to the privileges accorded its staff members by the administration. One who professed to have high regard for the Foxfire staff stated: "I've never been one to criticize if they have a small class size or a small number of hours because they're self-supportive. All they are provided is a room. They provide their own money. It's not my prerogative to gripe on that. Foxfire has been self-supportive, so teachers should be supportive."

The other teacher made a similar observation: "They are paid by themselves and they don't go by the state requirements. That doesn't bother me. I think most people around here like Foxfire. They have their own rules and have their own [staff] meetings and attend the department meetings. They're out with kids at 9:00 at night. They do their fair share of work."

Wigginton's English department colleagues viewed his program very favorably. "His suggestions are usually on target and helpful," observed the department head, who described Foxfire as "a viable alternative to the regular English classes." When asked if he had any criticisms of the program, he responded: "I have no criticisms of it at all—*period*. If I did, I'd be biting the hand that gives the English department so much help. Any student they have in their classes reduces [our] class load. If it's ten, that's ten less compositions per week an English teacher would have to grade."

The lone demurrer in the English department was a veteran traditionalist whose criticisms indicated that she was misinformed about Foxfire I, Wigginton's introductory composition/grammar class: "I'm totally against counting anything as an English [credit] except traditional English courses. Foxfire I shouldn't be substituted as an English course. [Students] should have traditional grammar and composition." Yet even this teacher had plaudits for Wigginton and the *Foxfire* magazine program: "I definitely don't think it's fluff. Look at the books and magazines. There's a lot of hard work. What he's done as a high school teacher is mind-boggling. He's an excellent teacher, and he's very concerned about kids."

NOTES

1. Herbert Kohl to Foxfire staff and board members, 24 September 1979.

2. Mickey Justice, a 1971 graduate, now a truck-engine mechanic, was one of these students. He recalls: "Wig and I beat the bushes on weekends looking for stills and people to interview, gathering information on how the stills were built so he could diagram [the whiskey-making process]."

3. Wigginton's argument is plausible. Most of the articles in the files that are unequivocally his authorship were written during the first five years of the project. Other articles of lesser complexity than the moonshining piece, drafts of which appear in Wigginton's hand, are the following: "Beekeeping," *Foxfire*, Fall 1971, 161–73; "A Quilt Is Something Human," *Foxfire*, Winter 1969, 5–7, 44–47; "To Save a Piece of History," *Foxfire*, Fall/Winter 1968, 10–14, 117–23; "An Old Chairmaker Shows How," *Foxfire*, Winter 1969, 11–16, 53–54; "Chimney Building," *Foxfire*, Fall 1970, 125–33; "To Save a House," *Foxfire*, Summer 1969, 6–8; "Faith Healing," *Foxfire*, March 1968, 15–24, 61–70; "Happy Dowdle," *Foxfire*, Spring/Summer 1971, 10–27; "The Annual Old Time World Championship Fiddler's Convention 1968," *Foxfire*, June 1968, 4–5. It is worth

noting that Wigginton did not write any of these articles in the name of his students. He has stated that he left these pieces unsigned because his signature might have conveyed the misleading impression that students had been only marginal participants.

4. Eliot Wigginton, ed., *Foxfire 5* (Garden City, N.Y.: Anchor Books/Doubleday, 1979), 208–25.

5. Wigginton's introduction to *The Foxfire Book*, 13; reprinted in *Moments* (Washington, D.C.: IDEAS, 1975), 116–17.

6. Wigginton, ed., *Foxfire 2*, 15.

7. Eliot Wigginton, ed., *Foxfire 6* (Garden City, N.Y.: Anchor Press/Doubleday, 1980), 14–15.

8. Eliot Wigginton, ed., *Foxfire 3* (Garden City, N.Y.: Anchor Press/Doubleday, 1975), 12–13.

9. Ibid., 13–14. In his "Report to the Boards," 9 September 1974, Wigginton explained that the company had offered Foxfire $25,000 for the film rights.

10. *Hands On* 4, no. 1 (1980): 4–5.

11. Diane C. Thomas, "The Foxfire Empire: Eliot Wigginton's Complex Battle to Preserve a Simpler Way of Life," *Atlanta Journal and Constitution Magazine*, 9 April 1978, 15.

12. In an interview with the author, a Rabun County school board member confirmed that the board had responded to a storm of community protest by ordering the guard to leave his gun at home.

13. Presciently, Foxfire legal-board member Mike Clark had predicted the effects of consolidation on Foxfire several years prior to the move to Rabun County High School:

> I can't help but feel that when consolidation does take place, it will have a tremendous impact upon the nature of the Foxfire project. I think this will occur not only because of the change of location but also because of the size of the new school, the lack of intimacy, and most importantly, the lack of a community based school which local people identify with and relate to as their school. (Clark to Eliot Wigginton, 10 May 1974)

> I get the feeling that a large amount of the actual work load in Foxfire is carried by the boarding students who have little else to do and find Foxfire to be the most stimulating thing in their lives (and I'm damned glad it's there). But is it realistic to expect the same kind of time and energy to be put into Foxfire by students who may have to go through a two or three hour bus ride every day to get home from school? (Clark to Wigginton, 23 May 1974)

14. *Hands On* 4, no. 1 (1980): 4–5.

15. A former Foxfire student stated that students were involved in a 1978 suit against Foxfire Log Homes: "A group of students went up to Otto [N.C.] and told them they were infringing on our trademark. They told us to take a hike. As a class, we called Rich Bennett, our trademark lawyer. He sent them a letter [telling them to take down their sign]. When they didn't . . . , he wrote them, "Take down the sign or there'll be six inches of legal paper on your desk

on Monday morning." [Again] they didn't take down the sign and there was a stack of legal papers on their desk on Monday. It went all the way to court, and the federal marshall made them take down the sign. They never paid our legal fees because they went bankrupt."

16. A 1980 graduate voiced her frustration about the relative impotence of students in Foxfire organizational affairs: "They always asked our opinion, but whatever the final authorities wanted, they'd get. It made you feel like you were wasting your time." Furthermore, she suggested that student decision making was limited to trivialities: "Heck, one summer we made the major decision whether we were going to put carpet in the chapel or not."

17. Wigginton, *Moments,* 16.

18. Erik Erikson, *Identity: Youth and Crisis* (New York: Norton, 1968), 53–70.

19. For more on this phrase, see Colin M. Turnbull's discussion of the potentially vital role of old people in the education of adolescents, in *The Human Cycle* (New York: Simon and Schuster, 1983), 225–27.

20. Page and Wigginton, eds., *Aunt Arie,* xii–xxxiii.

21. Ibid., 205–6.

22. Ibid., 202.

23. Turnbull, *Human Cycle,* 255.

24. Ibid., 228.

25. See Erikson's discussion of diffused identity, *Identity: Youth and Crisis,* 131–35.

26. These statements by Voiles and Woodall were submitted for an in-house evaluation study conducted by two Foxfire staff members in the early 1980s. The study was aborted because the questionnaire form was seriously flawed (for example, it contained a yes-no format). Because the questionnaire also contained a section for comments, I decided it might provide *some* reliable information. When I requested access to the completed questionnaires, the staff was unable to locate them. After interviewing Voiles and Woodall, I found an unpublished paper, "The Foxfire Evaluation," n.d., by Paul Gillespie, which contained the statements they had entered in the comments section of the questionnaire. These individuals had given me the same information, but I have not quoted it as extensively.

27. "Rabun County Board of Education Report," September 1984. Wigginton also did not mention that of the high school's 874 students in 1983–84, more than one-third had participated in Foxfire-sponsored classes (Foxfire enrollment lists, 1983–84).

28. In the summer of 1984, the following wage scale was in effect: first-year student employees, $117.25 weekly (minimum wage for 35 hours); second-year, $135.00; third-year, $150.00.

29. Tammy Blume, "Foxfire on the Road," *Foxfire Reflections,* May 1984.

30. As reported in the *Clayton Tribune,* 17 Oct. 1985, average SAT scores for 1983–84 seniors at Rabun County High School were verbal, 376; math, 411; total, 787. The Rabun County mean total score was 35 points lower than the Georgia state average. In 1984–85, Rabun County's average scores were

verbal, 370; math, 419; total 789. This total was 48 points below the Georgia average, 117 points below the national average.

31. Ernest Boyer adumbrates this crisis in college admissions procedures: "The particular courses a student takes are not important for getting into most colleges, although they may be critical to success once a student is there. Half the colleges set no specific course requirements, and only one quarter consider the courses taken in making a decision for or against admission" (*High School: A Report on Secondary Education in America* [New York: Harper and Row, 1983], 252).

32. "Rabun County High School Student Policies," 1983–84.

33. *Clayton Tribune,* 16 May 1985.

34. Ibid.

35. Wigginton, "Report to the Boards," 15 May 1985.

SIX

Community Issues and Effects

Over the past twenty years, Foxfire has promoted (and thrived upon) an intimate relationship with the people of Rabun County and the surrounding mountain communities. In this chapter, key issues and effects that have emerged in the context of this extraordinary union of school and community are described and analyzed. First, there are issues and effects that have resulted from Wigginton's commitment to community-based economic development under Foxfire's aegis—an elusive goal to which he devoted six years of planning and spent a small fortune trying to make operational. Second, there is the issue of whether Foxfire has, intentionally or unwittingly, exploited the Appalachian elders whose knowledge and wisdom have been the project's mainstay. The corollary issue is whether these Foxfire contacts have benefited from the relationship. Finally, there is the issue of where and how Foxfire has invested the ample royalties it has earned from information provided by native Appalachians. The evidence presented within each of these categories suggests that Foxfire has proved to be a boon, rather than a boondoggle, to the communities with which it has long been associated.

The Rise and Fall of the Mountain City Project

Fittingly, the catalyst that initiated Foxfire's Mountain City Project was the speculative activity of a local banker and his associates who had purchased a plot of land along U.S. Highway 441, adjacent to the Clayton Church of God in Mountain City. The deed of purchase attests that these individuals acquired the property on 2 June 1977 for $33,500.[1] When Wigginton learned that a supermarket chain intended to purchase the property, he negotiated with the new owners and by 1 August had agreed to pay a whopping $85,000 for the 8½-acre tract.[2] The threat of a large supermarket being built on the site was not the cause, but the signal for Wigginton to buy land in the town's business district. To relieve pressure on the Foxfire Center from tourists, Foxfire's legal board had previously authorized him to purchase new property on which to locate a retail outlet.

The land that Wigginton bought was the site of the old Mountain City Hotel, which had burned years before. It had been one of the two tourist hotels in the small town that had fronted the Tallulah Falls Railroad. On summer evenings the young musician, sometimes moonshiner, Buck Carver had played guitar to Leonard Webb's banjo and John Harkins's fiddle on the hotel's "big old veranda." In 1977, all that remained from that era was the hotel's metal water tower.[3]

Shortly after purchasing the hotel property, Wigginton presented to the various Foxfire boards a written plan for developing the site, which he justified as a logical "next step" beyond the preservationist role served by Foxfire. In his introduction, he wrote: "Though this new move may, on the surface, strike you as being a rather frivolous and expensive extra involvement, all of us here are convinced that, looking five years down the road, it is absolutely appropriate and necessary for the directions in which our organization is moving."[4]

Next Wigginton outlined his ideas for creating an educational center where adolescents could learn marketable skills under Foxfire's auspices. In the planning stage, he wrote, was a furniture factory that would employ local high school students to manufacture reproductions of traditional Appalachian furniture. Also envisioned were a cable television studio, a greenhouse and environmental gardens, a community conference area, a print shop, a log house for displaying Foxfire furniture, and a retail outlet for other Foxfire products.

Wigginton expressed his commitment to laying the foundation for a community-managed enterprise that would provide not only meaningful career employment to local people, but also a realistic alternative to uncontrolled strip development: "Hopefully . . . this new acquisition will eventually be a community-run model of tasteful highway-fronted economic activity . . . a welcome relief from the Pizza Hut/Kentucky Fried Chicken mentality that now threatens to overwhelm our county's section of [Highway] 23-441."[5]

There is circumstantial evidence that local realtors planned to take advantage of the Foxfire development in Mountain City. A knowledgeable Foxfire staff member related the following information:

"That was one of the highest prices paid in Rabun County per acre. When that happened it opened all the surrounding land to parasite development. It caused two other sites to be purchased for speculative purposes. These developers thought that if Foxfire went through with the plan it would draw tourists to the area, and they were going to provide two other tourist businesses. I know the developers. As the Foxfire development hasn't materialized, these developers have sold off the sites."

One of the developers supposedly involved in this scheme acknowledged in an interview that he and his partner had purchased tracts of property in Mountain City at the same time Wigginton obtained the hotel property. While the developer stated that his purchases were unrelated to Wigginton's, he also confided that a Foxfire development "would help stop people from going further north [to the Great Smoky Mountains]. It's name recognition. If I had that name on a business, man, I could stop traffic on 441."

As noted previously, Foxfire's MARBARLA project had nodded in the direction of social action with its disclosures about the problems attendant upon increased tourism and social dislocation in Rabun County. Although MARBARLA did not attempt to resolve community problems, its inherent strengths were the sustained involvement of students in the investigation of social issues and in the creation of publishable articles. Moreover, the young women of MARBARLA made, or participated in, the key decisions that resulted in the "Betty's Creek Issue" of *Foxfire* magazine. For example, they pressured Wigginton, and won the point, to publish their findings as an entire issue of the magazine rather than as a series of colored-stock center-sections in separate issues.[6]

For all its limitations as a vehicle for economic and social reconstruction, *Foxfire* magazine was a focal point of student activity. Students participated in every phase of magazine production—topic selection, interviewing, photography, transcription, editing, layout, and cover design; at Rabun Gap they had even participated in major organizational decisions, e.g., closing the Foxfire Center to tourists. Significantly, over the six years that Foxfire devoted to planning for community development (1977 to 1983) students were conspicuously absent, either as discussants or beneficiaries of the Mountain City Project.

One notable exception was Wigginton's "Mountain City class" at Rabun County High School in 1979. The pedagogical shibboleth for that year was "empowerment" of students. In his introduction to *Foxfire 5*, Wigginton argued:

It is impossible to be involved in education of this sort for any length of time and not be cognizant of the larger, overarching goal of education itself—a goal that goes far beyond the creation of a set of books and a series of record albums. Though our approaches may differ, here our mission as teachers is clear. It is, quite simply, to help our students master the information they must have to be able to take their destinies into their own hands. Said another way, it is to help our students come as close as is humanly possible to having control over their own futures. To start our students toward a life-style that matches their expectations. To move them toward the kind of independence that prevents their being eternally dependent on others. To give them tools for the long fight, and at the same time give them the human sensitivity they must have if they are to be part of the solution instead of part of the problem. There's a good word for it: empowerment.[7]

The twelve-week class included four juniors whom Wigginton described as "good students who are bored with school, unchallenged and who know how to get by with a minimal amount of work." One of his goals, he stated, was "to get the kids excited about reading and writing through the project." The primary aim, however, was to create in students an awareness of change—why and how it occurs, what its political mechanisms are, and how individual citizens can participate effectively in public decision making about change.[8]

The gloomy prospects of Rabun County's economy (a microcosm of the Appalachian region) guided Wigginton's conceptualization of the class. As he noted in his address to the 1979 National Workshop for Cultural Journalism in St. Louis, the bulk of the land available for private use in the county "is being grabbed as fast as it can by people from Tallahassee and West Palm Beach and Miami and Fort Lauderdale and Savannah . . . who want a place to build a summer home. . . . And what's left for the local kids is very little; and what little is left is so inflated in price that they cannot afford to buy it." In sum, the changes engulfing the community were on terms unfavorable to the economic destinies of Rabun County youngsters.[9]

As a first step in learning about change, each student in the new class selected a neighboring town that had experienced a recent growth spurt or period of social dislocation, e.g., Helen, Georgia, which had transformed itself from virtually a ghost town into a replica Alpine village, with over a hundred tourist shops and restaurants, a tawdry display of pseudo-Bavarian and Swiss architectural styles. The purpose of these investigations, typically interviews with mayors and other community officials, was to collect data and slides to present at a meeting for the people of Mountain City in an effort to get them involved in making decisions about the kinds of changes they wanted and did not want in their town. The students conducted a door-to-door campaign to get Mountain City's 450 residents out to the event.

Wigginton has colorfully described the night when his students addressed the town of Mountain City and the events that followed that meeting:

> On the appointed night eighty-six people turned out. The meeting was held in the auditorium of what had once been the town's elementary school. The four students that were in the class and Sherrod [Reynolds] and myself and the mayor were in the front of the room. The students gave a presentation to the community [using] maps to show how the city had changed over the last few years, and then the students ran their slide shows. One of the most revealing sections came from the mayor of Helen, Georgia. . . .
>
> Then they presented three other towns through their slides and quotations from leaders. Afterwards they opened up the floor for discussion. Mountain City had absolutely no zoning. Anybody who wants to [can] go into Mountain City and buy a piece of land and do anything he or she wants with it, no questions asked. And that creates some problems. So that was discussed.
>
> After the meeting was over everybody stood around and talked for about another hour. We got a great slide of the mayor and City Council huddled anxiously way back in the corner by themselves having a little council meeting trying to figure out what it was that had just happened to them. But one of the end results of that thing was the creation of a planning committee made up of twenty-four local residents.
>
> There were three other meetings that followed that one. Local people pulled themselves together then, and the first major activity they sponsored in association with the kids was a major town-wide cleanup where 125 people turned out, scoured the town, [and] hauled numerous truck loads of garbage to the dump. Everybody turned out and mowed their lawns and trimmed their trees, and if they had old stuff they had been meaning to throw away for years but had never done it, they could haul it out to the side of road, and when the crews came through, they'd grab it and throw it in the trucks. We took away bed springs and a row boat, dish washers, you know, all manner of garbage. And then at the end we had a big festival, a community celebration. We had a square dance and a greased pole climb; we had kids spitting watermelon seeds, and a tobacco-spitting contest. Tom McFalls, who's here with us, won first place in the tobacco-spitting contest. Spat a wad twenty-four feet. If you want to find out what that little festival was like, just talk to Tom McFalls about it. A great experience.[10]

Although plans were made for the continued involvement of students in Mountain City, specifically in addressing the problems of parasite development that would likely follow Foxfire into the town, these plans never came to fruition. The Mountain City class remained a "one-shot" effort to maintain high student visibility in the project.

Despite Wigginton's rhetoric of empowerment, neither he nor his staff offered any further social action courses or projects that linked students directly to what the teachers had on the drawing board for Mountain City.

In a proposal to the Kresge Foundation in 1979, Wigginton described the project, which by this time had dropped the furniture factory and added what he called, rather vaguely, "a small industrial complex linked to the industrial arts department of the high school." This complex, he stated, "will eventually be able to hire at least twenty young people who wish to stay in this area instead of having to move to Atlanta to find work."

Wigginton also included terse descriptions of the television studio and community conference area, which would also house Foxfire's tape archives; the print shop, which would be run by "former students who will have graduated from a trade school in the printing trades"; the cluster of "historic log buildings," which would house Foxfire's retail outlet, mail-order business, and the Rabun County Historical Society. Wigginton's father had drafted a site plan for the project, which Wigginton envisaged as a city park that would serve as a community "focal point" much in the fashion of the timbered courthouses and gazebos of an earlier era. The projected cost of the entire project was $1,352,200.[11]

Cleverly, Wigginton devised a plan that, if successful, would ensure a steady flow of operating funds, allow Foxfire to build its endowment, and support the Mountain City project all at the same time. In a proposal to NEH for a $900,000 matching grant, Wigginton stated that the funds would be used "to offset the bulk of our operating expenses for a three-year period so that the majority of our book royalties can be added to our existing endowment fund, thus building it to the point where its income could sustain much of our work, even if the books stopped selling entirely."

Under the terms of the three-to-one matching grant proposed by Wigginton, Foxfire would raise $900,000 against the $300,000 donated by NEH. Wigginton expressed confidence that private foundations would provide Foxfire's share. "We are convinced," he wrote, "that we could do the entire Mountain City project with grant funds stimulated by the challenge grant, cover most of our operating costs with a combination of the NEH funds and other grants, put the bulk of what will surely be increased royalties checks into the endowment, *and* handle the operating costs of the new buildings through the sales each will generate."[12] In early June 1979, NEH notified Wigginton of the $300,000 award.

Several months prior to receipt of the NEH grant, Wigginton had solicited funding from the Charles Stewart Mott Foundation for a director of development and an administrative assistant to raise the NEH challenge money for the Mountain City Project.[13] In a letter to his boards, Wigginton described the strain he was under trying to teach and to raise development funds at the same time: "We are either going to have to find and hire an administrator/fund-raiser/business manager to work with us full time, or I am going to have to stop teaching and carry that responsibility myself. It is becoming increasingly impossible for me to do both jobs well, alone."[14]

In the late fall of 1979, the Mott Foundation notified Foxfire of a $32,200 award for establishing a Grants Management Office (GMO),[15] and Wigginton hired Joe Haban, a former Rabun Gap boarding student, to head the new office, serving as a multipurpose administrator.

Shortly after hiring Haban, Wigginton and his staff began to explore the possibility that Foxfire might better serve the local economy as the catalyst for a community development corporation (CDC) rather than as an employer for its own enterprises. Although they planned to conduct feasibility studies for establishing small businesses that would be extensions of selected Foxfire divisions, they also envisioned the creation of a CDC as an independent entity under whose financial umbrella community-owned businesses would originate. In letters and grant proposals from the early 1980s, however, the distinction between the Foxfire and CDC-owned enterprises becomes blurred, suggesting a lack of specificity in the conceptualization of the project. Ironically, the "economic development analyst" who might have conducted feasibility studies and sorted out the planning details was never hired.

The impetus behind this decision to help create a CDC was Wigginton's realization that Foxfire-owned and operated businesses could never provide the kinds of white-collar, managerial jobs that would make working for Foxfire genuinely distinguishable from doing manual labor in a local plant. Wigginton has described how Mike Clark, director of the Highlander Research and Education Center, introduced Foxfire to the CDC idea and got the organization to rethink its role in community development:

> We didn't even hear about CDCs until Mike Clark at Highlander started talking about them on down the line. We didn't even know there was such an animal until fairly late in the process. . . . Mike began to lay some guilt trips on us and some of the board members about the fact that all this was going to be well and good for Foxfire but to what extent would it help to

educate other community people who were not connected with Foxfire about how they themselves could start businesses of their own and get some control of their own economic destiny.

In other words, it's like empire building. You become the big cheese and you hire community people to work with you, but in terms of those community people you hire getting an education about how to take control of their own futures, you don't make any contribution to that effort at all. What you ought to be looking at rather than lining your own pockets is community education, and that's where that CDC business began to come in.

The CDC seemed to everybody to be philosophically the better answer because you've got an independent entity, not Foxfire, doing the same things but doing them in a different way where the people themselves are making decisions about what kinds of things they want in their lives, and what kinds of things are going to improve the quality of their lives. And Foxfire isn't doing the whole thing—creating the programs or creating the options and then hiring somebody and, realistically, probably paying them six dollars or seven dollars an hour. [In that case] we're no better than Burlington.

As envisaged by Wigginton (and several of his staff and legal board members), the CDC would mobilize indigenous talent and resources to create, with seed funds, locally controlled businesses in which the CDC would hold investment shares ranging from 5 or 10 percent to 100 percent.[16] Initially, the CDC would build its investment pool with grants from federal, state, and philanthropic sources; following the expenditure of these funds, its continued existence (in theory, at least) would be contingent solely upon the success of the businesses that operated under its auspices. Likely candidates for CDC support included a furniture factory, a dry cleaning business, a printing shop, and a housing corporation. At the outset, the CDC would be headquartered on Foxfire's Mountain City property.

The first step in launching the CDC was to hire an economic development analyst to direct the project and to conduct the necessary feasibility studies. The private foundations (Ford, Lyndhurst, et al.) that Foxfire solicited to fund the CDC office, however, flatly rejected the proposal on the grounds that Foxfire had a lucrative endowment (over $500,000) that could, and should, be used to get the CDC underway.[17]

Funded for a second year in 1981–82 by the Mott Foundation, the Grants Management Office continued its fund-raising efforts to meet staggered NEH deadlines for the $900,000 matching grant. Throughout 1981, Joe Haban remained sanguine (at least, publicly) that the CDC would become a reality. In a report to the Mott Foundation,

Haban assured his benefactors that "our goal of creating a Community Development Corporation is still a priority item."[18]

By early 1982, however, Foxfire had once again begun to realign its community development priorities—this time refocusing on strategies for marketing and retailing Foxfire products. Feasibility studies provided free to Foxfire by the School of Business at Georgia State University (Atlanta) indicated that if Foxfire were to create a new business entity, it should be "a publishing company with a mail-order marketing program."[19]

The Georgia State marketing studies coincided with a decision by Wigginton and his organization to rejuvenate and restructure the Foxfire Press as a regional publishing house. Preparatory to securing the funds that would guarantee the viability of this venture, Wigginton created the Foxfire Journalism Internship Program, under whose aegis journalism interns would produce a series of new manuscripts that would differ significantly from the format of the Doubleday *Foxfire* series. A $15,000 grant from the Georgia Council for the Arts provided the money to pay the salary of a single intern, Linda Garland Page, a member of the original *Foxfire* editorial staff at Rabun Gap–Nacoochee School. During her year's internship, Page worked with Wigginton to collect, edit, and organize for publication the transcriptions of taped interviews with Aunt Arie Carpenter, who had died in 1978. Joe Haban described the press and the mail-order business that would be attached to it as "the first entity of our rural economic development program"—confirming the organization's renewed emphasis on its *own* businesses as alternative sources of employment to local wage-scale and piecework industries.[20]

An unusual arrangement between Foxfire and E. P. Dutton facilitated the establishment of Foxfire Press. Recently purchased by John Dyson, Wigginton's longtime friend from his student days at Cornell, the New York publishing house generously provided $400,000 to support the Press for four years, in exchange for the rights to eight nationally publishable Foxfire titles (books, plays, calendars, and related items) *or* $400,000 in royalties from the sales of one or more of the publications.

The contract was beneficial to Foxfire for two other reasons as well. First, Dutton would publish the volumes for distribution in its national trade-book market, while allowing Foxfire to buy them, at publisher's cost, to resell through the Foxfire Press mail-order business. Thus Foxfire circumvented the standard author-publisher contract, which allowed authors to buy books from the publisher at 60 percent of the retail value—an amount considerably above the actual publication costs. Moreover, as Joe Haban has noted, having the Dutton mail-order rights gave Foxfire further opportunities to provide employment for community people: "If we want to create jobs in Rabun County and we can't sell books through the trade, how does that create jobs? You get involved in direct response marketing—mail order. The only other marketing vehicle, if you [don't] sell in the trade, is mail. Since Dutton doesn't sell through the mail and we can't get involved in the trade, then fulfillment [of the mail orders] would create jobs."

Second, Dutton would not only provide free technical assistance in managing the press, but also would make Foxfire an equal partner in decisions about the design of the volumes. The first book jointly published under the agreement was *Aunt Arie: A Foxfire Portrait* (1983), which won a Christopher Award as a work contributing significantly to the uplift of the human spirit.[21]

Unlike the Foxfire Press, the community development corporation idea foundered. Wigginton and his staff lacked both the expertise and, ultimately, the commitment to launch such an entity. Although Haban finally located some philanthropic support for the CDC—a $30,000 grant from the Public Welfare Foundation—the Foxfire staff balked at hiring a CDC director with the funds. After a round of interviews with applicants, the staff could not reach a consensus on the *type* of individual to hire—a Rabun County native with strong local ties or an outsider with expertise in community development projects. Finally, the organization acted on the advice of a skeptical community development consultant and abandoned the idea at the end of 1982.[22]

Wigginton has summarized the failure of Foxfire's endeavors to become the catalyst for a CDC in the following terms:

> The thing that got the CDC thing thrown off the rails was that as we began to look into it more and more deeply, I began to feel—and a lot of other people began to feel, too—that [Mike] Clark had us on the wrong horse, because we couldn't find in the whole United States of America a CDC that was working. There's not a CDC in this country that's paying its own way. They're all dependent on federal grants and . . . that kind of thing, and there aren't any that are working. So how come that's such a good goddamn model? That's no good.
>
> The one CDC that people were really excited about, like Joe [Haban]— justifiably so—was this big one in Mississippi called the Delta Corporation. And it turns out that they've come to the same conclusion as all the rest of industry in this country—which is that since they're on the dole, they've got to get off the dole and they've got to bring in management experts from New York, which they've done. And they've got to hire people and pay them

minimum wage and turn out the goddamn products. And they're no better than any other industry except, presumably, the workers have a bit more say. But where the tire meets the road, it's a whole bunch of black people putting together bicycle wheels. That's where it is. You can go look at it, and that's what it is. It's a string of little factories with people doing assembly work and making minimum wage. That's not the alternative. That's not the option.

And Bill Duncan himself, as a consultant of ours, said, "I think you guys are doing the wrong thing. I think what you ought to do is just shut up and keep on doing what you're doing. And as [soon as] you can hire another person [hire him or her]. What you've got to remember is that, presumably, the kinds of jobs you are giving people are better in terms of quality than minimum-wage piecemeal work. They go to staff meetings [and] they participate in the organization and have a say, and the quality of the lifestyle and actually the size of the salary [you] pay people [at Foxfire] is a good bit better than the average. You're already having the kind of impact that you're talking about wanting to have through a CDC."

The final site plan for the Mountain City Project was researched and designed by Alan Levy, an apprentice landscape architect, in 1982. The plat included buildings for the Foxfire Press, a community historical center, a mail-order center and retail outlet, a model solar home, a craft area, and a blacksmith shop. Additionally, space was allocated for a garden center, an amphitheater, picnic areas, and a pond.[23]

Despite increasing opposition from his advisory and legal boards, which believed that Foxfire was straying from its educational mission, Wigginton argued that the Mountain City Project was inherently educational. For example, the Press would be an extension of *Foxfire* magazine activities at Rabun County High School; the mail-order center would provide training for students in the business department; and the amphitheater would be available for use by the drama department. Wigginton also envisaged an alternative school on the site for adolescents who could not function well in a traditional school; these students would receive academic instruction within the context of the project's variegated activities.

The first building to appear on the property was a solar house, designed by Paul Muldawer, a nationally prominent architect, and intended to be a model for alternative housing in Rabun County, where trailer homes are abundant. When they engaged Claude Rickman, a local contractor (and former Foxfire student), to build the house, Wigginton and Haban believed that the model would be "the basis of a Community Development Corporation program to make available low-cost, energy efficient housing to low-income families in

Rabun County."[24] A CDC housing development corporation could have attracted federal housing grants for reducing the mortgages on these homes from $40,000 to $30,000—providing $10,000 per unit to families who remained on the property at least five years.[25]

In the summer of 1983, Wigginton announced the purchase of the Rothell House, an antebellum "dogtrot" log house, which he had found in Toccoa, Georgia. A foreman and four Rabun County High School students in Foxfire's summer jobs program began to disassemble the structure and to mark every log for reassembly thirty-five miles away in Mountain City. Today the Rothell House stands on a knoll on the Foxfire property, across a small creek from the solar house, in the shadow of the old Mountain City Hotel water tower. The chinking, roofing, and windowing of the two-story building remain to be completed. Foxfire's legal board has put a halt to further work on the reconstruction.[26]

The Foxfire Press set up its offices in the solar house in 1983. To date, it is the only enterprise on the Foxfire property. Wigginton hired Tanya Worley, a young marketing analyst from northeast Georgia, to organize the Press mail-order business. Her strategy was twofold: first, to increase the number of *Foxfire* magazine subscribers; second, to market Foxfire products by mail to these individuals.

Worley's task was formidable. Magazine sales, which had never been high, had dwindled from a mid-1970s peak of approximately 4,500 to 2,840 by the fall of 1983. Using money from the Public Welfare grant (originally earmarked for the CDC), Worley conducted a survey of *Foxfire* subscribers, from which she compiled a profile of selected reader preferences. After she had matched the *Foxfire* customer profile to those of seven other periodicals, she purchased a random sampling of five thousand to ten thousand names from the subscriber list of each company and then mailed a Foxfire advertising package to each targeted subscriber—a total of fifty thousand names. Worley anticipated enough of a response to be able to identify the most propitious lists for marketing Foxfire products. The next step would have been to purchase entire lists and to continue testing with other companies.

Worley's strategies did not work to the satisfaction of Wigginton or his legal board. With $20,000 expended in the list testing project, she received only 375 orders for Foxfire products from the fifty thousand names solicited—less than a 1 percent response rate. Chagrined by these results, Wigginton halted any further list testing, in effect, divesting Worley of her job as marketing director. The Fund simply did not have the money to invest in the kind of list testing necessary to create a viable marketing program.[27]

Worley remained with Foxfire until November 1984. She was instrumental in organizing one further initiative, the Southern Regional Catalog Marketing Conference. On 7 July 1984, representatives of Foxfire, the Highlander Center (New Market, Tennessee), the Southern Highlands Handicraft Guild (Oteen, North Carolina), Georgia Mountain Crafts (Gainesville, Georgia), and Appalshop (Whitesburg, Kentucky)—all 501(c)(3) public service agencies—met in Cullowhee, North Carolina, to discuss the feasibility of marketing Appalachian products through a regional catalog. The conference was organized and sponsored by Foxfire.

Wigginton informed the conferees that the private foundations were distressed that Appalachian organizations were having difficulty marketing the goods the foundations were helping them produce. He predicted that money would continue to tighten until these organizations resolved their marketing problems. While money would no longer be available for indigenous products, the foundations would likely support a cooperative marketing venture of Appalachian organizations.[28]

The result of this conference was the creation of a catalog called *The Mountain Collection,* a collaborative marketing venture. In his December report, Wigginton proclaimed the project a "solid success." Paid for with Public Welfare funds, the catalog had practically defrayed its publication costs of $4,800 in its first two weeks, generating over $4,000 in gross sales. Wigginton optimistically stated, "If the response continues at the rate it has been so far, we may well undertake an expanded version of the same idea next Fall."[29]

Significantly, the legal board's decision to discontinue the Mountain City Project did not vitiate a project that Joe Haban had initiated in the summer of 1984. Haban had hired a consultant to work with him on grant applications which the Rabun County Commissioners submitted to the state for badly needed housing rehabilitation funds in the county. In November, the Commissioners announced receipt of an Emergency Jobs Bill Grant ($251,000) for renovating fifteen houses in the Hell Cat Creek community of Mountain City and a Community Development Block Grant ($225,000) for thirteen houses along Screamer Street, a predominately black community in Clayton. These grants would also provide jobs for thirty-three unemployed laborers in the county.[30] The chairperson of the Board of County Commissioners acknowledged that his group would not have applied for the grants without Foxfire's intercession: "They brought the subject up, and we supported it one hundred percent." ·

In his lobbying efforts with county officials, Haban posited that the housing rehabilitation program could, with the proper leadership and support of local government, grow into a bona fide county development office. Such an office would become the conduit for state and federal grants for a diversity of projects, such as county beautification, seed money for locally owned and environmentally tasteful businesses, or seminars and legal services for new businesses. To date, the county commissioners have not taken any measures to act on Haban's recommendations.[31]

Frustrated that Foxfire would not complete the community development project for which he had been hired as a fund-raiser and administrator, Haban resigned from the staff in May 1984. Before leaving, however, he set in motion a final community project, which came to fruition in the summer of 1984. Haban administered the paperwork and handled the preliminary negotiations that garnered federal funds available under the Job Training Partnership Act to give sixteen needy high school students summer employment. The project's coordinator, for whom Wigginton provided office space at the Foxfire Center, remarked that "the program would not have existed had Foxfire not taken the initiative."

Knowledgeable community people close to Foxfire have observed that most Rabun County residents are uninformed about the organization's community service role. "Most people don't have any idea what Foxfire [means] economically to this county," stated a Foxfire community advisory board member. "Before I was on the board, I was a supporter of Foxfire, but I had no real understanding of what they did. I told Wig, 'Wig, a majority of the county doesn't know what you're doing.'"

Several have suggested that Foxfire, despite its impressive record of stewardship, is perceived by community residents as remote and aloof. "I have the impression that people think they're a bit distant," stated a community businesswoman whose son had participated in Foxfire. "I feel like there's not an appreciation in the community for the value of Foxfire. There's been a lack of communication here."

Like most of us, Rabun County residents do not concern themselves with school affairs until they have a compelling reason to do so. The sparse public attendance at monthly school board meetings suggests as much. If Foxfire taught sex education or radical labor theory, it would evoke far more community awareness than it does as an uncontroversial cultural journalism project to which the community has grown accustomed. In other words, what some informants have interpreted as "distance" between Foxfire and its community may simply be a function of Foxfire's status as educational business as usual.

The Issue of Community Exploitation

In his controversial letter to Foxfire, Herbert Kohl accuses Wigginton and his legal board of exploiting the mountain community by not sharing their organization's wealth with the poor people whose knowledge created it. He intimates that the profits of Foxfire's investments accrue to the benefit of Foxfire and exploitative corporations rather than the community. Once again Kohl broaches interesting and substantive issues that demand a thorough and impartial examination.

Kohl states his position on the issue of the disposition of Foxfire's ample royalties in the following terms:

> Who gets the financial benefits from the books? It is usual to pay people to use their material, to publish their words and their writing. Given that the Foxfire Books are not scholarly works that appeal to academic audiences but well-packaged trade products, it seems that the people represented in the books should get the benefit. It is sensible for Foxfire to keep enough of the money to keep the project going, but when all the money goes into the land, staff salaries, and other development projects, it seems to be a case of exploitation. Kenny Runion does not seem any richer for being known by several million people. I believe that the Foxfire Board has a moral responsibility to recommend that Foxfire give a fair and retroactive share of the royalties to people who appeared in the books and to make sure that they get a share of future work.[32]

As noted previously, Kohl has the rhetorical habit of phrasing complex issues as definitions. In this case, if the Foxfire "contacts" are not being paid, they are (by definition) being exploited. This tautology leaves no room for the non-pecuniary benefits that may have accrued to the community's poor and elderly, and it belittles the fact that Wigginton has used virtually all of the money for community service projects. The following discussion elucidates this controversial issue, primarily by examining Foxfire's relationship with the people it has allegedly exploited.

During the Rabun Gap era, Foxfire was actively involved in improving the quality of life for its elderly contacts. For example, *Foxfire* magazine provided free advertising for elderly contacts like Kenny Runion, John Conley, Harley Thomas, and Claude Darnell. In their spring issue for 1972, the editors announced that "individuals (not shops and industries) in our area who have something they would like to sell that they think would be of interest to our readers may list it here." Foxfire also advertised the products of Appalachian craft artists affiliated with the Tallulah Falls Craft Co-op (a federal VISTA project) and Georgia Mountains Arts Products, Inc. (e.g., the spring and summer issues of *Foxfire,* 1974). Moreover, as a free service to its elderly contacts, Foxfire took the orders generated by the magazine articles and advertisements, paid the artists, and shipped their products—at Foxfire's expense.

On the porch of her home in a secluded hollow near Betty's Creek Valley, an elderly Marinda Brown described the relationship she and her husband Harry had with Foxfire:

> We lived close to the [Rabun Gap] School and were willing to cooperate with what they had started out to do. One of our granddaughters was with Foxfire when it started. We knew we were helping ourselves as well as helping the children in keeping up our heritage. My husband and I were doing craft work, and they helped us get advertised so we could sell our products, and that was an immense help. I was doing looming work, and Harry was making and caning chairs. Then he did the upholstery work, and I did the weaving for that. Foxfire has put us in touch with a lot of people and we've enjoyed the friendship of the people who've bought the crafts. And we've enjoyed the students coming by.

Hobbyist broom maker Monroe Ledford, a favorite Foxfire contact from Macon County, North Carolina, praised Wigginton and his students for their efforts in helping his business:

> They treated me nice, the Foxfire people did. I was kind'a doing it for their benefit, too. Foxfire was advertising my brooms in their magazine. They'd come and pick up the brooms and bring me the check. I had so many brooms to make I had trouble keeping up with the orders. I was in the construction business then. [The broom making] kept me busy rainy days when I couldn't work and at night. It turned out to be an awful nice hobby for me. After I retired, it was something to do, you know. I appreciate the Foxfire more than I can express.

In a previously cited incident, Foxfire helped Appalachian raconteur Harvey Miller by publishing a compilation of 'his newspaper columns and giving him the copyright and 1,500 free copies. Miller's daughter Ethel expressed her gratitude in a letter that appeared in the introduction to the "News from Pigeon Roost" issue:

> I want to personally thank Mr. Eliot Wigginton, founder and editor of Foxfire, for the kindness that he has shown Dad, for the interest he has shown in his writing and for the hard work he has done to make the publishing of some of Dad's articles and stories possible. It has been a

pleasure to work with him and the students, and having them in our home. Dad has had many disappointments in trying to get a book published but through the help of the many people he has written about and Eliot, this book is a dream come true for Dad, myself, and all the family.[33]

As observed in the previous chapter, Foxfire has played a unique and significant role in dispelling adolescent stereotypes of the elderly and in giving youth a method of eliciting the experience of old age in the service of their growth. There is persuasive evidence that the elders who made such a strong and favorable impression on the Foxfire youngsters have also benefited from these relationships.

In many cases, the students who conduct the interviews and work on assembling the articles are relatives of the elderly contacts. In 1978, a Foxfire staff member at Rabun County High School observed several instances of this phenomenon occurring in a single issue of the magazine:

One of the aspects of our program that I have always felt to be of paramount importance is the relationship between our students and our contacts. The interaction of high school students with those who are sometimes sixty years their senior is indeed something to witness. It is even more gratifying to see students working with those older people who are also their grandparents as happens to be the case in providing most of the material in this issue, for example: Tony Whitmire working with his grandfather, Numerous Otis Marcus, in showing how to make an ax handle; Libby Burney interviewing her grandmother, Addie Bleckley, about her life; John Crane recording the recollections of his grandmother, Betty Crane; and Lorie Ramey finding out from her grandfather, Percy McKay, how to drive moles out of the yard or garden.[34]

No contact ever gave more to Foxfire or generated more book sales than Arie Carpenter, the octogenarian whose life history is the focus of the critically acclaimed *Aunt Arie: A Foxfire Portrait.* If anyone stood to be exploited by Foxfire, it was Aunt Arie, widowed and poor and semiliterate, a charming relic from the cultural past. Yet every account, from former students to community elders to Wigginton himself, confirms that Foxfire treated Arie with filial love and respect.

"Every Christmas a bunch of kids would go up to her house and have a Christmas party for her—string popcorn on the tree and all that stuff," recalled Bit Kimball. "Wig and some of the guys would get the tree for her. It was a kind of fellowship thing. There were not presents or anything like that—just celebrating with her."

Fay Long, a Foxfire contact from the Mulberry community, where many of Aunt Arie's friends lived, recounted that "Arie used to live for Wig. They [Wigginton and his students] would go over and work her garden. In the fall of the year, they would dig her potatoes and did it without payment. That was love to her."

Stella Burrell, a Mulberry resident, added: "People who didn't have family took [the children] under their wings and made them family. Arie became a grandmother figure to Wig and to the Foxfire kids. She fell in love with them, and they with her. I'm sure it made her last days happy."

Wigginton and his staff regularly attended Arie's hospital bedside after her health began to deteriorate. In his introduction to *Aunt Arie*, Wigginton recalled the time he had taken her to the doctor in Clayton to check about a problem with her feet:

> She had . . . told me on numerous occasions, somewhat apprehensively, about a lump on her chest that seemed to be growing, but for which she refused treatment. Since I had her in the office of a competent doctor anyway, I forced her to allow him to examine her chest. He came out of the examining room shortly afterwards and told me that the tumor had to be removed as soon as possible. As I drove her home, we talked about it, and though I was expecting a major argument, it was almost as though her letting someone look her over had broken the ice, and she was not as resistant as I had feared she might be. Her major worry all this time had been that, like Ulysses [Arie's deceased husband], if she ever checked into a hospital, she'd never come back out; but Dr. King had helped her understand the need for the operation, and I assured her that Ruth and Nelson [Arie's relatives] and I would be with her every day, and that with the operation she might have years more at home, whereas without it she might not. Finally, in her driveway, she said, "All right, Sir. Trade made."[35]

Although Wigginton accepted Arie's donation of a handmade corded bed as a museum piece for the Foxfire Center,[36] he would not allow her to bequeath her eighty-acre farm to Foxfire because he feared that critics might accuse him of cultivating Aunt Arie with the intent of acquiring her property.

Rabun Gap Foxfire staff and students pitched in to help other elderly contacts with garden and yard work. In some cases, they even bought their groceries and paid outstanding bills. Rhonda Black Waters recalled that "when we went on an interview, we'd ask them if there was anything we could do. Maybe they'd say, 'I need to work in my garden next week.' And we'd see who was free the next week and load up a car to go and help. We used to have too many volunteers and couldn't take everybody."

Stella Burrell, whose Rabun County ancestry dates back to the early nineteenth century, observed that Foxfire students served the local community in a fashion similar to the old-time church family. Mrs.

Burrell, now a grandmother, recalled that during her childhood, the young people in the local churches "visited the elderly and cleaned house, cooked and washed dishes, and did whatever they could." Changing times and values have diverted church youth from this helping role: "They have their ball games and band practices to attend."

Of interest is the finding that only one elderly Foxfire contact (of nearly fifty interviewed) stated that she should have been paid by Foxfire—all were asked how they felt about *not* being paid for their information (see Appendix B for discussion of sampling procedures and interview schedules). "If they charge for the books, they should pay for my information," this spry ninety-three-year-old dissenter explained on the porch of her log house. "If it's worth going after and getting, it's worth paying for. When I'm working for the company and they're charging like they are for those books, then they should pay me something." The others, however, gave no indication that they felt abused by Foxfire. Even the dissenter stated: "I enjoyed their company. They're the nicest folks around."

That these people do not perceive themselves as exploited is, by itself, insufficient evidence to warrant a claim that they are not, in reality, being exploited. It is an oft-repeated irony that the victims of exploitation become defenders of the status quo that oppresses them. Yet in Foxfire's case, the perspectives of the Appalachian elderly count for something, perhaps a great deal, and should not be casually dismissed.

The evidence of interview testimony suggests that the Foxfire experience has benefited the elderly contacts in three general (and related) ways. First, it has provided a pleasant interlude in their lives as a vehicle for the joy that comes in sharing an arcane or deeply personal knowledge that is prized by its recipients. Furthermore, it has orchestrated moments of companionship and reassurance for the lonely and neglected among their number.

Nearly a year before his death in August 1985, Foxfire contact Buck Carver discussed his relationship with Eliot Wigginton and Foxfire, avowing that Foxfire was "the best thing that's ever happened to Rabun County." Seated on his bed in a nursing facility in Clayton, Carver spoke of the great pleasure he had derived from working with the Foxfire students: "I just love to talk to people about the old ways. When I had a car, I used to drive to the school and talk to the kids, and I really loved that. It's a pleasure for me to get with those little ol' kids and talk to them. And they enjoy it, too."

When asked how he felt about not being paid for his time, information, and labor, he responded that "it's not been a burden to me. It's been a pleasure. Several things I've done for him [Wigginton], such as putting that still and furnace up there on 'the land' [Foxfire Center], he wanted to pay me for, but I didn't want it. I didn't do it for the money." Moreover, Carver stated that Foxfire had no business paying any of the contacts: "They don't deserve no pay. They're helping to preserve a way of life that's vanishing fast. I feel I'm getting double pay by preserving our old-time methods. I think that's the way the others feel. He [Wigginton] has published nothing that hurt us—especially the moonshining. It don't throw no black mark on us at all. I think it made more people understand why we done it. It was necessary."

Jake Waldroop, a ninety-four-year-old mountain man who lived on a bottomland farm in North Carolina's Nantahala Forest, recounted that he had given Foxfire information on numerous subjects, from bear hunting to timbering to fishing. This gentle, soft-spoken man, in frail health and barely able to walk, described with an unmistakable tone of affection the visits to his farm paid by the Foxfire students: "I enjoyed it when I was able to take them out and show them the biggest poplar trees in the world. I enjoyed taking them to the pasture and showing them my cattle. I've enjoyed every minute working with them. I love to talk to them."

Elmer Hopper, a 1970 Rabun Gap School graduate, now a land developer, recalled the enthusiasm with which the contacts greeted the Foxfire students and their eagerness to pass along their unusual skills: "I'd never realized that old people would be as open to the high school people as they were. Never once can I remember going up to one of those old people and having them give us a negative reception. It just tickled them to death to tell us how to hew a log, butcher a hog, or make a cornshuck doll. We were asking them questions about things that had been stored up but had never been asked about before. They nearly all had something that had been hidden for years."

Second, Foxfire has given the elderly contacts a measure of recognition and notoriety that has enhanced their individual sense of self-worth and cultural pride. For example, "Aunt Addie" Norton, a warm and vibrant ninety-five-year-old Mulberry resident, expressed her pleasure at being a Foxfire celebrity:

> I've been fooling with that outfit a long time—about fourteen years. There's several of us people in North Carolina that's stuck with it all the time. I like it. I've got some mighty good friends through Foxfire. And it's caused my picture to go all around the world. It means a lot to a lot of people. It's caused many a person to be recognized that wouldn't have been recognized.

Say an old lady like me, without much education. It makes you feel good to know that people recognize you and think enough of you to put your picture in the magazine and several of the books. Take Aunt Arie over here—she got publicity she'd never got if it wasn't for Foxfire.

Addie Norton also spoke with pride about Foxfire's portrayal of the moral character of the native Appalachian: "I live in the mountains and I'm proud of it. [Foxfire] says there are certainly some good hillbillies (if there *are* hillbillies). Yes sir, there are some good ones. You won't find any better people in the United States. I'm glad I'm a hillbilly if it takes goodness. I've got neighbors that come in and do things for me, son, and they don't ask nothing for it. And that counts for something. Hillbillies love one another. I was raised as poor as Job's turkey, but I'm still a hillbilly and love it."

At her home on Scaly Mountain, N.C., "Aunt Bessie" Miller, aged ninety-five, talked about the recognition she had received from being featured in *Foxfire* magazine: "So many folks that knowed me is getting to see my picture. People that gets the book write other people and tell them how to get it. Now that I'm in it, people is a'saying, 'Now I want a book when you get it.' Somebody called me the other day and told me somebody is a'wanting it. There's a lot of people that's got this. It's been in stores around and people's bought it, they tell me."

Lassie Bradshaw, the manager of the Tallulah Falls Craft Co-op and a friend of Foxfire since the Rabun Gap era, spoke of the boost in self-esteem that Foxfire had given the elderly practitioners of the traditional mountain culture: "I've heard people bad-mouth Foxfire, but it's people who just don't know it. I feel like some of these people they've talked to are kind'a ashamed of how they used to live, and it's given them a new outlook, saying, for example, 'Golly, I know how to make pickled beans and not everybody knows how to do that.' I think it's given them an incentive to be proud of their culture. And to see their pictures in *Foxfire* and to know that thousands of people are reading that—gosh!"

Third (as noted in Chapter 5), the Foxfire experience has given the mountain elderly the *opportunity* to serve their community in constructive roles (e.g., community teachers and role models) that reduce the sense of marginality many old people feel.

One of America's most respected folk potters, Lanier Meaders (featured in *Foxfire 8*) has been a close friend of Foxfire since its inception. In the living room of his home outside Cleveland, Georgia, seated near a potbellied stove, Meaders spoke of the benefits he had received from his association with Foxfire. He recalled the time when

Wigginton and a student had hauled his pottery in a trailer to a craft festival at the Smithsonian Institution in Washington, D.C. More important, he discounted any suggestion that Foxfire owed him anything: "I feel that I *have* been paid. Everybody ought to contribute something to society. If I've helped other people to get a start in making a living, so much the better for me. I feel good about that." Other contacts made similar observations. For example:

> I don't care if they don't pay me. I don't charge nothing for talking. If I can be any help to anybody, son, that's what I want to do. (Addie Norton)

> I think about it as helping children who go to school. I wouldn't expect anything out of it myself. (Daisy Justice, Betty's Creek community)

> I didn't look for no pay. We're just glad to help them out. I like to do things for people. You know, you have to be a neighbor to have a neighbor. (Lessie Conner, Dillard)

Others have even suggested that Foxfire's cultural preservation is a public service, worthy of support without financial remuneration to its contributors. For example, Bob Vickers, the county's probate judge for thirty-five years, said tersely that he believed the contacts should not have been paid because "it's a duty of the citizens to promote the county."

Lassie Bradshaw provided an eloquent statement to the same effect: "I feel like if they came down here and said they would pay me if I gave them information, I wouldn't be as interested because it's something I *want* to do. It's not something you can buy. Foxfire has picked up on our culture that would have died and kept it alive. I would be insulted if they came down here and said, 'We'll pay you,' and I think that's the way most of the people feel."

Some of the benefits claimed by Foxfire's contacts defy generalization. For example, "Aunt Nora" Garland, a faith healer whose ministrations for bleeding and burns are described in *The Foxfire Book* (352–55), related that readers have called from as far away as Virginia soliciting her powers "to stop the blood." "That's a benefit," she stated. "It's a service for me and for the people who need it. It makes me feel good. A lot of people wouldn't know about this if it weren't for Foxfire."

Ellison Wall, a Rabun County native who expatriated for thirty-five years and then returned in 1977, talked about the building of the road to the top of Black Rock Mountain during the Depression. According to Wall, when he moved back to Rabun County, he noticed that a state marker had been erected at the base of the road, naming it the "Talmadge Trail" (after U.S. Senator Herman Talmadge). Given that the road had been planned, financed, and built by Joseph F. Gray, a local entrepreneur, philanthropist, and civic leader, Wall, who had worked for "Colonel" Gray, took umbrage that his friend's contributions had been ignored by state officials: "I stopped and looked at that marker, and I expected to find Joseph F. Gray's name at the top. When I didn't, that teed me off. I looked for a marker at the top of Black Rock, and I didn't find that either."

Wall's son Kim was a student in Wigginton's magazine class at the time, and together they discussed with Wigginton the idea of collaborating on an article that would give Joseph Gray the credit he deserved. "It was one way to get it out in the open," Wall stated. The article appeared in the Spring 1980 issue of *Foxfire* (32–40). Entitled "J. F. Gray: A Forgotten Man," it included a picture of Ellison Wall standing beside the Talmadge Trail marker.[37]

One of the contributors to *Foxfire 7*, a volume devoted exclusively to mountain religions, was Rev. J. C. Quilliams, minister for the Tiger, Georgia, Church of God. Rev. Quilliams spoke proudly of being featured in the book: "I only regretted that my dad was dead when that book came out. He had been so thrilled and tickled that his son was going to be in [it]. My mother was eighty-three, and when it came out and we finally got it, I took it up to where she lives in Cartoogechaye [Macon County, N.C.], and she was thrilled to death. She told me how my dad would have loved to have seen it."

This diverse testimony to the variety of ways in which Foxfire has benefited its contacts weakens the cogency of Herbert Kohl's critique of Foxfire. Yet there is also evidence suggesting that since Foxfire's move to Rabun County High School, its students have not maintained the personal closeness with community elders that characterized the project's remarkable tenure at Rabun Gap School. A reasonable assumption is that the same societal and school factors that have distanced students from the locus of decision-making power within the Foxfire organization have also exacted a toll in the close personal relationships that formerly inspired students to share their leisure time with the elderly. There are exceptions to this trend, but, for the most part, Foxfire students today do not assume the helping role that was a hallmark of the project's early community involvement.

A Foxfire staff member who has observed the project at both schools made the following observation: "I think a continuing closeness with the people after we've interviewed them is something that's been lost. You can look at the books. How many contacts receive the kind of closeness from Foxfire as Aunt Arie, Maude [Shope], and Aunt Addie? Part of it is getting the students to go with you. It's that after-school thing. The kids just don't want to do it. They're just doing an assignment."

Several of the Foxfire contacts agreed that things have changed since the organization left Rabun Gap School. "I saw more of 'em before they left the valley," said a Wolffork resident. "I hardly ever see any of 'em now." Another stated: "He [Wigginton] broke off from Rabun Gap like a stick a'breaking. It hurt a lot of us. Out of the clear blue, we were gone. I haven't seen Wig since they left up there, and that would be seven or eight years."

In 1984, the Foxfire staff sponsored several activities to honor their elderly contacts. Over Mother's Day weekend, they feted approximately three hundred guests with barbecued chicken and bluegrass music at their annual "Contacts Picnic" at the Foxfire Center. In August, Foxfire staff provided free tickets and transportation for the contacts to a performance of the *Foxfire* play in Highlands, North Carolina. In November, they honored the contributors to *The Foxfire Book of Appalachian Cookery* at a dinner party in Atlanta (featuring smoked venison and bear ribs) and escorted them to a performance of the *Foxfire* play at the Alliance Theater. Back in Rabun County, on the following Sunday, they entertained these same individuals at a community tea to which all the Foxfire contacts were invited. These activities, initiated and coordinated by adults, with only token assistance from students, indicate that Wigginton and his staff acknowledge their huge indebtedness to the contacts and make an effort to stay in touch with these people. Yet this does not alter the fact that today's Foxfire students have a less active community-service role than their predecessors at Rabun Gap School.

In the living room of her trailer home in the hills above Rabun Gap, a former Foxfire student from the early 1970s discussed how the project had changed over the years: "I don't see them helping anybody. I don't see them out in the gardens. I think when you lose your personal touch, you're going to sink your ship. It made you feel good, put you on a damn high, knowing you had helped somebody who needed it and really appreciated it. I think that personal touch—getting out and extending that helping hand—was the core. Friendships with the contacts and showing them you cared. There's a difference between acknowledging the contacts in print and showing up with a hoe in your hand."

In the company of Foxfire students on several interviews in 1984, I observed an insouciance on their part toward the elderly, evidenced by their statements that the interviews had been a waste of time if they did not get the information they were seeking. For example, on a July morning I accompanied several students and a free-lance journalist on a trip to Habersham County, Georgia, in search of information about old-time broom machines. The two elderly gentlemen whom the students interviewed, however, could only provide information about modern broom machines, much to the disappointment of the two boys who had arranged the session. The students left the factory before the end of the morning, and that was their last communication with the two elders, who seemed, at least, to have had a pleasant time demonstrating their skills at "new broom making."

Significantly, the failure of the interview (in several respects) did not deter the journalist from posing the students with the old men for photographs and making a hoopla over the fact that under Foxfire's aegis, young people and old people were at last bridging the generation gap. "I was looking for some great quotes, and I got them," she confided to me after her interview with the students. While it sells magazines, this slapdash style of reportage, typical of much of the literature on the subject, reinforces popular misconceptions of Foxfire.

The finding that the interest and investment of students in improving the quality of life for community elders have diminished in the past decade should not be interpreted to mean that Foxfire has become an exploitative organization. Neither Wigginton nor his staff has control over the cultural factors that have contributed to the increasing narcissism of youth. They have exacerbated the problem, however, by not building into the program periods of reflection and discussion about the experiences that young people have with the elderly.

The weight of the evidence suggests that Foxfire has not exploited the Appalachian elderly. Given that the *intent* of the program since the outset has been community improvement, given that the Foxfire contacts (as a group) have benefited over the course of Foxfire's history, and given that Wigginton has used Doubleday book royalties exclusively to support educational programs (including college scholarships and summer jobs), cultural preservation, and community development initiatives, it is difficult to conclude otherwise, even though Foxfire, and not the community, has made all the decisions concerning the allocations of these funds.

Moreover, utilitarian arguments strongly favor Wigginton's position. First, dispensing the funds on an equitable basis without creating rivalries and hard feelings among the contacts, who are a closely knit group, would be extremely difficult. Second, and Kohl stipulates this point, "giving a little to each individual will not have the same impact as keeping the money and helping the community." Perhaps this should have been a community decision from the outset, as Kohl suggests, but Foxfire's action in the name of the community hardly qualifies as exploitation.

Foxfire's Investment Policy

A related and important issue also broached by Kohl is Foxfire's investment policy. Kohl directed the following questions to Wigginton, ones that previous investigators have failed even to raise in their superficial analyses: "Where is the Foxfire money being invested? In corporations exploiting land and people and resources in Appalachia or in other parts of the world? How much of the money is invested in ways that are likely to serve the poor people in the community since without them there could be no Foxfire."

In 1984, Foxfire had its $1.8 million endowment invested in two portfolios, one in New York, with the firm of Anthony, Tucker and Day, and one in Atlanta, with the Trust Company Bank of Georgia. Significantly, all of its investments were in institutions *outside* Rabun County—on the face of it, a startling fact that warrants an explanation.

Not surprisingly, Wigginton and his legal board have cogent reasons for sidestepping Rabun County banks. First, they argue that local banks lack the investment expertise of a behemoth urban firm such as the Trust Company Bank, which can virtually guarantee a steady and substantial increase in the endowment from year to year. Second, they state that local banks invest primarily in the local economy without diversifying their investments; a sharp downturn in the Rabun County economy, they argue, would deplete the endowment. Third, and this point carries great weight with Wigginton, local banks loan their money to land developers who, in Wigginton's view, rape the mountain environment, inflate the price of land beyond the means of Rabun County natives, and displace the indigenous population by promoting an influx of land-hungry retirees and second-home owners. "These are things we're philosophically not at ease with," he has remarked. "The fact of the matter is that a large percentage of the money [in local banks] goes to Floridians to build condominiums."

Furthermore, Wigginton argues that even if Foxfire were to invest its money in Rabun County financial institutions, it would have no say in their lending policies. Earl Dillard, the scion of an elite mountain family that owns valuable resort properties (and for whom the town of Dillard is named), told a reporter for the *Wall Street Journal* in 1975 that Wigginton had "not the chance of a snowball in hell" of being appointed to the bank of which he was a board member.[38] Shortly before his death in 1985, Dillard related to me that he had not intended for people to think that he held a grudge against Wigginton, arguing that he had merely described a reality of local politics: "They've misconstrued that. It insinuates that I was against Foxfire. I'm not anti-Foxfire. Hell, it's one of the greatest things that's ever happened to Rabun County. I just knew Wig couldn't get on the board of directors. You can't get in that society unless you're born in it."

There is little evidence to suggest that the community at large either knows or cares about Foxfire's investments. When asked what criticisms they had heard about Foxfire or what recommendations they would make to improve the project, only three present or former Foxfire community advisory board members mentioned its investment policy. A Rabun County native, also a Foxfire contact, voiced one of the few trenchant criticisms about Foxfire's outside investments: "Money that comes from Foxfire should be put into Rabun County and not invested in other states and other parts of the country. Charity starts at home, and the money should stay at home. If there's any investments, it should be done in the locality where it comes from. That's the only thing I hold against it. They are taking our money and investing it in New York and other places when they could be getting the same return by putting it in the county and creating jobs for people."

Prominent business leaders in the community were reluctant to criticize Foxfire's investments, acknowledging the many services provided by the organization. One businessman offered the following subdued criticism: "I feel they should be keeping their money locally. The local banks have the trust facilities now to handle Foxfire's investments. [My bank] reinvests its deposits in local businesses, local real estate and local consumer loans. [Foxfire investments] would benefit the local economy. The dollar invested there would turn three or four times. There is no interest rate basis for it to be invested outside the county." Others indicated that what Wigginton did with Foxfire's money was his business, although one added: "Frankly, I'd like the money to be here. We can handle that trust."

That Foxfire puts its money outside Rabun County is not the only incongruity in its investment policy. The investments themselves, many in the stocks of electrical utilities, seem strikingly at odds with the conservationist philosophy that the *Foxfire* magazines and books represent in the public mind. For example, the New York portfolio lists stocks with such companies as Boston Edison, Commonwealth Edison, Middle South Utilities, Pacific Power and Light, Philadelphia

Electric Company, and Virginia Electric Power Company—all of which operate nuclear power facilities.

The rationale underlying these "un–Foxfire-like" investments is, to beg the pun, utilitarian. Foxfire has put its money in a geographically dispersed selection of stocks that promise the best—and safest—return on its investment. It has chosen to use the interest and capital gains to build an endowment that will ensure the continuation of its educational programs and community services beyond the time when *Foxfire* publications are viable sources of income.

It should not be interpreted that Foxfire has entirely ignored the principle of "socially responsible" investments. In 1981, Wigginton directed the Trust Company Bank to seek out companies that had high growth potential and reputations as being "non-polluting."[39] Wigginton asserts, however, that genuinely "socially responsible" investments have been virtually impossible to find. For example, Foxfire invested in Eastman Kodak, a supposedly non-polluting corporation. "[Now] it turns out," states Wigginton, "that Kodak is a major polluter in Kingsport, Tennessee."

NOTES

1. Rabun County Records, Book I-6, 46.

2. Foxfire legal correspondence, 1 August 1977.

3. See Wigginton's introduction to *Foxfire 8* (Garden City, N.Y.: Anchor Press/Doubleday), 10–11. A recreational vehicle park marks the spot where the Blue Ridge Hotel once stood. Before it was torn down, the hotel was used for the closing scenes in the film *Deliverance.* In an interview, Buck Carver, an elderly Rabun County resident and repository of local history and lore, provided additional information on both hotels.

4. Wigginton, "Report to the Boards," 27 September 1977.

5. Ibid.

6. Wigginton, *Shining Moment,* 270–71. In an interview, Barbara Taylor Woodall recalled: "We [MARBARLA] held out. We didn't think it [the "Betty's Creek Issue"] would serve its purpose or have its impact if it were split up. Wig didn't like it, but he listened and went along with it."

7. Wigginton, ed., *Foxfire 5,* 8–9.

8. Wigginton, Foxfire working paper, [1979].

9. Wigginton, "Empowerment through Education," speech delivered to National Workshop for Cultural Journalism, held at Washington University, St. Louis, Mo., 9–12 August 1979, in *Hands On* 3, no. 2 (1980), unpaginated.

10. Ibid.

11. Foxfire proposal to Kresge Foundation, 8 March 1979. Foxfire's request for $381,600 from Kresge was denied.

12. Foxfire proposal to National Endowment for the Humanities, 8 June 1978.

13. Foxfire proposal to Charles Stewart Mott Foundation, 1 February 1979.

14. Wigginton, "Report to the Boards," 28 August 1979.

15. William S. White to Eliot Wigginton, 13 November 1979.

16. Foxfire GMO memorandum, 13 October 1980.

17. Foxfire, fourth periodic report to Charles Stewart Mott Foundation, 30 January 1981.

18. Foxfire, fifth periodic report to Charles Stewart Mott Foundation, 28 May 1981.

19. Foxfire, sixth periodic report to Charles Stewart Mott Foundation, 11 January 1982.

20. Ibid.

21. Wigginton, "Report to the Boards," 2 July, 12 September, 20 December 1982.

22. Foxfire proposal to Public Welfare Foundation (Joe Haban to Charles Ihrig), 12 May 1982; Foxfire seventh periodic report to Charles Stewart Mott Foundation, 12 July 1982; Haban to C. B. Fair III, 22 July 1982; Haban to Rebecca Davis, 22 February 1983.

23. A copy of the plat appears in Wigginton's introduction to *Foxfire 8*, 16–17.

24. Joe Haban to Robert S. Collier, 20 May 1982.

25. Information provided by Foxfire GMO, 8 February 1984.

26. Wigginton, "Report to the Boards," 28 February 1984.

27. Relevant Foxfire Press documents include: "Foxfire Reader Survey," 26 August 1983; "Recommendations for Expanding the Number of *Foxfire* Magazine Subscribers," 1984; "Direct Mail Recommendations," 1984. Tanya Worley elaborated the details of her marketing program in two interviews, 20 January 1984, 2 January 1985.

28. I was an observer at this conference, held at the Mountain Heritage Center, Western Carolina University, Cullowhee, N.C., 7 July 1984.

29. Wigginton, "Report to the Boards," 5 December 1984.

30. *Clayton Tribune*, 3 November 1983. Also "Foxfire Reflections" (community newsletter), March 1984. It should be noted here that blacks constitute only .8 of one percent of the Rabun County population (Bureau of the Census, *1980 General Social and Economic Characteristics* [Georgia], 35).

31. *Clayton Tribune*, 19 January 1984.

32. Herbert Kohl to Foxfire, 24 September 1979.

33. *Foxfire*, Winter 1974, preface.

34. Paul Gillespie, *Foxfire*, Summer 1972, 102.

35. Wigginton and Page, eds., *Aunt Arie*, xxxi.

36. Wigginton, "Report to the Boards," 27 February 1974.

37. Ellison Wall hopes to persuade state officials to erect a memorial to Joseph Gray in the state park on Black Rock Mountain. Seated at the kitchen table of his Mountain City home, he remarked: "I will some way, somehow,

have Col. Gray recognized on Black Rock. I have to go through the State Park Commission in Atlanta, and I may have to go to the Governor. I'm the type of guy who fights with the truth and can back up everything I say. I'll get this done."

38. Neil Maxwell, *Wall Street Journal,* 2 July 1975.

39. Christina Bird, Trust Company Bank of Georgia, to Joe Haban and Paul Gillespie, 8 October 1981.

SEVEN

Organizational Issues and Effects

Several intriguing issues and effects emerge when the focus of analysis shifts to the Foxfire organization itself. The most salient of these deal with Eliot Wigginton's role as a high school teacher. How has Wigginton been able to survive for twenty years in a rigidly conservative ambience? What are the elements and hallmarks of his relationships with students? What *is* the pedagogical style of one of America's best-known teachers? As the focus moves from Wigginton to his staff, other issues arise. How has Wigginton's philosophy been interpreted, and acted upon, by other Foxfire teachers? What are the implications of Foxfire's "town meeting" style of organizational management? The answers to these questions provide an illuminating, if not entirely flattering, portrait of the Foxfire organization and its internal politics.

Focus on Eliot Wigginton

The Conservative Politics of Radical Classroom Reform

As a reform-minded pedagogue, Eliot Wigginton begs comparison with other teacher-reformers of the 1960s who, like himself, tried to create humane classrooms in which cultural distinctiveness was respected (and encouraged) and where alternative approaches to the memorization and recitation of textbook information were given an enthusiastic, if not always circumspect, hearing. In his early writings Wigginton identified himself with a small coterie of reformers that included Jonathan Kozol, Pat Conroy, James Herndon, and Herbert Kohl—public school teachers whose best-selling exposés of schooling in the 1960s epitomized, in the words of one observer, "more of a literary than an educational movement."[1] Indeed, these critics did not inspire a revolution against repressive and mind-deadening schooling and, with the exception of Wigginton, they even suffered the indignity of being fired for their heterodoxies. To understand how Wigginton has survived as a teacher-reformer in an ultraconservative rural community, it is first necessary to analyze the experiences of the so-called radical romantics Kozol, Conroy, Herndon, and Kohl to identify styles of reform that have *not* worked in either urban or rural school systems.

Of the radical reformers of the 1960s, Jonathan Kozol was the most obstreperous and the least cautious—perhaps because the Boston ghetto school that inspired *Death at an Early Age* was, as Robert Coles has written, "a disgraceful hovel—overcrowded, something out of a Dickens novel,"[2] where rattan-wielding teachers, broken windows (in the dead of winter), and the stench of urine from leaky toilets conspired to brutalize the black children whom Kozol took to heart.

A Harvard-educated novice teacher in 1964–65, Kozol taught a fourth-grade class in a dingy and boisterous auditorium, which he shared with several other teachers. Compounding the stultifying effects of the decaying school ambience, the Boston School Committee had mandated, as part of its so-called compensatory education program, the use of a hopelessly outmoded, standardized curriculum that took no account of ethnic and cultural differences.

To remedy this state of affairs, Kozol introduced, with good effect, the work of modern poets and artists, including Robert Frost, Paul Klee, William Butler Yeats, and Langston Hughes. Kozol intimates that his use of Hughes's poem "Ballad of the Landlord," a paean of black ghetto despair, resulted in his firing by the Boston School Committee on the grounds that he had taught materials not listed in the approved course of study. Yet a close inspection of *Death at an Early Age* suggests that the School Committee may have used the Hughes poem merely as a pretext to conceal its real reasons for firing Kozol.

Outside the ghetto school where he worked, Kozol engaged in civil rights activities and political demonstrations that courted the displeasure of city school officials. His arrest at the Boston Federal Building, in the company of workers from the Student Nonviolent Coordinating Committee (SNCC) and the Congress of Racial Equality (CORE) who were protesting alleged civil rights violations in Alabama, was reported to both his principal and the Boston School Committee deputy superintendent. Kozol also helped organize an unofficial meeting for parents and teachers at which he and a black teacher "told the parents, in answer to their inquiries, about the classes in the cellar, those in the auditorium, the outdated curriculum, the dilapidated materials and outdated textbooks and the overall worthlessness of the compensatory program as a viable means of making up for the deficiencies of a segregated school."[3] Moreover, he participated in another meeting of teachers and parents, who resolved to picket the Boston School Committee and complain to Kozol's principal about the horrendous conditions at the school. Compounding these larger "crimes" were Kozol's peccadilloes of wearing an equality pin at the height of Boston's racial unrest in 1965, regularly driving one of his students home (despite criticism from his principal and the School Department supervisor), complaining to the School Department that his school's curriculum "seemed to me to be very poor," and (one might finally add) teaching materials not listed in the approved course of study.

Death at an Early Age exposed the intransigence and callousness of the Boston School Committee and, by implication, white-dominated urban school systems throughout the nation. As a social commentary of the civil rights era and a fine descriptive narrative, it remains an important volume. Yet it also bespeaks the fate of the radical school reformer who transgresses the conservative norms of the power elite who control schools: Kozol was fired, and schooling went on much as before in the Boston ghetto.

As a first-year teacher on Yamacraw Island, near Beaufort, S.C., Pat Conroy encountered a similar and equally unforgiving bureaucratic intransigence in a rural context. Yamacraw was quite literally a backwater—an all-black, impoverished (and embarrassing) island appendage to the lily-white mainland school district. In his best-selling book *The Water Is Wide* (later a film entitled *Conrack*), Conroy described his sometimes painful, sometimes exhilarating year as a teacher-reformer who refused to compromise with racial segregation in any guise.

When he arrived at Yamacraw in the late summer to begin teaching at the elementary school, he was appalled by the "litany of ignorance" he encountered: "Six children who did not know the president. Eighteen children who did not know what country they lived in."[4] Beaufort County school officials, he soon learned, had no intention of improving education on the island; in fact, they fully supported the punitive style of Mrs. Brown, a stern black teacher who shared the school building with Conroy and who saw to it that the black children of Yamacraw did not aspire to be more than the mudsill of white society. Conroy writes: "It was a yes-sir, no-sir world I had entered. Math and spelling papers hung from the bulletin boards. Everything was Mickey-Mouse neat and virgin clean in the classroom. A map of the world, contributed by a Savannah bank, hung on one wall. Near it was a poster which read EDUCATION IS THE KEY TO SUCCESS. A picture of a large key drove the point home. On Mrs. Brown's desk was an item that caught and held my eye. It was a leather strap, smooth and very thick. It lay beneath a reading book."[5]

Throughout the year, Conroy petitioned the district school superintendent to do something about the conditions on Yamacraw, leapfrogging the district staff to lay his grievances directly at the superintendent's doorstep, sometimes in letters, sometimes in person, always "self-righteous, angry, undiplomatic, unapologetic and flaming." In one telling passage he summarized his unrelenting recalcitrance in dealing with his adversary: "Colonel Conroy, the chieftain of my clan, issued a hard-shell rule in my youth that the most unforgivable of sins was for a Conroy to beat around the bush, put garlands of roses around his thoughts or ideas, or—horror of horrors—for a Conroy to drop to his knees, pucker his potato-famined lips, and kiss somebody's rosy red behind."[6]

Despite the fact that the superintendent and his allies wanted Conroy out of the district, his pleas for social justice on Yamacraw had struck responsive chords not only in the black community, but in the conservative white community as well. After all, the latter reasoned, he was only asking for a better school building, better school materials, and free gasoline so he could commute from his newly bought house in a staid aristocratic section of Beaufort out to Yamacraw. In short, he posed no threat to integration and white supremacy—at least not until he decided to board three Yamacraw children in his home so they could attend junior high school on the mainland.

The school board fired Conroy, without community resistance, when it learned that he had taken a week's leave of absence to work as a consultant for the South Carolina Desegregation Center. In his peroration to *The Water Is Wide*, Conroy recounted, with regret, the lessons he had learned as a teacher-reformer who had gone a bridge too far:

> I saw the necessity of living and accepting bullcrap in my midst. It was everywhere. In teachers' manuals, in the platitudes muttered by educators, in school boards, in the community, and most significantly, in myself. I could be so self-righteous, so inflexible when I thought that I was right or that the children had been wronged. I lacked diplomacy and would not compromise. To survive in the future, I would have to learn the complex art of ass-kissing, that honorable American custom that makes the world go 'round. Survival is the most important thing. As a bona fide ass-kisser, I might lose a measure of self-respect, but I could be teaching and helping kids. As it is, I have enough self-respect to fertilize Yankee Stadium, but I am not doing a

thing for anybody. I could probably still be with the Yamacraw kids had I conquered my ego.[7]

Unlike Kozol and Conroy, James Herndon, a first-year teacher at a predominately black junior high school in the San Francisco Bay area, did not "make waves" or participate as a fifth columnist against the power elite. Herndon erred by allowing unconventional and disorderly behavior in his classroom—part of a strategy to build solidarity among a group of functionally illiterate seventh and ninth graders who had low self-esteem and lacked racial identity. In *The Way It Spozed to Be,* Herndon justified his methods as follows:

> There they were, about fifteen or so kids, all in a cluster, standing, shouting at each other, Verna in the middle shouting at all of them—a hundred demands, questions, orders, all at once. You couldn't make it out at all. Probably there were a hundred shouted irrelevancies, threats and insults, too. But the fact is this outcry was orderly in intent and in effect, for in about four or five minutes it was all over, readers were sitting down, they had books, the audience was getting ready to listen. I doubt very much if 9D [the official designation for this particular class] could have been organized to read a play in five minutes by an experienced teacher with a machine gun.[8]

Herndon eschewed the advice of the "experts" like the substitute teacher who counseled him to return his students to the meaningless rote work that created the semblance—and sham—of being orderly, the language arts consultant from "downtown" who bandied Skinnerian platitudes about motivating students to do such work, and the principal who recommended that he take voice lessons to improve his self-projection in front of disruptive students.

Herndon's class was loosely structured and, for the most part, spontaneous. Acknowledging that his students had learned nothing from the workbooks and ditto exercises of this or previous years (some could not even read the names on an absentee list), he made this work voluntary in his classes and allowed the students to read aloud children's plays (with the attendant cacophony of shouts, threats, insults, and bickering) and to compose in "slambooks," journals in which students wrote essays or epithets about each other's personal appearance, habits, tastes, and idiosyncrasies. While slambooks were banned by other teachers, Herndon encouraged them because they were so popular with the students and were the only vehicle that generated enough interest to get them writing.

Herndon offers no information to suggest how effective his unorthodox strategy was in improving the reading and writing skills of his students. Perhaps the point is immaterial. In his first year Herndon was groping for ways to improve his individual students' sense of self-worth and to make schooling a positive experience for them. While he may have erred by pandering to their whims (e.g., allowing "edibles" during the weekly movies in his classroom), he seems to have been successful in laying a foundation for group solidarity and cooperation that might have facilitated a vast improvement in the basic skills of his students had he been allowed another year or two with them. And certainly what he offered them seems to have been no worse than the mindless rote/copy work for which they had been promoted from year to year, albeit as social misfits and functional illiterates.

Herndon's principal fired him because he allegedly could not control his classes. Herndon might have survived in this school had he followed Conroy's advice to zealous teachers and courted favor with school officials or at least negotiated his strategy with the principal. In a telling statement, he wrote: "It was just as if one of us was of some other species, a Martian perhaps; I imagine he had the same problem with me."[9] When the principal and district officials visited Herndon's classroom, they saw disorder and disruption; lacking further information, they concluded that Herndon was inept and should be dismissed.

The last in this group of young teacher-reformers who helped raise national consciousness about the abuses of American schooling is Herbert Kohl, a penitent reformer. Having endured being fired as a student teacher and then being involuntarily transferred after his first year of teaching,[10] Kohl decided to deal gingerly with school administrators when he took charge of a class of sixth graders in a Harlem ghetto school in 1962. In his best-selling book *36 Children,* Kohl reported: "I learned to keep quiet, keep the door of my classroom shut and make believe that the class and I functioned in a vacuum, that the school around us didn't exist."[11]

As a supplement to the conventional sixth-grade texts, Kohl brilliantly structured a curriculum based on the life experiences of his students, shepherding them to write expressive essays, poems, cartoons, and fantasies that reflected the grim realities of slum life. He cleverly taught vocabulary, using etymology and mythology as contexts for word meanings; guided students in compiling novellas and short stories; and orchestrated an in-class newspaper that included expressionistic (and violent) cartoon art and writing. The best of these pieces integrated elements of Greek mythology, sophisticated vocabulary, and ghetto culture.

Responsibly, and with regret, Kohl acknowledged to his students that what they were learning in his class would likely not improve their standardized test scores, the criteria by which they would be judged and labeled throughout the remainder of their schooling. To ensure that they scored well on these tests, he taught them how to take standardized tests, using old tests he had borrowed from friends and colleagues. The results were impressive—one- to three-year gains in reading for his students.

Despite his year of demonstrated success as an innovative teacher, Kohl learned that the incompetence and ennui of Harlem's ghetto schools vitiated the gains he had made with the children. Visits from his former students who had entered junior high confirmed that their new teachers discouraged and stifled the kind of creativity they had displayed under Kohl's tutelage, leaving them embittered and disillusioned with school and their lives. As one former student stated: "Mr. Kohl, one good year isn't enough."[12]

Disillusioned, Kohl lasted only another year before quitting the public schools of New York, leaving the following epitaph in *36 Children:* "My choice was to remain within the system and work with the children, or leave and try to change it from without. I stayed. Though now I am convinced that that system, which masquerades as educational but in Harlem produces no education except in bitterness, rejection and failure, can only be changed from without."[13]

Since the mid-1960s, Kohl has remained at the forefront of the assault against conventional schooling—as a writer, private school teacher, and creator of alternative educational programs. In the early 1970s, Kohl endorsed Eliot Wigginton's pedagogy, calling Foxfire "one of the best things going."[14] And on the eve of the publication of *The Foxfire Book,* he told Wigginton: "Your magazine continues to be extraordinary and to be of great use to many of us—both because of its content and because of its intent."[15]

Yet by the late 1970s, Kohl had become disenchanted with Foxfire, in part, because Wigginton and his staff refused to get involved in labor union activity in Rabun County. Kohl joined Foxfire's national advisory board in the fall of 1977, but he appears to have been stymied by the organization's refusal to accept his anticorporate-capitalism credo, even in a minor key. As the final point in his letter of resignation to Foxfire, Kohl implied that Wigginton had a moral *and* pedagogical duty to address the issue of nonunion labor in the local factories: "I understand that there is a union drive going on in the local Burlington plant and don't recall any talk about unions or labor struggle in Foxfire. I do know it has existed in the community. Are there any other issues that have been avoided? What does it mean educationally to avoid difficult issues? What is the effect it has on the total learning program? On one's students?"[16]

Kohl criticized Wigginton from the perspective of an outsider—both in terms of Rabun County and the public schools. As an insider in both worlds, Wigginton had a different perspective on the limits of what his school and local community would tolerate. In his estimation, pro-union activity in a rural county whose citizenry was suspicious of organized labor was outside those boundaries.[17]

From the outset, Wigginton has maintained a conservative posture in his dealings with school administrators—affecting at least the appearance of conformity to their policies. Unlike Kozol and Conroy, he did not "go roaring into a school, try to change it, and get fired in the process."[18] And unlike Herndon, he negotiated with school officials and accepted their terms *before* implementing an alternative pedagogy.

Once the popularity of *Foxfire* magazine had given Wigginton a strong base of community support within the local community, his position at Rabun Gap School was relatively secure. Wigginton tested the limits of administrative tolerance, however, with his occasional peccadilloes and sidestepping of rules and regulations. When asked why the administration had not fired Wigginton for such nettlesome activities as putting an upside-down American flag on his Bronco jeep, smoking in front of students, or appearing for Sunday dinner at the school dressed in a faded pair of blue jeans when coat and tie were required dress, a school disciplinarian of that era remarked: "We would confront him, and he would agree with us. If I had a boy I [had] caught smoking and he said he had gotten them out of Wig's pickup, I'd tell [Wig] he couldn't keep his cigarettes there. He'd say, 'Okay, I won't do that anymore.' There were enough positive things going on with the Foxfire program. We liked [it] and if we could eliminate the adverse things to students, we wouldn't throw out the baby with the bath. We had a good baby."

Former Foxfire students recalled the daily tensions that existed between Wigginton and the boarding school administrators. One described the mischievous way in which Wigginton conformed to the dress regulation for teachers after being confronted by the boarding school president about his unconventional attire: "Wig could never have made it on the ten best-dressed list. Every day he wore an old, worn woolen sweater, a flannel shirt and jeans or khakis—casual-type dress. I can remember [the school president] opening the door and telling Wig, in front of us, that he had to wear a tie. So the next day he showed up wearing a tie—but he still had on his worn sweater and jeans. He always cooperated. If they told him to wear a tie, he'd wear a tie. Now can you imagine going to a hog killing in a three-piece suit and Florsheim shoes?"

In a cautionary note to the teachers of Foxfire-like projects, Wigginton enumerated the lessons of his experiences as an innovator and advised a conservative and discreet approach to classroom reform. Observing that Rabun Gap School administrators had reminded him "on a number of occasions" of the tenuousness of his position, Wigginton counseled the teachers to "swallow their daily ration of garbage" and not to risk being fired by upbraiding the administration or other teachers, or by flouting the rules and regulations. A facade of conservative behavior, even looking the other way in the face of an injustice, he intimated, was necessary in the service of a radical reform. With respect to his own project and students, and by implication to those of other teachers as well, he wrote: "Hopefully, it will be strong enough to counteract some of the bad effects of the rest of their school experience. It's damn sure it won't have a chance if I get fired."[19]

Wigginton's Relationships with Students

Eliot Wigginton brings to Foxfire a remarkable energy and zeal, as well as an enormous capacity for sustained productivity, which has not diminished over the past twenty years despite the strains and abrasions of administering Foxfire, constantly working with students, and teaching as many as five classes per quarter or semester. He has devoted much of his time away from the classroom, including weekends, summers, and holidays, to the following activities: editing (with his students) eight of the nine *Foxfire* volumes and *Aunt Arie: A Foxfire Portrait;* writing two books about Foxfire and its pedagogy; editing two collections of interviews published by Doubleday for Reading Is Fundamental and the Highlander Center—and donating the royalties to these organizations; serving on the advisory boards of the National Endowment for the Humanities, the National Endowment for the Arts, the National Trust for Historic Preservation, et al.; traveling with students to scores of educational conferences, schools, colleges, and universities (thirty-five in 1983–84) for speeches and workshops; and teaching a graduate-level educational course at a nearby university.

Living alone in his two-story log house on the side of Black Rock Mountain, Wigginton does not have family responsibilities to distract him from his single-minded dedication to Foxfire. Indeed, he has often remarked that his students *are* his family, suggesting that he does not dissociate his personal life from his work with young people. A surfeit of evidence from interviews, letters, and related documents underscores the point.

Over the years students have been frequent visitors to his home, first at the Hambidge Foundation on Betty's Creek, later at the Foxfire Center. "We'd go to his house after school," Linda Page recalled. "I think it was real appealing to students to go to a teacher's house and have a good time." For some of them, particularly boarding students at Rabun Gap School, Wigginton's home was a refuge and halfway house. Interestingly, this became a heatedly debated issue between Wigginton and the administration when a youth named Kenny, who had been expelled from the school, appeared on Wigginton's doorstep. Having learned of Kenny's return to Rabun County, the administration reminded Wigginton of the school's policy concerning expelled boarding students: "You may not be aware of a long standing rule that when a young person has been dismissed from school, he or she is not to be back on campus without permission for a year. This generally does not apply to someone who is not invited to return as a result of [an] end of year evaluation, but does apply to those dismissed during the year. Kenny would be in the latter category" (17 April 1974).

Wigginton's beleaguered response conveys his empathy for and devotion to youth—and his impatience with the rule-minded administration:

> I've known about the rule for some time regarding students being on campus that have been kicked out of our school. Essentially, I agree with it, and I try to abide by it.
>
> Kenny was with me for five days, and the three times he was on campus were all occasions when it was, I felt, necessary that he be with me. In all three cases, he was there only briefly (once to pick up my campus family and several other students that I was taking up Pickens Nose on an all-afternoon trash cleanup; once to catch Tommy Wilson so that he could watch Kenny for me during the days; and once on Wednesday to pick up the students I was taking to Wyoming. I planned to drop Kenny off at his home in Gainesville [Georgia] on our way to the airport. At no time was he left free to wander around. At no time was he unsupervised or unattended.
>
> On Friday night I was at dinner with Mary Nikas, the new head of the Jay Hambidge Art Foundation, who has asked me for some help in finding two employees for the Foundation. I returned home about 10:00 P.M. to find Kenny asleep on my couch. He had nothing with him but the clothes on his back: no toothbrush—nothing. Kenny may have been many things, but he was never one to be sloppy about his dress and appearance, so I was sure he had run away. He kept mentioning wanting to find Ernest, so I felt it was necessary to keep him with me if only to prevent his heading toward Clover

[South Carolina]. On one of the trips through campus, I stopped by the Bennetts and without his knowing it, asked Margie to call his mother to find out if she knew where he was.

Margie got me by phone that night at Pat's [Rogers] house. She confirmed that he *had* run away—he was not on Spring break from school—and that the State Patrol was looking for him. Apparently he had gotten into some sort of a family fight at home and had run. His father was looking for him too, and she was afraid that if he found Kenny, he'd probably hurt him pretty badly as he had done it before and wouldn't hesitate to do it now. His mother didn't want him to know where Kenny was for fear I might get hurt too, and she asked me, through Margie, to hold him here while she found his father and got him off the trail. She also asked that I watch him closely, being afraid that he was planning to run away to Florida with Ernest as he had threatened to do that previously.

So I worked out a system whereby Tommy would be at work every day on the Foxfire land, and when I came down the hill on each morning, I'd leave Kenny with him to help out (to avoid bringing him on campus), and then Tommy would take him to Clayton every night and leave him with Pat until I could get there and pick him up. As evidence of the care I took to keep him *away* from campus, I submit Steve Smith, who knew he was around, pestered me constantly to be allowed to see Kenny, but never even got to say hello.

Kenny never knew that I had checked to see whether or not he had run away. He finally told me the story himself, as I knew he would, and agreed to call his mother (which he did from Pat's house) and return to Gainesville of his own free will with us on Wednesday.

I think the thing that bothers me most about this whole episode is that no one even bothered to ask me first if there was a problem or a way they could help me out before jumping to criticize my action. I admit that I am far from what one would call a model Christian myself, but in a school that prides itself on its Christian love and example, I would have expected better treatment for a kid in real trouble.

Problem though he is, I still treat Kenny as part of my family and as welcome in my home whenever he needs someone to turn to. I'd like to believe there are other people on this campus that feel the same way (and would express concern for the kid first, rather than the rule) because there are times, like this one, when I can really use some help and support instead of suspicion. [23 April 1974]

A poignant statement in a letter written to Herbert Kohl in 1978 discloses the anguish that Wigginton has occasionally endured as a consequence of having integrated so thoroughly his personal and professional lives:

One of my ex-students is living here with me now (has been for two months) waiting until the new semester opens at a nearby trade school I have been able to get him into. He's pretty heavily into drugs, and is a constant drain also, but I think I can deal with it. Another student has written wanting to drop out of college and come back here to work with us full time, so I've got to deal with that next week. And my favorite kid of all time . . . just lost his father and got put into an orphanage in South Carolina by a mother who could care less. I went to see him last week. Shit.[20]

His attempt to create a viable community development project on the old hotel property in Mountain City attests that Wigginton's commitment to his students extends into their adult lives. A former staff member has observed: "Wig has a love for his kids that goes beyond the classroom. He knows that some of them can't live in Atlanta and, hell, they can't live here either because there're no jobs. Wig feels an obligation to help these kids get started in business. He has loaned kids money and signed notes at the bank for things like trucks—there is no better evidence of Wig's sincerity in wanting to help these kids financially. He wanted an agency [a CDC] to help these kids get started. He wasn't interested in building Foxfire into a conglomerate."

At a table in the rear of her restaurant near Dillard, a young woman, a former Foxfire student who requested anonymity, explained that Wigginton had cosigned with her mother a $15,000 loan (his responsibility was $7,500), which enabled her to start the business. "From day one when I thought about doing the shop," she stated, "he was behind it. He even looked at the layout and gave his opinions. And one day he just said, 'Hey, I believe in you and [your husband], and I believe you'll be a success.'"

As revealed in their letters to Wigginton, former students have turned to him for assistance and empathic support that goes far beyond the letters of recommendation routinely expected of high school teachers. For example, in one letter, a former student writes: "I have a good job now and I will pay you your $200 soon. I would like to say thanks for everything and especially your long wait for that money." Others have confided their personal and family problems to a trusted friend. Writing of her parents' bitter divorce, one states: "I know you're right here with me going through all the hell."

Wigginton has corresponded with several former students who have been sent to prison. He has also written letters in their behalf. In one case, Wigginton offered a Foxfire scholarship to a high school dropout who was about to be released from a work camp. Then he wrote a letter to the director of a local trade school in support of the youth's application. In another case, Wigginton appealed to a state clemency commission on behalf of a youth who was serving a felony sentence in a so-called reformatory. "Don't let the name fool you," the youth told Wigginton. "It's a full-fledged penitentiary, forty-foot wall and all."

Many of the letters and cards (of nearly a thousand in Wigginton's personal file) are reminiscences of the good times and escapades of high school. They are also a sharing of present actualities and dreams for the future. The most interesting are those written by youths who have temporarily dropped out of college to seek out new experiences or to reflect upon the future and sort priorities—the psychosocial moratorium, described by Erik Erikson as a phase "during which the young adult through free role experimentation may find a niche in some section of his society, a niche which is firmly defined and yet seems to be uniquely made for him."[21] To a former Rabun Gap boarding student wrestling with his identity crisis on a moratorium in New Orleans, Wigginton offered the following assurances: "I know you're going to turn out okay. In fact, one of the . . . greatest satisfactions in my life is watching you guys turn into normal, sensitive, caring human beings who are going to somehow matter, each in your own way, and each in your own style."

In the case of Varney Watson, a talented local musician, Wigginton extended a helping hand to a close relative of one of his students. After hearing Andrea Burrell sing one of Watson's songs in a Foxfire class at Rabun Gap School, Wigginton had it copyrighted in Watson's name and enlisted the school's music teacher to notate the music (Watson could not read music).[22] He also published the songs in *Foxfire* magazine, hailing Watson as "the finest young native songwriter we've ever met."[23] On a rainy July evening, Watson, who now runs an insurance business in Mountain City, recounted over a cup of coffee the story of how Wigginton helped him with both his musical career and his self-confidence:

> It was about 1972. I was working at the Burlington textile mill for ten hours a day, six days a week, on a project crew for $2.50 an hour. Times were tough. I didn't have any money. My wife and I sold Coca-Cola bottles to live on—and I'm telling you, pinto beans to live off of aren't worth a crap. At that time I had three kids all within four years of each other in age. My wife wasn't working. I was renting my house and didn't own anything.
>
> And then Wig talked to me about my song writing and got me enthused about more than working at the textile mill, introduced me to his contacts, and sent my songs to prominent writers like Pete Seeger, Guy Carawan, and Ralph Rinzler at the Smithsonian. Once at a Foxfire national advisory board meeting at the Dillard Best Western motel, I met Guy Carawan, Sam Stanley, and Myles Horton, and we stayed up till 4:00 in the morning

playing. [With Ralph Rinzler's help] they fixed it so I could go up to the American Folk Festival in Washington, D.C. I made enough money out of that to buy a new guitar.

Wig introduced me to Buddy Renfoe, [who] was working for the Department of Agriculture, and I wrote a song about my grandpa for a movie Renfoe was making, basically telling about the impact of the industrial revolution on the older generation in the mountains. It wasn't an *anti* song; it just told about how they had been overwhelmed by change. The movie was something like "Roots of the Nation."

All this was stuff Wig directed at me. He went out of his way, taking his own time and trouble for me. He got on the train to come listen to me play at the folk festival. When I saw him in the crowd, it made me feel good, you know. It wasn't like this brought me out of poverty or anything like that, but I think it gave me a lot of self-confidence and a better feeling about the stuff I was writing. It made me see more things than just the local arena between the county lines.

No testimony better articulates or exemplifies the profound influence that Wigginton has had in the lives of many of his former students than a letter he received in the fall of 1985 from a teacher who had been a student at Rabun Gap School in 1966 (some paragraph indentions have been added):

Dear Wig,

I have just received the first copy of FOXFIRE that I have seen in years. I ordered it for my class. That does not include the books. I always get those when I see them at the bookstores. Two things really struck me when I scanned the magazine at lunch. One was the fact that the magazine is twenty years old this year. Give me a break!!! I am supposed to be thirteen, not thirty-three. (I had a birthday last month—and so did you—) Which makes you—forty-two? Anyway, the very thought of twenty years zipping by astounds me. The second thing also runs in that same thought. . . . Olin [pseudonym] hardly had male hormones the last [time] I saw him, and with a beard he not only looks very good, but is definitely not the boy I knew in school. Being twenty years older looks better on some people than others.

It has been five years since I last saw you. It was no big deal, but I think sitting on your porch, having a beer, and talking is one of the nicest memories I have of you. The other two main nice thoughts that I have concerning you are incidents which were insignificant, but I remember them. I baked a birthday cake for you when I was in the ninth grade [at Rabun Gap School]. I had permission from Mrs. Hanson, and an act of God, to go to the Burdens' house. I baked it over there. I also remember when you went away for a year to work on your masters. It was important to me then that you took the time to answer a letter that I wrote to you. I guess I am mentioning these things now because I have given them a lot of thought recently. . . .

Over the last years I have thought about you very much. Parts of my life seem to be in a time warp, some areas are easily forgotten, and some are worth remembering. Some of the things I do and like about myself are direct results of having known you at an impressionable age. I have kept a journal since ninth grade. In college I dumped [threw out] some high school and college years that I had . . . in notebooks, but I have [entries] over the last ten years. I know that they will never be important to anyone else, but since I will probably never have kids, I think that I would like my nieces to know some day that I was a real person. I want them to know that I was mixed up as a kid and many times as an adult. I want them to know that I was interesting, witty, sensitive, sexy to a few people along the way, and always very human. I don't want them to ever have to feel the pain, intense shyness in new situations, or neurotic things that I felt when I was a kid. So much of that seems so far away, not only twenty years, but light years.

. . . In the last ten years, I have not become a great teacher, but I have become a caring teacher. I think that I am sensitive to the needs of my students. I try to communicate with parents on a level that does not ever seem ostentatious. That was what I disliked about many teachers in my last years of school. . . .

Whenever I think of characteristics of a good teacher I always think of you. I don't know if you ever do or did feel that you might not be effective, but I remember you more than any adult in my past. You were possibly the first person I ever had a crush on, definitly [sic] one of the first people I put on a pedestal, and always will be one of the people I would like to be remembered by. I find myself wanting to share brunch and hours of conversation with you. You've always been a private person, but I would like to know you as a person and not just as the object of years of hero worship. I think that's what made having a beer on your porch important to me. Our lives run in such different paths that they may never cross again—physically anyway. I do hear of you occasionally in papers, television, and most recently from a quick character sketch on tv. That was uptown, Wig.

It's odd that someone I never see should matter so much to me and to the person I try to be in a classroom. If you leave no other personal legacy (Foxfire excluded), it will be that you were a very concerned person who cared about kids. When the kids grow up they remember that—and love you for it.

Wigginton's Pedagogical Style

As might be expected, Wigginton's philosophy of education has altered as a result of his maturity and twenty years of experience in the classroom. What has not changed are the key elements in that philosophy, e.g., the counter-Freudian view that adolescence is a period of benign growth, as opposed to "storm and stress"; the assumptions shared with John Dewey that the meaningful learning of an intellectual skill or body of information occurs only in the context of its application to a problem that is perceived by the student as his or her own, that the interest in the problem will suffuse the process necessary for its resolution, and that the problem must originate within, or be relevant to, the student's out-of-school experience; and the proposition shared with humanist psychologists that a student's sense of self-worth is an essential factor in successful school learning, as well as a necessary antecedent for intimacy and empathy.[24]

What has changed are his expectations about the efficiency of the *Foxfire* magazine as a vehicle for delivering basic academic skills and for salvaging youths cast off by and alienated from school:

> One reason the magazine was started is that it *can* serve the needs of [those students] well. What we wouldn't do now we would have done years ago. We would try not to have a Foxfire class dominated by those kids. Years ago I would have taken them all in a magazine situation. If they come into class from the beginning and know the purpose is to publish an article, the [magazine] can be structured so even the least capable academically can come up with something publishable by the end of the quarter and get a good experience and it'll be good for them.
>
> But the realization I've come to is that it's a mistake to allow a class to be largely composed of those students because of the chemistry between them [and the other students] and what they do with each other when they're together. The process of doing anything substantial is so inefficient and so exhausting [with the two groups together], you don't get the kind of mileage out of the project that you ought to. They undo everything.
>
> [As an alternative] you can put together a "dirty dozen" class. If I had the time and thought there'd be enough mileage, I could make a situation work that was just those kids and nobody else. But I think the end result would be more affective than cognitive. The kids would wind up at the end of the quarter and feel good and it might have been an important experience. But if you *really* tested them in terms of having made substantive progress in basic skills they're supposed to acquire, if you're *really* honest with yourself, I don't think it'd be there. I think it is for those kids an inefficient way to get the job done.
>
> You have to stop and say to the principal: "Look, you tell me what I'm supposed to do. If my job is to teach basic skills that is one thing; if getting kids feeling better about themselves, that's another; if you tell me my job is to tell them about the blue-collar world and how they'll fit in as employees, that's something else. I can make all three happen simultaneously and I do, but if you tell me basic skills is my main job, I will tell you that a magazine is an inefficient way to get that job done. . . . If you tell me the most important thing in these kids' lives is self-confidence and getting over their resistance to language arts and [having] an attitudinal change . . . , I'll say, 'Fine, give them to me. I'll do this forever with these kids.'"

Wigginton also argues that the magazine is more appropriate for delivering "higher" academic skills, e.g., a major research paper that analyzes a technical process, than basic skills. Given the limited appropriateness of the magazine for poorly motivated, low-achieving students, he will now admit only a few of the so-called dirty dozen to the class—and only after he has decided "that it would really be useful for them at this point in their life and important that they get some serious strokes. I wouldn't take them because I'd deluded myself into thinking I'd have any real input in their basic skills. I can't lie to myself."

Wigginton also acknowledges that some of the students who come to him are unsalvageable, not only because of the intensity of their apathy and the abysmal level of their academic skills, but also because their other teachers have already given up on them. Tracy, the pseudonym of a student enrolled in Wigginton's Foxfire I class, is a case in point. Wigginton said of him:

He's so bummed out basically, and he is so negative about school and his own capabilities and so far behind in rudimentary skills [and] into such a mind-set in terms of listening to directions, taking constructive criticism, motivation [and] self esteem, that he is a major project—almost starting from ground zero. What's happened is he's trained himself to not listen, not care and not to participate or give any positive input or energy at all. He's been kicked out of a couple of classes this quarter [and] the teachers see him as a lost cause. When that happens, it's hard to turn around.

Tracy will be a dropout; he has an odd-job future. He probably won't return to school next year. He's a tenth grader. That means you're fighting the clock when you take him on. We're talking about a huge expenditure of energy and time. If you want to turn that situation around, you have to use all your tricks on that kid's head. Once the attitude is turned around, where you are now is with a kid who's got fifth grade skills and you send him to other classes with the changed attitude and unless every other teacher who has him is doing the same thing you're doing with him, in two days his attitude's back where you started because he realizes he can't handle the work.

The special situations being created inside schools, with small classes, are situations, say, for the gifted and talented or behavioral disorders. But Tracy doesn't qualify. He's bad off enough because he can't do high school work but not bad off enough to fall into any of those categories. He's one of a large group of kids in the United States out there on the low end of the scale—and they fall through the cracks. I can't do anything about it alone, and the average teacher can't do anything about it because she's got 150 other students.

The first rule of teaching is never turn your back on a kid. The reality of the situation is that unless the school shifts him into a special program and deals with him, all you've done is created between the two of you a halfway decent relationship where when you see him in the community ten years from now pumping gas or raking leaves, he's going to be able to say, "We had a good time together and I enjoyed your class, and I feel we're still friends, but you haven't substantially changed anything in terms of my ability to succeed."

So is it worth the time or investment? Eighteen years ago, I would have said, "Yes, and to not take him is an act of criminal negligence." But [I said that,] not having worked for eighteen years with a lot of these kids. What I'm saying is that until the school sets up some kind of support system what I've realized is that I'm just the Lone Ranger and the energy I've got—which is not infinite—can be much better applied.

One of the better applications of his time and energy has been the development of Foxfire I, the introductory composition course that incorporates the elements of magazine production in the explicit service of teaching the elements of style, grammar, and syntax. This course serves several purposes for Wigginton.

First, it is a replicable translation of his educational principles in a form that should appeal to teachers who are interested in an innovative, yet inherently conservative, alternative for teaching basic composition. Given that *Foxfire* magazine was originally intended as an educational reform in only *one* school in a tiny corner of rural America, its replication in over two hundred cultural journalism projects throughout the United States has made it a relative success; yet in absolute terms, its success has been very limited—a few hundred projects hardly constitutes a revolution in teaching practice. The concept's limited appeal to date is attributable partly to the enormous demands cultural journalism projects make on teachers, already overburdened with too many students and too much administrative minutiae, partly to the well-documented reluctance of most teachers to adopt any innovation that requires students to assume an active role in their own learning,[25] and partly to the national mood of "back to basics" that militates against any innovation that does not explicitly teach academic skills. In developing the Foxfire I course, Wigginton has addressed each of these concerns while remaining faithful to the basic tenets of his original philosophy.

Second, the course is a sorting and recruiting ground for students' entry into the magazine class. At the end of the winter and spring quarters of 1984, Wigginton announced that he had compiled a list of students who would be allowed to register for Foxfire II, based upon their performance in Foxfire I. He softened the blow for those whose names were omitted from the list by telling them: "There may be students who want to sign up for Foxfire II, but they haven't shown us they will work, and we don't know if we can use them. If your name's not on the list, come and see me. Between now and [registration day], the instructors will be watching you to see how you work." At all events, only a few habitually disruptive or poorly motivated students surfaced in the magazine class during either of the remaining grading periods in 1984.

Third, Foxfire I provides a common-sense framework for giving students with marginal language arts skills a positive, yet structured, experience in composition. When he changed the primary focus of Foxfire I from magazine production skills to descriptive and expository writing, Wigginton created a set of activities commensurate with the level of skills that he predicted his students would bring to his course:

> The *majority* of my students would be below national averages in language arts skills, would come to me having already decided they did not like English for whatever reasons, would be almost completely resistant to the "what are the elements of a paragraph" didactic approach to writing, and would be as restless as a roomful of weasels. They would know already that the rules of English make no sense (give me the past tenses of "bake," "take," "make" and "break" and tell me how logical our language is), and that the Emily Post propriety of "It is I" and "This is he" is stupid, and perhaps even dangerous given the fact that any person who used such language would be branded forever and cast into darkness.[26]

Wigginton has keyed the syllabus of Foxfire I to Rabun County High School's twelve-week quarter system (in effect from 1977 to 1984), which required three composition courses, three grammar courses, and three literature courses for graduation. The major—and perhaps fatal—weakness of such a curriculum structure is that it does not hold each teacher responsible for integrating the various components of English in their classes; in fact, it encourages a system whereby grammar is taught outside the context of student writing, and literature is divorced from its nexus with composition. In Foxfire I, Wigginton has avoided the fallacy of bifurcating composition and grammar by rigorously marking and grading students' writing mechanics according to a standardized point scale, by using grammar sheets compiled from students' papers to explain grammatical and syntactical errors, and by providing tutorial assistance to students with recurring problems.

What distinguishes Foxfire I from other high school and college composition courses is not only its incorporation of the elements of magazine production in the service of language arts skills, but also its use of traditional culture as an overarching thematic focus. In terms recalling Erikson's notation of the "evil image" of a culture, Wigginton explains why he included cultural understanding as a goal of the course:

> I had come to the firm belief that this understanding was vital partly through former student feedback, partly through my knowledge that not a single other teacher or course in the entire school was paying any attention to it at all, partly through observing the almost complete and needless ignorance of my students regarding their culture, partly through my realization that almost nothing in their lives was at work to counteract the negative national stereotype of the ignorant Southern Appalachian hick—and the effect of that stereotype on other people's opinions about them and their potential, partly through watching the astonishment and the grins on the faces of students I had had as they became caught up by and immersed in some traditional custom—and the joy and satisfaction with which some older person had introduced them to it, partly through my conviction that pride in background and roots has much to do with pride in self and with mental health and with never having to feel apologetic again for origins, and on and on.[27]

I observed Foxfire I on a daily basis throughout the entire spring quarter of 1984. At the outset, Wigginton announced that he had planned ten compositions for the class, which comprised twenty-two students in grades nine through eleven. As events proved, this was an unrealistic projection. Special school activities—a field day, an annual-signing party, a language-arts festival, and a play—forced the cancellation of four classes, and a tornado warning disrupted another. Wigginton's eleven absences from the class for trips with students and publishing meetings also disrupted the continuity of the course; for example, on four occasions his staff substitute filled the period with Foxfire-related films and slides and discussion of the work of the organization. Two other days were lost for class meetings—one for voting on minor organizational business and one for discussion of Foxfire courses to be offered under the school's new semester system, scheduled to begin in the fall of 1984.

Given these disruptions of the academic curriculum, the class completed only eight papers and the related grammar sheets (excluding the essay exam at the end of the course). The major culprit was the school's twelve-week quarter system. Schoolwide activities, class business meetings, and days off task are a normative, and not necessarily undesirable, reality of school life. Their effect on the curriculum, however, is compounded in a short academic session, the consequence being that students' time with an individual teacher is severely constricted.

The results of an analysis of Foxfire I, even in this truncated version, are twofold: first, insights about the implications and replicability of this unusual curriculum; and second, with supportive details from Wigginton's other classes, a portrait of one of America's best known and most respected teachers. An examination of the separate components of Foxfire I—composition/grammar, culture, and journalism—provides a context for discussion of these categories.

As stated previously, Foxfire I is distinguishable from Foxfire II, the magazine class, by virtue of its explicit focus on composition. In Foxfire II, with recorded culture as an end product, basic writing skills are ancillary to that goal and, in practice (albeit not in theory or testimonial rhetoric), are shortchanged. In Foxfire I, the agenda shifts to composition/grammar as the end product, an assurance by Wigginton, who now acknowledges the limited replicability of Foxfire II, that basic writing skills will be systematically addressed in a fashion that is consistent with his educational philosophy. From this perspective, culture and the elements of cultural journalism are subordinate (yet indispensable) to the goal of writing; in this minor-key reversal of Foxfire II, they become the means to the end.

For example, tape recording as a method of cultural preservation is the subject of a process analysis piece. In preparing his students for this paper, Wigginton demonstrates the setup and rules for use of the tape recorder. Next he moves about the room talking to the recorder from various distances and positions to demonstrate the effect of these variables on the quality of sound reproduction. Then, to show how technical gaffes during an interview can damage a tape, he directs a student to blow on the microphone (simulating the wind), to cover it with her hand, and to jostle and thump the machine. After playing the tape and discussing it with the students, Wigginton reviews the lesson's key points in a skeletal outline which the students will use as an organizing tool for their essays of three hundred to five hundred words.

The Foxfire interview, students' firsthand experience of the Appalachian culture, provides the opportunity for a variety of innovative papers. Given the difficulties of transporting twenty-two students at a time to four or five interviews during the academic session, not to mention the wrath of the teachers whose classes they would be missing, Wigginton invites the elderly contacts to visit his classroom. He directs the students to organize themselves into four or five groups, each of which will be responsible for conducting an interview, including setting up the tape recorder and taking photographs.

The following passage, taken from field notes, describes the interview with Fred Carpenter, a senior citizen from the Warwoman community whose information on chicken callers and ivy whistles became the subject of a process analysis paper:

> Fred is seventy-two years old, bedecked in a multicolored checkered shirt, white-haired, with a weather-beaten face mounted by an elongated nose. I find him to be a gentle, modest, and humorous man. Linda Page, from the Foxfire Press, introduces him to the students and gives them a list of topics about which information is needed for a forthcoming book on Appalachian toys and games. Wig explains to him that the interview will be taped and photographed, and the students will take notes. The fifteen or so who are here today are pressed horseshoe-style around Fred, who is seated in a desk at the front of the room. Claude has set up the tape recorder. Claude, Kelly, Steven, and Billy are the interviewers, seated a few feet opposite Fred, who gets lots of attention and laughs. Hedy and Donna take photos for color slides of Fred as he answers questions and makes the toys. Stanley and Al are responsible for the black-and-white shots that will be used for an article for the magazine. The hit of the day is Fred's homemade chicken caller, a device made by looping a rubber band inside and around the ends of a clothespin. When Fred blows between the two pieces of the clothespin, the resulting sound really imitates a chicken. He passes several of these around the room, and the students get them all going at the same time. "It sounds like a barn in here," yells Wig (laughing).

Wigginton goes far beyond relying on his contacts to teach Rabun County youngsters about the beauty and strength of Appalachian culture. During the first several weeks of the course, he accompanies the students in two groups on separate days to the Foxfire Center for a personal tour and an expert disquisition on the artifacts housed in the museum cabins on "the land."

Wigginton begins the tour in the grist mill, still operable when water from the reservoir above the mill is released down a flume to spill over the elm-wood water wheel. Inside this ancient edifice, he lectures on the ingenuity of the old-timers who handcrafted the gears that regulated the distance between the two grinding stones and the size of the ground corn granules.

In the wagon house, fronted by the property's split-rail fence, Wigginton shows the students an eighteenth-century covered wagon that once made the hazardous journey from the Shenandoah Valley of

Virginia through the Appalachians into Tennessee and was a gift to Foxfire from the family that had passed it along from generation to generation as an heirloom. He explains that the Appalachian wagon is much smaller than the Conestogas that headed west, because the only roads into the southern highlands in the early settlement days were narrow Indian trails.

In the oratorical style of a Luddite, Wigginton disparages the complexities of modern technology by comparing the ingenuity and simplicity of the old-time spare wagon wheel to the flimsy spare tire manufactured for his Chevy Citation, which, he asserts, will last for only fifteen or twenty miles on the road. Furthermore, it takes two hours to replace the damaged tire and to have it repaired at a service station. "In about ten seconds, you're back on the road," he says admiringly of the wagon wheel. "You sometimes wonder how much progress we're making. We may be going backwards."

Indoctrination in the service of enhancing students' pride in their cultural past is a salient characteristic of Wigginton's teaching style. He rarely misses an opportunity to extol the virtues of the mountain folkways or to remind students of the consequences of selling family heirlooms and artifacts to tourists or craft stores. A case in point is the quilt the young ladies of the Wolffork and Germany communities had sewed, embroidered with their names, and given as a wedding gift to Doc L. Justice and Lula Mosely in 1899. Having no children to whom she could pass the quilt, D. L. and Lula's daughter, Nan Powell, had given it to Andrea Burrell Potts, the former Foxfire student who owns the Tryphosia quilt store a few miles north of Rabun County. To ensure that the valuable quilt would remain in the area, Potts sold it to Foxfire, which has added it to the museum collection.[28]

While he and Margie Bennett held the quilt aloft in the Foxfire classroom, Wigginton explained to the Foxfire I students its family history and cultural legacy. Next he described how outside investors who have no kinship or community ties to southern Appalachian artifacts such as the wedding quilt exploit unsuspecting native sellers.

The problem I have with someone from, say, Jacksonville, Florida, buying it [the wedding quilt] for $45 is [that] the only reason she's buying it is as an investment, and she knows she can get ten to twenty times what she paid for it. If it were in better shape, it would sell for thousands. She has no connection with this county; what she sees is an investment. Something made out of love is being treated as a commodity, which it wasn't intended to be. We're trying to keep these things in the county. So much of it is going. If you've got one of these, don't let your mother take it to the Harvest

Festival in Dillard in October and sell it. If you let these things get away from you, you'll kick yourself for the rest of your life. I've heard too many people say, "I wish we'd kept it." I'm getting sick of hearing it.

Wigginton occasionally uses five or ten minutes of the class period to acquaint students with a list of Appalachian artifacts, the definitions of which older Rabun County natives would know immediately—terms such as *piggin, slop arm, granny woman, thrash, finial, maul, leather breeches,* and *puncheon.* He also explains such technical processes as the "fine art" of moonshining and hewing a log. For the latter, he drags a wooden beam to the center front of the room, takes a broadaxe in hand, and demonstrates the proper hewing stroke. He tells the students that some of the residents of affluent Sky Valley have had a sawmill operator cut the hewing scars in the log beams used in the construction of their houses—imitations that are easily detectable.

As noted in Chapter 4, Wigginton addresses the theme of culture writ large by having the students, as an oral class exercise, create a creature, specify its physiological characteristics, and select its environment as background information for a paper on culture. Then each student selects a specific need that biology or the environment has imposed on the creature and describes in an essay how the creature meets that need in the context of the chosen environment. Wigginton's teaching point in this clever exercise is that culture is the totality of nonphysiological adaptations made by a group of people of like characteristics to their environment.

This exposition of culture provides a conceptual framework for discussion of the origin and purpose of Appalachian folkways and the impact of change on the region's indigenous culture. At this point, Wigginton also usually introduces the Scotch-Irish settlement of the region and the highlights of Rabun County history. The last two papers in the course and the final exam build upon Wigginton's lectures and class discussions of the regional culture.

One of these papers is a letter written to Bil (spelled with one *l*) Dwyer, author of the booklet "Thangs Yankees Don' Know."[29] Although Dwyer asserts that this compendium of "dialect, lawin', greens, recipes, squar' dancin', beauty aids, wild life, remedies, signs, stills, and *Folks-Fire* [emphasis added] things" is accurate and even considered scholarly in some circles, Wigginton argues vigorously that the volume is a distortion of Appalachian culture and purveys conventional stereotypes of the region. Wigginton charges that not only has the author disparaged Foxfire's work in countering these stereotypes, but he has also used one of Wigginton's copyrighted diagrams of a moonshine still without authorization.

The critique of "Thangs Yankees Don' Know" is included in a lesson that focuses on the meaning and implications of the term *stereotype*. First Wigginton writes the epithet *nigger* on the board and reads a derogatory passage about blacks included in Margaret Morley's *Our Carolina Mountains* (Boston: Houghton Mifflin, 1913). Next he asks the students to compile a list of things that come to mind when they think about blacks, and he writes these on the board—an exercise that elicits guffaws and derisive laughter from those students who routinely disparage blacks as "niggers." Remarks such as "They're similar to apes" and stereotypic items such as watermelon, possum, rhythm, lips, and "spearchucker" appear on the board. Then Wigginton puts the term *hick* on the board and reads selections from Morley's book that portray the southern mountain folk as barbaric and lazy. "This is what she said about mountain people, i.e., you guys," Wigginton remarks. "Sure it's true," he adds facetiously. "It's written in this book right here. It's got to be true. No wonder mountain people get cold in the winter—they don't chop wood." With both sets of stereotypes in front of the students, Wigginton states: "If you agree with what she says about Negroes [Morley's term], you have to agree with what she says about you guys," his point being that all stereotypes are inherently illogical, the products of fear and ignorance. "Believe this," he says (pointing to the term *nigger*), "and you have to believe this" (thumping the board under the term *hick*).

This discussion has set the stage for Wigginton's introduction to Dwyer's booklet. He begins with the author's presentation of the mountain argot, asking the students if they know what *twinkles* are—a term defined by Dwyer as pine needles (p. 4). The students respond that they haven't heard the term before. The next term is *cooter,* which Dwyer defines as a turtle (p. 5).

The kids have a different meaning than the one Dwyer gives. "It's puss," Allyn tells me. There is a huge uproar of indignation here at Dwyer's account of mountain talk. "You guys hear of these things?" asks Wig. "No!" is the boisterous reply. Also at issue is the regional pronunciation of poison ivy—*pizen ivory* in Dwyer's rendition (p. 15). Al, whose family is rooted in these parts, turns to me and pronounces the term correctly. "This guy sucks," he says loudly. Someone asks, "Where does this guy live?" "Highlands now," responds Wig, who then says, "You guys want to write him a letter?" "Yes!" "Okay, tomorrow, we'll write him a letter." Billy adds, "Let's write what *cooter* is on his driveway."[30]

Wigginton has written that he has mailed composites drawn from these letters "a number of times now" but has never received a response from the author ("No matter, it's still a good exercise."). Wigginton underscores the point that students are particularly aware of the necessity for grammatical correctness in their letters: "I return the papers, asking, 'If your letter contains grammatical mistakes, and we put it in an envelope and send it to him, what happens?' The immediate and obvious response [is], 'It just makes him right when he says we're stupid.' Grammar sheets that day take on a slightly different meaning."[31]

As a humanist educator, Wigginton has strived to create nonpunitive learning environments where mistakes are treated as benign wellsprings for intellectual and emotional growth. In a speech given to the National Workshop for Cultural Journalism in 1979, Mike Cook addressed this aspect of Wigginton's pedagogy: "As a student, one of the things I got the most out of was the fact that we were allowed to do things on our own, and if we screwed up, then we screwed up, and we had to cover for it."[32]

Wigginton's patience and belief in the instructional power of mistakes was evident when two advanced Foxfire students working on an article on old-time butter churns forgot to turn on their tape recorder and lost an entire interview with a craftsman in Alto, Georgia. The students, Greg and Al, had driven the fifty miles from Rabun County to Alto ahead of Wigginton, who arrived just after they had completed the interview. When he discovered that the tape was empty, Wigginton conferred with the boys:

> Did you guys not have *play* and *record* pushed down when you were recording?" "No," says Greg. "That's okay," responds Wig. "Don't worry about it." Greg and Al both look at each other, and Al looks at me with a sheepish smile, both boys obviously embarrassed. We finally leave at around 1:00. I lead out as I've seen a barbecue place down the road toward Cornelia, and the others follow. Al and Greg have packed lunches and drinks; Wig and I get some food at the counter and join them for a picnic in the shade off the highway. Wig talks with the boys and tells them he likes the way they got everything set up and conducted the interview. Then he reminds them that they learned something today about the proper use of the tape recorder: "Now you won't make *that* mistake again."

Similarly, in Foxfire I, Wigginton has structured a classroom situation in which students can make mistakes without fear of failure or retribution. For example, he will not assign a final grade to a paper that he has marked for errors until the student has exercised or waived the privilege to correct it and to improve the content for a higher grade—a privilege that often makes the difference between a passing and a failing grade. To ameliorate further the defeatism lower-level students bring to their writing, Wigginton assigns separate and equally weighted grades to grammar/syntax and content, e.g., seventy-six/B+. Students who have below-average grammatical skills will rarely fail a paper because of this weakness alone.

In grading writing mechanics, Wigginton deducts points according to the severity of the error, e.g., minus three for a spelling error, minus fifteen for a sentence fragment—a common procedure in college-freshman composition courses. On the first day of the new session, a startled Foxfire I student remarked: "Gosh, you can make negative." "Yes, you can," responded Wigginton. "And many of you probably will on the first paper, but you have the opportunity to rewrite and get it right."

On his first paper in the College English class, where the same marking/grading system was used, a senior scored a negative seventy-six on grammar, primarily because of repetitive comma splice and sentence fragment errors. Wigginton told the student, "You had *one* humdinger—two comma splices in sentences back to back." "That's the lowest grade I've ever seen," exclaimed another student. The senior revised the paper and raised the grammar grade to a respectable eighty-seven. Commenting on Wigginton's rigorous grading, this relieved student remarked stolidly: "This guy had my paper for lunch."

When discussing their papers with students, Wigginton focuses on their strengths as a point of departure for remediating their mistakes. For example, as he handed back the second set of papers in Foxfire I—a description of old-timer Johnny Eller—he told the class: "These papers are markedly better than the first set, the grammar particularly. Only four below passing [and] these are, in every case, people making the same mistake [repeatedly]. Once they fix it, we're home free." Similarly, as he handed back their graded letters to Bil Dwyer, he remarked: "In terms of grammar mistakes, there are almost none. There is only one paper below sixty-five and that was close. These are good. Anybody [who] wants [his or her] letter sent to Mr. Dwyer can take it home and correct it so we can send it next week. If you're from the Appalachian region and don't know how to spell it, you don't look so good."

Wigginton provides ample reinforcement and encouragement, even for students he does not appear to like. The following comments appeared on three of the graded papers of one such student in Foxfire I:

This is one of your best papers. It is worth rewriting to fix a few errors. *Good* improvement.

Your work is getting better. If we could just get your run-on sentences under control, we'd be set.

Good start. Some details left out (as noted), but this is much cleaner work. Great improvement! Keep it up!

He is particularly attentive to shy and withdrawn students as evidenced by his behavior toward Eddie [pseudonym], a tenth-grade student in the class. Wigginton accorded Eddie special treatment, although he was not obtrusive about it—e.g., an occasional pat on the back, a reference to a "nice detail" in Eddie's paper in front of the class, a chat with him (seated on the floor) in the hallway, and the offer of a summer maintenance job with Foxfire.

Wigginton had noticed at the outset of the quarter that Eddie, the grandson of two favorite Foxfire contacts, appeared withdrawn from and disinterested in the class.

Eddie didn't say one word until [the discussion] of the flying jennys. He came up real quietly and said he and his family had built one of those and told me he once had an accident and got hurt on it. That was the first thing he said in here. [He was telling himself,] "Oh, we made one of those! There's a connection now between me and this class." I wanted a strategy to get him involved. I started building more and more of that kind of thing into what we were doing. Since he was getting more and more comfortable, I wanted to build on [that]. I gave him the color film and *my* camera, helping ensure great pictures, and when the pictures came back, I put one in the Foxfire slide show and I told him I'd done that. All I'm trying to do is to zing enough things in his direction that I keep him coming forward and coming out. Giving him extra encouragement in the margins of his compositions. One of the big reasons is I've heard he's thinking about dropping out of school. I want him to have a place now where he can get some reinforcement and encouragement and we can reach a point where we can begin to talk about it.

Wigginton brings to his management of the classroom not only his resonant baritone voice and confident demeanor, but also his reputation as a fair teacher who genuinely likes and trusts young people. Consistent with other elements of his pedagogy, his style of classroom discipline is nonpunitive and informal. Observing Wigginton on a daily basis over an entire year—in class, on trips, at the Foxfire Center—I noticed that he rarely raised his voice with students, never once lost his self-control, and only once yelled angrily at a student ("Hey, get that drink out of here!").

The following excerpt from field notes, descriptive of his students on their worst behavior, captures (albeit only in glimpses) Wigginton's use of voice modulations, pauses, and gestures to keep control of the class. The exercise to which seven disorderly students on the left side of the classroom were supposed to be attending was a grammar sheet.

There is talking on the left side of the room. Holding the grammar sheet, Wig stretches his right hand toward the boisterous group as he continues to talk about errors in the students' papers. Next he glances to the left side, and the chatter stops. As he explains the improper use of the coordinating conjunction *and* as an introductory element in a sentence (unless used for emphasis), Wig writes several examples on the board. Again there is chatter from the left side. Wig says loudly and firmly, but without shouting, "Look right here!" Next he lowers his voice: "See what's wrong with number four." To get the recalcitrant students' attention, he hits his grammar sheet on number four, making a loud smack. Somebody on the left has farted (or simulated the noise). Wig looks at the left side. Someone says, *"shh."* Wig looks again. Next the chatter resumes. Turning away from the left side, he says firmly, "Listen!" Steve and Claude are giggling now (apparently over the noise). Billy, Al, Allyn, and Claude redirect their attention to Wig. Stan talks with Allyn, eliciting a remark from Wig, "You listening?" Stan turns once again to Allyn and then directs his attention to the grammar sheet. Steven and Claude talk while Wig reads aloud from the grammar sheet, asking questions of the students, standing now on the left side of the room. These students have not really disrupted the class—they don't seem to be disturbing the kids at the center and the right of the room, who have been extremely quiet this period. Their behavior is *self-disruptive*, but Wig has not let their persistent giggling and chatting distract him from getting the class through the grammar sheet.

This outbreak of restless behavior occurred early in the quarter. A week later, Wigginton laid down a hard and fast rule that silenced the disorderly students in the class and marked a turning point toward a different kind of behavior on their part. Perhaps it is the undeniable reasonableness of the rule, perhaps the intensity with which Wigginton delivers the admonition, perhaps a combination of both that elicits the desired behavior. The rule pertains to the students' conduct during an in-class interview, expressed in words similar to the following: "One of the things you don't do is to pass notes or to talk or to indicate that you're bored with a person we're interviewing. I'll not allow a student to do anything to embarrass a visitor. If that happens, then when you come to class the next day, I will give you a note and you will report to the guidance counsellor, who will assign you to another class. You will no longer be in this class. If you don't believe me, try me. We'll see on Wednesday [the day following the interview] if we have a full class."

Over the remainder of the quarter, the entire class cohered as a generally orderly, cooperative, task-oriented work unit. Wigginton's pacing of his instruction, incorporating two or more activities on a given day (interviews become a collage of activities); his own frenetic demeanor in class—constantly moving about the room, his hands and arms in almost perpetual motion (between classes Wigginton releases his abundant energy by moving furniture, slapping students on the back, and joking with whoever happens to drift into the room—he cannot sit still); the credibility in his voice when he tells students that their work in his course is important; the urgency he conveys when he tells them that there is precious little time to do all this work (statements such as "We're about three compositions behind in this course. We're going to start a whole new chunk. This is the race to the end of the year."); and the intensity of the activities themselves tended to keep most of the students focused on the tasks at hand.

The following passage, describing the class during which Wigginton introduced photography to the students, preparatory to their interview with Johnny Eller and the subsequent description paper, underscores most of these points. Wigginton put Owen Riley, a friend of a staff member and a skilled adult photographer, to good use during the period:

> Before class, Stanley and Wig exchange greetings, and Wig grabs his shoulders playfully. Wig tells Owen to hold his slide presentation to twenty minutes. Cannon has taken a seat with his Mountain Dew. "We need to get started," Wig says, with his fingers to his lips. "We have about twenty things to do. You guys sit tight." Wig tells them that Owen's slides will take twenty or twenty-five minutes, that after the demonstration he will pass out cameras to groups of five or six students. Allyn says, "Is five okay? We've got our group." Owen presents his slides, telling students to "focus on the eyes" for portrait shots, to which Wig responds, "That's a good point: Always focus on the eyes. I've never heard that." Owen also suggests that the students take their light readings on a hand preparatory to portrait shots. Wig tells the class that they'll practice that in a few minutes. Wig has Owen stop on a portrait to make the point that "what you see [through a single-lens reflex camera] is what you get." Gives advice, something like, "Give the subject some space so you don't cut off part of an arm or face," and "Look around the edges to see if a powerline is in the picture." Wig is standing in the far corner of the room at the edge of the darkroom. "Please don't bring Cokes and ice cream in here," he announces, very soft-spoken. "There's too much [danger that negatives, prints, cameras, and layouts] can get gunked up with that crap and syrup." After the slides, he announces in a stronger

voice, "Okay, give me five groups." The students form four self-selected groups. Each group has at least one camera. Wig directs their attention to Owen ("Everybody listen!"), who demonstrates how to hold a camera. Allyn is talking and laughing. Wig has a serious look on his face as he looks in Allyn's direction. Next Owen has students set the shutter speed of their cameras to 1/60 of a second on ASA 400. He advises them not to photograph below 1/60 without using a tripod; also tells them to squeeze rather than push the shutter release. Owen explains the relationship of the F-stop ring [light meter] to the focus ring [depth of field]. Wig, Margie [staff member], and Denise [staff member] work with the various groups. Owen demonstrates using the hand to take a light reading for portrait shots. Wig explains that this technique will exclude extraneous room light that might result in an inaccurate reading. In their groups the kids focus on each other and set their light meters [F-stop setting]. Next Wig says to Owen, "We've got ten minutes." Denise volunteers as a subject for the students and sits at the front of the room. Al and Stanley are talking, kidding, almost turning over a desk. Wig asks, "Are you guys listening?" Stanley responds, "Yes." He and Al turn toward Owen. The photographing of Denise is done in two platoons. Owen directs the students to get close to her. There is plenty of movement here—perpetual motion. Kids are moving all over the front of the room with their cameras, shooting. Owen orchestrates this with commands: "Go high, go low." Wig adds, "Some of you guys go low." Wig puts his hands on Cannon's throat, giving him a mock choke, and Cannon, leaning back and down in his desk, puts the camera up to Wig's face; Wig then gives him a pat. Wig instructs the students to attach the cameras to their cases. "Good timing," he says, the bell having rung as the last camera snaps into its case.

With five weeks remaining in the course, Wigginton instructed the students that each of the groups would be responsible for transcribing the parts of the tape of its in-class interview that pertained to a toy or a game, printing the photographs, drawing and labeling diagrams, and compiling an index of the material as the basis of an article that would be completed by Foxfire II students. He told them, "On the days I say *group work*, you all will break up into your groups. One person should bring out the negatives, diagrams, tapes, and transcriptions. Decide today who will do the diagrams. One other [student] will help. Each time we break up into groups I'll send one from each group into the darkroom to print. Obviously, I can't let four groups into the darkroom at the same time."

These groups met several times, and some group members worked after school and at home. During the in-class sessions, the work tended to be focused and intense as students worked individually and in pairs printing in the darkroom, mounting photographs, diagramming, and transcribing. Wigginton himself taught six students how to use the darkroom, and they taught their peers. Observing the groups at work near the end of the quarter, Wigginton remarked: "It doesn't look bad. It almost looks organized. Of course, it could all fall apart in a few minutes." This did not prove to be the case.

As conceptualized and implemented by Wigginton, Foxfire I achieves a balance of cognitive and affective objectives—the kind of curriculum integration advocated by John Dewey in *Experience and Education* (1938). In this lucid volume written explicitly for practitioners, Dewey scolded progressive educators who had bastardized his philosophy by emphasizing too heavily the emotional needs of their pupils in the so-called child-centered schools of the 1920s and 1930s. In jettisoning the traditional curriculum, which Dewey had found too inflexible and too concerned with subject matter at the expense of other educational aims, the progressives had erred toward the opposite extreme of building curriculum on the unbridled impulses of children. The resolution of the curriculum dilemma, Dewey suggested, lay between the extremes in an integration of cognitive and affective skills.[33]

For Wigginton, Foxfire I resolves the progressive's dilemma of how to make curriculum more responsive to students' emotional and personal growth needs, without the sacrifice of academic rigor that has proved to be the case in Foxfire II. In an era of "back to basics," when a major underpinning of educational reform is the assumption that cognitive and affective skills are antipodal and it is better to sacrifice the latter rather than the former, Foxfire I is one of those rare curriculum reforms that attempts to harmonize the two.

Given its well-defined academic focus, Foxfire I should appeal to a larger audience than the small but hardy band of teachers in the cultural journalism network. In *Sometimes a Shining Moment*, Wigginton presents a sixty-page, heavily anecdotal curriculum guide that leads readers day by day through the twelve-week course. The guide is less a model than it is an inspiration and font of ideas for practitioners interested in creating alternative teaching approaches that address composition/grammar skills.

The most replicable elements in the course, ones that teachers could readily adapt to their own pedagogical styles and interests, are the use of the elderly as community teachers and the use of indigenous culture and/or local history as a thematic leitmotif around which to structure writing exercises. The elements of magazine production are more problematic, hence less replicable. Not only must teachers negotiate the use of their schools' photographic equipment, they must also have enough expertise to be able to teach the rudiments of photography to young people and to answer their questions as well. Observational data collected in Foxfire I and analysis of Wigginton's curriculum guide suggest that photography is an effective motivational tool for marginally academic students, but it is not indispensable to the intellectual-skills objectives of the course; in fact, the most inventive papers are drawn from interviews and related cultural themes.

For example, Johnny Eller's rugged face and thick, hoary beard, which contrasted sharply with his reticent and soft-spoken demeanor, made him a colorful and entertaining subject for descriptive writing. Jack Prince, a lively raconteur, held the students' attention with his demonstration of making a cornstalk airplane, the subject of a process analysis essay on an Appalachian toy. When attached to a string and swung in a rotation above the head, the plane "flew," with propellors spinning and whirring.

Similarly, other essays that build upon the theme of culture are not dependent on magazine skills. In one exercise, Wigginton shows the class an old, battered front half of a plastic doll's head. He then specifies that they are "to assume a first-person stance and pretend they *are* the object. I instruct them to tell me their life story from their creation in the mountains through the changes they've witnessed, and their reaction to those changes, to the present."[34]

On the other hand, magazine production skills are an indispensable component of the group projects, given that the students are laying the foundation for a publishable article. These activities reflect Wigginton's sustained commitment to the motivational power of an end product that will be viewed by an audience beyond the classroom. As yet Wigginton has not formulated Deweyan group-process goals for Foxfire I, such as democratic decision making and social problem solving. Given the present hegemony of basic skills, it is unlikely that critics will take him to task for this omission.

In *Democracy and Education* (1916), John Dewey rejected the notion that effective teaching could occur in a heavily structured environment with a teacher "pouring in" subject matter to be passively absorbed by students.[35] Indeed Dewey envisioned a different kind of classroom and a different role for the teacher: "The alternative to furnishing ready-made subject matter and listening to the accuracy with which it is reproduced is not quiescence but participation, sharing in an activity. In such a shared activity, the teacher is a learner, and the learner is, without knowing it, a teacher—and upon the whole, the less consciousness there is, on either side, of giving or receiving instruction, the better."[36]

In a fashion consistent with Dewey's philosophy, Wigginton brings to his teaching an attitude of "becoming the learner." He has referred to this reversal of the teacher's authoritarian role as "the ginseng connection," a phrase coined in memory of a Saturday outing to hunt for ginseng with a community student whom he had previously labeled a "loser." After the student had taught him how to identify and dig the well-camouflaged root and recited the folklore of "sang digging," Wigginton had a different perspective on what a teacher's role should be. "Instead of being a 'pal,' someone with whom it was safe to clown around, I had stumbled into a different kind of relationship of a much deeper quality. For one thing, our roles had been reversed and suddenly I was the pupil, he the teacher. I was amazed at the depth and quality of his knowledge about the woods. He knew far more on that score than I, and I could not help but respect him. He had his areas of knowledge and ignorance, and I had mine, and in that respect, we were equal, each potentially able to share something with the other, to the enrichment of both."[37]

The themes of "role reversal" and "learning partnerships" are recurrent in Wigginton's published writings. For example, in *Foxfire 2*, he made the following statement about teachers who had asked him for specific instructions on starting a Foxfire-like project: "How can I answer questions like that, knowing that the only way it can work is for the teacher to push back the desks and sit down on the floor with the kids and really listen to them for the first time, and see what they can all come up with *together* that *might* work in the context of their own particular school and community—and then try to find ways to make it work for as long as it seems worth doing—and then find another."[38]

Wigginton is not spouting idealistic jargon, as attested by present and former students whose descriptions of him create a portrait strikingly similar to Dewey's model: the mature and knowledgeable teacher *qua* student. For example, a 1984 graduating senior remarked: "He [Wigginton] seems more like a student than . . . a teacher. He works with you in the classroom so you don't feel like he's trying to be like some authority over you; so it makes for a comfortable atmosphere. He's sitting there beside you working on the same thing. He's not lecturing or [saying] do page so and so and hand it in at the end of the period."

Similarly, when asked to compare Wigginton to her other teachers, another Foxfire senior stated: "Everything about Wig is different. He goes out of his way to teach us [something] and to make sure that we've learned it, and he doesn't stop until he knows that we've learned it. And he really cares about his class. We're real to him. He's on our level but yet he's mature. By that I mean that he can make jokes and laugh with us about things. And he really understands how we feel. Yet he's mature enough to know when it's time to stop joking and improve the things that are not the way they should be for us to learn."

Wigginton is not the quintessential Deweyan teacher—at least not yet. Ironically, he had been evolving Foxfire for nearly fifteen years before undertaking a study of Deweyan pedagogy. As discussed in the next chapter, most of the points of convergence between his philosophy and Dewey's, e.g., the emphasis on the learner's out-of-school experience as a foundation of instruction, have been fortuitous. As of this writing, Wigginton is still grappling with Dewey and trying to move the entire Foxfire project in directions consistent with Deweyan pedagogy.

Finally, like all progressives, Wigginton assumes that formality, construed as desks arranged in neat rows facing the teacher, with students postured upright at attention, is an impediment to learning. Students assume a variety of postures in his classroom, as does Wigginton himself. The following interaction between Wigginton and a student in his College English class epitomizes his informal, yet task-focused, style of instruction. The students were working on the first draft of a personal narrative.

> There is a silent busyness here, Ruth's pencil noise in the background the only sound. Wig is standing and looking at the students during this silence. Then he moves to Curt, positioning himself on his haunches, listening to Curt's story about his auto accident on ice. Wig has now moved into a sitting position on the floor, facing Curt, placing his hands behind him for leverage. Curt is lying back in his desk, with his feet straight out in front, touching the floor. Curt continues to talk and Wig listens. Then Wig takes a seat in a desk about five feet from (and at a forty-five degree angle to) Curt, who says that the point of his essay is the lesson he learned about driving on ice. Wig confirms that this should make a good narrative. Curt then tells the entire class about his accident; Wig is standing with his hands in his pocket, smiling. "I think I'd trade you in—take you back to the factory and get a new model," says Wig. Curt responds, "I had one [accident] they [Curt's parents] don't know about." Wig's laughing rejoinder is, "I don't want to know about it."

One of Wigginton's trademarks, although it has raised the ire of rule-minded administrators, is his consistently informal dress, irrespective of the occasion, typically a casual shirt or threadbare sweater, faded blue jeans, Foxfire belt buckle, and desert boots. Whether he is addressing conferees at a sit-down dinner or students in Foxfire I, Wigginton invariably wears a pair of jeans. The only time I saw him wearing a coat and tie during the entire year was at a dinner at the Alliance Theater in Atlanta, celebrating E. P. Dutton's release of *The Foxfire Book of Appalachian Cookery.* Tanya Worley had cajoled him into dressing up for the occasion because the Atlanta press and critics were attending the dinner. Before the festivities, I found him seated on a divan on the second floor of the theater and made a joking reference to his sartorial finery, to which he dourly responded, "Shut up."

Focus on Other Foxfire Staff

In expanding Foxfire to include divisions in Appalachian folklore/ music (later music performance), community television production, and environmental science/outdoor education, Wigginton had two goals in mind: first, to attract students at Rabun County High School who were not interested in magazine production; second, to "stretch" the experience of his magazine students into other areas where their cultural journalism skills could be applied.[39] He also intended that the new divisions incorporate the key elements of his philosophy by providing "experiential" (community-based) programs in which students would learn intellectual and personal growth skills while creating marketable products appropriate to the subject matter of each division. At the outset, however, Wigginton erred by not making these philosophical tenets explicitly clear to his new staff, and by not mandating that they develop curricula that were consistent with the Foxfire concept Wigginton had articulated in his pedagogical treatise *Moments,* written in the latter days of his Rabun Gap School tenure.

In that volume Wigginton had described a four-stage developmental model for guiding adolescents from egocentric to sociocentric ("beyond self") perspectives of the world and human relationships. He argued that to be capable of genuine intimacy with (and empathy for) others, the individual must first have acquired a strong sense of self-worth and a stable identity. An effective way to serve these goals, he postulated, was to provide a nonpunitive schooling environment *and* a vehicle through which students would learn targeted intellectual and personal growth skills in the service of a quality product that would be displayed to an audience beyond the school.

By learning academic skills in their application to a product in which students had both an honest share and a psychological stake, the resulting good feelings and sense of achievement would be neither hollow nor superficial. Wigginton assumed that the quality of a young person's schooling experience was a determining factor, for better or worse, in the development of his or her global sense of self-esteem.

The surest grounding for self-esteem in that context would be demonstrated academic achievement. Wigginton believed that cultural journalism provided the motivation for learning and applying "basic" skills as well as creating a publishable end product that gave students visible proof of their personal and academic competence.[40]

The second level in Wigginton's model, the refinement of basic communications skills, built upon and reinforced the first level of self-esteem and demonstrated competence. Community-based journalistic activities, he assumed, provided the opportunity and impetus for students who were growing increasingly confident in their own abilities to engage in intimate and mutually rewarding relationships with community elders, the hallmark of stage three. These activities were also a catalyst for strengthening the individual student's sense of community and cultural identity, as well as for eliciting genuine concern about the future of the community.[41]

The model was a spiral—discursive, "with a constant movement between the levels."[42] Wigginton's final goal, or "developmental ideal,"[43] was the autonomous, responsible, and caring young adult of stage four. The building blocks of the spiral were the positive formative experiences that he called "moments" or "touchstones," experiences that ranged from having an article published in *Foxfire* to hoeing potatoes in Aunt Arie Carpenter's garden.

As stated earlier, observations of other Foxfire staff teachers confirmed that by 1984, Wigginton's philosophy as adumbrated in *Moments* had been bastardized, ironically within his own organization, not because the core ideas were inappropriate to such content domains as Appalachian folklore, community television, and environmental science, but because the staff had been allowed, and in some cases encouraged, by Wigginton to develop programs that were not consistent with the original philosophy. For the most part, these courses had a decidedly nonacademic focus: they provided either technical training (the case in community television) or behavior modification/social adjustment (the case in environmental science) or leisure-time enrichment activities (the case in outdoor education and music performance). This observation should not be construed as implying that these staff members did not have good intentions or did not provide useful services to the school and community. It is to say that the Foxfire organization, lacking a unifying philosophy, did not have clear educational goals and even acted in some ways that were antithetical to the school's goals of teaching students academic skills and effective study habits.

At a staff meeting on 5 March 1984, Wigginton handed the teachers in each of the Foxfire divisions a tentative timetable for developing curriculum guides for courses they were teaching that had an academic content or could be tailored to include such content and were potentially transferable to other locations. These materials would be available to teachers who requested guidelines for tailoring the ideas in Wigginton's forthcoming book, *Sometimes a Shining Moment,* to their own courses or for creating Foxfire-like courses. Wigginton's course guide for Foxfire I was to appear as an entire section of the book. On this occasion, he issued the following mandate to his teaching staff:

> The intent behind the creation of the very first issue of *Foxfire* was to overlay (and replace) the academic agenda of an English course with an experiential/community-based component, the assumption being that that component would create a better delivery system for the academic agenda. Until proven to be a bankrupt or unworkable assumption, other major courses developed by and funded by Foxfire will follow the same line of reasoning. If we find we must retreat to traditional methods to teach the material effectively, there is no reason for Foxfire to continue to pay for the courses. That's what the state is for. Let them pay the teachers. If we find ourselves abandoning the academic agenda, likewise there is no reason for Foxfire to continue to pay for the courses. We should not be primarily a "salvage" or a "Dr. Feelgood" organization in lieu of the academic mission. "Salvage" and positive self-esteem occur most forcefully in the context of academic/skills gains.[44]

After seven years at Rabun County High School, Wigginton had belatedly given his staff a mandate that would necessitate a drastic refocusing of their courses and teaching styles. My observations in the class of each staff teacher that was most amenable to restructuring along the lines requested by Wigginton illuminated the disparities in the philosophy that had guided Foxfire in its incipiency and the reality of its practice in the Foxfire divisions. The resulting data also indicated that the strengths and interests of his teaching staff are *not* in the academic realm.

During the winter quarter 1984, I spent a week in George Reynolds's classes in folklore, instrument building, and music performance; I also spent a week in Mike Cook's community television classes. After Wigginton had delineated Foxfire's educational goals at the 5 March staff meeting, I decided to focus primarily on one class taught by each of these individuals throughout the spring quarter. In Reynolds's case, I chose Appalachian folklore because, at least on paper, it had an explicit academic focus and could become the basis of a transferable course. Throughout the year, on several occasions I also accompanied Reynolds on trips with his various string bands and attended their community performances.

Cook's courses posed a problem because they were expressly non-academic, although each could have been tailored to include an academic agenda. I chose the lower-level television production course because, unlike the upper-level course in which students worked on projects independently of Cook, it gave me the opportunity to observe his teaching style both in the classroom and on interviews with students in the community. During the quarter I also made occasional visits to his upper-level class and interviewed the majority of his advanced students.

Unlike Reynolds and Cook, who tolerated with patience and a modicum of good humor having an observer/evaluator in their classes for nearly twelve weeks (not an easy burden to bear), Bob Bennett was manifestly unfriendly to my presence at Foxfire. Fearing a conflict that might jeopardize my relationships with the other staff members as well as the school administration, I stayed out of his classes for the first month of the spring quarter. I was not comfortable with this decision, and in early April I told Wigginton that excluding Bennett would leave a gap in the final report. He agreed with my assessment and supported my negotiating with Bennett, vowing that he would intervene in my behalf if the negotiations stalled.

Bennett and I met at his cabin on 9 April for dinner and a strained discussion of the goals of my research, after which I received his begrudging consent to observe the outdoor education class. The following day I assured him that I would appear only occasionally in the class, and restricted myself to six visits during the remainder of the quarter. Our relationship remained strained, and I tried to be as unobtrusive as possible when observing his teaching.

By the end of the 1983–84 academic year, I had compiled observations of Bennett's teaching in only twelve class periods (four in environmental science, six in outdoor education, one in the seventh-grade introduction to Foxfire, and one in the Foxfire-sponsored running course). Yet these sessions provided sufficient evidence that his courses, as they were currently structured, were not applications of the Foxfire philosophy even though Bennett provided services that were applauded by students and faculty alike.

George Reynolds's string-band and ensemble groups, comprising students in his music performance classes at Rabun County High School, were highly visible and popular in the local community. From 1977 to 1979, Reynolds had taught a listening/lecture/discussion course in Appalachian music that did not include a performance component. In the fall of 1979, he dropped this course in favor of a music performance class, and in the spring of 1980, the Foxfire String Band was born. By the fall of 1981, Reynolds was teaching separate courses in string band, beginning music performance, instrument building, and record production.

In 1984, the members of the original string band, all but one of whom had graduated, used the name Foxfire Boys String Band to distinguish themselves from the high school–based Foxfire String Band. As mentioned previously, the Foxfire Boys attracted regional attention with their performances at the Grand Ole Opry and the Knoxville World's Fair and on two tapes produced under the Foxfire Records label. The Foxfire String Band performed twice weekly at local restaurants during the lunch hour (they were paid with a free meal) and at community benefits. The Cat's Meow was an eighth-grade ensemble which mixed gospel, pop, and bluegrass instrumentals in programs for local elementary schools.

A fourth string band included three male students who had learning disorders and were enrolled in the school's special education program. Reynolds organized these boys into a cohesive bluegrass band which performed at local elementary schools, an annual community festival, and a charity fund-raiser at a local fire station. A special education teacher who taught math and science to the three students stated that Reynolds and the music performance class had exerted a profound influence on their individual sense of self-worth:

> These kids don't think of themselves as handicapped. George has boosted their egos and proved to them they [can] do something worthwhile. . . . I just don't believe the difference it's made in the children. Their attitude is just great. It gives them something to look forward to, and they know George is their friend. Their learning how to play is what this county's about, and these kids are going to fit right in. There's a lot of music makers here. I couldn't think of another kind of class that could help these children better in terms of when they finish here. . . . And when they graduate, that's what you want—for these kids to be socially adjusted.

Yet for all his good intentions, Reynolds could not offset the reality that the students had only marginal vocal and instrumental abilities; even his expert accompaniment on guitar and bass could not mask their deficiencies. The following excerpt from the field notes includes my own mixed reactions to the band, which performed on a cold, drizzly February afternoon in the auditorium of a local elementary school.

Seated on the stage steps, I tape record the performance. When I hear "Do Lord," which the band performs in front of a microphone, I cringe. They're flat—bejeezus, they're bad. I try not to smile. Their enunciation is imprecise. All the while George is standing behind them, playing bass and smiling. Despite their lack of talent and off-key mumbling of words, there is something moving about these kids singing "Bringing Mary Home." Some of the sixth graders in the audience whoop it up when the boys play "Foggy Mountain Breakdown." "Meet Me Over on the Other Side," a vocalization without instrumental accompaniment, is terribly flat. At the end of the concert the principal congratulates his own students as an excellent audience, and he thanks them for giving the performers some needed experience.

By mid-spring, Reynolds had discontinued the band's community performances. It was evident that the community, which had high standards for its music makers, did not share his educational goals. Confiding his fear that the youths had "an inflated notion" of their talents, he remarked: "When you take them out you want them to be ensured of success. I was afraid that when they got out in front of John Q. Public, [they would not be well-received]. Old John Q. isn't as kind as the audiences we get in the [elementary] schools. The little kids were nice. . . . To be frank with you, even over at Satolah, their next-door neighbors told me that they want the Foxfire Boys String Band, but they expressly said not to bring [the other band]; they wouldn't work out. They're improving, but they're not at the point where I'm going to put them in front of John Q. Public."

The care and concern that Reynolds showed for the students in his bands was evident in the testimony of a senior in the Foxfire String Band, an orphan who had been reared in a series of foster homes. "George is a friend as well as a leader [and] a teacher, too. He hauls us around to all our pickings on long trips and during school. George has took me and Arlene [another band member] all the way home sometimes. That's twenty-eight miles from here. George doesn't have to do any of this as a teacher, really. He takes it upon himself to start a band and sticks with it, and he'll see you through. He helps you with the good and the bad. He's a terrific man. He'll give you recognition when you're good and sometimes he won't—just to make you better."

He also described the influence of music performance in other aspects of his life: "The Foxfire String Band has offered me the opportunity to get up in front of people and entertain. I get free publicity for myself and the chance to get to meet professional musicians and to go to places like Virginia and to have the chance to get to the top. Performing gives me a chance to meet people. . . . It's bettering myself in meeting people. . . . I wouldn't be what I am today without it as far as my singing and playing. I wouldn't be half as good as I am now. I'd probably be in more construction and cabinet-making [courses]. I might have even quit school. That's how much it means to me. It gives me something to do. I love it."

The opening of the *Foxfire* play at the Alliance Theater in Atlanta on 17 October 1984 provided the occasion for accompanying and observing Reynolds and the Foxfire String Band on a "road trip." The students were scheduled to provide entertainment in the Alliance foyer before and after the play, as well as during the intermission.

Prior to the performance, Reynolds took the students to the Country Inn Restaurant, located several blocks from the theater/museum complex on Peachtree Street. Dressed in their school clothes (one of the students was bedecked with a yellow trucker's cap, a malodorous, blue-and-white-checkered, short-sleeved shirt, and jeans), the Rabun County students were ill-prepared, and some were ill-dressed, for the haute ambience of the restaurant (linen service, silver settings, crystal, multiple utensils, and assorted china plates), where a celebration dinner honoring the *Foxfire* play's Atlanta opening was in progress. The following reconstruction describes how Reynolds, with some help from the observer, used the occasion to teach the students about urban manners and etiquette.

The kids order soft drinks; Joe, the only eighteen-year-old in the group, who is also attending trade school this year, orders a beer. He admits knowing nothing about mixed drinks and asks me to recommend one. "Gin and tonic," I say, "but you can't get it here, Joe. You're a minor." After getting George's consent to order a beer, Joe asks, "How do I get the waiter's attention. Do I yell at him?" "No," says George, "Just raise your hand, like this. He'll see you."

A very polished, genteel waiter services us, describing the menu (*ad nauseam*) on the hand-held chalk board. A thorough professional, the waiter delivers his monologue on the menu like a robot. The kids are stymied by the names of the haute cuisine. "John, can I get a grilled cheese sandwich here," Tom asks me. "No, Tom." "How about a hamburger?" "No, Tom." Eventually everybody makes enough sense of the menu to place an order. George, who says he's never eaten escargot before, orders that as an hors d'oeuvre. Most of the others have a soup of some sort. "It's snail," George announces. "A delicacy." "Ugh," says Jody. Joe asks if he can try one. "That's pretty good." George offers one to Jody, who reluctantly eats it, says it's okay, but adds he doesn't like the idea of eating a snail. I tell George that these kids have seen *The Temple of Doom*.

Oh Soon, whose father is a business executive, has been in this kind of restaurant before. She explains to any who will listen that elbows stay off the table but forearms are appropriate there. After George departs to the restroom, Jody's French onion soup arrives. Jody seems mystified, not recognizing that there is soup under the layer of Gruyère cheese. "What do I do?" he asks. I try to help him: "Stick your spoon through the cheese and spoon out the soup." "Like this?" he asks. "Yes, you've got it." George has returned, and Jody who is eating the soup very gingerly, turns to him for confirmation: "Is this right, George?" "Sure is," says George. Finally, Jody asks, "Do I eat the cheese?"

Reynolds had salvaged what had augured to be a culinary disaster. In this epicenter of Atlanta society, the students ate their dinners without further ado, mastering hors d'oeuvres and bread plates alike. Even the waiter, whom I had imagined guffawing with his colleagues in the kitchen about the "yokels" in the dinning room, seemed to be enjoying himself with the students by the end of the meal. Perhaps Reynolds acted irresponsibly in not preparing the students for the culture shock awaiting them at the Country Inn; certainly their dress was inappropriate and occasioned the stares of stuffed-shirt onlookers dressed in suits and cocktail gowns. On the other hand, he mitigated the awkwardness of the situation by behaving as if nothing were awry, coaching the students through the meal and patiently fielding all their questions. For rural mountain adolescents, this proved to be a *sui generis* exposure to high-stepping society.

In his 5 March directive to the Foxfire staff, Wigginton had classified Reynolds's string-band concept under the rubric, "valuable, but not particularly transferable." On the other hand, he included folklore as one of the Foxfire courses that "was not only valuable in our school situation but also transferable."[45] These assessments were ironic because they constituted a *reversal* of Reynold's own teaching preferences and priorities.

The folklore class taught by Reynolds in the spring of 1984 bore scant resemblance to the Foxfire philosophy. The key elements of that philosophy (the creation of a quality end product through the application of intellectual skills) were either ignored or given token attention (the explicit linkage of subject matter to the local community). These omissions were exacerbated by Reynolds's lack of thorough planning and his frequent lateness either to the class or in getting it underway.

Given the small size of the class—only five students—Reynolds had ample opportunity to teach a course along the lines prescribed by Wigginton; instead, he resorted to the lecture materials of previous quarters—materials that drew heavily upon the key structures and concepts of folklore, e.g., *magic* (imitative and contagious), *culture* (folk, popular, and elite), *narrative* (personal experience, anecdote, and legend), and *truth* (factual truth, "human truth," and philosophical truth). One of Wigginton's reasons for hiring Reynolds had been to add a professional folklorist to his staff—a response to Richard Dorson's criticism of the *Foxfire* books, which Dorson considered "unprofessional" partly because Wigginton and his students had ignored the essential structures of academic folklore in their handling of folkloric materials. Yet Wigginton had not intended that Reynolds teach folklore in a traditional lecture-based format and in a fashion that did not require students to participate actively in their own learning. The closest students came to such participation were rambling discussions that required little if any preparation on their part and perfunctory homework assignments (e.g., present a list of twenty-five examples of "cool" and "uncool" behavior), which Reynolds rarely collected or rigorously examined.

Directed by Wigginton in 1976 to create a program of Appalachian music with research and writing components, and, if possible, a record company, Reynolds had accomplished these objectives by 1980. He had started Foxfire Records, produced two albums of Appalachian music (*The North Georgia Mountains* and *It Still Lives*), and organized the Foxfire String Band. The record company idea was the closest that Reynolds came to applying the key elements of the original Foxfire philosophy. Here students not only participated in every phase of record production, from locating traditional musicians to marketing the albums, they were also involved in the oral history research that provided the narrative commentary for the inserts. Yet Foxfire Records did not prove to be a viable marketing idea. The two albums produced between 1978 and 1980 collectively sold fewer than nine hundred copies; even the two Foxfire Boys String Band tapes enjoyed only a marginal success, with eight hundred copies sold by the end of 1984. Moreover, the tapes of the Rabun County Gospel Singing Convention and the Christian Harmony singers were expected to generate few sales.

After 1982 Reynolds discontinued the record production class at Rabun County High School. The educational benefits of the program did not justify the huge expenditure of time and money necessary to produce a single album. During the summer of 1984, Reynolds and a former student (assisted by a member of the Foxfire String Band) compiled taped interviews with members of the Rabun County Gospel Singing Convention for publication as an entire issue of *Foxfire* (dated Winter 1984).

At two staff meetings during the summer of 1984, Wigginton voiced his concern that music performance had received too heavy an emphasis at the expense of other academic/intellectual skills that could, and should, be addressed by Reynolds in his classes. He stated that he expected Reynolds to develop a course that included skills (e.g., research and writing related to music) that would help the Foxfire music students get to and succeed in college: "I want to see what the music component does in terms of the . . . skills the school, by law, is supposed to address." While he acknowledged the value of the present music program to the school and community, Wigginton also stated: "You have an obligation to do whatever you can do in terms of getting [your music students] ready for college. The kind of music program that you're [currently teaching] isn't going to be as transferable as we would like it to be. . . . You can still do the music but give me one good transferable course."

With good reason, Wigginton did not mention folklore as the course Reynolds should be restructuring. Since the 5 March staff meeting at which Wigginton had included folklore as a "transferable" Foxfire course, the social studies department had removed it from the list of courses that fulfilled departmental graduation requirements, contending that folklore did not adequately address academic skills. In Wigginton's view, Foxfire could not justify funding an elective course that would likely attract only a handful of students. (In the fall of 1984, Wigginton and Reynolds jointly taught an English-credit course in Appalachian literature, which was keyed to state competency objectives.)

Wigginton's directive put his teaching staff in a quandary: the division instructors had spent years fashioning their courses along lines that were, in some key respects, inconsistent with the philosophy now being mandated. The fault lay with Wigginton who had failed to imbue his staff with this philosophy at the outset and had allowed individual teachers to pursue their own curriculum interests willy-nilly without pedagogical guidance. Moreover, Wigginton had not held his staff accountable for maintaining academic standards, as suggested by the paucity of discussion about curriculum matters at weekly staff meetings[46] and his habit of not evaluating each staff member's teaching performance. The result of these omissions was an entire organization at personal and philosophical loose ends in 1984.

The staff member least resistant to Wigginton's refocusing of Foxfire's educational goals was Mike Cook. For several years, Cook and Wigginton had discussed a Rabun County landownership study that would fill a gap in the research conducted by the Task Force of the Appalachian Alliance in the mountain counties of six Southern states. Such a study would not only integrate the components of television production (e.g., videotaped interviews) with narrative writing, but also would teach students how to do courthouse (read *primary source*) research and manage tax and demographic data.

A participatory research effort involving citizens from throughout the region, the Appalachian Alliance Task Force study had focused on the problems of absentee landownership and development in both the mineral-producing and tourist counties. The task force conducted extensive courthouse research in eighty counties of the six states and reached the following major conclusions. First, the dearth of an adequate tax base to support quality schools, roads, and public services in the mineral-producing counties was attributable, in large part, to the failure of absentee corporations to pay their fair share of property taxes; aided by their allies in state government, these absentee owners had taken advantage of antiquated tax laws to avoid paying the considerable sums that rightfully belonged to the counties. Second, federal ownership of huge tracts of forest land in the tourist counties excluded this valuable property from business and housing development (and subsequently from the county tax base); federal payments in lieu of taxes provided only a fraction of the tax revenue the property could have generated under private ownership. Third, nonunionized factory labor and seasonal labor in the mountain tourist industry dominated the labor markets in the tourist counties; the low annual wages in both sectors removed the element of competition among the industries that might have elevated per capita income.[47]

Curiously, the Appalachian Alliance had ignored the mountainous northeast quadrant of Georgia in its report. Wigginton and Cook hoped to redress this omission by having the television production students apply the task force's research methodology to an examination of the role of landownership patterns in shaping Rabun County's economy. The publication of this methodology provided the impetus for Cook to initiate such a study with his students.

On 27 March 1984, Cook and five students met after school in Wigginton's classroom to discuss the Appalachian Alliance study and the methodology developed by Highlander Folk Center staff members John Gaventa and Bill Horton. These students did some preliminary work on the study as an extracurricular activity in April, gathering information about county government and local school financing. Concerned that the students' research might occasion suspicion in the community about their motives, Wigginton advised them in words similar to the following: "We need a good tight answer as to how this information will be used. To get it tight and to offset the implication that we're trying to expose something, make it a tape for eighth-grade history and twelfth-grade government."

Two of these students conducted off-camera interviews with county officials during the summer, and by the late fall the group had compiled information from the county tax digest. Cook also sent two students to a two-week summer workshop at the Highlander Center in New Market, Tennessee, where leading social activists conducted consciousness-raising activities for high school students with respect to environmental issues, civil rights, and community politics and economics. The students also met with Bill Horton and other land study experts and examined the landownership files at Highlander, which had been the headquarters for the Appalachian Alliance task force.

Yet by the late fall, the study was making only marginal progress. "I haven't been doing much on it," said one participant, also a student in Cook's advanced community television class. "It's kind of at a standstill. There's so much different stuff we've got to do from last summer—editing and stuff" (i.e., editing tapes for Foxfire Video Productions that were unrelated to the landownership study).

As a thorough scrutiny of his introductory television course (Video I) and occasional visits to his advanced course revealed, Cook had incorporated the key elements of Wigginton's philosophy (e.g., community-based activities focused on creating a high-quality end product, an audience beyond the classroom, a nonpunitive, supportive learning environment) in his teaching, with the critical exception of academic skills. In the introductory course, he first taught students the fundamentals of setting up and operating video equipment and television lights, interviewing, and editing; after mastering these technical skills, the students worked individually or in small groups to plan and develop a television program for broadcast on the local cable station.

Accompanied by Cook, the students took their equipment into the Rabun County community to tape programs on topics as diverse as the Rabun County Animal Shelter, Sheriff Chester York, and weaver Marinda Brown. The following passage from my field notes briefly describes one such interview:

> I meet Mike after school at South Rabun Elementary and transfer to the Foxfire station wagon for the trip to Tut Woodruff's with Mike, Patricia and Jesse. Tut is a Coca-Cola heiress who lives on Lake Burton. I help lug the equipment into Tut's lake house, still in the process of construction. Patricia and Jesse set up on the sun deck, Patricia on sound and Jesse on camera, and Mike makes some adjustments to the lens.
>
> Tut is a sixty-one-year-old hang-gliding enthusiast who owns a mountain

in Rabun County called Hang Glider Heaven, which is sanctioned by the United States Hang Glider Association. She is seated with her back to the water and the mountains beyond. Patricia rolls the camera, and Jesse gets the interview underway with the loquacious Tut. Mike absents himself. Unaware that the microphone she's wearing doesn't pick up much extraneous noise, Tut tells the kids to cut off the video as trucks go by the house: "Now we've got some noise, so you can shut off the camera for a minute." Mike shakes Jesse's hand after the interview—he's been listening from behind the door that leads from the sun deck into the house—and says, "You did a real good job, Jesse." Next Tut stands on the sun deck and yells through her megaphone to passing boats while Jesse shoots cover shots of the lake and mountains and Tut's yelling and waving.

Cook's advanced course was distinguishable from the introductory course, as follows. First, Video II students had already mastered all the fundamentals and were honing their skills in developing new projects; second, Cook's presence was not required on most interviews—unless the student did not have access to a car. For example, two students carried the video equipment into the mountains to tape an operating liquor still (without the proprietor's knowledge) and then cajoled an active moonshiner to talk about his craft while positioned behind a screen so that only his shadow was visible to the camera.

In both courses the educational focus was explicitly *technical* and not academic. Moreover, Cook allowed some students to miss assignment deadlines without an excuse and even to produce hastily contrived tapes—all without significant penalty. One senior's comments suggested that for some advanced students, community television (a ten-hour credit) was a virtually painless and effortless way to acquire two electives: "We've never come up short yet. We can put a rush job on ours. When we feel like doing it, we'll do it. We goof off, but when it comes down to it, when we've got no other option, we do it—as it's coming now when we've got fifteen days left [in the quarter] and we've got to get something done. In other words, we'll probably be working our butts off 'til the end of the quarter. We can always tell when Cook gets mad. If we sit around for two weeks and do nothing, that's when we know we have to start straightening up the shelves or get out a show."

This criticism is not to suggest that other students did not take their video work more seriously. For example, a shy, reclusive ninth-grade student for whom community television was an extracurricular activity as well as a class, spoke with obvious pride of craftsmanship about his program on bluegrass musicians, the tape of which he showed in his home community of Satolah: "I thought I did a real good job on it.

It looked good. They [the student's family] really liked it. Mama was proud of it; Daddy was too. [The musicians] saw it. A lot of people around the community saw it. They just sat and watched. They liked it. It felt real good that I did a good job of it. I was real proud of that. They were the first interviews I'd done for tape."

A serious problem in both courses (two classes of Video I and one two-hour block of Video II) was the excessive amount of time students spent *not* working on their productions. In the Video I course, the problem arose in the final three to four weeks of the quarter when students were either scheduling follow-up interviews with their subjects or taking turns at the editing machine, laboriously culling and sequencing their tapes and adding the audio narrative. One conscientious student explained the problem as follows: "I had a lot of space between them [two interviews]. I couldn't get in touch with Mr. Ramey [her subject]. . . . During that time [three weeks], I didn't have anything to do."

In Video II, the time-lag problem was, in large part, a function of scheduling. In 1982–83, the course had been scheduled as a two-hour block to accommodate the traveling time necessary to get the students to and from the Foxfire television studio in downtown Clayton. When Cook abandoned the studio and moved his program back to the high school, an adjustment was not made in the school schedule to reflect the change; consequently, he had a two-hour block of time in which to keep students focused on a single activity. During a given hour, the observer could expect to find some students working on their projects, others engaging in a variety of off-task behaviors, such as reading a romance novel or congregating on the media center promenade with friends.

Like Wigginton's magazine class, Foxfire community television productions had become repetitious and formulaic. From quarter to quarter, students turned out the same type of product, with differences only of degree, not of kind. For example, two students in Video II, one of whom had been in the program several years, were allowed to produce a simplistic, unimaginative tape of an interview with the county's parks and recreation director.

The Rabun County Landownership Study represents, at the rhetorical level, a shift in a new direction that would incorporate academic skills into the community television program. Yet by year's end, as the testimony of a major participant suggested, Cook had not given the study a working priority over the other materials the students were producing.

Of Foxfire's three division heads, Bob Bennett, the environmentalist/outdoor educator, was the furthest removed from the philosophy Wigginton had articulated in *Moments* and reaffirmed at the 5 March staff meeting. Outdoor education and running, albeit popular and useful physical education courses, were expressly unrelated to the Foxfire learning concept. In his two-hour environmental science/outdoor education block, Bennett sought to help a handful of disaffected ninth- and tenth-grade boys adjust to the social and academic demands of school life—a laudable project, but divergent from Wigginton's expressed goal of creating an academically sound, community-based environmental science course that would be transferable to other schools.

Labeling Bennett's course "almost a special education situation," Wigginton remarked: "A smarter and more efficient way to use that block would be a serious environmental class. What I'm consistently asking myself is am I . . . getting my money's worth? What you have is between one third and one half of his salary being expended on four or five people. That's a lot of money."

Bennett's work with this select group of students, nonetheless, drew praise from teachers, guidance counselors, and students. A guidance official described Bennett's contribution to the school:

> The kid he looks for is the one who's on the verge of being kicked out of school—the most obvious hell-raiser and rebellious type of kid, disruptive of classroom proceedings, interfering with the learning of others. These are the ones we try to give to him. You can imagine the relief some of the teachers have to get rid of those kids. . . . What [Bob] tries to do is to get their heads back on straight. He works on the chips on their shoulders. He tries to get them to work with other people, not to resent authority, and take personal pride in themselves. After a quarter or two—with most—their grades [in other classes] go up.

One of Bennett's former students who had made a smooth adjustment to school life described Bennett's influence:

> In my other classes I didn't feel like doing my work. I was making bad grades. One of my science teachers talked to Mr. Bennett, and that's why I was put in that class. I was in the tenth grade at the time. He was really somebody who cared about what was happening to me. . . . I got in the class with a bunch of different people with different problems. With Bob nudging me, I'd nudge others. Later he pulled me aside and congratulated me on assuming leadership and more or less put me in charge of the group to guide it [and] keep it rolling. The nudge was a moral[e] boost [that] made me feel like I should work, if not for myself, for him. . . . He gave you a feeling of confidence about yourself.

Wigginton terminated Bennett's block course at the end of the 1983–84 academic year, substituting in its place an environmental science course that incorporated text materials, field trips, and environmental studies in the local community. In the spring of 1984, Bennett began preliminary work on the course, assisted by a biology teacher at the high school; yet he was not comfortable with the change.

Bennett's disquietude was apparently rooted in the discrepancy between the organizational ethos that had fostered and guided the development of his courses and Wigginton's new mandate to shore up Foxfire's academic foundations. His personal dilemma was that of an individual who had a strong rapport with adolescents and a plethora of creative technical skills but lacked the formal training and accreditation required by the state to teach an academic course.

Bennett taught the new environmental science course in 1984–85 and developed a curriculum guide geared to state competency objectives; however, in the spring of 1985, he resigned from Foxfire. Prompting his resignation was the county superintendent's mandate that all Foxfire teaching personnel obtain certification or be released from the high school. In a letter to his boards, Wigginton described the turn of events as follows:

> Bob has made the decision not to become certified. Instead, he has accepted a job offered him by the Rabun Gap–Nacoochee School. Paid by Rabun Gap, he will be helping students conduct independent study projects, guiding environmental studies programs, and coaching track and cross country. A new science teacher recently hired by RCHS will take over the environmental science courses he initiated there, and will be supervising activities on the ropes course Bob built with Project Adventure. A cross country coach will also be hired by the county to take his place. We have given the school's new environmental science teacher permission to use the cabin Bob and his students built for the program. . . .
>
> The staff change is a serious one since Bob has been with us for eight years. In two ways, however, it carries with it unexpected benefits. First, Bob initiated the environmental courses and the cross country team at RCHS, under funding from Foxfire. As testimony to the popularity of these programs, they will be continued, but with state and county funding rather than funding from us.
>
> Second, Bob will not be severing his connections with Foxfire. Rather, some of the Rabun Gap students' independent study projects will be conducted using our resources, and through Bob's work, Rabun Gap and Rabun County students may soon be working together again as they used to during the days before the new RCHS complex opened.[48]

The Politics of Egalitarianism in a 501(c)(3) Organization

A related source of organizational tensions in 1984 was the factional-ism that existed between two groups—the Foxfire Press/Grants Man-agement Office and the Foxfire Fund. Although legally part of the Fund, the Press maintained a separate budget drawn from the $400,000 royalty advance from E. P. Dutton in 1982. Similarly, the Grants Management Office, which was closely allied to the Press by virtue of the latter's community development role, relied primarily on external funding from the Charles Stewart Mott Foundation and the Public Welfare Foundation. Doubleday royalties supported Foxfire's educational programs at the high school. This tripartite funding ar-rangement paralleled the physical insularity of the various Foxfire entities. As a Foxfire teacher observed: "In terms of organization, the Press feels like it's an island up there [in Mountain City], we feel like we're an island at school, and they [Grants Management Office] feel like they're an island on 'the land.'"

Comments by Foxfire teachers who opposed Foxfire's expansion into community development suggested that the conflict between the two factions was rooted in their divergent views of what the organiza-tion's community role should be. "I was afraid it would pull us in another direction," one stated. "And it has. It's spread too thin."

On the other hand, Press/GMO staff complained about the lack of support and cooperation from their colleagues who worked at the high school. Not only did this group feel beleaguered, but some of its members also charged or insinuated that other Foxfire employees were underworked and overpaid. "A lot of the staff are on the gravy train," stated a Foxfire administrator.

Significantly, this intra-staff conflict was *not* evident during any of Foxfire's numerous staff meetings (including its three-day staff retreat on Lake Burton) held throughout 1984. The bitterness and acrimony surfaced only in the context of interviews or private conversations with staff members. This organizational tendency to avoid *overt* con-flict was both a reflection of and response to Wigginton's style of administrative leadership.

At one level, Wigginton managed an egalitarian organization in which each staff member from the administrative secretary to the Foxfire teachers to Wigginton himself cast an equal vote. At their weekly staff meetings, virtually devoid of any discussion about peda-gogy until the fall of 1984, Foxfire employees discussed and adjudi-cated administrative matters, from budgets and insurance to hiring a conservator to maintaining the unpaved road at the Foxfire Center.

The purpose of these meetings, Wigginton remarked at a teacher workshop, was "to make sure everybody is going in the same direction."

Curiously, Wigginton reserved even the pettiest of administrative details for staff discussion. On one occasion the staff debated whether or not Foxfire was responsible for paying the $124 owed by a former Foxfire maintenance man to a local convenience store. The store's owner had charged that he had allowed the debt to accrue because he knew the maintenance man worked for Foxfire, implying that the organization had a moral responsibility to pay the debt. A Foxfire staff member resolved the immediate crisis (although not the underlying issue) by volunteering to pay the $124 on behalf of the former maintenance man, who had moved to West Virginia.

Three staff members provided testimony that Foxfire was *not* the democratic organization that Wigginton professed it to be; in fact, their responses suggested that on major issues they voted *with* Wigginton simply to avoid conflict.

> There are things I've felt we shouldn't go into but I've just kept my mouth shut. When you voice objections to Wig, it creates a problem. I think we have a very dictatorial staff. If the [legal] board views it as a town meeting kind of thing, that's because Wig lets us share the blame. We are allowed input. It's a heck of a lot more democratic than that situation at the high school where people have no input. (Staff Member A)

> Wig decides everything. If Wig wants it, he goes ahead and does it. We're going to vote [for] it because there's no use doing it any other way. (Staff Member B)

> If Wig really wants something, he gets it. We'll go along with him. (Staff Member C)

Conflict avoidance at Foxfire was a two-edged sword. For his part, Wigginton refused to confront staff members whose actions defied organizational policy. For example, a staff member absented himself with impunity from ten of the twelve curriculum-planning meetings held throughout the fall of 1984. Wigginton privately admitted his unwillingness to confront the refractory teacher despite the salience of these meetings to the development of the Foxfire curriculum guides.

At a staff meeting held on 17 July 1984, Wigginton presented a letter from a legal board member (dated 6 July) that reflected his own views about strengthening the entire Foxfire curriculum. An excerpt from the letter reads as follows: "I am somewhat old fashioned in that I believe on average that the thorough teaching of the three R's provides an individual with the best tools to succeed. Development of talent skills, craft skills, art skills, sport skills, mechanical skills, etc., are, of course, important but clearly secondary to the three R's in primary and secondary education. Certainly the 1980s have shown us that 'doing our own thing' doesn't pay the rent."

Significantly, Wigginton used the letter as a mouthpiece to restate points he had made at the 5 March staff meeting and later at the 6–7 June Foxfire staff retreat. His action conveyed two implicit messages: He was dissatisfied with the progress staff members had made in carrying out the mandate he had issued at the 5 March staff meeting; he *assumed* that his staff would resist the mandate, knowing that he would not enforce it unless it were explicitly validated by Foxfire's legal board—an action that would shift the onus of enforcement from Wigginton to a higher authority. A week later, Wigginton remarked to me: "What pisses me off is that I've been making clear for some time now exactly what's demanded. One reason I haven't moved sooner on this is that now I have the board and Karl Mathiasen [a business management consultant to Foxfire] and other sources telling them the same thing. I have something I can go to the staff with and tell them, 'Look, I'm getting this from the board and Karl Mathiasen and that's the way it is.'"

Whatever the reasons behind an individual staff member's vote (or other expression of approval) on issues in 1984, the fact remained that issues, as well as administrative minutiae, were examined and discussed *ad nauseam* at Foxfire staff meetings. Moreover, a given issue was likely to be tabled to another meeting where, after protracted discussion, it was likely to be tabled to yet another meeting. A case in point was the circumlocutory debate surrounding the proposed hiring of a conservator for the Foxfire Center log house reconstructions and museum collections. Discussion of whom to hire for the position began on 12 March, continued through 30 April (six staff meetings), and terminated with the decision to hire a Rabun County High School teacher as a summer maintenance man.

A former community advisory board member and longtime friend of Foxfire commented on the organization's penchant for excessive deliberation: "My only concern over the years is that they move slow. . . . I've accepted it. It used to bother me—rehashing things over and over." An incredulous consultant to Foxfire, after observing a three-hour staff meeting, remarked: "Are *all* the meetings like this? You must be bored stiff."

Asked by Wigginton to share my tentative impressions of the organization at its June staff retreat, I commented on the staff's tendency to sidestep pedagogical issues and to focus on administrative matters that had only marginal bearing on the organization's educational programs and could have easily been handled by a single staff member. (Here my role temporarily changed from an observer to an advisor.)

Wigginton responded to this criticism in the fall of 1984 along two fronts. First, although he continued his practice of allowing staff debate and voting on organizational issues, he infused a measure of discipline in the weekly meetings by authorizing a newly hired staff member to organize, with input from other staff members, an agenda for each meeting and to enforce the time limit prescribed for discussion of each item. Second, he bifurcated the staff meetings, relegating administrative matters to the first half and reserving the second half for planning the course guides that were to be available for dissemination after the release of his book to teachers in the fall of 1985.

Throughout the watershed year of 1984—the year that witnessed the end of Foxfire's Doubleday series, the organization's first budgetary crisis, the shift in direction from community development to national curriculum dissemination, the attendant modifications of the Foxfire curriculum at Rabun County High School, and the end of the era of benign neglect by county and state school officials—it was evident that Foxfire was about to enter a new phase of its history that would require firm and decisive administrative leadership if the organization were to accomplish its educational goals.

This assessment builds on a model developed by Nancy E. Franco and associates—prominent observers of the patterns of nonprofit organizations. According to the model, there are four stages through which the "non-profit" must pass, each stage a prerequisite for the next. The first stage, "creativity," aptly describes Foxfire during its Rabun Gap era.

> The founder or founders are usually highly creative entrepreneurs who are committed to the organization's goals. They attract a few other highly committed people and jump into long hours of work rewarded by the importance of the cause and a modest salary. Thus, the management's focus is the cause; the organizational structure is informal; top management style is highly individualistic; control systems are limited to direct, often tangible results; and the rewards are primarily mission and meaning. . . . The flexibility that the informality and commitment permit is essential for the new organization to establish itself.[49]

The model is equally useful as an analytical tool for examining Foxfire's first crisis—at heart a crisis of leadership engendered by the array of factors underlying Wigginton's decision to strengthen Foxfire's academic agenda. "It is usually a crisis of leadership," Franco et al. assert. "Stronger management is necessary, but creative founders are often neither interested in nor temperamentally suited to this kind of managerial direction. As a result, it is usually very difficult for them to let go of their 'baby' and allow the organization to bring in more effective managerial staff."[50]

Apropos of the model, Wigginton is ill-suited, both by temperament and previous experience, to provide the strong leadership that will be necessary to ensure formal accountability on the part of his staff to the organization's redefined educational standards. He once remarked, "What I want to do is teach. I'm not an administrator. I'm not a boss. I'm a teacher. That's what I do best."[51] A former Foxfire staff member tersely summarized Wigginton's administrative dilemma as follows: "Wig is a good, decent man, but he can't manage worth a shit."

Equally apropos of the model, it is unlikely that Wigginton will ever relinquish or even share his position as "first among equals" at Foxfire. While not entirely a cult of personality, Foxfire is *his* "baby." A staff member who resigned from Foxfire in 1985 put it this way: "There must be someone on staff with the knowledge and experience to oversee the organization in a more professional manner. . . . Wig is not the man for that job. . . . He admits that, but still neglects to do anything about the problem."[52]

The model assumes that the only rational response to the stage-one crisis is a more dictatorial style of leadership and an end to the era of informality—a necessary precursor to the "direction" stage characterized by centralized authority and directive managerial leadership. The crisis of the direction stage is excessive rigidity in governance, the rational response to which is increased staff autonomy and the passage to a third stage called "delegation." Yet this decentralization of authority typically fragments the nonprofit organization into staff "fiefdoms" in which organizational goals become secondary to individual project goals. This last crisis begets the fourth stage of "consolidation" in which individual and organizational goals are finally harmonized, albeit in a climate of dictatorial management and bureaucratic red tape.

It is a given that Foxfire can survive in an attenuated form, at least for another twenty years, entirely on the strength of its $1.8 million endowment. Moreover, renewed national interest in Foxfire stimulated by Wigginton's book to teachers may even generate foundation support that will allow the organization to maintain the present level of its programs indefinitely. But if Wigginton intends to make the leap from rhetoric to reality by creating a set of transferable courses that effectively integrate academic and personal growth skills (a balanced equation), he must disabuse himself of the illusion that his present ambivalent style of leadership will suffice to achieve this goal.

As indicated previously, the skills and interests of his teaching staff are nonacademic. To infuse academics into a curriculum top-heavy with technical skills and "feel good" activities, Wigginton must enforce a realignment of staff priorities. If individual staff members cannot keep pace with his demands or prove refractory, he will have to replace them. In sum, Foxfire's successful transition to the "direction" stage hinges on Wigginton's ability to step out of character and subordinate personal loyalties to his teaching staff to his ideals for the organization.

NOTES

1. Daniel Tanner and Laurel N. Tanner, *Curriculum Development: Theory into Practice* (New York: Macmillan, 1980), 125.

2. Jonathan Kozol, *Death at an Early Age: The Destruction of the Hearts and Minds of Negro Children in the Boston Public Schools* (Boston: Houghton Mifflin, 1967), viii.

3. Ibid., 133.

4. Pat Conroy, *The Water Is Wide* (Boston: Houghton Mifflin, 1972), 275.

5. Ibid., 23.

6. Ibid., 196.

7. Ibid., 299.

8. James Herndon, *The Way It Spozed to Be* (New York: Simon and Schuster, 1965), 167.

9. Ibid., 165.

10. Herbert Kohl, *Growing Minds: On Becoming a Teacher* (New York: Harper and Row, 1984), 31–34, 48–49.

11. Herbert Kohl, *36 Children* (New York: New American Library, 1967), 42.

12. Ibid., 205.

13. Ibid., 163.

14. Herbert Kohl to Eliot Wigginton, 29 September 1970.

15. Kohl to Wigginton, 2 January 1972.

16. Kohl to Foxfire, 24 September 1979.

17. There are few regional precedents against which the wisdom of Wigginton's decision to avoid social controversy might be assessed. As social historian David Whisnant has noted, the reform agendas of the Appalachian folk and settlement school movements of the early and middle decades of this century were not oriented toward radical school change. While eastern Kentucky's Hindman Settlement School and western North Carolina's John C.

Campbell Folk School, Whisnant's primary examples, provided programs of basic (and conventional) education for impoverished mountain children and job opportunities for adults in their crafts industries, the leaders of both schools focused their energies on traditional craft revivalism in lieu of more profound social, political and economic issues—in Hindman's case, exploitation of the region's mineral wealth and indigenous labor by absentee owners; in Campbell's case, the dislocations caused by tourism and the expanded federal presence in the southern highlands (See David Whisnant, *All That Is Native and Fine: The Politics of Culture in an American Region* [Chapel Hill: University of North Carolina Press, 1983], 69–78, 178, 261).

Two educational movements, however, did not avoid social controversy and paid a heavy price for their radical activities. The first was the Macedonia cooperative community, founded by Quakers in north Georgia's Habersham County (adjacent to Rabun County) in the late 1920s. According to Whisnant, Macedonia experienced a "modest success" as a mountain farmers' cooperative, but lost its community support (and its vigor) when it affiliated with "the national and international radical pacifist movements" during World War II and invited political activists to join the community (Whisnant, *All That Is Native and Fine*, 178).

The Highlander Folk School, located first in Summerville, Tennessee, and later in New Market (in the foothills of the Great Smoky Mountains), exerted a powerful national influence as an organizing center for southern textile workers, coal miners, teamsters, and various industrial groups from 1935 to 1952. Founded by Myles Horton, a labor organizer influenced by the socialist theories of Reinhold Niebuhr and the pragmatism of John Dewey and William James, Highlander became, in the words of Horton's biographer, "a practical educational program that sent countless new leaders into the fight to build unions" (Frank Adams, *Unearthing Seeds of Fire: The Idea of Highlander* [Winston-Salem, N.C.: John F. Blair, 1975], 72).

In 1952 Horton and his colleagues shifted their focus from labor union organizing to the struggle for black civil rights. Highlander workshops helped blacks to organize and educate themselves for voter registration drives throughout the South, particularly the Freedom Summer of 1964. Horton was also instrumental in establishing the Citizenship Schools, which taught reading and writing in black schools, and had reportedly educated one hundred thousand blacks by 1970.

Over the years, militantly conservative Southerners, including the Ku Klux Klan, have resorted to arson and other violent acts in their attempts to drive out Highlander. When burnings and beatings failed, Horton's enemies resorted to quasi-legal tactics. In a county court proceeding held in Altamount, Tennessee, in the early 1960s, the prosecution won a specious ruling "that Highlander had sold beer and other items without a license, that the school was operated for Horton's personal gain, and that it had practiced racial integration in violation of Title 49, Section 3701 of Tennessee law forbidding such practice" (Adams, *Unearthing Seeds of Fire*, 140). Horton denied the first two charges but vigorously affirmed the third. The court placed Highlander's property in receivership and liquidated it at a public auction. Undaunted, Horton relocated the center first in Knoxville and later in New Market, where, as the Highlander Research and Education Center, it continues its work of organizing and educating poor people to speak and act for themselves.

18. Eliot Wigginton, "Up against Success," *Exchange* 2, no. 1 (1974): 17.

19. Wigginton, ed., *Foxfire 2*, 12.

20. Wigginton to Kohl, 22 September 1978.

21. Erikson, *Identity: Youth and Crisis*, 156.

22. *Foxfire*, Winter 1971, 221–24.

23. *Foxfire*, Summer 1974, 147–49.

24. See Wigginton's discussion of these elements of his philosophy in his introduction to *Foxfire 6* (Garden City, N.Y.: Anchor Press/Doubleday, 1980), 7–24; Wigginton, "Is Your School Doing Its Job?: Lessons from the Foxfire Experience," *Southern Exposure* 10 (January/February 1982), 53–59; and Wigginton, review of John J. Mitchell, *The Adolescent Predicament*, in *Nameless Newsletter* 1 (March 1978), 21–23.

25. A case in point is the National Science Foundation's seven-volume report on the status of mathematics, science, and social studies education (1978), fully cited in Appendix A (Bibliographical Notes) and discussed in Chapter 11 of my study.

26. Wigginton, *Shining Moment*, 329.

27. Ibid., 333.

28. Tammy Blume, "Foxfire Reflections," May 1984.

29. Bil Dwyer, *Thangs Yankees Don' Know* (Highlands, N.C.: Merry Mountaineers, 1975).

30. In fairness to Dwyer, it should be noted that Horace Kephart, a sojourner in the Great Smoky Mountains in the early 1900s, reported that "a 'cooter' is a box-tortoise, and the noun is turned into a verb with an ease characteristic of the mountaineers" (*Our Southern Highlanders* [New York: Outing Publishing, 1913], 203).

31. Wigginton, *Shining Moment*, 375.

32. *Hands On* 3, no. 2 (1980), unpaginated.

33. John Dewey, *Experience and Education* (New York: Macmillan, 1938), especially 1–11, 77–85.

34. Wigginton, *Shining Moment*, 378.

35. John Dewey, *Democracy and Education* (New York: Macmillan, 1916), 46, 220–21.

36. Ibid., 188.

37. Wigginton, *Shining Moment*, 71–72.

38. Wigginton, ed., *Foxfire 2*, 10–11.

39. Eliot Wigginton, "The Foxfire Concept," in *Teaching Mountain Children: Towards a Foundation of Understanding*, ed. David N. Mielke (Boone, N.C.: Appalachian Consortium Press, 1978), 211.

40. Eliot Wigginton, *Moments: The Foxfire Experience* (Washington, D.C.: IDEAS, 1975), 17–54.

41. Ibid., 70–91.

42. Ibid., 16.

43. Parks, "Foxfire: Experiential Education in America," 284.

44. "Timetable 1984," Foxfire staff document, 5 March 1984.

45. Ibid.

46. From January to August 1984, the focus of Foxfire staff meetings, with few exceptions, was administrative matters. Apparently, this had become an organizational pattern, as evidenced by the dearth of references to curriculum in the minutes of 1983 staff meetings.

47. Appalachian Landownership Task Force, *Who Owns Appalachia? Landownership and Its Impact* (Lexington: University Press of Kentucky, 1983).

48. Wigginton, "Report to the Boards," 15 May 1985.

49. Nancy Franco, Susan Gross, and Karl Mathiasen, III, "Passages: Organizational Life Cycles," Management Assistance Group, Washington, D.C., May/June 1982, 1.

50. Ibid., 2

51. Wigginton made this remark in a videotaped interview conducted by a student, February 1984.

52. The resigning staff member submitted this statement in a letter to the Foxfire boards, 16 September 1985.

Aunt Arie Carpenter (Courtesy Foxfire)

Eliot Wigginton (Photo: Owen L. Riley, Jr., courtesy Foxfire)

The Foxfire Center on Black Rock Mountain (Courtesy Foxfire)

George Reynolds (left) and members of the Foxfire String Band (Courtesy Foxfire)

Eliot Wigginton (center) with students in a Foxfire I class (Courtesy Foxfire)

The Rothell House on Foxfire's Mountain City property (Courtesy Foxfire)

Foxfire student Chet Welch (left) interviewing an elderly Appalachian woman (Courtesy Foxfire)

Appalachian contact Johnny Eller (right) explaining old-time toy making in a Foxfire I class (Courtesy Foxfire)

Eliot Wigginton (right) with community elders at the annual Foxfire Contacts Picnic (Courtesy Foxfire)

The play *Foxfire* at the Guthrie Theater, Minneapolis, with (left to right) Hume Cronyn as Hector Nations, Jessica Tandy as Annie Nations, Richard Cox as Dillard Nations, and Catherine Cortez as Holly Burrell (Photo: Bruce Goldstein, courtesy Guthrie Theater)

Foxfire contact Jake Waldroop (right) and his prize Hereford bull (Courtesy Foxfire)

Foxfire contact Buck Carver and his miniature liquor still (Courtesy Foxfire)

A scene from Foxfire's early years: (left to right) Elizabeth Rickman, Andrea Burrell, and Emma Buchanan interviewing Andrea's grandmother, Pearl Martin, about old-time soap making (Courtesy Foxfire)

Wesley Taylor (left) and Mitch Whitmire (right) with Leonard Webb (center) and his gourd banjo (Courtesy Foxfire)

PART THREE

Issues and Effects Writ Large:
Foxfire and the Global Contexts
of American Education

EIGHT

Foxfire and the Progressive Tradition

Foxfire's Progressive Dilemma

On 23 August 1984, in preparation for the 1984–85 academic year, Wigginton assembled his staff for a full day's discussion of a strategy for revising each division's curriculum along lines that were consistent with the basic tenets of Deweyan philosophy, as well as with the objectives of the Georgia Competency-Based Education/Basic Skills Test (CBE/BST). After six months of periodic harangues about the necessity of bolstering Foxfire's academic agenda, Wigginton presented at this meeting a set of revision guidelines for his staff members to follow—guidelines that were to apply to *all* Foxfire courses. A description of this pivotal meeting provides a context for discussion of Wigginton's links to the progressive education movement, with particular attention paid to John Dewey's seminal works, and for analysis of the lessons of this tradition for the Foxfire experience.

Preparatory to discussing the specifics of curriculum revision, Wigginton reminded his staff of the reasons underlying the creation of the Foxfire concept and presented a terse statement of the organization's educational mission. He began with a disquisition about his salvation as a floundering tenth-grade student at the Hill School by teacher Jack Tyrer, who helped him publish an essay in the school's literary magazine:

> That act of generosity on his part is the reason why I became a ninth-grade teacher. Jack Tyrer, when he realized I was going under, didn't come up and put his arm around me and pat me on the back. Instead he indicated that he was going to prove to me that I could do competent work in an academic context. He watched what I did over a period of time and gave me encour-

agement and stretched me to a higher level. He became the agent for me to handle the kind of material I hadn't been able to handle before. That was why *Foxfire* magazine started—to prove to students that they could achieve in an academic context. Those are the roots of the whole project.

There are some fairly sophisticated delivery systems to this craft [teaching]. We believe we are capable of coming up with a more powerful delivery system for teaching academic skills. That delivery system involves the linkage of those academic skills and the community and the application of those skills in the service of creating products judged by those people to have worth. At the same time, we serve the community also. What we're about is the creating, refining, and polishing of that delivery system and sharing it with others. Presumably, we care about kids wherever the hell they are. Presumably, we care about other kids than just those in Rabun County. All of us presumably buy into that philosophy and that stance that we care about kids in a broader context.

To illustrate what had happened to Foxfire since its move to Rabun County High School, Wigginton enlisted John Dewey's criticism of the overreaction of many progressive educators of the Depression era to traditional modes of education that emphasized the pouring in of facts and figures to docile students, ignoring their individual needs and capacities. But the progressives, in attacking formalism, had erred in the opposite direction by devaluing subject matter and intellectual skills. Wigginton intimated that Dewey's criticism of progressive education, expressed in *Experience and Education* (1938), was apropos of the Foxfire curriculum. Dewey's lesson to Foxfire, he stated, was that both sets of objectives—cognitive *and* affective—were integral to a sound curriculum: Take the middle ground.

In a forthright appraisal of his own handling of *Foxfire* magazine, Wigginton admitted he had lost sight of the academic agenda (a term used by Wigginton to describe concepts and understandings as well as reading, writing, and computational skills) in the rush to publish a quarterly magazine: "It's not a bad course but it's got some flaws addressing objectives that are real important. That's one of the reasons [until this year] it hasn't counted as an English [graduation credit]. . . . I let the demands of putting out the magazine set the entire agenda, and once in a while I hit an objective. . . . Instead of aiming at education, we're aiming at *product*. . . . That's what's happened to Foxfire II, for sure."

In Wigginton's own estimation, Foxfire II had not realized its potential as a delivery system for academic skills and higher-order cognitive processes; instead, over the years, he had allowed individual students to continue producing the same kind of article. What had been ignored was the spiraling from lower-order to higher-order thinking and the attendant reflection that would enable students to transfer skills learned in Foxfire II to other courses and other projects.

The first step toward reaching a Deweyan balance or "middle way" in curriculum development was for the staff to "brainstorm" four lists of objectives that would apply to *all* courses across the Foxfire curriculum. The first list comprised the state CBE/BST objectives necessary for success on the statewide minimum-competency exam required for admission of a student to the junior class. The second list addressed academic and reasoning skills deemed necessary for success in college, yet useful for non–college students as well, e.g., note taking, organization of data, and test-taking skills. The third list included skills a student would need to prove of real value to an employer, e.g., efficient use of time and resources, self-direction, management and supervisory skills.

The final list had two components: first, a statement of the skills included in the other three lists that each staff teacher could honestly say were already being addressed in each of his or her courses; secondly, a statement of the skills that *could,* with minor restructuring of the course, be incorporated in its activities. What was required, in other words, was a "fine-tuning" of existing courses to deliver minimum-competency cognitive skills as well as cognitive *and* affective skills deemed essential for success in college and/or the work world.

Wigginton's attempt to harmonize Foxfire and Deweyan philosophy focuses attention on the utility—and necessity—of a theory of pedagogy to sound educational practice. Further afield, yet significantly, it leads to reflection on the role schools of education have to play in the widely proclaimed "crisis of quality" in the nation's public schools.

Nearly a decade ago, a few educational researchers began to draw some parallels between Wigginton and Dewey. For example, in superficial analyses, Sitton,[1] and later Parks,[2] discussed the general affinities of Foxfire to Dewey. Surprisingly, none of these investigators bothered to ask if Wigginton had *consciously* designed Foxfire as an application of the principles of John Dewey, or any other theorist. The answer to this question, first broached by Wigginton himself in *Sometimes a Shining Moment,* raises a troublesome question about the quality and utility of teacher education programs on the nation's campuses.

In 1981, after fifteen years of managing Foxfire, Wigginton had his first serious encounter with Dewey while engaged in background reading for his book to teachers—and discovered that he had reinvented the proverbial wheel:

One paragraph into *Experience and Education* by John Dewey and things began to crystallize. By the time I finished it, I was shaking my head in amazement. On every one of its less than a hundred pages, insights had leaped out into the air and I had found myself pounding the arm of my chair and saying, "That's *right*, dammit, that's *exactly* right. That's just the way it is." All those discoveries I thought I had made about education, Dewey had elucidated into complete clarity fifty years and more before. And he showed me how incomplete my own philosophy still was. I read more, and the same thing happened over and over, to my chagrin and awe.[3]

Wigginton's chagrin is attributable to his realization that teachers everywhere are mired in "philosophical quicksand," having no thorough understanding of or allegiance to a pedagogical approach other than the traditional imparting of textbook and lecture information, unless, like himself, they are fortunate enough to have *independently* discovered the universal laws of learning. Wigginton places the blame for this dilemma squarely on schools of education, citing his own preparation for teaching as a case in point:

Why didn't I hear what Dewey et al. were saying when I was first introduced to them at Cornell? Well, Dewey, for example, struck me as being unreadable. And he wasn't the only one. Thus I skipped most of the readings. The professor certainly was precious little help in deciphering them. All this was combined with the fact that the courses in which philosophy and methods were taught happened to be among the most boring courses I've ever been part of. Most of us skipped class frequently—and passed anyway. Added to this was the vital fact that we had no experience base by which to judge or which to *apply* those readings. We were taught, in short, precisely as we were later to teach using those deadly high school texts. My high school students had no experience through which those texts could come to life, and thus they remained gray and lifeless in their hands.[4]

Wigginton makes no attempt to disguise his contempt for schools of education, most of which, he avers "quite simply, should not be allowed to graduate teachers at the present time. And given the size of the job ahead of us, they should not be allowed to do so until education has been turned into one of the most rigorous, demanding, creative and respected majors on campus."[5]

This criticism perhaps explains Wigginton's reluctance to pressure his staff to acquire certification during Foxfire's early years at Rabun County High School, when "benign neglect" of such matters on the part of state and county school officials was the rule. In sum, beyond fulfilling a bureaucratic requirement, he believes most education courses are useless. Given Wigginton's personal dedication and commitment to teaching, the high esteem in which he is held by other teachers, and his reasoned advocacy of public education (not to mention the sheer cogency of his argument), his criticism should not be taken lightly.

Wigginton's avowed fealty to Dewey and his affinities to Deweyan theory, which preexisted his understanding of its basic tenets, make that philosophy a logical benchmark for assessing Foxfire's strengths and weaknesses as a pedagogical system. The following discussion makes explicit points of convergence and divergence between Wigginton and Dewey and draws upon research in the emerging field of "experiential education" to provide empirical support for its conclusions. Included in this discussion as contexts for the analysis of Foxfire are a description of Dewey's pedagogical theory, a brief historical perspective on progressive education from Dewey's era to the present (emphasizing the pitfalls and dilemmas of this style of education), and an overview of the current educational reform movement.

Deweyan Pedagogy

Dewey was an epistemologist whose theory of knowledge was founded upon a conception of the universe as unstable, uncertain, "precarious and perilous." An advocate of evolutionary theory, he rejected dualistic philosophical systems that viewed the human mind as a psychic entity, separate and distinct from the body. According to Dewey and his fellow pragmatists, mind had emerged in human society as a functional response or biological adaptation to an environment constantly in flux.[6]

Dewey rejected interpretations of evolutionary theory that led conservative social theorists such as William Graham Sumner to advocate government laissez faire and the abandonment of social welfarism. As historian Lawrence Cremin notes, Dewey's views were melioristic; in short, he believed that society should intervene to ensure its benefits for all its members.[7] In this view, social reform itself was an adaptive response of the human organism. Like his contemporary, French psychologist Jean Piaget, Dewey believed that human development was the accretion of life experiences (read *learnings*) that resulted from the ongoing resolution of dissonance in the individual's environment. Each experience provided a substratum for the ones that followed, the net effect being a "spiral" of increasing complexity. Dewey argued that every act of significant, or reflective, thought began with a difficulty or perplexity (an "indeterminate situation"). It involved a doing and an undergoing: the learner acts to solve the problem, and the environment responds. For example, the child who puts her hand on the burner of a hot stove to satisfy her curiosity about the pretty red glow quickly learns the connection between the act and its consequences; that is, she learns the *meaning* of the act.[8] Pragmatist Ernest Bayles has called this understanding of the connectedness of things and events *insight*.[9]

Reflective thinking is the first cornerstone of Dewey's system. Dewey's famous model of reflection, or the "complete act of thought," is a reconstruction of a biologically evolved, discursive problem-solving mode that productive human beings apply in their daily lives. Its essential features, he argued, are those of the scientific (or experimental) method.

According to Dewey, reflective thinking is the only way that meanings are understood and "grasped" by the learner; it is the mode of thinking underlying the doing and undergoing spiral of experience. Reflective activity is evident in a rudimentary form in infant behavior and develops in different directions (dependent upon the individual's life experiences) and with increasing sophistication throughout the life cycle. Hidebound in their determination to inculcate fixed bodies of subject matter, schools ignore the natural tendency of the child to learn by resolving dissonance and to become emotionally engaged in a problem the solution of which is within her intellectual capacity. Consequently, reflective activity attained in one direction is paralleled by "bad thinking" in other directions. Nonreflective activity, unchecked by educative influences, accounts for the body of prejudice and unexamined ("unwarranted") belief that prevails in society.[10]

Extrapolated from his various writings, the following are the phases or elements of reflective activity, which, according to Dewey, should be incorporated by all teachers in all classrooms: First, an ongoing activity that has already captured the student's interest; second, a "genuine problem" that arises within the course of this activity and engages the student's curiosity (by creating dissonance) and stimulates further thought;[11] third, refinement of the difficulty or perplexity to specify precisely its dimensions; fourth, the formulation and elaboration of an idea (what Dewey called a "suggestion") into a tentative solution to the problem—an *hypothesis*;[12] fifth, testing the validity of the hypothesis by an application—by "overt action" and observation of results or by "imaginative action" and contemplation of results;[13] sixth, a review or summary of the entire process that resulted in a conclusion or course of action "to see what is helpful, what is harmful, what is merely useless" as an adjunct in dealing "more promptly and efficaciously with analogous problems in the future."[14]

Dewey believed it counterproductive to intellectual growth for educators to treat subject matter as a body of truth that had an absolute or universal value external to the individual learner's needs and capacities. He believed it folly to assume that the logic inherent in the scholar's ordering of disciplinary knowledge could be intuited by the learner if it were merely inculcated by the teacher or text in its predigested entirety, memorized by the learner, and regurgitated at the appointed hour. Dewey attacked the formalist assumptions underlying most schooling at the turn of the century—assumptions that treated subject matter as an *end* rather than a *means* to thinking. Subject matter, he argued in the major corpus of his writings, acquires its value (and utility) in the service of reflective activity.

Dewey distinguished between the *logical* and the *psychological* ordering of knowledge, in other words, between knowledge as synthesized by the scholar on the frontier of a discipline and knowledge as meaningfully grasped by the young learner. With respect to the latter, to *psychologize* subject matter is to make it available to the child as an instrument for resolving a problem or intellectual dilemma that has arisen in the course of a continuous activity which is planned and guided by the teacher. The outcome of this reflective process will be understandings (or elaborated meanings) of concepts and principles.[15] Dewey believed that knowledge applied in such a fashion will not only be retained, but will acquire "an absorbing value" of its own. In this restricted sense only does subject matter become an educational end.[16]

The anti-intellectualism that has traditionally pervaded educational progressivism and undermined its credibility should not be laid at Dewey's doorstep. As a careful analysis of his major works reveals, Dewey vigorously affirmed the school's responsibility to communicate subject matter—disciplinary information, concepts, and generalizations. Indeed, as discussed previously, Dewey inveighed against romantic naturalists who made child activity an end in itself rather than a means for the acquisition of cognitive skills and communicated information.

Dewey argued that the teacher should be not only an expert psychologist who could readily identify—and tailor instruction to—the needs and capacities of individual students, but also a subject matter expert, armed with disciplinary knowledge "abundant to the point of overflow."[17] Dewey's commitment to academic scholarship was reflected in his policy for hiring elementary-grade teachers at his laboratory school at the University of Chicago (1896–1904):

It was assumed, at first, that an all-round teacher would be the best, and perhaps it would be advisable to have one teacher teach the children in several branches. This theory, however, has been abandoned, and it has been thought well to secure teachers who are specialists by taste and training—experts along the different lines. One of the reasons for this modification was the difficulty getting scientific facts presented that were facts and truths. It had been assumed that any phenomenon that interested the child was good enough, and that if he were aroused and made alert, that was all that was expected. It is, however, just as necessary that what he gets should be truth and not be subordinated to anything else. . . . The school, accordingly, is endeavoring to put the various lines of work in [the] charge of experts who maintain agreement and harmony through continued consultation and cooperation.[18]

Dewey took great pains to explain that the problem with traditional education (and his criticism is apropos of today's schools) was not its heavy emphasis on intellectual development, but rather the isolation of subject matter and intellectual skills from the life experience of the learner.[19] Dewey assumed, first, that the learner must have some previous experience *and* interest to which subject matter can be directly linked if it is to be meaningfully learned; second, that subject matter is meaningfully learned only in the context of its reflective application to a problem—practical or intellectual—that has its origins in a situation of dissonance within the life experience of the learner. Thus, learning is an active process—it is doing.[20] And ever mindful of the social ends to which knowledge should be put, Dewey wrote: "It is a mistake to suppose that the mere acquisition of a certain amount of arithmetic, geography, history, etc. which is taught and studied because it may be useful at some time in the future, has this effect, and it is a mistake to suppose that acquisition of skills in reading and figuring will automatically constitute preparation for their right and effective use under conditions very unlike those in which they were acquired."[21]

The teacher's role is not, as many progressives assumed, to step aside and let the child pursue her natural impulses (spontaneous interests) willy-nilly, but rather to convert impulses to educational purposes by creating activities that incorporate these interests, elicit reflective activity, and require the use of disciplinary knowledge, reading, writing, and computational skills. In Dewey's arcane terminology: "A purpose differs from an original impulse and desire through its translation into a plan and method of action based upon foresight of the consequences of acting under given observed conditions in a certain way."[22] Ignoring this fundamental distinction between impulse and purpose, many of the child-centered schools of Dewey's era, pilloried by academicians and caricatured in the popular press, remained at heart anti-intellectual.

In an oft-quoted passage in his magnum opus, *Democracy and Education*, Dewey declared that education is "that reconstruction or reorganization of experience which adds to the meaning of experience, and which increases the ability to direct the course of subsequent experience."[23] Implicit in this dictum is Dewey's notion of the spiral curriculum, the second cornerstone of his pedagogy, made explicit in his other writings. For example, in *Experience and Education*, Dewey wrote:

> It is . . . essential that the new objects and events be related intellectually to those of earlier experiences, and this means that there be some advance made in conscious articulation of facts and ideas. It thus becomes the office of the educator to select those things within the range of existing experience that have the promise and potentiality of presenting new problems which by stimulating new ways of observation and judgement will expand the area of further experience. He must constantly regard what is already won not as a fixed possession but as an agency and instrumentality for opening new fields which make new demands upon existing powers of observation and of intelligent use of memory. Connectedness in growth must be his constant watchword.[24]

The sensible curriculum, argued Dewey, is that which spirals from one level of knowledge to the next, elaborating previously acquired information, concepts, and generalizations, and increasing the acuity of reflection. Its soundness resides in the teacher's subject matter expertise, attentiveness to the needs and capacities of learners, and ability to arrange the learning situation ("objective conditions") so that previous learnings transfer (generalize) to new cases and situations. It is incumbent upon the teacher to orchestrate the conditions under which ideas transfer to higher intellectual levels; if left entirely to the student, learning transfer becomes a "sheer accident"—if it occurs at all.[25]

The third cornerstone of Deweyan pedagogy is the idea of the continuity of experience. Dewey believed that education and life experience were synonymous—and he equated both with growth. Thus, he was stymied by the conventional practice of schools to ignore the learner's out-of-school experience in their curricula and methods of instruction: "There is a tendency to connect material of the schoolroom simply with the material of prior lessons, instead of linking it to what the pupil has acquired in his out-of-school experience. . . . As a result, there are built up detached and independent systems of school knowledge that inertly overlay the ordinary systems of experience instead of reacting to enlarge and refine them. Pupils are taught to live in two different worlds, one the world of out-of-school experience, the other the world of books and lessons. Then we stupidly wonder why what is studied in school counts for so little outside."[26]

Dewey described two pervasive kinds of classroom instruction, both of which he believed were counterproductive to intellectual growth. The first was classroom instruction that was so fragmented as to present each lesson "as an independent whole," disconnected from "other lessons in the same subject, or other subjects of study." The second was the better of two evils, but still pedagogically deficient because it isolated subject matter from out-of-school experience: "The student is systematically led to utilize his earlier lessons to help understand the present one, and also to use the present to throw additional light upon what is already acquired."[27]

The alternative to these practices, he suggested, was a curriculum that bridged the two worlds—hence his injunction to teachers that they "become intimately acquainted with the conditions of the local community, physical, historical economic, occupational, etc., in order to utilize them as educational resources."[28]

Dewey argued that neglect on the teacher's part to take account of out-of-school (read *community*) experience in instructional planning leaves the integration of the two worlds of experience to chance: "Save by accident, out-of-school experience is left in its crude and comparatively unreflective state. It is not subject to the refining and expanding influences of the more accurate and comprehensive material of direct instruction."[29]

The quintessential pragmatist, Dewey did not believe that an experience possessed an absolute value or truth in itself. Its value was inherent in its quality of being conducive to the learner's further growth. By this criterion, many life experiences were "noneducative" or "miseducative"—experiences that did not "progressively realize possibilities, and thus make individuals better fitted to cope with later requirements."[30]

To the category of unproductive experience, Dewey also assigned activities that isolate subject matter from life experience or "tend to land [the learner] in a groove or rut and thereby narrow the field of further experience."[31] Responsibility resides with the teacher for arranging the conditions of learning to ensure the synthesis of subject matter and out-of-school experience in a spiral curriculum that elicits and disciplines reflective activity.

The final cornerstone of Deweyan pedagogy is the social function of education. As Cremin has noted, Dewey's pedagogical theory was more than a revolt against traditional school practice (formalism); it also envisioned the school as a lever of social reform.[32] In his early works, Dewey explicitly linked his social and political philosophy to his pedagogical theory. The school, he argued, should be organized as "a miniature community, an embryonic society" permeated throughout with "a spirit of social cooperation and community."[33] In a democratic school, the unifying aim of the curriculum would be "the growth of the child in the direction of social capacity and service."[34] Dewey's reform advocacy was gradualist and orderly rather than violent or revolutionary, and it became more sharply focused and prominent in his writings during the 1930s Depression era.

As noted previously, Dewey believed that on the intellectual side schools should accord reflective thinking their highest priority. Social intelligence he defined as the application of this mode of thinking by a *group* of learners in a problem-solving situation that evokes inquiry and hypothesis testing. It is through the agency of cooperative activity, Dewey argued, that social dispositions are formed. As he stated: "Only by engaging in a joint activity, where one person's use of material and tools is consciously referred to the use others are making of their capacities and appliances is a social direction of disposition attained."[35]

Dewey believed that if the promise of democracy for the realization of the potentialities of all its members was to be fulfilled, the schools would have to take an active role in training young people in the habits and attitudes appropriate to what he called "associated living." Deweyan scholar David Sidorsky summarizes Dewey's position as follows: "It is noteworthy that Dewey believed that the schools of democracy could be a model for democratic society. They could exhibit a form of life in which conflicting views would be mediated by intellectual inquiry, and in which social policy would result from the free participation of all elements of the school community. This kind of freedom and democracy would inevitably be more difficult to achieve in the larger political and economic institutions of the society. But schools could demonstrate the potential direction of a free, democratic society."[36]

The social and economic dislocations of the 1930s gave Dewey a greater urgency to promote the creation of "a more just, more humane, and more secure" social order.[37] He advocated a "pretty complete overhauling of the curriculum from the fifth grade through high school" (although he never prescribed a specific kind of curriculum) and an infusion of schooling with a social purpose.[38] Dewey implied that the reconstructed curriculum at each level, particularly in the high school, would incorporate an examination of social and economic problems, attend to underlying causes and potential solutions, and substitute "methods of inquiry and mutual consultation for the methods of imposition and inculcation."[39] He envisaged a new generation of reflective thinkers accustomed to cooperative social problem-solving strategies. To this end the task of the school was "to develop the insight and understanding that will enable the youth who go forth from the schools to take part in the great work of construction and organization that will have to be done, and to equip them with the attitudes and habits of action that will make their understanding and insight practically effective."[40]

Consistent with his view of reality as a constant flux, Dewey refused to specify precisely the kind of society that would result from the widespread application of experimental method to the social field. He indicated that it would be "a society which is continuously plan*ning* rather than a plan*ned* society"—a cooperative, collectivist state in which the largess of science and technology would serve social rather than individual ends.[41] Dewey concluded that education would play a key role in the progressive reconstruction of society: "This need for a society in which experimental inquiry and planning for social ends are organically contained is also the need for a new education. In one case as in the other, there is supplied a new dynamic in conduct and there is required the cooperative use of intelligence on a social scale in behalf of social values."[42]

Dewey's grand vision for American education has never gained a substantial following even within the ranks of progressive educators, who for generations have either ignored his theory or bastardized it to suit their varied agendas for curriculum change. Since the 1920s disparate factions of pedagogical reformers have flown the progressive banner. Their differences notwithstanding, these groups have shared Dewey's antipathy to the rigidity and extreme didacticism of traditional schooling. Contrary to Dewey's philosophy, however, they have also manifested a tendency to overemphasize the affective side of the child's education, leaving intellectual development largely to chance. At worst, their programs have been virulently anti-intellectual.[43]

Dewey is commonly regarded as having inspired programs that he neither envisaged nor would have endorsed. Dewey's critics have reinforced this perception, particularly historian Richard Hofstadter, who attributed many of the shortcomings of progressive education to Dewey's prose style:

> It is commonly said that Dewey was misunderstood, and it is repeatedly pointed out that in time he had to protest against some of the educational practices carried on in his name. Perhaps his intent was widely, even regularly violated, but Dewey was hard to read and interpret. He wrote a prose of terrible vagueness and plasticity, which William James once characterized as "damnable; you might say God-damnable." His style is suggestive of the cannonading of distant armies and one concludes that something portentous is going on at a remote and inaccessible distance, but one cannot determine just what it is. That this style is, perhaps symptomatically, at its worst in Dewey's most important educational writings suggests that his great influence as an educational spokesman may have been derived in some part from the very inaccessibility of his exact writings.[44]

Hofstadter's colorful polemic is a red herring. What should be at issue is the *substance* of Dewey's work, not his occasionally pedantic style, the difficulty of which Hofstadter exaggerated. A sounder argument would have given Dewey credit for his good ideas, but would have put the blame where it belonged—on progressive educators who were wont to eschew the careful scrutiny Dewey's pedagogical works demanded or perhaps who never even bothered to read Dewey.

Wigginton and Dewey Compared

Highly publicized research on the quality of schools in the 1980s suggests that American education is in a sorry state. Reports of national studies headed by Ernest Boyer (*High School*), John Goodlad (*A Place Called School*), and Theodore Sizer (*Horace's Compromise*) have drawn two major conclusions about the status of education: (1) the nation's schools are "emotionally flat" and uninspiring places to attend; (2) teachers rely almost exclusively on textbooks, lectures, and seatwork to pour in information to predominately passive and tractable students.[45] In short, schools of the 1980s are a distant mirror of the institutions Dewey so stridently attacked at the turn of the century. Whether a class is "relevant to student needs" (in theory, progressive) or grounded in traditional academic content, the likelihood is that the center of gravity is weighted heavily toward the teacher, who is expected by his or her superiors to maintain an authoritarian posture (in the interest of discipline) and to "cover the text" (even at the expense of higher-order intellectual skills).

These studies have fueled a widely shared belief that something must be done immediately to ensure America's competitive edge in the international market place. This concern has been manifested in nearly 350 national- and state-level task force reports, and a plethora of legislative initiatives. All have mandated that the purpose of schools is to give students a rigorous grounding in academic content and intellectual skills—the "essentials" for competent adult living in an information society.[46]

Eliot Wigginton's is one of the few Deweyan voices to be heard in what has been called "the great school debate" of the 1980s. His vision for schooling, however, is not antithetical to the intellectual goals of many "back-to-basics" advocates. Apropos of the conservative educational milieu in Georgia, he has modified Foxfire by keying its community-based activities to the objectives of the state's competency testing program—a clever defensive strategy, which strives for a Deweyan balance between cognitive and affective skills. Wigginton firmly believes that Deweyan "experiential learning" is the most promising pedagogical system for motivating students to acquire higher-order intellectual skills, an appreciation for and understanding of organized subject matter, and a range of personal growth skills.

As noted previously, at several staff meetings in 1984, Wigginton declared that the entire Foxfire program (with the exception of Foxfire I and College English) needed an infusion of intellectual rigor. My own observations during this period confirmed that parts of the program were reminiscent of the brand of progressivism that Hofstadter and other academicians had vehemently criticized. As taught in the winter and spring of 1984, such courses as folklore, outdoor education, string band, television production, Appalachian instrument building, environmental science, and *Foxfire* magazine were largely devoid of academic content and lacked a conscious focus on intellectual skills.

In his book to teachers, published in October 1985, Wigginton forthrightly describes the flaws in his handling of the magazine class. Not surprisingly, these weaknesses are points where the curriculum has deviated from Deweyan prescriptions. The following discussion highlights the points of convergence and divergence between Deweyan theory and Foxfire practice.

1. *Reflection*. Reflective activity beyond the mechanics of laying out a magazine (for example, which photographs, of what size, to put where) was conspicuously absent in Wigginton's classes. Given the

contact students have with the Appalachian elderly, as well as their exposure to the vanishing mountain culture and the region's problems, teacher-guided reflection is necessary to ensure that they glean the social learnings mediated by each experience. Dewey called it "the need of constant review, in the sense of looking back over what has been done and has been found out, so as to formulate the net outcome, thus getting mentally rid of debris, of all material and acts that do not sustain the outcome. . . . The ongoing process of experience should be periodically arrested to make a survey of what has been going on and to secure a summary of its *net* accomplishments."[47]

Since the early 1980s, there has been a burgeoning of loosely associated "experiential learning" projects across the country. Included under this rubric is a diversity of program types: cultural journalism, career internships, community service, social/political action, and Outward Bound–like adventure education. The available, albeit scanty, research evidence suggests that these out-of-classroom educational experiences contribute to the self-esteem, general emotional growth, and social responsibility of students.[48] Significantly, proponents' claims for the success of these programs are based almost entirely upon short-term measures of affective growth.[49]

An interesting finding of these studies, with implications for Foxfire, has been the importance of reflective activity in securing the personal growth and social skills mediated by an out-of-classroom experience. For example, Conrad and Hedin reported in their national study of twenty-seven experiential education programs that "systematic and directed reflection," through the agency of "a formal (and at least weekly) seminar," was the most powerful variable in promoting affective growth.[50] Similarly, psychologist Stephen Hamilton has written: "The need to supplement activity with reflection in order to enhance its educational value is perhaps the most firmly grounded assertion that can be made about experiential learning, an idea rooted in Dewey's theory and supplemented by the research of [James] Coleman and his associates."[51]

2. *Spiral curriculum—attention to subject matter and intellectual skills.* In the 1984 spring quarter, Wigginton allowed a student, Scott, to enroll in four Foxfire courses: photography, Foxfire II, video I, and folklore. The consequence of this decision was that Scott was not exposed to any substantive academic or intellectual skills work in at least four of his classes at Rabun County High School—those he took in the Foxfire program. In these classes he was not required to read any books, write any papers that were rigorously critiqued or marked, or do any real

homework. In short, on the intellectual side, Scott's Foxfire experience was virtually bankrupt. In a frank statement in *Sometimes a Shining Moment,* Wigginton acknowledged that Scott had not been well served by his program:

> One summer we decided to move a magnificent log house [the Rothell House] and document the process for the summer, 1984, issue of *Foxfire.* Scott, one of the students on the construction crew, photographed the dismantling of the structure step by step; and that fall, in the magazine class, he began to process those negatives at the same time that he was photographing the phases of reconstruction that went on all fall with a crew of community adults hired to take the place of the students who were now back in school. He was buried in photographs and diagrams. Before the class ended, he finished most of those and much of the layout, and he had started work on the captions. Too late, I realized the captions were a disaster; Scott left our course still spelling *chimney* "chimbley." He had learned a few valuable things, granted, but as a student in a magazine class who was producing a publishable article, he fell through the cracks in terms of some of the things he should have learned—*could* have learned if I had been more attentive. He left us writing not one whit better than when he came to us. And he knew it. And although Scott learned a great deal about one type of traditional log structure, he learned nothing about the other types or about the broader picture of Appalachian culture in general. His knowledge of Appalachia was fragmentary and episodic, all based on one tiny tile in a huge mosaic he never saw whole and entire. He knew a good bit about that one tile, but he knew little of the overall picture to which it contributed its tiny spot of color. He was immersed completely in a project to which I never successfully added context. We were all too busy, too distracted by the pressures of deadlines.[52]

In the same chapter, his peroration to the book, Wigginton publicly acknowledged what Herbert Kohl had suspected and what my observations confirmed: *Foxfire* magazine had become formulaic and repetitious. Dewey's curriculum spiral, the gradation of increasingly complex skills and knowledge, had been violated: "We had often fallen into one of the most insidious traps of all: that of allowing the production of an issue of the magazine to be sufficient as an end in and of itself. . . . I had some students who had not even equated in a primitive way the process they had just gone through to produce an article with the process of writing a research paper for another teacher. There was almost no transfer of acquired skills to other tasks or classes."[53]

3. *Continuity of experience.* Here Foxfire practice bears a close similarity to Dewey. Experiential learning is the essence of Wigginton's program. For twenty years Foxfire students have entered the Appala-

chian community to record its oral history, survival arts, folklore, and traditions—what one observer has labeled "salvage ethnography."[54] For twenty years they have also served as ambassadors for the project, traveling in every state and throughout the Caribbean, serving as consultants to fledgling projects and speaking at schools, colleges, workshops, conferences, and even before a Congressional committee.

As Wigginton has admitted, one of Foxfire's weaknesses has been his neglect to guide students to grasp the connectedness of their individual experiences to broader fields of experience accessible through texts, lectures, and class discussions. Ideally, states Wigginton in his self-critique, there should be an "ebb and flow. Back and forth. Lecture and text to project and application and reflection."[55]

4. *The social function of education.* Dewey believed that the participation of students throughout their schooling in cooperative ("conjoint") activities that promoted individual and group reflection would foster the adult social dispositions and habits of thought necessary for the continuing reconstruction of the society.

Like Dewey, Wigginton believes in the power of education to ameliorate social injustice. Unlike Dewey and more radical social reconstructionists, however, Wigginton does not harbor any grand vision of a collectivist society. In short, Foxfire has evolved as a community-specific reform strategy, both in Rabun County and in other locations where the learning concept has been implemented. Unlike Dewey, Wigginton has created a practical reform agenda that has proved replicable in a wide variety of geographic and ethnic settings. In Rabun County, he has even attempted a symbiosis of education, cultural preservation, and community economic development, each element functioning (at least in theory) in the service of the other.

Wigginton shares with Dewey the belief that the school should carry forward the constructive social values of earlier generations—cooperation and interdependence, empathy, self-reliance (in the sense of individual competence), and social responsibility. The diminution of these social values, he posits, has cost the human spirit dearly. In the early years of Foxfire, Wigginton wrote: "I'm afraid we've become a nation of nomads with no sense of that security or serenity that comes from being able to say, 'Here is where I belong. Here is my place, my time, my home, my birthright, my community. Here I am loved and known, and here I love in turn.' . . . Somewhere along the way, we've lost something fine. Perhaps in our search for personal satisfaction and pleasure, we've dug so deeply into ourselves that we've forgotten each other. . . . Soon we are a community of isolated islands ('Who are those people that just moved in?' 'I don't know. We ought to go find out someday.') and the damage is done."[56]

Like Dewey, Wigginton views the school as a proper (perhaps the only) forum for transmitting the values that are indispensable to a well-integrated, harmonious society. As actress Jessica Tandy, who portrayed Annie Nations in the *Foxfire* play, has correctly observed, Wigginton's social vision is neither backward-looking nor utopian: "I think that something very important . . . in Wigginton's philosophy is that change is inevitable. You cannot stop change. It is going to happen. And so what's the answer? You must take the best of what you had and bring it into the changed situation. . . . It's no good saying, 'Ah, the old times were wonderful and oh, if we could have them back.' It's up to you to readjust your sights . . . and keep the best."[57]

Wigginton's advocacy of Deweyan pedagogy carries the assumption that the purpose of education should be more than merely academic learning. Like Dewey, he assumes that cognitive and affective development should not be separated—each is best achieved in the service of the other. The task Wigginton has set for his organization is to find ways to harmonize the two sides of adolescent development in every Foxfire course.

As a final point of comparison, Wigginton and Dewey share the aggravation of having had well-intended disciples misinterpret their pedagogical theories. In 1938, Dewey was piqued enough by the tomfoolery being carried on in his name to write a blistering critique of progressive educators who had debased the academic side of schooling. He presented an eloquent statement of his pedagogy in *Experience and Education*—one that even the dullest of educators could understand. Unfortunately, his painstaking admonitions were ignored, and inverting Dewey has remained the vogue in progressive education to the present day.

Similarly, Wigginton's teaching staff at Rabun County High School unbalanced the Deweyan equation. Increasingly sensitive to the lessons of the past, Wigginton now has started to use Dewey's critique of progressivism as a benchmark for restructuring the entire Foxfire curriculum. In *Sometimes a Shining Moment,* he has reaffirmed the good sense of hewing to Dewey's middle road in curriculum development. Indeed, one of Wigginton's most significant contributions to the current educational debate has been to direct attention to the appropriateness and feasibility of Deweyan pedagogy as the basis of classroom reform and school improvement.

Whither Foxfire?: The Reality behind the Rhetoric

During the academic year 1984–85, Wigginton announced several changes that he expected would strengthen the *Foxfire* magazine program. First, students were now required to write detailed introductions to their articles. "We want you to really tease out a description of the character," he told one class. "What we want is a piece that stands on its own as an article." In his book to teachers Wigginton expressed his dissatisfaction with the expository writing his magazine students were accustomed to doing: "In the past, students often went on an interview, made no notes, and some weeks later drafted a half-page 'We went to see Mr. Gillespie and he told us about his general store and he was a nice man and we liked him' introduction that Margie or I would help the students expand slightly and then approve. The students had completed a piece of writing, it was grammatically and factually correct, and though short of all it could have been, it was deemed sufficient."[58]

In the fall, Wigginton and Bennett set aside several classes for group discussion of the elements of a sound introduction. During two periods students critiqued and suggested revisions for the introductions that their peers had written for forthcoming articles. The introduction to an article on mountaineer Roy Roberts profited from its critique by Wigginton and the students, whose suggestions were incorporated in the final draft. An excerpt from this lively piece reads as follows:

We went back to the shelter and sat around the cement picnic tables, and he [Roy Roberts] began to show us how to make some of the toys he used to play with as a child. . . . Once he had found the right wood, he sat and whittled while he reminisced until late in the night. After showing us how to make two different kinds of whistles and a pop gun, he decided he needed a different stick of wood. So off we went, romping through the woods at ten o'clock at night with no flashlight in the pitch black darkness. He left us sitting there, wondering what was going on. We could hear him thrashing around and breaking branches. By the time we had figured out what he was doing and had started out after him, he was already back with a satisfied grin on his face, holding a perfect stick for his next toy.[59]

Second, students would be expected to incorporate library research in their articles, providing the "proper historical or cultural context" for their interviews.[60] Presumably, as their research skills improved they would produce articles of increasing complexity—Dewey's curriculum spiral.

Third, in the service of state-mandated mathematics competencies, students would be required to do a cost analysis of their articles, based on the cost of the materials used in the production of the article, transportation expenses, and labor costs (figured at the Foxfire summer employment rate of $3.35 per hour). They would then be required to compare their costs to those of a hypothetical article of twelve pages with fifteen photographs (39½ hours of labor at a total cost of $1,460 for materials, printing, and mailing, plus $265 for wages).[61]

Fourth, as an ongoing reflective activity, students would analyze their community experiences in the light of Appalachian history and culture; in turn, they would relate their insights to other fields of experience. For example, they would "evaluate their own—and their culture's—attitudes about *other* cultures and deal with those, to help them see that just as they have been wrongly stereotyped, so too have they wrongly stereotyped others, and to help them see that great men and women refuse to be contained by the tradition in which they were raised."[62]

A review of issues of *Foxfire* magazine through the winter of 1986, however, indicates that the magazine program has not changed significantly since I completed my observations in December 1984. A case in point is the fall 1985 issue of *Foxfire,* which includes eighteen articles focused on traditional observances of Christmas in Appalachia. The student-authored introduction contains elements of the detailed narrative description that Wigginton expects of his older students. An excerpt reads as follows:

> Christmas Day, 1915. A new snow has fallen overnight outside a one-room handbuilt log cabin tucked into a valley somewhere in the hills of the Appalachian Mountains. Roosters crow as the rising sun slowly spreads its light across the white ground and the family inside begins to stir. The six children in the loft have been awake for hours whispering about Santa Claus and quietly laughing over the tricks they played on their neighbors while "serenading" the night before. They can hardly contain their excitement as they anxiously await the sound of their father grinding the morning coffee—their cue to get up.[63]

Yet taken as a whole, the issue is a disappointment. Of its eighteen articles, fifteen are introduced by two- and three-paragraph essays, most devoid of rich detail. One veteran Foxfire student was even allowed to submit a two-paragraph introduction that tells readers only where her grandmother was reared, where she moved to, and what her hobbies were—listless writing from a student capable of stronger work. In short, Wigginton's intention of having students tease out details about their interview contacts—physical appearance, idiosyncrasies, environment—has not been realized in most of these introductions.

The *Foxfire* issues are also devoid of library research. The single (and notable) exception is a "scientific explanation" of foxfire, the luminescent fungus for which the magazine was named (Spring 1985). Written by a senior in Wigginton's College English class, this entertaining article (which also served as an English term paper) combines research from scientific texts, encyclopedias, interviews, and literature. The author leads the reader from the folklore inspired by the phenomenon to its use as a literary device by Mark Twain in *Huckleberry Finn* "to establish a mysterious, secretive, even a magical atmosphere"; then to a description of the "most common fungi responsible for foxfire"; lastly, to an explanation of the chemical processes that cause the fungi to glow in the dark. We are told that foxfire is the spore stage in the life cycle of several species of mushroom—a tiny parasite that aids in the decomposition of wood and "resembles a stain that has been applied to the wood." Its glow is a by-product of photosynthesis, the emission of excess ultraviolet energy.

The young writer cleverly uses a description of his research methodology as an organizational strategy for presenting his findings. He tells us that folklore and literature were not much help in explaining foxfire, and when scientific sources proved too complex or left unanswered questions, he turned to local biology teachers for help. Moving from source to source, he raises new questions and finds new answers. This strategy piques readers' curiosity and holds their interest from one level to the next. For example: "After reading about foxfire in these books [folklore and literature], I was still uncertain about it. I still did not know what foxfire really was. Many things in nature glow and are luminescent. Certain kinds of salt water fish glow in the dark as well as the more obvious lightning bug."[64]

My observations throughout the fall of 1984 suggested that Wigginton was not prepared at that time to enact substantive changes in the magazine program. With the exception of several class periods that called attention to upgrading the quality of the expository writing, systematic group instruction in English was conspicuously absent. The only stage of the writing that required students themselves to assume the burden of revision was the introduction—and most students only had to write *one* expository essay between September and December.

The exceptions were the few students who also wrote essays for the Foxfire community newsletter. As stated in an earlier chapter, one-to-one instruction and assistance in editing the transcriptions (the bulk of most articles) was largely didactic. Throughout the entire process, teachers and students never paused to make the reflective links that would bind their individual experiences and give them perspective.

Moreover, in the bustle of production, Wigginton and Bennett seemed to lose track of what some of their students were doing from day to day. Lori, a bright, personable student, was a case in point. Enrolled in *two* magazine classes (one for English credit), she spent over two months in these courses dividing her time between transcribing tapes (her main activity) and printing photographs.

There is no denying that making effective changes in the magazine program will take time. Wigginton's absence from June 1985 to January 1986 in the service of Foxfire's endowment campaign may have slowed the change process even further. The time factor notwithstanding, my findings from the fall of 1984, coupled with the evidence gleaned from issues of *Foxfire* magazine in 1985, indicate that the program will not significantly change until Wigginton squarely faces the issue of publication deadlines. By his own admission the pressure of deadlines has resulted in a product focus to which educational processes have become subordinate.

There seem to be several alternatives for resolving the dilemma— although none is an easy solution. First, retain the quarterly publication schedule and extend the class to a two-hour block. It is a given that Wigginton and Bennett cannot teach English, lead reflective discussions, and direct student research (in and out of school) within the constraints of daily fifty-five-minute classes and quarterly publication deadlines. There simply is not enough time.

Second, retain the quarterly publication schedule, while incorporating the College English class into the magazine program, thereby relieving the regular magazine classes of the full burden of production. It certainly makes good sense for Wigginton to require his College English students to explore community resources for research papers. The experience of the student who wrote the article on foxfire suggests as much. This solution, of course, would require Wigginton to restructure College English and perhaps make Foxfire I an entry requirement.

The third solution would be to reduce the number of publications per year, and subsequently the number of articles, freeing class time for the activities that would make Foxfire a bona fide Deweyan curriculum. This solution seems relatively facile and fraught with fewer logistical headaches than the other alternatives. A carefully worded letter should be sent to subscribers (and there are only 3,000 of them) explaining the publication change in the light of Foxfire's educational mission. This might well take care of the nagging pressure to continually meet production deadlines that detract from Foxfire's ability to reach its own potential as an excellent manifestation of Deweyan principles in action.

NOTES

1. Sitton, "Foxfire-Concept Publications," 119–27.

2. Parks, "Foxfire: Experiential Education in Rural America," 293.

3. Wigginton, *Shining Moment*, 280.

4. Ibid., 281.

5. Ibid., 282.

6. John Dewey, *Experience and Nature* (New York: W. W. Norton, 1925), 41–45, chaps. 2, 7. A helpful guide in interpreting this statement of Dewey's metaphysics is John Childs, *American Pragmatism in Education: An Interpretation and Criticism* (New York: Henry Holt, 1956). See also John S. Brubacher, *Modern Philosophies of Education* (New York: McGraw-Hill, 1950).

7. Lawrence A. Cremin, *The Transformation of the School: Progressivism in American Education: 1876–1957* (New York: Viking, 1962), 99–100, 115–216.

8. Dewey, *Democracy and Education*, 163–64.

9. Ernest Bayles, *Pragmatism in Education* (New York: Harper and Row, 1966), 17–19.

10. John Dewey, *How We Think: A Restatement of the Relation of Reflective Thinking to the Educative Process* (Boston: Heath, 1910, rev. 1933), 10–11, 23–29, 78–79, 205–9.

11. Dewey, *Democracy and Education*, 192.

12. Dewey, *How We Think*, 107–11.

13. Ibid., 97–98, 112–15.

14. Ibid., 128; also, 75, 77–78, 189.

15. John Dewey, *The Child and Curriculum* (1902), in *John Dewey: The Middle Works: 1899–1924*, vol. 2, ed. Jo Ann Boydston (Carbondale: Southern Illinois University Press, 1976), 285–87. For further general discussion, see Dewey, *Democracy and Education*, 179–92, 212–27.

16. Dewey, *How We Think*, 225–26.

17. Ibid., 274–75; also Dewey, *Democracy and Education*, 184.

18. John Dewey quoted in Katherine Camp Mayhew and Anna Camp Edwards, *The Dewey School* (New York: Atherton Press, 1936), 35–36. Dewey helped the Camp sisters write this volume, and he gave it his endorsement.

19. For example, see Dewey, *Experience and Education*, 48–49.

20. Dewey, *Democracy and Education*, 217.

21. Dewey, *Experience and Education*, 47–48.

22. Ibid., 80.

23. Dewey, *Democracy and Education*, 89–90.

24. Dewey, *Experience and Education*, 90.

25. Dewey, *How We Think*, 66–68, 187–88.

26. Ibid., 259.

27. Dewey, *Democracy and Education*, 191–92.

28. Dewey, *Experience and Education*, 36.

29. Dewey, *Democracy and Education*, 192.

30. Ibid., 65. See also Sidney Hook, *Education and the Taming of Power* (LaSalle, Ill.: Open Court, 1973), 92–93.

31. Dewey, *Experience and Education*, 13–14.

32. Cremin, *Transformation of the School*, 119.

33. John Dewey, *The School and Society* (1899), in *John Dewey: The Middle Works: 1899–1924*, vol. 1, ed. Jo Ann Boydston (Carbondale: Southern Illinois University Press, 1976), 11–12.

34. Ibid., 55.

35. Dewey, *Democracy and Education*, 47.

36. David Sidorsky, ed., *John Dewey: The Essential Writings* (New York: Harper and Row, 1977), xxxii.

37. John Dewey, "Education for a Changing Social Order," National Education Association Proceedings (Washington, D.C.: The Association, 1934), 751.

38. Ibid., 749.

39. John Dewey, "Education and the Social Order" (a pamphlet published by the League of Industrial Democracy) in *Intelligence in the Modern World: John Dewey's Philosophy*, ed. Joseph Ratner (New York: Random House, 1939), 689. See also John Dewey, "Education and Social Change," *Social Frontier* 3 (1937): 235–38.

40. Dewey, "Education and the Social Order," 695.

41. John Dewey and John L. Childs, "The Social Economic Situation and Education," in *The Educational Frontier*, ed. William H. Kilpatrick (New York: D. Appleton-Century, 1933), 72.

42. Ibid., 64.

43. Herbert M. Kliebard, *The Struggle for the American Curriculum, 1893–1958*, chaps. 6, 9; Cremin, *Transformation of the School*, 215–20; Diane Ravitch, *The Troubled Crusade: American Education, 1945–1980* (New York: Basic Books, 1982), chap. 2; Hook, *Education and Taming of Power*, chap. 6; Tanner and Tanner, *Curriculum Development*, chaps. 8–9.

44. Richard Hofstadter, *Anti-Intellectualism in American Life* (New York: Knopf, 1963), 361.

45. Specifically, Ernest L. Boyer, *High School: A Report on Secondary Education in America* (New York: Harper and Row, 1983), 141–53; John Goodlad, *A Place Called School: Prospects for the Future* (New York: McGraw-Hill, 1984), 105–13; Theodore Sizer, *Horace's Compromise: The Dilemma of the American High School* (Boston: Houghton Mifflin, 1984), 54–56. For an excellent historical analysis of the failings of the American high school, see Arthur G. Powell,

Eleanor Farrar, and David K. Cohen, *The Shopping Mall High School* (Boston: Houghton Mifflin, 1985), chap. 5.

46. For example, *A Nation at Risk,* the report of the National Commission on Excellence in Education (Washington, D.C.: U.S. Department of Education, 1983), in which the commission asserted that the level of academic quality of the nation's public schools would determine whether or not America regained its position of scientific, technological, and military supremacy, lost, the commission assumed, to Japanese and Soviet encroachments. See also the Task Force on Education for Economic Growth, *Action for Excellence* (Washington, D.C.: Education Commission of the States, 1983).

47. Dewey, *How We Think,* 189.

48. Charles Conrad and Diane Hedin, *Executive Summary of the Final Report of the Experiential Education Evaluation Project* (St. Paul: University of Minnesota, Center for Youth Development and Research, n.d.). See also John P. Hill, "Participatory Education and Youth Development in Secondary Schools" (Position paper prepared for Better Schools, Inc., 1983).

49. Diane Hedin, *The Impact of Experience on Academic Learning: A Summary of Theories and Review of Recent Research,* Report No. 9 (Boston, Mass.: Institute for Responsive Research, n.d.).

50. Conrad and Hedin, "Impact of Experiential Education," 71.

51. Stephen F. Hamilton, "Experiential Learning Programs for Youth," *American Journal of Education* 88 (1980): 184.

52. Wigginton, *Shining Moment,* 390.

53. Ibid., 395.

54. Sitton, "Foxfire-Concept Publications," 50.

55. Wigginton, *Shining Moment,* 408.

56. Wigginton, *Foxfire 2,* 15–17. Cf. Dewey, *School and Society,* in *John Dewey: The Middle Works,* vol. 1, ed. Boydston, 7–8; Dewey, *Democracy and Education,* 20.

57. *Foxfire Glow* transcription.

58. Wigginton, *Shining Moment,* 395–96.

59. Kyle Conway, "'I Done Some Work in My Time,'" *Foxfire,* Spring 1985, 4–5.

60. Wigginton, *Shining Moment,* 395–96.

61. See Margie Bennett, "Meeting the Objectives," *Hands On* 7, no. 1 (1985): 26–29.

62. Wigginton, *Shining Moment,* 397.

63. Kelly Shropshire, "A Christmas Card from Foxfire," *Foxfire,* Fall 1985, 130–31.

64. Curt Haban, "Why Does Foxfire Glow?," *Foxfire,* Spring 1985, 26–29.

NINE

Foxfire and Adolescence

A pervasive stereotype describes adolescence as a period of "storm and stress" when normal development is marked by tumult, rebellion, and asocial behaviors. Stamped with the imprimatur of scientific theory in the works of the psychoanalytic school, the stereotype has been reinforced by the mass media, which routinely sensationalize occurrences of adolescent misbehavior. Since its appearance in the quasi-scientific treatises of G. Stanley Hall in the early 1900s, this view of adolescence as pathology has remained a salient underpinning of schooling in America. In the 1960s social learning theorists even suggested that the paradigm had become a self-fulfilling prophecy for youth—a cultural expectation forced upon and acted out by teenagers.[1]

Over the past ten to fifteen years, numerous investigators have assailed the doctrine of "storm and stress," marshalling reams of quantitative data to belie the stereotype. The counterpoint view is a paradigm of adolescence as a period of benign growth and emerging potentiality, unsullied by psychological upheaval and turmoil. Social psychologist John P. Hill summarizes the results of these recent investigations:

> The cumulative result has been the consensus that adolescence is not universally a period of storm and stress; that the development of intensified relationships with peers does not normally mean that affectional ties with parents break down or that adolescents' values come to differ much on important matters from those of their parents; or that adolescents cease to seek advice and appreciate the standards of parents and other adults. Within families there has been little *evidence* of a generation gap. Rebelliousness is not normal in Western societies. There is no universal "identity

crisis." Available evidence suggests strongly that we could all do with a dedramatization of adolescence.[2]

The paradigm of adolescence as benign growth/potentiality challenges conventional educational practices that cast adolescents in passive classroom roles and fail to mobilize their potential for constructive social service. The proponents of this view are widely respected social scientists and educators—all advocates of responsible social roles for youth and adolescents. Eliot Wigginton and his staff have built their educational programs upon the assumption, shared with these scholars, that adolescence, with its attendant enthusiasm, creativity, and idealism, has the potential for uniquely valuable social contributions.

In the first part of this chapter the two opposing paradigms of adolescent development are examined, their implicit and explicit assumptions are delineated, and attention is paid to the quality of the research evidence supporting each position. This discussion provides a documented perspective for viewing Foxfire in the context of the school environments in which it has operated for two decades.

Adolescence as Pathology: G. Stanley Hall to the Present

The paradigm of adolescence as pathology first appeared as a fully articulated theory in G. Stanley Hall's seminal—and massive—two-volume work, *Adolescence* (1904). One of America's first academic psychologists and a founder of the American Psychological Association, Hall wrote at a time when psychology was emerging as a separate discipline from philosophy. Hall had studied Hegelian idealism at the University of Berlin from 1867 to 1870, and his "recapitulation" theory of adolescent development synthesized elements of Hegelianism, Darwinism (a theory he embraced in the 1890s), and nineteenth-century Protestant morality.[3] Historian Joseph Kett has described the theory as follows:

> In Hall's version, recapitulation postulated that the child passed through or retraced in its development the course already taken by the "race." Taking his cue from the fact that some of the materials used by children in play, sand and wood, were once the tools of primitive man, Hall speculated that adolescence corresponded to a period in prehistory marked by large-scale migrations. For the race and for the individual, it was a time of upheaval, giving rise to myths and sagas, poetic descriptions of traumatic uprooting. In a similar way, the dictates of racial experiences attracted the adolescent to tales of heroic leaders and battles. Some contemporaries thought that Hall was speaking figuratively, but he understood the law of recapitulation

literally. The adolescent was not merely like savage man. An almost Jungian collective consciousness determined aspects of adolescent behavior which were responses to inexorable commands out of the past.[4]

The biological underpinning of the theory was the evolutionist doctrine of "ontogeny recapitulates phylogeny," according to which the individual organism (ontogeny) recapitulates the evolutionary history of the species (phylogeny).[5] For Hall the doctrine provided an analog for Hegel's idea of "the parallel development of individual consciousness and the consciousness of the human race."[6]

Hall's introduction to *Adolescence* suggests his ambivalence about the period, which he broadly defines as covering the ages fourteen to twenty-two. On the one hand, he hails the period as "a new birth, for the higher and more completely human traits are now born." Moreover, "these years are the best decade of life." Yet adolescence is also fraught with peril: "Development [compared to childhood] is less gradual and more saltatory, suggestive of some ancient period of *storm and stress*, when old moorings were broken and a higher level attained."[7]

It is the latter view that dominates Hall's theory and casts such a pall over his writing. Indeed, we are told that the historical epoch being recapitulated was "emotionally unstable and pathic," its vestiges manifested as emotional volatility and dramatic mood fluctuations, which Hall believed normal for youth.

In a characteristic passage, Hall wrote that "the emotions develop by contrast and reaction into the opposite." The "normal" youth is described as a brooding Schiller, whose gaiety and euphoria fluctuate with melancholy, dysphasia, and pain. Suicidal thoughts are not uncommon: "The sad Thanatopsis mood of gloom paints the world in black." Yet doom and gloom is short-lived, displaced by a volatile exuberance: "There is gaiety, irrepressible levity, an euphoria that overflows in every absurd manifestation of excess of animal spirits, that can not [*sic*] be repressed, that danger and affliction, appeals to responsibility and to the future, can not [*sic*] daunt nor temper."[8]

Hall described the average teenager as unstable, selfish, asocial, inclined to delinquency, tortured by sexual and aggressive drives, irresponsible, and untrustworthy. If injurious effects were to be avoided, Hall argued, adolescent storm and stress had to be restrained, its biological irruptions sublimated into constructive channels. Otherwise, these impulses would appear later in the life cycle as "feral traits or even animalism."[9] Not only did this jaundiced view of adolescent growth heavily influence Hall's generation, it also prefigured the widespread acceptance of Freudian/psychoanalytic theory, which proffered a similar description of adolescence.

Freudian psychology is broadly defined as "a dynamic psychology that studies the transformation and exchanges of energies within the personality."[10] Freud postulated the existence of three personality structures, which regulate the ebb and flow of psychic energy: the id, ego, and superego. As the seat of instinctual drives and impulses, the id represents the "pleasure principle" and continually seeks gratification through the agency of the ego. Representing the "reality principle," the ego is the perceiving, thinking, reasoning self; "in a well-adjusted person the ego is the executive of the personality, controlling and governing the id and the superego and maintaining commerce with the external world in the interest of the total personality and its far-flung needs."[11] The superego comprises two structures, the ego ideal (the seat of goals and ideals) and the conscience (the seat of guilt), which restrain the excesses of the id and give direction to the ego.

A second major component of Freudian psychology is the stage theory of psychosexual development. Freud argued that the life cycle comprises five stages: oral, anal, oedipal, latency, and genital. In each stage the individual must accomplish developmental tasks that are prerequisites for later stages. Failure to negotiate the tasks at any stage retards emotional growth at later stages.

The psychosexual stages of particular importance in the psychoanalytic study of adolescence are the oedipal, latency, and genital stages. According to Freud, in the oedipal stage the boy cathects his mother as the object of sexual energy and directs aggressive energy toward the father, whom he regards as a rival for his mother's affections. Yet the boy also fears that the powerful father will castrate him as punishment for the fantasized incest. Castration anxiety causes him to repress his oedipal and hostile impulses.[12]

No longer burdened with anxiety and guilt, the boy identifies with his father and internalizes (introjects) parental values, creating the superego. Freud believed that a similar process takes place in female development. Incestuous love for the father and attendant penis envy gradually subside at the end of the oedipal stage, although the girl does not fully repress these urges. Both male and female enter the latency period temporarily freed from the discomfitures of biological impulses. The resurgence of the impulses at puberty causes the storm and stress of adolescence (the genital stage).[13]

Freud's descendants in the psychoanalytic tradition drew heavily upon his conceptualization of psychosexual development, extending and elaborating his theory in their own analyses of adolescence. Two eminent figures in the psychoanalytic study of adolescence since Freud's death have been his daughter, Anna, and Peter Blos. Primarily on the strength of Anna Freud's reputation, the doctrine of adolescent storm and stress has held the status of dogma among psychoanalytic theorists from the 1930s to the present.[14]

In her seminal work, *The Ego and the Mechanisms of Defense* (1936), Anna Freud described the perpetual internecine struggle of the id and ego. Faced with an onslaught of sexual and aggressive impulses (instinctual impulses) from the id, the ego activates its defenses to prevent an overthrow by its rival. "The instinctual impulses . . . pursue their aims with their own peculiar tenacity and energy, and they make hostile incursions into the ego, in the hope of overthrowing it by a surprise attack. The ego, on its side, becomes suspicious; it proceeds to counterattack and to invade the territory of the id. Its purpose is to put the instincts permanently out of action by means of appropriate defense mechanisms, designed to secure its own boundaries."[15]

The ego is most vulnerable at the onset of puberty, when the instinctual drives dramatically increase in strength and quantity. The beleaguered ego constructs an unprecedented array of defenses, which are expressed behaviorally as emotional volatility, turmoil, and rebellion. In a passage reminiscent of G. Stanley Hall, Anna Freud described the symptoms of "normal" adolescence: "The height of elation or depth of despair, the quickly rising enthusiasms, the utter hopelessness, the burning—or at other times sterile—intellectual and philosophical preoccupations, the yearning for freedom, the sense of loneliness, the feeling of oppression by the parents, the impotent rages or active hates directed against the adult world, the erotic crushes—whether homosexually or heterosexually directed—the suicidal fantasies, etc."[16]

One of the behavioral peculiarities closely examined by Anna Freud was asceticism, a trait she associated with reduced eating or the postponement of excretion.[17] While she insisted that asceticism was not indicative of a neurosis, her argument was not persuasive. Like G. Stanley Hall's, her descriptions of the oscillation of the "normal" adolescent personality between the extremes of "instinctual excess"—in this case, between asceticism and libertarianism—had undeniably pathological overtones.

Anna Freud believed that storm and stress was a marker of normal development. Indeed, the absence of these symptoms—particularly rebellion—was taken to be abnormal and believed to warrant psychiatric intervention.[18] She acknowledged the problem her interpretation posed for clinicians: "I refer to the difficulty in adolescent cases to draw the line between normality and pathology. . . . Adolescence constitutes by definition an interruption of peaceful growth which resembles in appearance a variety of other emotional upsets and structural upheavals. The adolescent manifestations come close to symptom formation of the neurotic, psychotic or dissocial order and merge almost imperceptibly into borderline states, initial, frustrated or fully fledged forms of almost all the mental illnesses. Consequently, the differential diagnosis between the adolescent upsets and true pathology becomes a difficult task."[19]

Peter Blos attends more carefully to the nuances of psychosexual development than Anna Freud, for whom the details were only marginally interesting. In fact, Blos's meticulous explanation of the oedipus complex from its first appearance in early childhood to its final resolution in late adolescence makes painfully laborious reading.

In Blos's complex theory, the major developmental task of adolescence is "the shedding of family dependencies [and] the loosening of infantile object ties in order to become a member of the adult world."[20] In his magnum opus, *On Adolescence: A Psychoanalytic Interpretation* (1962), Blos postulated that in normal development, the adolescent ego diverts the psychic energy (libido) that has formerly bound it to the parental ego and, by degrees, cathects extrafamilial objects in the following order: first, peers and idealized role models (e.g., sports heroes); second, the ego itself (narcissism); third—and finally—heterosexual, extrafamilial relations.[21] The ego's attachment to and preference for extrafamilial, heterosexual relations signifies a full and lasting renunciation of oedipal wishes and the achievement of individual autonomy from the family group.

Complicating, as well as giving impetus to, the individuation process is the resurgence of the oedipus complex, which activates subconscious anxiety and fears of regression to preoedipal childhood dependencies: "Oedipal wishes and their attending conflicts come to life again. The finality of this inner break with the past shakes the adolescent's emotional life to the center; by the same token, this break opens up to him unknown horizons, raises hopes, and generates fears."[22]

According to Blos, the ego's progressive individuation from familial object ties has unpleasant behavioral correlates—"attendant and well-recognized states of chaos"—throughout adolescence.[23] For example, the adolescent narcissist vehemently renounces familial values: "The parent . . . now becomes undervalued and is seen to have the shabby proportions of a fallen idol. The narcissistic self-inflation shows up in the adolescent's arrogance and rebelliousness in his defiance of rules, and in his flouting of the parent's authority."[24]

In the mainstream psychoanalytic tradition, adolescence is generally described as an affliction: "One is in the grip of erratic and, at times, uncanny emotions, subject to storms of affect—rages, depressions, enthusiasms, and the like—which seem to have a life of their own."[25] An underlying assumption of the psychoanalytic paradigm is that biological changes at puberty have direct and unmediated psychological effects. Psychiatrists Peterson and Taylor have described the direct-effects model as follows: "Direct causal linkages are proposed between physiological (e.g., neuroendocrine) changes as antecedent variables and certain psychological phenomena of adolescence as the dependent variables. Because primary importance is attributed to physiological causes, other causal, intervening variables (such as psychological structures, cognitive processes, or sociocultural influences) are not included as significant features of this model."[26]

These investigators have found no evidence in the literature on behavioral endocrinology to support the psychoanalytic assumption of biological determinism. In fact, the weight of the evidence supports a mediated-effects model that includes the adolescent's subjective experience of pubertal changes, as well as familial, peer, and sociocultural attitudes and expectations.

In his pioneering psychoanalytic studies of ego identity formation, Erik Erikson has built upon and extended Freudian theory to include a psychosocial model of development—seven stages between early childhood and old age, which are analogs of the Freudian psychosexual stages. Erikson has described his model as "an emergency bridge between the so-called 'biological' formulations of psychoanalysis and newer ones which take the cultural environment into more systematic consideration."[27] In short, he argues that epigenetic growth—the sequential unfolding of "the maturing organism"—is *mediated* by environmental and sociocultural factors that govern psychic health at each growth stage.

Yet Erikson's conclusions about the nature of adolescence, based largely on his study of patients (pathographic data) and the biographies of famous persons who experienced upheaval in adolescence (e.g., George Bernard Shaw and Martin Luther), do not dispute the mainstream psychoanalytic tradition. For example, Erikson observes "the similarity of adolescent 'symptoms' and episodes to neurotic and psychotic symptoms and episodes." Like many other psychoanalysts, he assumes that adolescence is "a normative crisis."[28]

The conventional wisdom that normative adolescence is tumultuous has promoted a dangerous confusion among clinicians between pathology and normality. In the late 1960s psychiatrist James Masterson criticized his colleagues for their uncritical acceptance of the theory of "symptomatic adolescence" promulgated by Anna Freud and others. In his longitudinal study of a sample of outpatient adolescents, from ages sixteen to twenty-one, Masterson found that adolescent turmoil was often symptomatic, not of normal development, but of psychiatric illness. This is to say, he wrote, that "many symptomatic adolescents are not going to 'grow out of their difficulties.'"[29] He admonished clinicians of the dangers of casually dismissing manifestations of psychic disturbance as normal adolescent behavior: "The tendency to attribute symptomatology among adolescents to temporary, developmental 'turmoil' rather than to psychiatric illness may dangerously delay the therapeutic intervention required to prevent the development of greater psychopathology."[30]

Adolescence as Benign Growth/Potentiality

Over the past two decades, adolescent psychologists have compiled persuasive evidence that normative adolescence is a period of benign growth, neither volatile nor tumultuous. Contrary to the stereotype/ traditional psychoanalytic view, these studies suggest that the majority of American youths are neither volatile, hostile, nor alienated from adult society. In fact, storm and stress is atypical behavior for the period—the developmental path least taken.

From Anna Freud's day to the present, psychiatrists and psychoanalysts have based their conclusions about adolescence on their clinical experiences.[31] The neo-Freudians have assumed that morbidity is an exaggerated form of normality—hence their generalizations from patients diagnosed as depressive, paranoid, schizophrenic, and psychopathic to "normal" adolescents. Their goal, as stated by Sigmund Freud, has been to "extract from psychopathology what may be of benefit to normal psychology."[32] Given that these investigators have not used representative sampling procedures, however, their inferences about normative adolescence as tumultuous are suspect. On the other hand, all studies that have been based on a representative sampling of adolescents dispute "the turmoil theory."[33]

The longitudinal study of adolescence conducted by Offer and Offer is a strong case in point. The Offers based their findings on a sample of "normal or typical middle-class midwestern, adolescent males," selected on the basis of scores on ten scales of a "Self-Image Questionnaire." The subjects were "those who seemed to be functioning primarily at a middle range in most areas of personal and social adjustment. The aim of the selection was to find a modal male population and to eliminate from the research subjects exhibiting extremes of psychopathology, deviancy, or superior adjustment."[34]

The research team for this study tracked seventy-three students throughout the high school years and collected follow-up data on their subjects for the post–high school years (1962–70) as follows: sixty in the first year, forty-six in the second year, forty-one in the third year, and forty-six in the fourth year. The investigators conducted psychiatric interviews with each subject at least once per year from 1964 to 1969, administered a battery of psychological tests and self-rating instruments, interviewed parents, and had teachers rate the subjects.

As their most significant finding, the Offers identified three developmental paths within the modal population of male adolescents: continuous growth, surgent growth, and tumultuous growth. While each path manifested its share of growing pains, only tumultuous growth, which characterized just 21 percent of the sample, resembled the turmoil associated with the psychoanalytic conception of adolescence. The authors hypothesized that "the tumultuous youth behaves in a similar manner throughout his life. Tumult is aggravated during transitional periods, and in that sense adolescence and adulthood qualify as protagonists for those who are prone to meet change with emotional upheaval."[35]

This is not to suggest that adolescence is devoid of disquietude or discomfort—for either young people or their parents. The familiar phenomenon of the young adolescent's self-preoccupation is a case in point. David Elkind, who has examined adolescent egocentrism, regards it as a universal and typically benign manifestation of the individual's passage from lower-level cognitive capabilities (concrete operations) to abstract reasoning (formal operations).

> Formal operational thought not only enables the adolescent to conceptualize his thought, it also permits him to conceptualize the thought of other people. This egocentrism emerges because, while the adolescent can now cognize the thoughts of others, he fails to differentiate between the objects toward which the thoughts of others are directed and those which are the focus of his own concern. Now it is well known that the young adolescent, because of the physiological metamorphosis he is undergoing, is primarily

concerned with himself. Accordingly, since he fails to differentiate between what others are thinking about and his own mental preoccupations, he assumes that other people are as obsessed with his behavior and appearance as he is himself. *It is this belief that others are preoccupied with his appearance and behavior that constitutes the egocentrism of adolescence.*[36]

Elkind has observed that egocentricism wanes in middle adolescence (by the age of fifteen or sixteen) as the individual's growing powers of cognition (aided by increased social experience) make possible the distinction between real and imaginary audiences. "In a way the imaginary audience can be regarded as a hypothesis—or better, as a series of hypotheses—which the young person tests against reality. As a consequence of this testing, he gradually recognizes the difference between his own preoccupations and the interests and concerns of others."[37]

Elkind's interpretation suggests that many of the growing pains associated with adolescence have begun to subside by the high school years. In their well-regarded study, the Offers found that the early stages of adolescence (ages twelve to fourteen) were the most noisome for parents, who reported outbursts of "bickering" from their pubescent youngsters—usually over trivial matters. Significantly, adolescents evidence far less hostility and aggression toward adults than psychoanalytic theory would imply. Even this "moderate rebellion," which parents find a huge irritant, disappears during the high school years.[38]

A large body of evidence disputes the contention that adolescents are estranged from adult values—the position taken by James Coleman in his widely respected panel report, *The Adolescent Society* (1961). In their cross-cultural comparison of American and Danish adolescents, based on the results of a questionnaire survey of several thousand male and female teenagers (ages fourteen to eighteen) and their mothers, Kandel and Lesser found "close and harmonious relationships" between parents and their adolescent children in both cultures: "Overall adolescents feel very close to their parents. More than 50 percent in both countries report that they are 'extremely close' or 'quite close' to their mothers and fathers."[39]

The authors also noted that the individuation process (autonomy striving) does not estrange adolescents from parents: "The enhanced feeling of independence is associated with closeness to parents and positive feelings towards them."[40] This finding disputes the psychoanalytic assumption that extreme rebellion is a mark of normal adolescent development.

Studies conducted during the turbulent 1960s indicated, surprisingly enough, that the public image of militant, enraged youth was largely the product of a media-promulgated stereotype. For example, the Offers collected longitudinal data on the modal male adolescent population at the height of the student protest movement, yet they found no evidence of a generation gap: "Our evidence indicates that both generations *share the same basic values*. . . . This scale of values would include the religious, moral, ethical, and political standards of the individual. Further it would include the individual's goals and aspirations in life. . . . It would not include such superficial preferences as the kind of clothes one wears and how one wears them, the kind of music one listens to, or the kind of food one likes."[41]

Observers of student activism (defined as sit-ins, marches, etc.) in the 1960s found that student activists tended to share many of the basic values espoused by their parents, that they did not rebel against, but rather acted upon those values, perhaps in ways that were offensive to their parents.[42] For example, in a longitudinal study "at a large state university" (1964–68), Coopersmith and associates surveyed parents and students and found little evidence of a generation gap: "Relationships are generally congenial between youth and their parents, and . . . these youth generally admire and respect their parents' values and integrity. Few parents are seen as hypocritical, and most have given considerable decision powers to their offspring."[43]

Coopersmith et al. reported that only 10 percent of the students were campus activists—a finding congruent with the 9 percent to 15 percent figures reported by other investigators. Moreover, even within the activist group, the authors found evidence of shared beliefs and values with parents: "By and large, the young are not seriously deviating and rebelling against their parents but instead are attempting to implement the very beliefs they learned from their parents: beliefs in social justice, in the superiority of intellectual and aesthetic pursuits over material success, and in the need for increased freedom of expression and more humanitarian concern."[44]

This discussion should not be construed as a disparagement of the usefulness of such psychoanalytic constructs as "individuation" (Blos) and "ego identity formation" (Erikson). The point is, rather, that the behavioral manifestations of these processes are far more quiescent than the conventional wisdom suggests.

Researchers of juvenile delinquency have observed that "the frequency of delinquent behavior accelerates from late childhood through middle adolescence, then begins to level off, although it continues to rise until early adulthood before it subsides."[45] Their studies, based on self-reports, also indicate that over 80 percent of adolescents have committed at least one act of delinquency. At first glance, these findings would seem to support the paradigm of adolescence as a traversable pathology. Yet Gold and Petronio, who reviewed over one hundred studies on juvenile delinquency, point out that most delinquent acts are such peccadilloes as drinking (a status offense) and smoking pot. Moreover, "relatively few adolescents are responsible for most of the delinquent behavior committed by the cohort."[46]

In a national study for the Drug Abuse Council, Yankelovich and his colleagues examined drug usage among nearly two thousand high school and college students in the mid-1970s. These observers reported that while most adolescents and youth had experimented with drugs on at least one occasion, very few were abusers of these substances: "Drug experimentation and use is not limited to a small fringe of freaks, but is quite widespread. Two out of three college students (64 percent) and almost half of all high-school students (48 percent) have experimented at least once or twice with drugs, typically marijuana. About one third currently consider themselves regular users (26 percent in high school, 41 percent in college). Fewer smoke marijuana daily—six percent of the high school students, eight percent of the college students." Significantly, these adolescent drug users did not evidence pathological behavior: "The research shows that two correlates of drug abuse do not apply to most student drug users: signs of psychological disturbance associated with depression and a negative self-identity, and a readiness to abandon rather than revise the norms and values of the larger society from which the drug user feels excluded." The Yankelovich study indicated that drug use by this age cohort was generally restricted to social settings: "They use drugs for the same reasons that they and adult social drinkers use liquor."[47] Rather than rebelling against adult norms, adolescents seemed to be emulating them.

Jessor and Jessor reported a similar conclusion in their longitudinal study of adolescent drinking patterns in a small Rocky Mountain city. They found that by the senior year in high school, 78 percent of their large random sample of students were drinkers. Given the premium put on social drinking by adult society, their findings indicate that drinking behavior is a transition marker of normative development—a manifestation of youth's aspirations for adult status.[48]

Finally, for all the media hoopla about rampant and escalating substance abuse among adolescents in the mid-1980s, "the most reliable recent surveys suggest that both drug and alcohol use actually may be declining."[49] Representative findings reported for the period 1975–83 by the University of Michigan Institute for Social Research indicate a nationwide decline among high school seniors in "overall illicit drug use." For example, current marijuana use ("some use in the past thirty days") dropped from 39% in 1979 (peak level) to 32% in 1983. Given its expense, cocaine has never been a drug of preference for this population; after a "dramatic increase" from 5.6% in 1975 to 12% in 1979, annual cocaine use declined to 11.4% in 1983. With respect to licit drugs, alcohol use "has remained relatively stable in this population" (69% reporting use in the prior month); cigarette use has dropped precipitously.[50] The vast majority of adolescents, it seems, are neither "potheads" nor "junkies"; nor are they impervious to the consequences of substance abuse.

The weight of research evidence in adolescent psychology over the past two decades belies the paradigm of adolescence as a pathology.

> Our theoretical portrait used to have adolescents racked by overwhelming forces they could barely contain, while the majority of adolescents were in fact living rather humdrum lives bounded by cars, clothes, and stereotyped relationships. . . . Development during adolescence is slow, gradual, and unremarkable. Maturation in adolescence most often takes place in steady, silent, and nontumultuous ways. Adolescents may appear to us to be bland, docile, or limited in vision because we expect (or want?) them to be other-wise. But our task at this point is to accept and understand the gradualness of ego growth and to respect the cataclysmic ego changes that hardly make a sound.[51]

The research evidence further suggests that not only do most ado-lescents exhibit, at worst, only mild rebellion, but they also value independence, honesty, and responsibility.[52] Moreover, they want to be treated as adults.

Evidence from historical and cross-cultural anthropological studies of adolescence indicates that adolescence is a cultural phenomenon restricted primarily to Western societies. Indeed, in some non-Western cultures, "the transition from childhood to adulthood may be as brief as one ritual."[53] Historians generally agree that adolescence in the United States was invented "largely as a response to the social changes that accompanied America's development in the latter half of the nineteenth and the early twentieth century."[54] In fact, in antebellum America, social status, not age or physiological characteristics, had determined how society regarded the individual. For example, the sixteen-year-old district school student was considered a "child"; a college student of the same age was regarded as a "youth."[55]

G. Stanley Hall first popularized the term *adolescence* in his two-volume tome on the subject, published in 1904.[56] By World War I, compulsory education, child-labor laws, and the juvenile court system had institutionalized adolescence and defined as it as the years between the onset of puberty and the ages sixteen to nineteen.[57] Enacted for humanitarian as well as practical reasons, these laws forced teenagers out of increasingly competitive and specialized labor markets that over the years had steadily upgraded the educational qualifications necessary for entry even at the lowest skill levels. By the 1950s the overwhelming majority of the teenage population age fourteen to seventeen was remaining in school.[58] Such has been the close association between teenagers and extended schooling that adolescence today is construed in the public mind as the years of secondary education. The extension of adolescence has been a mixed social blessing, to say the least. Certainly prolonged schooling is a sine qua non for attaining a satisfactory livelihood in postindustrial society. On the other hand, schooling routinely and consistently has contributed precious little to ensuring a smooth transition for adolescents from the world of childhood to productive adulthood.[59]

The passivity of student roles is a salient and well-documented feature of public education. Even after decades of federally funded educational reforms, conventional pedagogy remains heavily burdened with texts, workbooks, lectures, and student recitations/regurgitations. By treating adolescents exclusively as consumers, schools exacerbate the discontinuity between adolescence and adulthood. Moreover, they deny to young people opportunities to acquire dispositions for social service and to exercise responsibility at a level commensurate with their capabilities and experience.

Preoccupied with teaching cognitive skills, raising standardized text scores, and sorting children along lines of academic ability, schools roundly ignore the cultivation of sociality (a diffuse trait associated with such constructive behaviors as altruism, tolerance, cooperativeness, and community service) and the predisposition to take full responsibility for one's actions. If schools are to teach sociality, they will have to disabuse themselves not only of the tendency to view children as receptacles, fit only for the pouring in of knowledge, but also of the psychological underpinnings (the legacy of orthodox psychoanalysis and mass media stereotypes) which assume that youths must be controlled and restrained lest they wreak havoc in the streets.

Foxfire and Two Clinical/Theoretical Views of Adolescence

It is a short analytical leap from the tenets of Freudian psychology to the milieu of Rabun Gap School in the late 1960s and 1970s. Implicit in the petty rules and restrictions on the boarding students was the assumption that adolescence is inherently tumultuous, that young people are not to be trusted, that they must be constrained and closely monitored lest they do damage to themselves and society. The restrictions on student sexual behavior—no kissing, no unchaperoned dating, no meetings with the opposite sex that were not in public view—reflected a belief that youthful sexuality is dangerous and sinful.

Drawing upon sociologist Erving Goffman's researches in prisons and mental institutions, Eliot Wigginton has compared Rabun Gap School during the Foxfire era to an asylum institution. Goffman observed that such facilities evoke an "underlife" behavior from their inmates, the goal of which is "a reassertion of personal independence and self-worth."[60] The seriousness of underlife behavior—whether it is malicious or playfully mischievous—is determined by the severity of the confinement and the extent to which inmates identify with the goals of the institution.

Wigginton notes that the underlife behavior at the Rabun Gap public school "was the usual garden variety." Students asserted their independence by "smoking in the student parking lot, laying out of school, and getting the best of new or vulnerable teachers." There was rarely an escalation of misconduct, he explains, "because the school was small, generally humane, headed by a fine principal, staffed by some pretty fine teachers, and filled with students who were basically clean cut, cooperative, and polite."[61]

Wigginton states that the complexion of the school changed radically after the day students had gone home. Chafing under the weight of "majors" and "minors," the dormitory students escalated their underlife behavior, which had a malicious intent. "It was staggering," Wigginton writes. "Students who had been a joy in school turned into demons. It was the craziest thing I have ever observed."[62]

According to Wigginton, the houseparents developed a siege mentality. Failing to understand the causes of student impertinence and misconduct, they overreacted by inventing rules to cover the most trivial of infractions. A cycle of negativism ensued on all sides as the boarding students' fractiousness (real and imagined) begot more rules from the staff, which in turn begot another round of hostility from the students.

> Houseparents, separated from the real world by their jobs, lost all perspective. The war consumed them. I remember especially a directive one of the girls brought me from the dormitory bulletin board. Posted on January 14, 1974, it reflected the demented state of a housemother obviously out of control: "You have had a week to be stopping the use of 'baby' and 'man.'

Today minors will be given for their use on this floor. Example: 'Judy-man,' 'Nan-baby.' "[63]

One further aspect of the boarding school culture requires discussion: its religious underpinnings. As a former school official stated, the administration believed that an experience of religious conversion was the only path to salvation. This belief gave the campus rules a moral imperative that transcended their regulatory function.

Wigginton's file from his years at Rabun Gap includes the following memorandum from the boarding school administration, dated 16 October 1973, at the end of Christian Emphasis Week: "We are most fortunate in that we have the privilege of seeing spiritual harvest. Think of the ministers and missionaries who work years and do not have the opportunity to see the souls saved as we did last week. I wish it was possible for each of you to have stayed after the Friday night service and to have heard some of the testimonies of the young people."

Implicit in the boarding school's concern for saving young souls was a misanthropic view of humanity. Its revivalist beliefs assumed that the individual had no dignity or value apart from the conversion experience. Without a conscious rededication of one's life to Christ (being "born again"), one was damned.

The boarding school administration and staff were not advocates of Freudian psychology. It is interesting, however, to note the similarities between the psychoanalytic paradigm of adolescence and the assumptions underlying the treatment of many dormitory students at Rabun Gap School. At the confluence of religious misanthropy and Freudian psychology is a view of adolescence as volatile and untrustworthy. Both positions ascribe a profound (and sinister) influence to genital sexuality in shaping adolescent behavior. For the Freudian, the way out of the adolescent predicament is the sublimation of genital impulses in creative outlets. For the revivalist, the only resolution is religious conversion.

Throughout the Foxfire era, Rabun Gap School remained an oasis virtually untouched by the "new morality" values that had permeated most college and high school campuses by this time. Beyond their vacations and occasional weekend trips home, the dormitory students were isolated, confined, and carefully monitored by adults whose moralistic strictures were constant reminders of the sinfulness of human sexuality. It is not unreasonable to speculate that in such a moralistic environment, young people, particularly those with low self-esteem and foundering ego identity, would have been especially vulnerable to religious proselytizers. To draw upon the theory of observers who have analyzed religious conversion among adolescents, it may have been the case of Rabun Gap converts that "their adoption of the role of believer lent them the ego strength to abjure sexual behavior of any kind and perhaps sexual fantasy as well."[64] That a public affirmation of faith and spiritual renewal would have also given the convert a celebrity status in the eyes of school officials is evident in the following excerpt of a memorandum dated 14 November 1966: "More than thirty of the boarding students and some day students have accepted Christ during the Christian Emphasis Week. They need our prayerful support so that they might stand in their new found faith. They need our example so that they might grow to more effective Christian living."[65]

Time and a new administration appear to have changed Rabun Gap School since Foxfire's leave-taking in 1977. While the school (now fully independent) has retained its Christian emphasis, there has been a shift in its assumptions about human nature. Christian humanism has transplanted revivalism. Wigginton himself has acknowledged the positive direction the school has taken under its new leadership. "In all fairness, and from all I hear today," he has written, "the situation is dramatically different at the school now. There's a new headmaster, scores of new programs, enrollment is up, and there's a waiting list for admission."[66]

That Foxfire has epitomized and reinforced the benign view of adolescent development requires little elaboration of the evidence already presented. As previously documented, Wigginton and his tiny staff provided a sanctuary for restless and unhappy dormitory students at Rabun Gap School. As a group, the dormitory students responded to Wigginton's benevolence by supplying invaluable energy and enthusiasm for the fledgling magazine.

Throughout the twenty years of Foxfire, Wigginton has not only made young people (through *Foxfire* magazine) a vehicle for cultural preservation, he has also dispatched them across the country and abroad as representatives of Foxfire; he has routinely entrusted them with expensive equipment, funds, and even his own credit cards; he has given them a lion's share of responsibility for socially relevant projects (e.g., the "Betty's Creek Issue" of *Foxfire*, the Mountain City town meetings); and he has given them decision-making authority commensurate with their ability and willingness to assume meaningful responsibility.

While there can be no denying that in recent years Foxfire has

chosen the path of expediency in the interest of supporting the organization's burgeoning growth—a path that has necessarily relegated
less organizational power and responsibility to young people, the fact
remains that Wigginton has *not* altered his assumptions about the
nature of adolescence. Skepticism about the potentiality of youth is *not*
among the factors that have combined to diminish the vitality Foxfire
enjoyed during the Rabun Gap tenure.

Nowhere is the benign nature of adolescence—its need for sociality,
its capacity for empathy, its potentiality for social service—better illus-
trated than in the relationships Foxfire students have cultivated with
the mountain elderly. At one level, students have had a grand time
working in the gardens and underbrush of an elderly contact's home
or helping a craftsman like Monroe Ledford market his brooms. Yet at
a deeper, more profound level, some of them have regarded such
activity as a social responsibility. For example, Rhonda Black Waters, a
nurse in her early thirties who works with geriatric patients, recalled
her visits to the home of elder Anna Howard: "I'd go and check on her
about once a week, even when it wasn't with the magazine. It seemed
to mean a lot to her because if I missed a week, she'd send word
wanting to know if I was sick. She missed talking to me and having me
listen to her. Even after I had finished working with Foxfire, I kept in
contact with her. The day she died she sent word that she wanted to
see me. She had died about five minutes before I got up there. I felt
just like I'd lost my grandmother."

Despite the mounting evidence, supported by this evaluation study
of Foxfire, that adolescence is not a pathology, schools continue to be
built and organized according to this paradigm. Rabun County High
School in 1984 was a case in point, with its fortress-like (read *asylum*)
appearance, replete with gate guard; the administrator/drill sergeant
patrolling the halls with a paddle in his pocket; the requirement that
parents verify notes for students to leave school; the rule that students
(even seniors) could not be in classrooms after school unless attended
by an adult; the patronization of seniors with a privilege that gave
them a special corner of the lunchroom to call their own, yet ensured
that they would be in a place where their behavior could be monitored
by adults. The message to these young people could hardly have been
more explicit: They were not to be trusted.

As Wigginton stipulates, to some extent even the best of schools
must have asylum features, given their task of keeping hundreds, even
thousands, of students under one roof for six hours daily. Yet he also
makes the astute observation that good rules are those whose necessity
is self-evident for the achievement of the school's educational mission.

When I asked students and teachers why there was a guardhouse at the school entrance, they could offer only speculations. Its purpose was not self-evident—nor were the other regulations just cited.

It would be unfair to the educational hierarchy of Rabun County to suggest that its treatment of adolescents differs widely from that of other school systems. National research studies of schools have documented the salience of authoritarian roles and relationships in most high schools and the treatment of students, not as producers but as consumers. These findings suggest the premium that the nation's high schools put upon the maintenance of quiescence and docility in their students. They further imply the stranglehold that cultural stereotypes about adolescence have on our schools. Lastly, they are persuasive evidence that most schools rarely, if ever, put to constructive use the potentialities of this stage of the life cycle.

NOTES

1. Albert Bandura, "The Stormy Decade: Fact or Fiction?," *Psychology in the Schools* 1 (1964): 224–31. Social psychologist John P. Hill first called my attention to this paradigm in a guest lecture at the University of North Carolina at Chapel Hill in March 1983.

2. John P. Hill, "Participatory Education and Youth Development in Secondary Schools." See also Daniel Offer, Eric Ostrov, and Kenneth I. Howard, *The Adolescent: A Psychological Self-Portrait* (New York: Basic Books, 1981), 84–93. The authors briefly trace the rise and fall of "turmoil theory" and provide a useful bibliography.

3. Dorothy Ross, *G. Stanley Hall: The Psychologist as Prophet* (University of Chicago Press, 1972), 47, 56–57, 92, 125, 265–72, 326–33.

4. Joseph Kett, *Rites of Passage: Adolescence in America, 1790 to the Present* (New York: Basic Books, 1977), 218.

5. Ross, *Psychologist as Prophet*, 263.

6. Ibid., 266; also 47.

7. G. Stanley Hall, *Adolescence: Its Psychology and Its Relations to Physiology, Anthropology, Sociology, Sex, Crime and Religion*, vol. 1 (New York: D. Appleton, 1905), xii-xviii.

8. Hall, *Adolescence*, vol. 2, 75–77.

9. Hall, *Adolescence*, vol. 1, 322.

10. Calvin S. Hall, *A Primer of Freudian Psychology* (Cleveland: World, 1954), 6.

11. Ibid., 22.

12. Ibid., 115.

13. Ibid., 116–17.

14. Joseph Adelson and Margery J. Doehrman, "The Psychodynamic Ap-

proach to Adolescence," in *Handbook of Adolescent Psychology,* ed. Joseph Adelson (New York: Wiley, 1980), 113.

15. Anna Freud, *The Ego and the Mechanisms of Defense* (New York: International Universities Press, 1936; rev. 1966), 7.

16. Anna Freud, "Adolescence," in *The Psychoanalytic Study of the Child,* vol. 13 (New York: International Universities Press, 1958), 260.

17. Freud, *Ego and Mechanisms,* 152–58.

18. Freud, "Adolescence," 264–65.

19. Ibid., 267.

20. Rolf E. Muus, *Theories of Adolescence,* 4th ed. (New York: Random House, 1982), 100.

21. Peter Blos, *On Adolescence: A Psychoanalytic Interpretation* (New York: Free Press of Glencoe, 1962), 72–107.

22. Ibid., 88.

23. Ibid., 73.

24. Ibid., 91.

25. Adelson and Doehrman, "Psychodynamic Approach to Adolescence," 105.

26. Anne C. Peterson and Brandon Taylor, "The Biological Approach to Adolescence: Biological Change and Psychological Adaptation," in *Handbook of Adolescent Psychology,* ed. Adelson, 132–33.

27. Erik H. Erikson, *Identity and the Life Cycle* (New York: Norton, 1959, rev. 1980), 161.

28. Ibid., 125.

29. James F. Masterson, Jr., "The Symptomatic Adolescent Five Years Later: He Didn't Grow Out of It," *American Journal of Psychiatry* 123 (1967): 1338.

30. James F. Masterson, Jr., "The Psychiatric Significance of Adolescent Turmoil," *American Journal of Psychiatry* 124 (1968): 1552.

31. See discussion of this methodological fallacy in Daniel Offer and Judith Offer, *From Teenage to Young Manhood: A Psychological Study* (New York: Basic Books, 1975), 160–66. In *Identity: Youth and Crisis,* Erik Erikson states "that the conflicts we meet in our case histories in vastly aggravated form are, in principle, common to all individuals, so that the picture presented is only a distorted reflection of the normal adolescent state" (179).

32. Erikson, *Identity and the Life Cycle,* 131.

33. Adelson and Doehrman, "The Psychodynamic Approach to Adolescence," 113.

34. Offer and Offer, *Teenage to Young Manhood,* 7.

35. Ibid., 185. Daniel Offer's recent work has included the study of adolescent females. In a report of research covering the period 1962–80, Offer et al. conclude that "normal young people [of both sexes] in our culture enjoy life and are happy with themselves most of the time. . . . Normal adolescents generally believe that they have control over their lives" (*The Adolescent,* 46).

36. David Elkind, "Egocentricism in Adolescence," *Child Development* 38 (1967): 1029–30.

37. Ibid., 1032. See also Elkind, "Strategic Interactions in Adolescence," in *Handbook of Adolescent Psychology,* ed. Adelson, 432–44. In this delightful scholarly treatise, Elkind describes phoning, choosing one's friends, dating and ostracism as behaviors orchestrated to impress the imaginary audience.

38. Daniel Offer, *The Psychological World of the Teenager: A Study of Normal Adolescent Boys* (New York: Basic Books, 1969), 186–87.

39. Denise B. Kandel and Gerald S. Lesser, *Youth in Two Worlds: United States and Denmark* (San Francisco: Jossey-Bass, 1972), 74.

40. Ibid., 85.

41. Offer, 205.

42. Reviewed by Martin L. Hoffman, "Moral Development in Adolescence," in *Handbook of Adolescent Psychology,* ed. Adelson, 330–33.

43. Stanley Coopersmith, Mary Regan, and Lois Dick, *The Myth of the Generation Gap* (San Francisco: Albion, 1975), 139.

44. Ibid., 278.

45. Martin Gold and Richard J. Petronio, "Delinquent Behavior in Adolescence," in *Handbook of Adolescent Psychology,* ed. Adelson, 523.

46. Ibid.

47. Daniel Yankelovich, "Drug Users v. Drug Abusers: How Students Control Their Drug Crisis," *Psychology Today,* October 1975, 39–42.

48. Richard Jessor and Shirley L. Jessor, "Adolescent Development and the Onset of Drinking," *Journal of Studies on Alcohol* 36 (1975): 25–51, reprinted in *Adolescent Behavior and Society: A Book of Readings,* 3rd ed., ed. Rolf E. Muus (New York: Random House, 1980), 455–75. A similar finding is reported in Jere Cohen, "Adolescent Independence and Adolescent Change," *Youth and Society* 12 (1980): 107–24.

49. Richard Danzig and Peter Szanton, *National Service: What Would It Mean?* (Lexington, Mass.: Heath, 1986), 60.

50. Lloyd D. Johnson, Patrick M. O'Malley, and Jerald G. Backman, *Drugs and American High School Students, 1975–1983* (Rockville, Md.: National Institute on Drug Abuse/U.S. Department of Health and Human Services, 1984), 11–14, 99, 181, 186.

51. Ruthellen Josselson, "Ego Development in Adolescence," in *Handbook of Adolescent Psychology,* ed. Adelson, 188.

52. Reported findings of values surveys of large samples of teenagers in the public schools of Adelaide and Sydney, Australia, and New York City, by Norman T. Feather, "Values in Adolescence," in *Handbook of Adolescent Psychology,* ed. Adelson, 261–65.

53. Rolf E. Muus, "Puberty Rites in Primitive and Modern Societies," in *Adolescent Behavior and Society,* ed. Muus, 507.

54. David Bakan, "Adolescence in America: From Idea to Social Fact," *Daedalus* 100 (1971): 980.

55. Joseph F. Kett, "Adolescence and Youth in Nineteenth Century America, *Journal of Interdisciplinary History* 2 (1971): 293–94.

56. Ibid., 283.

57. Bakan, 979–96.

58. See Table 39, *Digest of Education Statistics 1987,* 50. For an excellent discussion of the factors that contributed to the upward trend in high school enrollments in a major American city, see David John Hogan, *Class and Reform: School and Society in Chicago, 1880–1930* (Philadelphia: University of Pennsylvania Press, 1985). These factors included diminished employment opportunities for youth, credentialism, rising educational aspirations and improved economic mobility of the immigrant working class, and the growth of immigrant-supported Catholic high schools (chaps. 2–3).

59. Recognition of this state of affairs in the 1970s prompted a spate of recommended programs for youth work and community service, e.g., James Coleman et al., *Youth: Transition to Adulthood* (University of Chicago Press, 1974); National Commission on the Reform of Secondary Education, *The Reform of Secondary Education: A Report to the Public and the Profession* (New York: McGraw-Hill, 1973); Kettering Commission on Youth, *The Transition of Youth to Adulthood: A Bridge Too Long* (Boulder, Colo.: Westview Press, 1980).

60. Wigginton, *Shining Moment,* 251.

61. Ibid., 253.

62. Ibid.

63. Ibid., 254.

64. See Gold and Petronio, "Delinquent Behavior in Adolescence," 528.

65. Wigginton, *Shining Moment,* 27.

66. Ibid., 253.

TEN

Foxfire and Southern Appalachia

In previous chapters, *community* has implied only a specific Appalachian microcosm: Foxfire's immediate sphere of influence within Rabun County and its environs. Yet the larger Appalachian community—the Appalachian macrocosm—must also be considered, for here Foxfire has exerted a profound influence as well. This chapter begins with the whirlwind changes that have swept over Rabun County in the past decade and stimulated changes in the Foxfire program. As indicated by a review of Appalachian historiography since the 1960s, the forces that have transformed Rabun County are part of (and congruent with) the larger Appalachian experience. This literature provides the background necessary for assessing Foxfire in its regional context.

Rabun County: The Appalachian Microcosm

In 1970 Houghton Mifflin published *Deliverance,* poet James Dickey's narrative saga of four city men pitted against the malefic forces of a wild, unforgiving river and brutish mountaineers. Although Dickey used fictitious geographic names, his few references to the river's location (e.g., 150 miles northeast of a metropolitan area, a county in the north Georgia mountains) suggest that the prototype for the novel's Cahulawassee River was the Chattooga River, which forms Rabun County's border with South Carolina. When Warner Brothers filmed the movie version of *Deliverance* on the Chattooga in 1972, the novel became inextricably linked to Rabun County.

In his descriptions of north Georgia mountaineers, Dickey intensified regional stereotypes that portray native Appalachians as an isolated race of bootleggers, moral degenerates, physical brutes, illiterates, and misanthropes. The following excerpts from *Deliverance* support this argument:

> These are good people, Ed. But they're awfully clannish, they're set in their ways. They'll do what they want to do, not matter what. Every family I've ever met up here has at least one relative in the penitentiary. Some of them are in for making liquor or running it, but most of them are in for murder. They don't think a whole lot about killing people up here. They really don't. (45)

> Everything in Oree was sleepy and hookwormy and ugly, and most of all, inconsequential. Nobody worth a damn could ever come from such a place. (55)

> In the comparatively few times I had ever been in the rural South I had been struck by the number of missing fingers. Offhand, I had counted around twenty, at least. . . . The work with the hands must be fantastically dangerous, in all that fresh air and sunshine, I thought: the catching of an arm in a tractor part somewhere off in the middle of a field where nothing happened but that the sun blazed back more fiercely down the open mouth of one's screams. . . . I wanted none of it, and I didn't want to be around where it happened either. But I was there, and there was no way for me to escape, except by water, from the country of the nine-fingered people. (55–56)

In the book's most memorable scene, two of the canoeists, Ed and Bobby, are confronted by two lawless mountain men in the woods beside the river.

> They came forward moving in a kind of half circle as though they were stepping around something. The shorter one was older, with big white eyes and a half-white stubble that grew in whorls on his cheeks. His face seemed to spin in many directions. He had on overalls, and his stomach looked like it was falling through them. The other was lean and tall, and peered as though out of a cave or some dim simple place far back in his yellow-tinged eyeballs. When he moved his jaws the lower bone came up too far for him to have teeth. "Escaped convicts" flashed up in my mind on one side, "Bootleggers" on the other. But they still could have been hunters.[1]

Hunters they are not. Forced at gunpoint to lie across a log, Bobby is viciously sodomized by one of the men (in the film, he is made to squeal like a pig). Lewis, another canoeist who has been watching from a thicket, kills the rapist with a broad-headed hunting arrow. The dead man's partner escapes to the high ground, and the subsequent death of one of the canoeists is attributed to him.

This graphic scene conveys a stark and frightening image of native mountaineers—a ghoulish stereotype that has attracted tourists to the region in the same way reptile farms and carnival freak shows attract them. This image, which has been applied to Southern mountaineers in general, has shamed and outraged the people who unfairly bear its stigma.

In the yard of his house, which overlooks a narrow farming valley several miles from the river, a middle-aged Rabun County man spoke of *Deliverance* as "a disgrace to this county." In the October twilight, he implied that something sacred to him had been violated: "My grandparents and great-grandparents are buried on the river—at the Holden Cemetery. I carried my uncle up there in a two-horse wagon over a swinging bridge to bury him. . . . My kids were raised on the river. I camped and fished with them from five years old on. And I logged the river forty years ago."

Beyond reinforcing stereotypes of the traditional mountain culture, *Deliverance* had a further social consequence for the people of Rabun County. After Warner Brothers released the film version of Dickey's novel, thousands of thrill-seeking tourists embarked upon the river's rapids and cascades, some (suicidally) in tire tubes, cluttering the banks with their beer cans, broken canoes, punctured rafts—and corpses. "That's probably the most dangerous river in the country besides the Colorado," remarked James Dickey. "People are going there partly because of something I wrote and some have been killed. . . . That river is haunted for me."[2]

The local citizenry has not taken lightly the intrusion of so many outsiders into their traditional fishing and camping grounds. "People in Rabun County don't get along with the 'river rats'—we don't like them," stated a former Foxfire student who was raised three miles from the river in Rabun County's Chechero community. "I was fishing there about four years ago at Bull Sluice [a dangerous cascade on the river], and a man asked me kindly to get my pole out of the water and get out of the way. He was a river rat. It's like the locals aren't supposed to be down there."

Angry locals have harassed the river rats, shooting rifle bullets over their heads and puncturing their rafts with fishing hooks. Some have even vandalized and burned property owned by a commercial outfitter. "We're mean to 'em," said the former Foxfire student. "It's *our* river the way I see it."

This kind of territorial defense has been observed elsewhere in Appalachia. Anthropologist James W. Jordan noted a similar harassment of tourists by local residents in his case study of Coker Creek, an enclave community in the Cherokee National Forest of eastern Tennessee. Jordan hypothesized that this behavior ("defended neighborhood ideology") on the part of local residents vented their rage and frustration in the face of the powerful federal agents who now controlled their traditional hunting and grazing lands.[3]

Such might be the case in Rabun County, where the U.S. Forest Service has taken drastic measures to curtail pollution and to regulate traffic on the Chattooga. Exercising eminent domain, federal agents have bought up the adjacent lands from Rabun County south to Lake Tugaloo, Georgia, and declared the area a "wild and scenic river." This action has penalized local citizens by restricting their access to traditional fishing and camping grounds. "We used to go in at Burrell's Ford and camp," stated an elderly Rabun County man. "You can't do that anymore. It's about five miles from where the gate's at. You can't take nothing above that gate anymore."

Landownership is virtually a nonissue in Rabun County politics, perhaps because so much of the land is deemed to be nonnegotiable. The U.S. Forest Service owns 63% of the surface land (148,530 of 236,150 acres), the largest percentage of any Appalachian county; Georgia Power Company, a subsidiary of Southern Railway, owns approximately 7%, including three recreation lakes and hydroelectric power dams; industrial corporations, e.g., Burlington Industries (Rabun Mills) and Sangamo Weston, own .2%, and .65% belongs to churches and other tax-exempt organizations.[4] This leaves a niggardly 29% of the county's land for housing, agriculture, and small business development.

By any measure, Rabun County is poor. For example in 1981, the county per capita income was reported as $6,790—compared to $8,934 for the state and $10,491 for the nation.[5] In 1983 Rabun's per capita income stood at 70% of the Georgia average; 62% of the national average.[6] According to 1980 census data, 16.9% of the county's population lived below the poverty level.[7]

In 1980, Rabun County had a labor force of 4,643, of which 36% were employed in manufacturing industries. Approximately 52% were employed in services related to tourism/recreation development (finance, insurance, real estate and services, wholesale and retail trades). In 1950, 38.5% of the labor force had been employed in agriculture, forestry, fisheries, and mining, compared with only 5.7% for this sector in 1980.[8] Like other areas of Appalachia, farming has been displaced by the shift in the county's economic base. Between 1978 and 1982, the number of farms continued to decline—from 163 to 143 with an average of 81 acres per farm.[9]

Before the coming of industry, Rabun County was much poorer

than it is today. A woman who had taught in the county schools for thirty-five years recalled those hard times and compared their conditions to the present.

> When I first started teaching in Rabun County in 1941, I taught one year at Lakemont [a community in the south end of the county]. The children did not have a penny to make a valentine with. I bought the construction paper for the valentines and they made them. Ice cream was a nickel in the lunchroom. They couldn't buy ice cream. There were holes in the bottoms of their shoes. They were very poorly clad. . . . I would get clothes for the children in the community. . . . Then after industry came—how many poorly clad children do you see at the high school? I'd say a dozen out of nine hundred. I do not think we have many hungry people in this county now. They have better homes. They don't sleep cold. A few, but a *very* few. They don't come to school without coats in wintertime. If they do it's by choice. Industry has raised the economic standing of this county and the educational opportunities for people beyond high school. Trade school is not beyond most low-income families now.

The textile industry arrived in Rabun County in the 1950s, attracted by the prospect of low-wage, docile, nonunion labor. The Clayburne shirt factory opened in Clayton, and Burlington Industries/Lees Carpets Division began its operations in Rabun Gap. Sangamo Weston, an Ohio-based manufacturer of energy-measuring instruments, opened a plant in the Wolffork Valley in the late 1970s. None of these wage-based industries has had to contend with unionization. Predictably, industry representatives argue that their employees do not want a union; as one observes: "The people have benefits without having the need for a union. The organizer comes around and the people don't need it. . . . Here the people are treated good."

A spokesman for Burlington Industries indicated that a large majority of his plant's salaried positions were filled by local people—yet of approximately 650 employees only about eighty were salaried. Of the wage earners, he reported, "eighty to eighty-five percent . . . are in the $6.00-$7.00 [per hour] range." A Clayburne representative stated that the six salaried positions at his plant belonged to people "born and raised in Rabun County." The plant's other 270 workers were paid a piece rate, with a guaranteed minimum of $3.45 per hour for new employees.

The behavior of Sangamo Weston, Inc., a subsidiary of Schlumberger, Ltd., has underscored the instability of the local economy. In 1977, Sangamo proposed to build a plant in Rabun County, forecasting an eventual 1,200 new jobs for local people. The Chamber of Commerce, which recruited the Northern-based industry, boldly predicted an additional $9 million in retail sales as a result of Sangamo's coming. Yet a vocal minority objected to locating the new plant in a beautiful farming valley, fearing that Sangamo, which allegedly had a poor environmental record, would pollute the area.

Privately, Eliot Wigginton and his Foxfire staff sided with those who believed that Sangamo posed an environmental threat. A former Foxfire student who worked for the industry at the time she was interviewed recalled "the only time I got mad at Foxfire": "They didn't want Sangamo coming in here. They fought it to the last stitch. . . . Margie and Wig talked to me one time, and they were saying it was going to pollute the water. But you know I've got to have a job."

The heatedly debated issue came to a head at the Rabun County courthouse on the night of 9 December 1977. The occasion was a meeting of the county planning board to adjudicate Sangamo's request for a zoning change of its Wolffork Valley property from agricultural to heavy industrial. After hearing both sides of the issue, the planning board would make a zoning recommendation to the county commissioners. The *Clayton Tribune* called it "one of the most widely attended public meetings that the county has ever had." An estimated four hundred to five hundred people jammed the courthouse.[10]

Sangamo was granted its request for a zoning change. Yet in the course of its short history, the promised benefits have not been delivered. In the fall of 1984, a plant representative, an in-migrant to Rabun County, extolled Sangamo's benevolence to its employees, but added that the corporation had ordered two layoffs in the two months prior to the interview. One of his observations seemed naive and stereotypic: "I could walk into the plant and say we're going to have to lay off five people in here, and they'd fuss about who's going to get to go home. This is the first place I've ever been that's been the case. They *will* get unemployment."

On 12 July 1985, Sangamo announced that it would close the Rabun County plant, beginning the phase-out in the early fall. A succession of layoffs had steadily reduced the plant's work force from a peak of 859 (early 1980s) to 250 by the summer of 1985. The corporation attributed the closing to poor sales of its electric meters.[11]

Sangamo's continuous layoffs and, finally, its closing have put almost a fifth of the county's labor force out of work. Other county industrialists have indicated that they may be able to provide work for a small minority of the employees laid off by Sangamo, but how the majority will fare remains an open question. The *Clayton Tribune* asserted:

"Both past and present job losses due to the closing of this plant stand to have a detrimental impact on the county in terms of increased unemployment."[12]

Yet many of those who have reliable jobs have trouble buying or holding onto property. The division of landownership in Rabun County, with the federal government and Georgia Power Company holding 70 percent of the property, has sharply escalated the value of the remaining land. Private recreation/resort development of mountain real estate has attracted an influx of wealthy retirees and second-home buyers and contributed to driving real estate beyond the means of many native residents.

> It makes it hard on the young generation coming up to own property. The price of it has got out of reason. You take a young couple starting out to build a house—Lord, the property is so much they'll be paying for it 'til they're seventy-five. (Betty's Creek resident)

> The property has gone immeasurable. People sell their property when times are hard, and it's gone. They sold it in a tight [under pressure]. . . . That's what fouled up everything. Property in this county is higher than any place I know of. (Mountain City resident)

> These damn realtors are a terrible plague. Once you get infested with them, they stick to you like a leech to a turtle shell. I don't think we need any more durn realtors. They ruining our county. . . . They've got land so dang high a native boy can't buy it at all. (Dillard resident)

> A lot of it is going to Florida people. If you look up on the mountains you'll see where they're building roads and houses. See that 'dozer over yonder on that mountain behind us? They got a road going way over it. Real estate people is a cause of a lot of it. They buy the land and sell it for three times what they give for it. That's caused taxes to go up. (Wolffork Valley resident)

> Locals live in trailer parks because we can't afford land. The way I see it is that there's not going to be any local people left. One reason is that the land prices are so high. (Rabun Gap resident who earned the average wage paid at Sangamo Weston and lived in a single-wide trailer home)

> People who have had land here for generations back are losing their land because of the taxes. Taxes are incredible. I know a lady who has to save all she can so she can pay her taxes. You have to hold onto your land because that's all you've got. (Boggs Mountain resident)

Census Bureau statistics for Rabun County corroborate the assessment of these native residents. For example, seasonal or migratory housing showed a 145.3% increase from 1970 to 1980. During the same period, year-round mobile homes or trailers increased 114.2%, while conventional year-round housing increased only 28.7%. The latter two percentages suggest that conventional housing is being priced beyond the means of many residents.[13]

According to a 1984 realty listing, available Rabun County lakefront and subdivision housing ranged from $69,000 to $160,000. Land lots on Screamer Mountain, overlooking Clayton, were priced from $4,500 to $11,500. Individual lots on Lake Burton, one of the recreation lakes, started at $22,500. Housing in the affordable price range for some blue-collar laborers ($22,000 to $40,000) was advertised under such ominous rubrics as "Oldie but Goodie," "Mr. Fix-it," "Price Reduction," and "Itsy Bitsy."[14]

In an interview, a Clayton banker (there are only two banks in Rabun County) acknowledged that housing is beyond the reach of the average Rabun County resident. Similarly, a Dillard realtor stated: "It becomes very difficult if you're working in a factory to buy an acre of land. It's just too expensive. Now it's reached a level where it can't go any further. . . . Property is being priced out of the range of any native . . . who hasn't inherited it."

In 1980 seasonal or migratory housing constituted 24.2% of total housing units in the county.[15] Today locals estimate that this figure is approximately 50% of the total. Rabun County natives resent this intrusion by outsiders, whom they derisively call "Floridians." One woman suggested the following behavior for flaring Rabun County tempers: "Shoot their dog or tell 'em you're from Florida."

There is evidence that the local stereotype of the affluent, condescending "Floridian" has a strong basis in fact. A case in point is Sky Valley, the wealthy resort community located in a wide valley four miles east of Dillard. Replete with nearly four hundred expensive houses (many of Swiss Alpine design), an Alpine-style ski lodge and ski slopes, a golf course, a community swimming pool, and tennis courts, Sky Valley is in but not of Rabun County. With the exception of the winter ski season, the resort is closed to the general public, including the average Rabun County resident. A spokesman for the company observed that the rules keep local "riffraff" out of the Sky Valley lodge, where prospective buyers are entertained. Referring to two blue-collar bars in Mountain City, he stated, "We don't want a 'Filthy Dave's' or 'D's Tavern' here."

Sky Valley is owned by a family of in-migrants from the Atlanta metropolitan area. A Rabun County man was an original partner in the development, but he later sold his interest to the current owners. With eighty-eight to one hundred year-round residents, the resort is an incorporated town and remains the only community in Rabun County where liquor by the drink can be legally purchased. Sky Valley comprises 12 percent to 15 percent of the county's tax base, yet receives few county services—a fact that chagrins its residents. A county commissioner argued that local government has a legal mandate not to provide services within Sky Valley: "When we get beyond that gate [we've] got a restricted area where it's against the law for us to use tax money for a place that everybody can't have access to."[16]

A lawsuit filed in 1985 by a Rabun County banker and his brother, natives of neighboring Habersham County, provides evidence that vacation and retirement home owners do not wish to be bothered by local economic issues and concerns. When the brothers petitioned the county government for a zoning permit to build condominiums on twenty-six acres along Lake Rabun, they aroused a storm of protest from the home owners on the county's lakes. An overwhelming majority of the approximately 1,500 cabins and cottages on the county's three recreation lakes—Rabun, Burton, and Seed—were owned by residents of metropolitan Atlanta and other Georgia cities. These "outsiders" packed the planning board and commission hearings and barraged county officials with protest mail. The president of the Lake Rabun Association, an Atlanta lawyer who had vacationed on the lake for thirty years, was quoted as follows: "What concerns us most is that once you allow this one, other condominiums will be built. With that type of high-density development, you'll have to cut more roads, more power lines and soon you will have ruined the natural setting that makes Lake Rabun so special."[17]

After hearing the brothers' petition, which included an environmental study showing that condominiums were a less harmful use of the land than single-family detached dwellings, the planning board recommended to the county commissioners that the lake be rezoned for higher density development. The planning board chairman was quoted as saying: "Everybody who builds a house on one of those lakes wants it to be the last house built in the county."[18]

The county commission, however, did not agree with the planning board. Concerned that development on the lakes was moving too fast and without sufficient regulation, it denied the petition at its public meeting of 12 July 1984. Its action was intended to preclude higher density development along the lakes. Subsequently, the banker and his brother filed suit against the county in federal district court to have the commission's decision overruled. In December 1985, the suit was dismissed because of irregularities in the plaintiffs' application for a zoning variance.[19]

Ironically, the beneficiaries of the county commission's ruling were not mountain people, but rather wealthy urban dwellers from outside the region. A Clayton merchant expressed the sense of powerlessness felt by locals in the face of outside control of mountain resources: "People from Atlanta make their living there and come up here to play. Yet they don't want us to be able to make a living *here*."

The strip development along Highway 441 in Clayton, the county seat, provides visual evidence of poorly regulated land use. Nearly one mile in length, the Clayton strip juxtaposes Kentucky Fried Chicken, Pizza Hut, Hardee's, Tastee Freeze, and Dairy Queen with two stop lights, a shopping center, two motels, three restaurants, four service stations, one gift shop, two convenience stores, two automobile dealerships, a trailer park, the Chamber of Commerce, and at least five realty companies. Some of the companies have exercised a token environmentalism by building replica log cabins or gabled, Alpine-design houses. Others have flagrantly disregarded the environment. For example, there is a three-story building of retail shops, painted olive-drab green, replete with a tin roof that slopes out over the front porch and spired gables on the third floor. In the parking lot stands a forty- to fifty-foot-tall windmill, painted white and topped by a red and white fan. Behind the building is the remnant of a mountain, now a huge red-clay gash.

Perched on a mountainside near the intersection of Highway 441 and Highway 76 East (which leads to the Chattooga River), the ill-named Panorama Condominiums afford a view to the west that includes the strip development below, the Winn-Dixie parking lot, and a gouged hillside of red clay in the distance. Further north on the highway, near another intersection, is perhaps the most grotesque scenery in Rabun County. A group of investors that includes the mountain elite as well as outside businessmen has bulldozed a mountain to make room for a new shopping center. All that remains is an eroding chunk of red clay rising nearly fifty feet from the valley floor, its right flank mounted by an earthen mound that leads to a rustic cabin on top. Residents report that the cabin and remaining trees belong to an obdurate local who has demanded an exorbitant price for the land.

Further evidence that this development has not been regulated surfaced in the late summer of 1984, when the town of Clayton was adjudged to be in violation of state and federal guidelines required for participation in the National Flood Insurance Program. At issue was the strip development in the flood plain of Stekoa Creek, which flows from north to south paralleling the highway. According to the *Clayton Tribune*, "Much of the building in Clayton has been going on without building permits coming into the picture."[20] The city council had violated flood insurance regulations by allowing building that was not above the one-hundred-year flood level of the creek. Disqualification from the program meant that the city was not eligible for any federal disaster relief "to build, buy or repair property in the flood plain areas."[21]

This penalty was not to be taken lightly. In the late spring of 1976, three feet of flood water had severely damaged the Clayton Elementary School. At that time the community was a participant in the federal flood insurance program, and less than two months after the flood, the Department of Health, Education, and Welfare authorized $205,000 to reconstruct the school and replace lost textbooks.[22] Without this federal insurance, the city council would have assumed liability for any damages that resulted from flooding in the community.

As in other areas of Appalachia, Rabun County's population at large has benefited only peripherally or not at all from the upsurge of tourist-related development. There are exceptions of course, but the consistently low income levels reported for the county in recent decades indicate that the profits are concentrated in relatively few hands—for example, in-migrant realtors, outside industrialists, and wealthy mountain elite.

The Appalachian Macrocosm

Over the past decade, historians and social scientists have provided extensive documentation of the exploitation of Appalachia's land and people by absentee corporations and their allies in state and local government. One group of these scholars has adhered to an interpretation of the Appalachian highlands, from southern West Virginia to northeastern Alabama, as an "internal colony" of urban-industrial America. A smaller, more radical group argues that Appalachia is an "internal periphery" within an advanced capitalist state; in this view, exploitation of the periphery is a systemic feature of advanced capitalism. Both schools of the "new Appalachian historiography" attribute a large share of the region's long-standing social problems—its pervasive welfarism, poor schools and inadequate teachers, marginal community services, unregulated land development, environmental abuse, and endemic sense of powerlessness—to the control and, in many cases, virtually untaxed expropriation of its wealth by the absentee interests.

These acute observers have exposed serious flaws in the long-standing interpretation of Appalachia as a "subculture of poverty," the quintessential expression of which has been Jack Weller's *Yesterday's*

People (1965). In this widely read essay, Weller asserted that the region's problems were a function of the outmoded social values of the mountain culture. He wrote, "The greatest challenge of Appalachia, and its most difficult, is its people."[23] Weller and others of his ilk advocated the reconstruction of the indigenous value system as a necessary precondition for economic progress in the region. Yet these proponents of the subculture of poverty model tended to ignore fundamental historical processes, to judge native Appalachians exclusively in terms of middle-class values, and to draw stereotypic conclusions about the region as a whole from nonrepresentative samples. Conversely, writers of the new Appalachian historiography look beyond alleged cultural deficiencies to situate the causes of Appalachia's difficulties in the forces for economic modernization impelled by the growth of industrial capitalism.

The demographic and interview data reported for Rabun County indicate that some of the same economic forces identified by these observers as having divested other native Appalachians of their land and power impinge here as well. At first glance, Rabun County and the coal fields of eastern Kentucky seem to have nothing in common. Closer inspection reveals that both are, in varying degrees, victims of a pervasive mind-set within American society that views Appalachian resources as "ripe for the picking." Such imperiousness was evident in the statement of a wealthy, in-migrant Rabun County realtor: "The problem is with the mountain people. They aren't taking the initiative to take control of their own destinies, and they're allowing people like me to do it for them."

The following discussion draws upon the research of Ronald Eller, John Gaventa, and other Appalachian scholars to review briefly the history of the region from the late nineteenth century, when agents of the timber, railroad, and steel companies first began their purchases of large tracts of mountain land, to the 1980s, when the Appalachian Landownership Task Force released its seven-volume report on the consequences of absentee ownership in both the coal-mining and tourist counties of Appalachia. This documentation of the historical forces that have shaped the region (forces that have also given stimulus to popular stereotypes of the Southern highlander) provides a matrix of social and economic factors useful for analyzing Foxfire's evolution in the context of a rural mountain community, as well as its significance for the entire region.

Industrial America began its intrusions into Appalachia in the postbellum period before 1900. Speculators and agents of northern-based industries and the "New South" manufacturing centers traveled

throughout the region buying up timber and mineral rights at remarkably low prices ($.25 to $3.00 per acre) from ignorant and unsuspecting mountaineers. In the coal fields of southern West Virginia,
eastern Kentucky, southwestern Virginia, and northeastern Tennessee, industry acquired not only unencumbered rights to the coal
beneath the ground, but also to the surface land and its timber. Unable
to read or interpret the fine print on the "broad form" deed he had
signed or marked, the mountain farmer was unaware that he had
actually conveyed his birthright to the coal barons. To add injury to
insult, the farmer remained the *de jure* owner and bore sole responsibility for paying the property tax. In such a fashion, northern and
"New South" capitalists took possession of the region's coal-producing
counties.[24]

A similar exploitation occurred in the region's abundant timber-
lands. Farmers sold their timber rights at outrageously low prices and
subsequently lost control of the land on which the trees stood. As
Ronald Eller has documented, between 1890 and 1920, "the lumber
barons purchased and cut over huge tracts of mountain timberland,
devastating the region's forests in one of the most frenzied timber
booms in American history."[25] The greatest despoliation occurred in
the Great Smoky Mountains, where "over 75% of the land came under
the control of thirteen corporations."[26] By 1909, the southern highlands were producing approximately 40% of the nation's lumber. This
proved a short-lived prosperity, as the timber barons were avaricious,
uncaring landlords who did not bother to reforest the timber strands
they had devastated. Having culled and denuded large areas of southern Appalachia, they shifted their operations to the Northwest after
World War I.[27]

Industrial development in the Appalachian Mountains from West
Virginia to Alabama provided the major impetus for the demise of the
region's family farms and the social values that were attached to an
agricultural way of life. Subsistence agriculture was a hard living, and
the mountain farmer was lured into the region's mines, sawmills, and
new textile factories by the promise of an easier, more rewarding life.
The reality proved otherwise, and by 1930 industrial America brutally
controlled the lives and destinies of the once self-reliant mountaineers.

Only a residuum of the value systems that were based on a family-
oriented barter economy has survived the transformation to a national
market economy. Community social happenings such as cabin and
barn raisings, corn shuckings, pea pickings, bean stringings, and quilt-
ing bees—recalled by a generation of elders in the *Foxfire* books—have

passed into the region's folklore.[28] The local firehouse barbecue/ fund-raiser is a distant mirror of these earlier social practices. Other cultural values that have been greatly diminished by economic change are the native Appalachian's attachments to the land, homeplace, family, and community.[29] The changing pattern of land ownership *and* use has been the key factor in undermining what was once a well-integrated social structure.

Eller has described the necessary intimacy that existed between preindustrial Appalachian farmers and their land: "From the earliest settlement, mountain residents relied almost entirely upon abundant timber, stone, and other natural resources for the construction of homes, barns, tools, furniture and farm implements, and upon the fellowship of neighbors and kin for most social activities. Everything about the mountain homestead reflected a society which had adapted and harmonized with its surroundings by making effective use of local resources and by altering traditional cultural patterns to fit new physical conditions."[30]

The shift in the region's economic base from family farming to industrialization, tourism, and second-home development has increasingly divested native mountaineers of their land and its natural resources. The trend of land divestiture begun by the coal and timber barons before the turn of the century has been escalated by the recent encroachments of multinational oil corporations, land-development companies, and—not insignificantly—the federal government. As documented by the Appalachian Alliance landownership study and other sources, these encroachments have accrued few benefits and many liabilities to the region's inhabitants.

Nowhere has corporate exploitation been more blatant or callous than in the Appalachian coal fields. Yet for all the mass media attention and exposés of deplorable health, safety, and environmental standards in the coal-mining counties, improvements have been marginal—and, more often than not, the miners themselves have been blamed for their poverty and ignorance. Moreover, the oil and coal corporations, aided and abetted by cowed (or bribed) governors and legislatures, continue to evade the taxes that would substantially improve the counties' schools and community services.

By World War I, large northern-based syndicates controlled large shares of Appalachia's bituminous coal fields. For example, the triumvirate of Consolidation Coal, Clinchfield Coal, and U.S. Steel had squashed its smaller competitors and taken over the richest mines in West Virginia, Kentucky, and Virginia.[31] The absentee corporations entrusted operation of the mines to their subsidiary coal companies or leased their holdings to independent companies in exchange for fixed royalties. These lower-echelon companies managed the "company towns" that kept the coal miners in a state of servitude and compliance.

Birthed by a company doctor, baptized in a company church, educated (poorly) in a company school, forced to live in a company house, and paid in company scrip redeemable only at a company store, the coal miner existed at the beck and call of the company "bosses," who also controlled the county sheriff and tax assessor.[32] Moreover, the company town monopoly discouraged attempts to diversify the local economy through retail or manufacturing enterprises. The upshot was the long-term ruination of the Appalachian coal region's economy and the outflow of wealth, including a large portion of the miners' wages, to absentee owners. As Eller notes: "The same modernizing forces that oversaw the transition in landownership and the emergence of a new economic order in the mountains also shaped the new social environment of the region. And like so much accompanying industrialization, that environment was not of the mountaineer's own choosing."[33]

According to Eller, from 1906 to 1935, coal-mining accidents claimed the lives of 48,000 men, 71 percent of whom died in roof falls. This carnage—over four-fifths the number of Americans killed in Vietnam—did not raise a public outcry. Moreover, with few exceptions, the coal bosses were not held responsible for the poor safety conditions that made coal mining the nation's most hazardous occupation.[34]

Coal's "big boom" in the United States lasted approximately from 1912 to 1927, after which the industry went into a decline from which it has never fully recovered.[35] The shift of coal's industrial consumers to cleaner and more cost-efficient energy sources (gas, fuel oil, hydroelectric power), coupled with the development of more economical uses of coal itself, forced the coal bosses to curtail employment.[36] In the 1950s mechanization of the industry helped the coal companies recoup some of their losses, but the net effect of automation was to put increasing numbers of miners out of work. Characteristically, the coal bosses made no attempt to ameliorate the plight of their former employees.

Ill-educated and unsuited for other work, the unemployed coal miners turned to federal welfare for relief. Writing in the 1960s, Harry Caudill described the sense of powerlessness and defeatism that pervaded the coves and hollows of the Cumberland Plateau, which he called a welfare state ("By the end of 1957 in some counties more than half the people were regularly eating Government relief commodities").[37] Caudill detailed the rotting and peeling wood-frame company houses, the "ever mounting piles of debris," the "rickety, sagging" schoolhouses, and the corporate insouciance that tolerated these conditions.

In 1965, during the Johnson administration, Congress created the Appalachian Regional Commission (ARC) to oversee federally funded economic development projects in Appalachia. ARC poured hundreds of millions of federal dollars into "bricks and mortar" development programs: highway construction, hospitals, water and sewage treatment plants, vocational educational facilities, and airports.[38] While there is no denying that ARC made material improvements in the region (an example is 1,831 miles of new roads by 1985), it is doubtful that the agency made any significant contribution to eradicating the *causes* of Appalachian poverty and powerless. ARC had a mandate to invest federal dollars, not in the areas of greatest need but rather in the areas deemed to have the greatest potential growth. Of greater significance, ARC did *not* have a mandate to address such matters as corporate evasion of property taxes in the coal fields. Indeed, issues surrounding absentee landownership—the source of the region's most critical problems—were never on the federal reform agenda in Appalachia.

Working in conjunction with the Appalachian Alliance, the Appalachian Studies Conference and the Highlander Center, a group of concerned scholars and citizens from throughout the region undertook a mammoth survey of landownership in eighty counties in a six-state region of Appalachia. In January 1979 ARC became a reluctant funding partner in the study, which was based upon an exhaustive perusal of courthouse documents in each of the counties. When the seven-volume task force study was finally released in the early 1980s, the ARC refused to endorse its findings, which exposed large-scale corporate tax evasion and governmental complicity in the corporate pillage of the region.[39]

The task force researchers have discerned a consistent pattern throughout Appalachia of "concentrated corporate ownership, with a great extent of absentee ownership."[40] The pattern is starkest in the coal-producing counties, where 79% of the mineral rights (on seven million acres surveyed) are controlled by absentee owners, 52% of whom are from out of state; 27% are from in state but out of county.[41] Moreover, "not only do the coal counties have greater corporate ownership than the other county types, but the level of corporate ownership also increases with the level of coal reserves."[42]

Nowhere is corporate neglect more glaring or its consequences more appalling than in the abysmally low property taxes paid annually by the owners of the region's coal mines. As reported by the task force, "Over 75 percent of the 3,950 owners of mineral rights in the survey pay under $.25 per mineral acre in property taxes. Some 86 [percent] pay less than $1.00 per acre. In the twelve counties in eastern Kentucky—which include some of the major coal-producing counties in the region—the average tax per acre of minerals is $.002. The total property tax on minerals for these major coal counties is a meager $1,500."[43]

A case in point is a subsidiary company of the Norfolk and Western Railroad, which according to the task force pays only $76 in property taxes to Martin County, Kentucky, for $7.6 million of unmined coal—hardly enough to buy a tire for a school bus.[44] A 1978 law passed by the Kentucky legislature taxes the coal owners at the rate of one-tenth of one percent for every $100 worth of unmined coal.

In his commentary on the Clear Fork Valley, a coal-mining area that straddles the border of southeastern Kentucky and northeastern Tennessee, Gaventa offers profound insights into the way power relationships are controlled and manipulated by Appalachia's absentee corporations and their allies. Since the 1880s, the counties of the Clear Fork Valley have been dominated by a single absentee corporation, the London-based American Association Ltd., owner of 85 percent of the land. By virtue of its hegemony in county politics, the corporation has controlled the agenda of local political issues—and made corporate taxation a nonissue.

Gaventa documents that the quiescence of the valley's residents in the face of corporate power is a function of their fatalism, a pervasive "sense of inevitability, a prevailing belief that nothing can be done."[45] Corporate hegemony has been maintained "not only through institutional barriers but also through the shaping of beliefs about the [prevailing] order's legitimacy or immutability."[46] In short, deeply ingrained presuppositions of the futility of political action on behalf of the poor serve to reinforce the status quo. As Gaventa notes, "public challenges by the non-elite, as candidates or as critics, are deterred by feelings of inadequacy, fear of reprisal, or simply the sense that the outcome is a foregone conclusion."[47]

Appalachia's problems with absentee landownership are not limited to tax dodging by the energy corporations and their devil-may-care attitude about the land and its people. In the region's tourist counties, the influx of second-home builders and the federal government's removal of millions of acres from the public domain (creating national forests, parks, and wilderness preserves) have accelerated social dis-location and severely restricted the land available for use by native Appalachians. Outside the national forests of the tourist counties, excessive (and often unregulated) land development by a combination of absentee corporations, local mountain elite, and "in-migrant" realty companies has diminished the area's natural beauty, inflated land prices, and overburdened existing water and sewage treatment facili-ties. Such has been the case in Rabun County, Georgia.

The federal government is the largest single landowner in Appala-chia, yet pays no property taxes to any of the region's counties. The Weeks Act of 1911 allocated a share of federal revenues to the moun-tain counties from timber sales and other uses of the land. This measure did not benefit those communities in which federal revenues from land use were marginal or nonexistent. In 1975, Congress pro-vided some compensation in the Payments in Lieu of Taxes Act, which guaranteed to the counties $.75 for each acre of federal land. In many cases, however, an *ad valorem* tax on federal property would generate more revenue to the county than payments in lieu of taxes. For example, the Appalachian Alliance Task Force found that "in Clay and Swain Counties in North Carolina, the two counties with the highest level of federal ownership, the $.75 per acre does not compare with the $1.05 per-acre tax that out-of-state corporate owners average paying or the $1.22 that out-of-county corporate owners average pay-ing."[48]

The federal presence in Appalachia has proved a mixed blessing. On the one hand, by setting aside over five million acres of forest-lands, the government has preserved large tracts of wilderness from the unconscionable abuses that have occurred in unprotected areas. On the other hand, the government (in addition to not paying taxes) has precluded development that would increase the tax base of the counties in which it holds land, displaced large numbers of native mountaineers by exercising eminent domain, and restricted access to traditional hunting and family burial grounds.

Prospects that tourism would leverage economic growth in the region have not materialized. In the tourist counties surveyed by the Appalachian Alliance Task Force, "absentee, government, corporate, and larger individual owners in the sample . . . control some 60% of the total land surface."[49] This increasing concentration of landowner-ship in a few large hands, coupled with "the seasonal and low-wage employment of resort and recreational development," has kept per capita income at a low level in these communities.[50] Moreover, the growing demand for vacation homes and recreational property has inflated the price of land and property taxes beyond the means of many native Appalachians.[51]

Foxfire's Implications in the Regional Context

Against this socioeconomic backdrop, Foxfire's significance for Appalachia in general, and Rabun County specifically, is threefold. First, through the sale of nearly 6.7 million of its books, it has thrust positive, counter-stereotypic images of the region into the public consciousness. Second, through its mobilization of Appalachian culture in the service of youngsters' social, intellectual, and psychological growth, it provides a working model for culturally appropriate educational reform throughout the region. Third, through its community service initiatives, particularly its attempt to launch a community development enterprise in Rabun County, Foxfire inspires a vision of how native Appalachians might regain a measure of control in the face of widespread absentee ownership throughout the region. In the remainder of this chapter, each of these points is delineated, beginning with the implications of Foxfire's representation of Appalachian culture.

Coincidentally, both *The Foxfire Book* and *Deliverance* originated in the same county, the former representing the very best, the latter the very worst about native Appalachians. Foxfire's portraits of traditional mountaineers as a hardy, intelligent, self-reliant, and loving people have provided a powerful antidote to the ugly stereotypes in Dickey's book, particularly the image conveyed by the bestial "rednecks" who terrorize his "civilized" protagonists. As Buck Carver eloquently stated of Foxfire: "It's enlightened some people that we're not the dumb sons of bitches . . . they've made us out to be."

Foxfire is a recent expression of a tradition of cultural preservation and celebration in the Southern highlands. Cultural revivalism was the stock and trade of the settlement, craft, and folk schools that proliferated throughout the region in the early decades of the twentieth century. Impelled by a sense of noblesse oblige, reform-minded aristocrats such as Katherine Pettit (Hindman Settlement School, Knott County, Kentucky) and Olive Dame Campbell (John C. Campbell Folk School, Brasstown, North Carolina) founded institutions for educating mountain children and for marketing craft goods produced in the schools' furniture shops, weaving sheds, and woodcarving rooms.

Yet, as documented by social historian David Whisnant, these women promoted a "hybridized" version of mountain culture by marketing handicrafts that were not indigenous, but for which there was a national market.[52] For example, at Brasstown, mountaineers carved wooden animals with their whittling knives, yet prior to the establishment of the Campbell Folk School, woodcarving had not been a native folk art.

Whisnant's most serious criticism, however, is that cultural revivalism deflected the genteel reformers from challenging the exploitation of the Southern mountains by corporate industrialists. This criticism, however, ignores that these women were ill-suited by virtue of both breeding and temperament for radical activity. Moreover, it diminishes the substantive contributions of the reformers, who acted in what they passionately believed were the best interests of their clients. The fact remains that the Campbell Folk School (as documented by Whisnant himself) provided humane jobs and basic education for mountain people. It also served as a catalyst for funding a local agricultural cooperative, a credit union, and a savings and loan association. The Hindman Settlement School provided similar services for its clients in Knott County.

Foxfire has endured strikingly similar criticisms. Herbert Kohl has taken Wigginton to task for not lobbying on behalf of unionized labor in Rabun County (see Chapter 7). Other critics have attacked the brand of Appalachian folklore that is purveyed in *Foxfire* magazines and books. One of the most vocal has been Charles L. Perdue, Jr., a folklorist at the University of Virginia, who accuses Foxfire of "packaging a consumer version of folk culture designed for a mass culture, middle-class, mostly white audience."[53]

What appears in *Foxfire* publications, Perdue charges, is a romanticized, mythic version of culture, selectively edited to appeal to reader nostalgia. *Aunt Arie: A Foxfire Portrait* is a case in point. First, the editors blended the richest fragments of the same story told by Arie at different interviews into a composite version. Second, they altered Arie's dialect to enhance the readability of her speech. The result, states Perdue, is "versions of stories [Aunt Arie] never told while living in a dialect she never spoke."[54]

There is no denying that Foxfire projects an innocent view of traditional Appalachian culture, ignoring its dark side—its anti-intellectualism, parochialism, and occasional violence. Perdue is also on solid footing in his assumption that Foxfire's financial success is attributable to the mass appeal this vanishing culture has for white, middle-class America:

The letters-to-the-editor column in Foxfire over the years reveal people all over the United States who are anxious and ready to accept the representations of traditional North Georgia culture found in Foxfire as their own mythologized past. It is much easier to accept one standard and popular view of our heritage than it is to deal with the complexity of cultural diversity and the realities of difference in migration, settlement patterns, environmental, religious and political factors. Thus, plans for traditional structures in North Georgia are used to build an outdoor toilet in Port Sanilac, Michigan, and a log cabin in Manatee County, Florida. A folklore student from the University of Virginia visited Canada a while back and found that craftsmen at a restored historic fort had learned their crafts from one of the Foxfire books. Our own National Park Service hired a couple to demonstrate crafts in the Shenandoah National Park and when the woman said she did not know how to weave, she was given a Foxfire book and told to learn from that! These examples and more that could be given illustrate the fact that a sizable portion of the American public is ready to accept folk culture as presented in Foxfire as its mythologized national folk cultural heritage.[55]

Perdue's interpretation is consistent with the marketing patterns of other cultural journalism publications. Of the hundreds of Foxfire-descendant projects, only four have published books (one of which featured a nonwhite culture), and none has approached the success of the parent project. The second most successful project has been Salt in Kennebunk, Maine, which published two books with Doubleday—*The Salt Book* and *Salt II*. These volumes featured articles on white New England ("Yankee") seaboard culture, with subjects ranging from lobstering and shrimping to rum-running to making snowshoes and maple syrup. The only book that originated in a predominately non-white-American culture is *Cama-i*, a collaborative effort of eight hundred Alaskan students, featuring "the wild mixture of lifestyles, of personal philosophies, of racial and ethnic backgrounds in southwestern Alaska."[56]

The culture that Foxfire mirrors has traditionally been associated with an inferior standard of education. The most recently published aggregate data indicate that Appalachia continues to lag behind the nation on measures of educational attainment and school retention.[57] Scholars and other commentators in the field of Appalachian education have attributed the poor quality of the region's schools not only to politicized school administrations and inadequate funding, but also to a pedagogy that is largely irrelevant to Appalachian life and work. In their analyses, Appalachia's classrooms are described, at best, as places "where textbook cliches abound and no one makes much effort to relate them even to the limited experiences of the students in the class."[58] At worst, Appalachian education is portrayed as an instrument of class conflict used to legitimate the hegemony of the dominant culture and the prevailing class structure by inculcating in mountain children an acceptance of the inferiority of their cultural heritage.[59] From the latter perspective, Jim Wayne Miller speaks of "culturally depriving schools, schools that deprive students of the opportunity to see their lives reflected in the school, their experiences and knowledge legitimized in the school setting."[60] Across this spectrum of criticism, proposed solutions range from "multicultural education" (Appalachian studies) to "revolutionary praxis" (radical consciousness-raising and social action).[61]

Through its celebration of Appalachian traditions and values, Foxfire can be properly viewed as an attempt to resist the denigration of mountain culture. As a working model of culturally appropriate educational reform, particularly as it strengthens its academic side, Foxfire should be an attractive alternative for all but the most hardened critics who believe that nothing less than socialism will bring fundamental change to the region.

Since Foxfire's dissemination efforts in the early 1970s, only a tiny fraction of Appalachia's teachers have experimented with cultural journalism. Evidently the region's teachers have decided that the material and psychological costs of this style of pedagogy outweigh the benefits; perhaps they have even rationalized that Foxfire has a "prior claim" to Appalachian folkloric preservation at the pre-college level. After several years of refining Foxfire I, his introductory writing course, Wigginton has distilled a simpler and more economical strategy than cultural journalism for implementing his educational principles. For reasons explicated in the next chapter, it now seems likely that Wigginton's revised pedagogy will attract a larger audience than previously among teachers both within and beyond Appalachia.

Documented in previous chapters is Wigginton's belief that Foxfire's mission should encompass more than education and cultural preservation. Since the late 1970s, his vision for the organization has been to integrate these functions with community economic development. Given the repudiation of this idea by Foxfire's legal board, however, its chances of coming to fruition, at least in the short term, appear remote.

The aim of the Mountain City Project was to generate viable career alternatives, enabling indigenous youth to remain in the county after high school without having to work in a local factory. It was finally decided that the most appropriate vehicle for implementing this idea would be a Foxfire-sponsored community development corporation.

The project foundered, in large part, because there were no existing school-related CDCs (nor any about to get under way) to which the organization could turn for guidance and inspiration. As previously noted, Wigginton and his teaching staff lacked the business exper-tise—and ultimately the commitment—to attempt such a project from scratch. Although Foxfire's grants management office enlisted private foundation support for a CDC director, the staff waffled on hiring anyone. Concerned that the organization was being diverted from education, its cost-conscious legal board intervened to halt further community development planning.

As events have proved, Foxfire's abortive community development project was a variant of the idea of school-based enterprises, invented and formulated as a model for rural education and development by Jonathan Sher in the late 1970s. Ironically, Foxfire abandoned its economic initiatives at the precise moment that elements of Sher's model were being implemented in other areas of the rural South. The network of expertise and financial support that might have helped Foxfire launch its CDC is currently being developed—perhaps too late to influence events in Rabun County.

A review of Sher's model of the school-based CDC is instructive for two reasons. First, it is a theoretical model for rural education and development that is potentially useful and appropriate for Appala-chian communities seeking a measure of control over their economic destinies. Second, its successful implementation and institutionaliza-tion in the communities where pilot projects have been initiated would give Wigginton added leverage in renegotiating a Foxfire-sponsored CDC, or a related project, with his legal board at some future date.

Sher has proposed three variants of his model of the school-based community development corporation (i.e., private, quasi-public, pub-lic), assuming that different communities will have different needs and preferences. His own bias leans heavily toward the publicly owned CDC, briefly described as follows:

> Under the auspices of the school board responsible for the operations of the local public high school, a community development corporation is incorporated as a wholly owned and operated venture of the local public school district. Its legal status would be that of a special purpose public educational institution, not unlike existing vocational schools, special edu-cation facilities, and adult education centers. Its staff would be public employees; its buildings would be public facilities; its programs would serve the public; and its practices would be matter of public policy. It is, in short, intended to be a public institution in every usual and legal sense of the term.[62]

As Sher notes, the publicly owned CDC would be eligible for support from a plethora of sources, e.g., state and federal rural development funds and programs. Its optimal governance structure would be a CDC advisory board, representing various community constituencies, with the district superintendent, CDC directors, and building principal serving as nonvoting, ex-officio members. Sher cautions, however, that "this advisory group is worthless unless the school board is willing to delegate (either legally or by agreement) the bulk of its programmatic policy and decision-making powers to the CDC advisory board."[63]

Under the auspices of the school-based CDC, students would conduct research to identify deficiencies in the local economy that could be remedied by new businesses. For example, they might find a demand for affordable, energy-efficient housing that could be met by a new construction company specializing in solar homes. Once a new business had been targeted, the CDC would serve as the catalyst for start-up funds. With appropriate faculty guidance, the new business would be created, managed, and controlled by students. Ideally, the business would be profitable enough to survive independently of the CDC, providing a bona fide career alternative for the students who operated it.

Chronicling the shortcomings of conventional vocational education programs, specifically their outdated agricultural programs or training related to urban employment, Sher argues persuasively that school-based enterprises have strong potential for providing relevant, experience-based entrepreneurial and leadership training, with the added motivation that students would be shaping their own futures in their home counties. In short, a successful school-based CDC would "complement or eventually supplant existing public vocational educational programs and institutions, while concomitantly becoming an integral part of the educational experience of most rural high schools."[64]

In 1982, Appalachian strategists and representatives of populist advocacy groups met at the Highlander Research and Education Center at New Market, Tennessee, to discuss economic development strategies for Appalachia in the 1980s. The conference identified three elements that must guide future economic development initiatives if native Appalachians are to be the real (rather than the alleged) beneficiaries: (1) empowerment of people through ownership of businesses, mines, and factories; (2) improvement of the quality of life by ensuring "meaningful job opportunities, economic security . . . and maintenance of cultural integrity"; (3) democratic planning and control of development initiatives.[65] Significantly, these elements are conceptual underpinnings of Sher's model of the school-based CDC.

The first applications of Sher's model were a school-based day-care center, feeder-pig operation, and construction company, all founded in a rural county in southern Georgia. The youth-operated day-care center, a state licensed training program, is still in operation, although ownership of the business has *not* reverted from the high school, the sponsoring agency in this case, to the young people who started it.[66] In North Carolina, under Sher's direction, an organization called N.C. REAL Enterprises (REAL is an acronym meaning "Rural Education through Action Learning") has recruited five school districts in the state's eastern section to participate in a pilot program of rural school-based enterprises. Among the various businesses underway are a screen-printing operation, a graphic arts/print shop, a New York-style delicatessen, a boat-rental business, and a retail/rental store for videotapes, records, and games. Here legal arrangements are being made to ensure that after a suitable incubation period, usually no longer than three years, students who founded the business will have the first option to buy it. Thus far, N.C. REAL Enterprises, which provides a capital pool for the projects, and local school boards, which provide seed funds and services in kind, have assumed the role assigned to the school-related CDC in Sher's original formulation of the school-based enterprise concept. If its proposals are funded, N.C. REAL Enterprises will expand Sher's model to ten other sites statewide, including five in the mountains, as well as to selected rural communities nationwide.[67]

Whether or not Foxfire will ever resume planning for community development remains an open question. Wigginton reluctantly yielded to his legal board's decision to put the Mountain City Project on hold. His zealous advocacy of community-based and controlled development programs, reflected in interviews, speeches, books, funding proposals, and private conversations, suggests that he will never put the idea to rest. For example, in an interview in 1982, he expressed his commitment in the following terms:

> It's a battle not to save a way of life *per se*. It's not a battle to preserve outdoor toilets and kerosene lamps. . . . But it's a battle to get local people to the point that they realize that they can continue to survive and have decent, sane and positive futures in this part of the country if they want to stay here and carry on some of the traditions and certainly some of the values and the customs that they've grown up with and grown out of—as opposed to people who throw up their hands and say, "This problem's too big for us. There's

nothing we can do." If I thought that it was over and I thought we didn't have a chance, I wouldn't be standing here today. I mean, there's got to be a chance. Otherwise I wouldn't have a reason to go to work in the morning.[68]

NOTES

1. James Dickey, *Deliverance* (Boston: Houghton Mifflin, 1970), 108. Cf. Wigginton's analysis in *Foxfire*, Winter 1973, 258–59.

2. *Miami Herald*, 29 January 1978, *Tropic* magazine, 16 ff.

3. James W. Jordan, "Frontier Culture, Government Agents, and City Folks," in *Appalachia and America: Autonomy and Regional Dependence*, ed. Allen Batteau (Lexington: University Press of Kentucky, 1983), 239–51.

4. Sources for this information included the Rabun County Tax Assessor's Office, Georgia Power Company, and the U.S. Forest Service, Clayton, Georgia.

5. "Economic Profile: Rabun County and Clayton Georgia" (Prepared by Chamber of Commerce, Clayton, Georgia, May 1984), 2.

6. Thomas W. Hodler and Howard A. Schretter, *The Atlas of Georgia* (Athens: Institute for Community and Area Development, University of Georgia, 1986), 254–56.

7. Reported in Sandy S. Cook, "The Structure of a Successful Community Development Corporation in a Rural Area: A Recommendation to the Foxfire Fund, Inc." (Master's thesis, Baylor University, 1983), 57.

8. United States Department of Commerce, Bureau of the Census, *1950, 1960, 1970, 1980 Census of the Population*, cited in Cook, "Structure of a Successful Community Development Corporation," Table 19.

9. 1982 Census of Agriculture, cited in *Clayton Tribune*, 24 May 1984.

10. The major source for background information on the Sangamo controversy is the *Clayton Tribune*, 24 November, 15 December 1977.

11. *Clayton Tribune*, 18 July 1985.

12. Ibid. Similar incidents of the failure of "branch industry" to deliver the anticipated economic benefits have recurred throughout the South. As reported in *Shadows in the Sunbelt: Developing the Rural South in an Era of Economic Change* (Chapel Hill, N.C.: MDC, Inc., 1986): "Southern states' traditional approach to industrial development—industrial recruitment—is not likely to ameliorate the adverse trends facing rural communities" (1).

13. U.S. Census Bureau, *1970 Housing Characteristics for States, Cities and Counties (Georgia)*, Tables 1, 2, 60, 62; U.S. Census Bureau, 1980 *General Housing Characteristics (Georgia)*, Tables 5, 46; all cited and analyzed in Cook, "Structure of a Successful Community Development Corporation," 61–62.

14. *Homes and Land of the Mountains: Serving S.W. North Carolina and N.E. Georgia*, 1, no. 8 ([1984]): 2, 12. In 1984, Sky Valley resort lots (½ to ¾ acre) generally ranged from $13,000 to $50,000.

15. Cook, "Structure of a Successful Development Corporation," 61–62.

16. *Clayton Tribune*, 23 August 1984.

17. *Clayton Tribune*, 28 February 1985.

18. Ibid.

19. *Clayton Tribune*, 19 December 1985.

20. *Clayton Tribune*, 21 June 1984.

21. *Clayton Tribune*, 6 September 1984; see also 5 July 1984.

22. *Clayton Tribune*, 3 June, 15 July 1976.

23. Jack E. Weller, *Yesterday's People: Life in Contemporary Appalachia* (Lexington: University of Kentucky Press, 1965), 7.

24. In his provocative, albeit undocumented commentary, *Night Comes to the Cumberlands* (Boston: Little, Brown, 1962), Appalachian native Harry Caudill described the hoodwinking of the farmers of the coal-rich Cumberland Plateau in eastern Kentucky, e.g., 61–74. Historian Ronald Eller provides scholarly documentation of the quasi-legal practices behind industry's takeover of the coal fields in *Miners, Millhands, and Mountaineers: Industrialization of the Appalachian South, 1880–1930* (Knoxville: University of Tennessee Press, 1982). For discussion of broad-form conveyances in the coal fields, see Warren Wright, "The Big Steal," in *Colonialism in Modern America: The Appalachian Case,* ed. Helen Lewis, Linda Johnson, and Donald Askins (Boone, N.C.: Appalachian Consortium Press, 1978), 161–75.

25. Eller, *Miners, Millhands, and Mountaineers,* 87.

26. Ibid., xxi.

27. Ibid., 104–10.

28. Cf. Walter Precourt, "The Image of Appalachian Poverty," in *Appalachia and America,* ed. Batteau, 86–110.

29. A seminal essay on the demise of traditional Appalachian values is Thomas R. Ford, "The Passing of Provincialism," in *The Southern Appalachian Region: A Survey,* ed. Ford (Lexington: University of Kentucky Press, 1962). For an undocumented counter-argument, see Loyal Jones, "Appalachian Values," in *Voices from the Hills: Selected Readings of Southern Appalachia,* ed. Robert J. Higgs and Ambrose N. Manning (Boone, N.C.: Appalachian Consortium Press, 1975).

30. Ronald Eller, "Land and Family: An Historical View of Preindustrial Appalachia," *Appalachian Journal* 6, no. 2 (1979): 96. See also Robert Coles, *Migrants, Sharecroppers, Mountaineers,* vol. 2 of *Children of Crisis* (Boston: Little, Brown, 1971), 7, 23.

31. Eller, *Miners, Millhands, and Mountaineers,* 152.

32. Caudill, *Night Comes to the Cumberlands,* 93–137, 174–75; Eller, *Miners, Millhands, and Mountaineers,* 182–98, 212–17.

33. Eller, *Miners, Millhands, and Mountaineers,* 198.

34. Ibid., 179–82.

35. Caudill, *Night Comes to the Cumberlands,* 141–215.

36. Eller, *Miners, Millhands, and Mountaineers,* 159.

37. Caudill, *Night Comes to the Cumberlands,* 267.

38. "Appalachia: Twenty Years of Progress" (special issue), *Journal of the*

Appalachian Regional Commission 83, no. 3 (1985): 41–88. This journal is an ARC publication.

39. John Gaventa and Bill Horton, "Digging the Facts," *Southern Exposure* 10, no. 1 (1982). Scholars have criticized the ARC for spending millions of dollars to pay outside consultants to conduct research unrelated to landowner-ship. For example, see Patricia D. Beaver, "Participatory Research on Land-ownership in Appalachia," in *Appalachia and America*, ed. Batteau, 252–66. Significantly, there is no mention of the Appalachian Alliance task force study in the ARC's twenty-year report, cited previously.

40. Appalachian Landownership Task Force, *Who Owns Appalachia?*, 11.

41. Ibid., 20.

42. Ibid., 23.

43. Ibid., 48.

44. Ibid., 61. Corporate tax relief in Appalachia is not limited to the coal industry. For example, in Alabama, the Appalachian timber interests suc-cessfully lobbied for an amendment "that had the effect of placing a 'lid' on the amount values could be increased through a court-ordered reappraisal program. . . . As a result . . . the large landholders still pay little for their land" (ibid., 47–48). Nor is kowtowing to extractive industries in Appalachia restricted to state legislatures. For example, in West Virginia, the executive branch effectively blocked judicial decisions that would have forced the legis-lature to tax the coal-mining corporations as a remedy for statewide inequities in school finance (Jonathan P. Sher, "Bringing Home the Bacon: The Politics of Rural School Reform," *Phi Delta Kappan* 65, no. 4 [1983]).

45. John Gaventa, *Power and Powerlessness: Quiescence and Rebellion in an Appalachian Valley* (Urbana: University of Illinois Press, 1980), 140–41.

46. Ibid., 42.

47. Ibid., 144.

48. Appalachian Landownership Task Force, *Who Owns Appalachia?*, 56–57. See also Si Kahn, "The Forest Service in Appalachia," in *Colonialism in Modern America*, ed. Lewis et al., 85–109.

49. Appalachian Landownership Task Force, *Who Owns Appalachia?*, 76.

50. Ibid., 77.

51. For example, see Anita Parlow, "The Land Development Rag," in *Colonialism in Modern America*, ed. Lewis et al., 177–98. The author describes the social and environmental consequences of land development in Watauga and Avery Counties, N.C., in the 1970s. Here the land boom in ski resorts and rental complexes (e.g., the Beech and Sugar Mountain developments) has skyrocketed land prices and "transformed [the counties] from farming valleys shielded by gently sloped mountains to a cacophony of strip development/fast food chains."

52. Whisnant, *All That Is Native and Fine*, 61–63, 169–70.

53. Charles L. Perdue, Jr., "What's Wrong with Foxfire?," *Nameless Newslet-ter* 2, no. 2 (1979): 30–31.

54. Charles L. Perdue, Jr., "The Americanization of John Egerton and Aunt Arie," *Appalachian Journal* 11 (1984): 440.

55. Perdue, Jr., "What's Wrong with Foxfire?," 30. Compare Henry D. Shapiro's description of Foxfire as reinforcing "a mythology of the Appalachian folk culture," in *Appalachia on Our Mind: The Southern Mountains and Mountaineers in the American Consciousness, 1870–1920* (Chapel Hill: University of North Carolina Press, 1978), 263–65.

56. Ann Vick, ed., *The Cama-i Book* (Garden City, N.Y.: Anchor Press/Doubleday, 1983), xv.

57. See *Appalachia—a Reference Book,* 2d ed. (Washington, D.C.: Appalachian Regional Commission, 1979), 70, 74; supplement to 2d ed. (1981), 27–28. See also J. Lamarr Cox et al., *Study of High School Dropouts in Appalachia,* Report No. RTI/3182-01/01 FR (Washington, D.C.: Appalachian Regional Commission, 1985), vii–xv. According to 1980 census data, percentages of dropouts in central and southern Appalachia (using the ARC subregional designations) were 38.0 and 30.0, respectively. The former was 59% higher than the national average; the latter, 25% higher (ibid., viii–xi).

58. Peter Schrag, "The School and Politics," in *Teaching Mountain Children: Towards a Foundation of Understanding,* ed. David Mielke (Boone, N.C.: Appalachian Consortium Press, 1978), 173. For a similar interpretation, see James Branscome, "Educating Appalachia's Poor," in *Appalachia: Social Context Past and Present,* 2d ed., ed. Bruce Ergood and Bruce E. Kuhre (Dubuque, Iowa: Kendall/Hunt, 1983), 281–84.

59. For variations of this interpretation, see Jim Wayne Miller, "A Mirror for Appalachia," in *Voices from the Hills,* ed. Higgs and Manning, 447–59; Edward H. Berman, "The Politics of Literacy and Educational Development in Kentucky," *Comparative Education Review* 22 (1978): 115–33; Roy Silver and Alan DeYoung, "The Ideology of Rural/Appalachian Education, 1895–1935: The Appalachian Education Problem as Part of the Appalachian Life Problem," *Educational Theory* 36, no. 1 (1986): 51–65; Una Mae Lange Reck and Gregory G. Reck, "Living Is More Important Than Schooling: Schools and Self Concept in Appalachia," *Appalachian Journal* 8, no. 1 (1980): 19–25.

60. Jim Wayne Miller, "Appalachian Education: Critique and Suggestions for Reform," *Appalachian Journal* 5, no. 1 (1977): 13–22.

61. For discussion of the former, see ibid.; also Alan DeYoung and Julia Damron Porter, "Multicultural Education in Appalachia: Origin, Prospects and Problems," *Appalachian Journal* 7, no. 1–2 (1979–80): 124–34. For the latter, see Jim Foster et al., "Class, Political Consciousness, and Destructive Power: A Strategy for Change in Appalachia," *Appalachian Journal* 5, no. 3 (1978): 290–311.

62. Jonathan P. Sher, "School-Based Community Development Corporations," in *Education in Rural America: A Reassessment of Conventional Wisdom,* ed. Jonathan P. Sher (Boulder, Colo.: Westview Press, 1977), 327.

63. Ibid., 337.

64. Ibid., 323.

65. Steve Fisher, "Economic Development Strategies for Appalachia in the 1980s," Highlander Research and Education Center, 14–16 May 1982.

66. See "Brooks County, Georgia: To Market, to Market," in *The Charles Stewart Mott Foundation 1982 Annual Report*. n.p., n.d.

67. Jonathan Sher to Mary Reynolds Babcock Foundation, 15 December 1986. In 1988, the meaning of the acronym REAL was changed to "Rural Entrepreneurship through Action Learning."

68. *Foxfire Glow* transcription.

ELEVEN

Foxfire and Styles of Curriculum Reform

This chapter features a comparison of two styles of curriculum reform. The first is the conventional style: reforms created and controlled by "experts," flowing downward through layers of publishers, consultants, and bureaucrats (eventually, it is hoped, to schools). The second is the "grassroots" style: reforms created and controlled at the classroom level, flowing *across* schools from teacher to teacher. Invented by a single teacher and disseminated through an informal network of teachers and students, Foxfire has become the archetype of this particular reform style.

Twixt Cup and Lip:
The Shortcomings of Top-Down Curriculum Reform

In 1978 the National Science Foundation released a comprehensive seven-volume report on the status of mathematics, science, and social studies education in America. The report contained approximately two thousand pages of data amassed from three studies—a national survey of teachers and administrators, a review of the relevant literature in the three fields from 1955 to 1975, and a compilation of case studies (including a follow-up national survey). Collectively these studies have great significance for curriculum planners and educational policymakers because they provide an extensive data base for assessing the influence of nearly two decades of federally sponsored, "top-down" curriculum reform.[1]

Interpreters of the National Science Foundation data have agreed that the scores of commercial, "teacher-proof" curricular packages sponsored by the National Science Foundation and the United States Office of Education from 1955 to 1975 effected few lasting changes in classroom practice. This finding prefigured the results of Goodlad's national study of schooling (*A Place Called School,* 1984), which found that America's pedagogy is generally a mechanical affair of a teacher and text imparting (in Dewey's words, "pouring in") information to a roomful of passive students. All of these studies indicate that class-room practice is largely devoid of student inquiry, discovery learning, or other innovative strategies that were embodied in the reform packages.

In his interpretation of the NSF survey data on the status of science teaching, Strassenburg concluded that "science courses are offered in most secondary schools at every grade level according to a pattern that has been common for at least forty years and has been altered only slightly in recent years. Reforms in science education have had little impact on precollege science classrooms." For example, the innovative Physical Science Study Curriculum and Project Physics were being used by only four percent and ten percent of high school physics teachers, respectively, "even though . . . 94% of schools that include only grades 10–12 teach some physics."[2] Strassenburg further noted that "textbooks . . . often are the single most important source of information in science courses." And in most cases, "teachers were attempting to transmit information to rather passive and not infrequently bored students."[3]

Gibney and Karns drew similar conclusions from the data on the status of mathematics education: "Despite the 'new math' thrust . . . there appears to be little change in mathematics instruction in grades K–12. . . . The single textbook is still the primary source of mathematics curricula. . . . Although most emphasis has been given to the development of inquiry teaching, little is taking place."[4]

Shaver and his colleagues reported the same bad news for the federally sponsored "new social studies" projects of the 1960s and 1970s: The conventional textbook continued to hold sway in the nation's social studies classes; teaching remained largely an affair of lecture and recitation. Moreover, "for students to demonstrate learning acceptably in discussions and on tests, they often have to reproduce not only the content but the language of the text."[5]

Significantly, the implications of the National Science Foundation studies for educational reform—planning, design, dissemination, and implementation—have been roundly ignored by the authors of the recent spate of reform proposals and by all but a handful of analysts in the education profession. After 1979, discussion of the reports (beyond an occasional reference in a journal article) disappears from the educational literature.

In its self-interest as the conduit of federal educational reform dollars, the National Science Foundation has chosen to ignore the unflattering results of the three national curriculum studies commissioned under its auspices in the late 1970s. A case in point is *Educating Americans for the 21st Century,* an NSF publication compiled by the National Science Board Commission on Precollege Education in Mathematics, Science and Technology. In over 250 pages of text, the commission devoted only *one* paragraph to discussion of the previous curriculum reform initiatives, the "ultimate impact and effectiveness" of which, the writer admits guardedly, "was far less than had been hoped."[6]

Without any serious reflection upon the lessons of the past, the commission called for another wave of "top-down" curriculum reform, for example: "The National Science Foundation structure provides a unique and valuable interaction between scientists and science educators. In the past this was very fruitful in producing high level, relevant and scientifically accurate science and mathematics curricula. It is urged that this powerful synergy and the expertise previously assembled by the National Science Foundation Education Directorate be utilized again."[7]

Endorsing the commission's goal to "provide all the Nation's youth with a level of education in mathematics, science and technology . . . that is . . . the highest quality attained anywhere in the world," the National Science Foundation has issued requests for proposals for reform initiatives ranging from precollege materials development and research (including applications of advanced technologies) to precollege teacher development to special activities (e.g., use of museums and science academies). With respect to improved instructional materials, the foundation has encouraged both innovative curricular packages "suitable for widespread distribution, preferably through the private sector" and "improved methods of delivering instruction, including technology-based materials, software, computer simulations of laboratory experiments, and television or videodisc-based materials."[8]

The lack of historical perspective evident in the current educational debate at both the federal and state levels is alarming. Ignoring (or not even bothering to read) the findings of the National Science Foundation studies or the evidence compiled by Rand Corporation researchers and other widely respected analysts who have examined the historical record, the school reformers of the 1980s are building their programs for changing classroom practice upon the same flawed assumptions that guided the reformers of previous decades.

An illuminating study of curriculum projects funded by federal programs of the 1960s and 1970s has been the eight-volume Rand report commissioned by the U.S. Office of Education (now the Department of Education). In the first phase of the four-year study (1973 to 1977), Rand researchers examined 293 local curriculum projects sampled from eighteen states. The projects were in their last or next to last year of funding. In the second phase of the study, the researchers examined "what happened to innovative projects after the end of the federal funding period [of three to five years]."[9] This group comprised approximately one hundred projects that had been funded as "innovative projects" under Title III of the Elementary and Secondary Education Act of 1965. In their summary of the findings, Berman and McLaughlin stated: "The adoption of projects did not insure successful implementation; moreover, successful implementation did not guarantee long-run continuation. . . . The net return to the federal investment was the adoption of many innovations, the successful implementation of few, and the long-run continuation of still fewer (with the exception of the special case of bilingual projects, where federal and state funding continues to be available)."[10]

Perhaps the most revealing conclusion of this report, one that should have raised the eyebrows of the new federal and state reformers, is the statement by Berman and McLaughlin that "effective implementation is more likely if adoption is done in a problem-solving manner, in which schools identify their needs and then seek solutions to them. But most federal dissemination efforts only made districts aware of new educational products, and not of their own needs. Unwittingly, federal policy thus fueled the preoccupation . . . with innovations for their own sake."[11]

The National Science Foundation's request for proposals to develop marketable, packaged curriculum programs and materials makes no mention of the real needs of local districts. The agency assumes—as it did thirty years ago—that effective pedagogical reform can be accomplished by identifying exemplary curriculum programs, creating teacher awareness, and providing in-service teacher training. Yet, as Sarason notes (taking his cue from Berman and McLaughlin), the complexities of the change process in local districts and individual schools have consistently vitiated this reform strategy.[12]

According to Sarason, innovative curricula and pedagogical approaches that attempt to get students involved in their own learning, e.g., problem-solving and discovery-learning strategies, necessitate structural changes at the level of the classroom—"changes in how teachers and children relate to each other."[13] In short, the adoption, even implementation, of a curriculum reform is no guarantee that it will be used as its designers intended. "It is probably true that the most important attempts to introduce change into the school culture *require* changing existing teacher-child regularities. When one examines the natural history of the change process it is precisely these regularities that remain untouched."[14]

The bottom line is that curriculum reformers, because they tend to be *outsiders* to the school culture—e.g., funding agencies, policymakers, consultants, academicians—have little understanding of schools and what is required to change the behavioral as well as programmatic regularities of the school culture. As discussed previously, they also tend to ignore the lessons of previous reform attempts.

Policy analyst Decker Walker has described the unfortunate tendency of curriculum policymakers to act unreflectively to resolve a perceived crisis: "There is generally not time for extensive study of the problem. Either a course of action is ready at hand and we merely search it out, or we must do the best we can with one jerry-built. Doing nothing and business as usual are unthinkable."[15]

In their thoughtful analysis of the current movement to improve schools, Stanford educators Kirst and Meister specify three criteria that characterize enduring educational reforms. First, they entail new organizational structures or require new cadres of specialized personnel. Teacher aides, vocational education programs, and programs for handicapped or bilingual students are examples. Second, they generate powerful constituencies. For example, "the driver training and health education courses that required physical changes in schools also created powerful lobbies of professionals as well as of non-school groups such as insurance companies and anti-alcohol organizations." Third, they are easy to monitor and "furnish accessible evidence of compliance." Examples include legislated changes in certification requirements.[16]

Pedagogical reforms—those that "addressed teacher practice within and between classrooms"—have not lasted. Included in this category of minimally implemented, unenduring reforms are "endeavors to alter teaching methods or strategies," e.g., computer-assisted instruction, individualized instruction, and inquiry learning.[17]

Given the current enthusiasm for improving educational performance with computer-assisted instruction—and the likelihood that the educational market will soon be inundated with CAI materials—Kirst and Meister's sober prognosis is as timely as it is heretical:

New reforms involving computerized instruction will probably [not last]. In schools where a computer science department is created with special facilities, equipment, trained teachers, and designated courses, the reform is likely to remain, because school structures will have changed as part of the innovation. However, when an individual elementary teacher or a secondary English teacher, for example, is asked to use the computer in order to augment traditional classroom instruction, the reform is less likely to be successful. No formal teacher constituency has yet developed to support technological innovations such as computers in instruction, nor has any discernible organizational change in school structures yet been required.[18]

In the wake of the recommendations of more than 280 state-level commissions in 1982–83, state governors, legislators, and educators have initiated an unprecedented number of school reforms. For example, forty-one states have increased their high school graduation requirements, with six states considering or proposing legislation; twenty have increased instructional time, with fourteen considering or proposing legislation; nineteen have mandated improved school discipline policies; thirteen have instituted academic requirements for extracurricular athletic participation; and thirty-five have raised teacher preparation/certification standards, with fourteen considering or proposing legislation.[19]

Events in North Carolina over the past several years exemplify a trend that is occurring nationwide at the state level of educational reform. In April 1984, the North Carolina Commission on Education for Economic Growth, chaired by Governor James B. Hunt, Jr., submitted to the legislature a proposal for sweeping reforms in the state's public schools. The legislature responded in its June session with an appropriation of more than $255 million for a plethora of reforms ranging from increased pay for teachers to upgraded equipment (including the establishment of computer laboratories in all schools) to the creation of a statewide network of mathematics and science centers for upgrading the certification of teachers in these fields.[20]

The Kirst-Meister model of reform longevity predicts that the nonpedagogical reforms being mandated at the state level, e.g., more rigorous certification requirements, "could . . . have a lasting impact" because they require organizational changes, create new constituencies of specialists, and are easily monitored. Predictions for the future of structural reforms that entail changes in pedagogy, however, are far less sanguine. As put by Kirst and Meister: "Among the 1984 reforms, those such as statewide graduation requirements expressed in Carnegie units (e.g., three years of math) will last. Although transcripts showing the number of units taken can be monitored, the content of new curricula to fill the units will be highly variable and difficult to monitor unless well-specified and well-publicized state tests linked to subject matters accompany this curricular reform."[21]

Classroom practice will not change fundamentally without the meaningful involvement of the teacher in the change process.[22] Berman and McLaughlin found that teacher involvement in *all* phases of project development correlated strongly with successful implementation of an innovation: "Where project activities and objectives reflected significant teacher input, the staff were more likely to invest the considerable energy needed to make the project work. The project, in short, was 'theirs.'"[23] Conversely, innovations that excluded significant teacher participation did not endure.

As documented by Berman and McLaughlin, the conventional pattern of curriculum innovation is top-down; reforms tend to be owned and controlled by "experts"—curriculum policymakers, academicians, and educational specialists. Classroom teachers are generally excluded from the decision-making processes that surround innovations. Ironically, they are the constituency that ultimately determines whether or not a pedagogical change will be implemented. As the historical record attests, innovations that are not adaptable to their needs will be set aside.

Grassroots Reform: The Foxfire Example

The obvious strength of grassroots (school-based) curriculum development is that teachers are directly involved in the planning and modification of an innovation. This has been the case with Foxfire and its descendant projects. Eliot Wigginton did not create Foxfire as a model for curriculum development. His original objective was to enliven the stodgy English curriculum he had inherited from the Rabun County Department of Education. What began as the reform of a single teacher's classes in a tiny rural high school, however, spread through word of mouth and a network of books, magazines, and newsletters created by teachers and students to school sites in forty-seven states (including the District of Columbia), as well as American Samoa, Puerto Rico, Guam, Haiti, the Virgin Islands, Jamaica, the Dominican Republic, Costa Rica, Japan, Australia (thirteen projects), and Scotland. By 1985 approximately 260 cultural journalism projects, initiated and controlled by teachers, had been launched.[24]

There exist few studies of the cultural journalism phenomenon from which firm conclusions about the dissemination of the Foxfire concept can be drawn. Sitton's "first appraisal" of the status of the

Foxfire-descendant projects is easily the best conceptualized and most thoroughly documented of the handful of "scholarly" monographs that have been written on Foxfire or its descendants.

Having analyzed survey data from the teachers at thirty-five project sites, Sitton described his study as a "teacher's-eye view" of program processes, and he stipulated that his report "perhaps contains more than a grain of wishful thinking derived from the sources of the data." Sitton could have mitigated this flaw in his research methodology by building in a reality check, i.e., by sampling student opinion, or conducting some site visits, or both. This structural limitation notwithstanding, the study provides useful demographic data on the projects—and the general impression conveyed by the remaining data is that the respondents had taken, in Sitton's words, "a long hard and at times critical look at their projects."[25]

Taught primarily by English and social studies teachers, the projects focused heavily on the past and generally excluded present-day social issues. Sitton found that most of the projects were located in small towns (43%) or rural areas (40%). He attributed this "rural bias" to a combination of two factors: the prevalence of distinctive folkways in rural communities and "the flexibility of working arrangements that are possible in . . . smaller schools."[26]

All but one teacher in Sitton's study reported having more informal and relaxed relationships with students involved in the project than with students in conventional classes. Most claimed to share project decision making with the students, and most reported that students had an active role in representing the project to community groups and other schools in the area.

The teachers reported having cordial, albeit occasionally strained, relationships with school administrators. Sitton summarized school-project relations as follows: "The schools appear to be relatively supporting of their projects in terms of schedule changes, arrangements whereby students may get scholastic credit for project work, arrangements whereby projects can use school equipment and school space, and undertake project work during the regular school day. Schools are much less willing to let the project teachers 'get out of anything,' to allow students out of other teachers' classes, or to let students off the premises during the school day to go on interviews. They are even less likely to give the project direct financial support, or at least very much of it."[27]

Sitton found that financial success and high community visibility were sources of friction with school officials. In the case of Salt advisor Pamela Wood, this friction escalated into a battle that resulted in her firing in 1977. Wood has charged that the school board in Kennebunk, Maine, resented having a financially successful, incorporated (hence autonomous) project in the local high school. Salt subsequently purchased a boatyard in Kennebunkport with advance royalties on *The Salt Book* and employed students and high school dropouts in apprenticeship programs that included cultural journalism, boat building, seamanship, and forest management.[28]

Sitton's study remains the only substantive piece of research on Foxfire or a related project. A dissertation study preceding his and one following have added little to illuminate how the Foxfire concept works in practice. Indeed, these latter studies are grist for the mills of critics who charge that dissertations in education are bereft of critical scholarship.

Nungesser's dissertation study at Ohio State University (1977) is better described as story telling than academic research. As his dissertation, Nungesser wrote a description of his experience in directing *Thistledown*, a Foxfire-type project in a small-town high school.[29] While the author adequately explained the details of project development, he failed to document his rhapsodical claims for the efficacy of the Foxfire concept in general and *Thistledown* specifically. Indeed, Nungesser built his dissertation upon a layer of unsubstantiated assertions—his own and those of other Foxfire advocates. The following is a sampler of explicit assumptions for which Nungesser provided no valid supportive evidence:

> Certainly, we must agree that given the weight of accountability being placed on education, especially those institutions in the public domain, an effective and accepted experiential program must be one that is closely related to the achievement of basic education skill-learning goals. . . . Foxfire fulfills these goals admirably. (48)

> *Thistledown*, and the 80-some other Foxfire concept projects, all exist entirely within their respective systems and meet, without difficulty, all the demands of traditional systems, as shown in this study. At the same time, however, they are practicing and using the best experiential methodology, upholding experiential principles and thus, neither the traditional demands nor the experiential ideas are being sacrificed. (308)

> . . . the traditional system can no longer look askance or ignore experiential learning as unsuitable for the system, for it *does* work and it is viable, as evidenced by the many ongoing and successful projects, such as *Thistledown*, now under way. (309)

The study was burdened from the outset with the problem of observer bias. Nungesser assessed a project he had created and nurtured himself; this fact alone made his conclusions extremely suspect. The report is further undermined by the author's uncritical acceptance of untested claims made on behalf of Foxfire and Foxfire-type projects, his unfortunate tendency to describe the projects as successful in the absence of evaluative data, and his failure to address any substantive pedagogical and sociological issues.

England's dissertation study at the University of Alabama (1979) is sounder from a methodological perspective than Nungesser's study, but its content is trivial. England, also an advisor to a Foxfire-type project, examined what he called "ideal characteristics of Foxfire-type projects as perceived by teacher advisors." This study entailed surveying twenty-seven of Sitton's respondents to learn how they thought their projects *should be* working (e.g., how many students should be in a Foxfire-type class, what student-teacher relationships should be, and so forth). This tactic yielded predictable—and banal—findings; for example, "The idea that a Foxfire-type project should have some equipment was expressed."[30]

England drew heavily from Nungesser and Sitton and built on the unexamined assumptions in both studies. Like these observers, he assumed, in the absence of evaluative data, that the Foxfire concept worked in practice as advertised in the testimonial literature (i.e., Wigginton's writings and journalistic accounts).[31] In this respect the previous "scholarly" literature on the Foxfire phenomenon is itself testimonial.[32]

There have been no external evaluations of the Foxfire learning concept. Foxfire's university-based allies have proved reluctant to test the claims made in its behalf. Some of these academicians have even carved niches for themselves in the educational literature, largely on the strength of unsubstantiated assertions about Foxfire and its descendants.

In 1979 University of Virginia folklorist Charles Perdue advocated that Foxfire subject itself to an evaluation: "As far as pedagogy is concerned, it would be very useful to know what has happened to *all* of the students who have been involved in the project. Where are they now? What has been the effect, if any, of the Foxfire project on their lives? Are they better off today for the experience? Is their community better? A comparative study of ex-Foxfire students with a control group of non-Foxfire students, would, I believe, give us a better informed basis from which to evaluate this particular version of experiential learning and cultural journalism."[33]

In an article responding to Perdue's challenge, Foxfire enthusiast Thad Sitton, also a university academician, acknowledged that an

evaluation was overdue: "We are badly in need of experimental studies of the effects of involvement in cultural journalism upon a variety
of outcomes—self-esteem, school attendance rates, basic skills, etc.
And if we can't prove the expected effects, we should better be ready
to determine why—and, if necessary, to 'change our act'!"[34]

Sitton's rhetoric, however, raised the ire of Duane Pitts, former
advisor to Cracklings, a Foxfire-type project in Valdosta, Georgia.
Specifically, he objected to Sitton's advocacy of using quantitative
measures in evaluating the learning concept: "In quantitative reports,
where does one place student enthusiasm? How does one figure into
such 'outcomes' the establishment of new friendships between the old
and the young, a growing sense of self-esteem, confidence, and new-
found respect? How does one measure the pride our elders feel when
asked to lend their knowledge and experience to the present?"[35]

Here the heated debate ended. Foxfire attempted a quantitative *self*-
evaluation in 1981. Untrained in designing measurement instruments,
staff members contrived a "yes or no," forced-choice format which
yielded unusable data from the former students who responded to the
questionnaire. By 1984, when I began my field study of Foxfire, there
had been no sustained efforts to examine critically any applications of
the learning concept.

Despite this dearth of evaluative data, the creation and spread of the
Foxfire concept provides a forceful example of the sacrifices dedicated
teachers will make for the sake of an innovation that makes sense to
them, that is easily adaptable to their particular circumstances, that
they own and control. Eighty-three percent of the teacher-advisors
who responded to Sitton's questionnaire indicated that their project
commitments did not relieve them of other teaching or supervisory
duties in the school. Moreover, they reported that project work took
place not only during regular class hours, but also before school
(29%), after school (86%), and on weekends (71%).[36] In short, most of
these teachers had voluntarily assumed additional responsibilities in
undertaking their projects.

There is no little documentation from which to adduce the dura-
bility of the Foxfire-type projects. Evidence from previous dissertation
studies and the cultural journalism newsletter suggests that many
projects are short-lived. For example, Sitton reported in 1978 that at
least three projects (of fifty-three to which he had mailed questionnaires) were defunct.[37] A year later, England reported that eight of
the thirty-five projects surveyed by Sitton had terminated.[38] Citations
in the cultural journalism newsletter over an eight-year period indi-

cate that of the twenty-eight Foxfire-type projects listed between the fall of 1974 and the spring of 1975, only seven had survived into the 1980s: Loblolly (Gary, Texas), Salt (Kennebunkport, Maine), Bittersweet (Lebanon, Missouri), Sea Chest (Buxton, North Carolina), Tsa' Aszi' (Ramah, New Mexico), Thistledown (Pataskala, Ohio) and Cityscape (Washington, D.C.).

According to incomplete Foxfire records in 1986, Project Blueberry (Wilbraham, Massachusetts) and the Paradise Project (Burlington, Vermont) had endured for a decade. These projects had not appeared among the original twenty-eight listed in *Exchange* in 1974–75. The Foxfire records also indicate that fewer than ten of all the other projects have survived as long as five years.

The existing literature on the Foxfire learning concept suggests a combination of four factors that must be present and harmonized for a project to survive: administrative support, community support, financial success, and student enthusiasm. Sitton's respondents indicated that their most serious problem was finances. Plagued by high production costs and low circulations, the journals struggled to stay "in the black." The following is a sampler of difficulties that have jeopardized or undermined Foxfire-type projects over the years:

> Some members of the school board do not approve. They say that they think the project is good, *but* they "don't want us to get too big." They are afraid of "losing control," whatever that means. I think they do not know how to handle our growth and popularity, and so put restrictions on my time hoping to contain us. . . .[39]

> When you have incompetent or retarded administrators they will try to torpedo a project that is not of their own doing, or will possibly reach out for the glory that is not earned by them. Our project was almost "killed" by two administrators because their names did not show on the credits! And a third one who was liaison between [the] administration and the project, tried to omit it from the curriculum because a story on him was scrubbed. . . . I've "back doored" these administrators and have gone directly to the board—successfully, but no telling for how long.[40]

> The magazine "came off" because two reliable types and I sweated our brains out. . . . After two years of fighting a losing battle, mainly with disinterested kids, I must close out.[41]

In *Sometimes a Shining Moment* (1985), Wigginton tacitly acknowledges that cultural journalism is an idea whose time may have come and gone. The emphasis in this volume is directed toward teacher adaptation and integration of the elements of magazine production into teaching a conventional academic subject. The publication of a high-quality product is no longer deemed essential to this particular style of learning.

The reasons underlying Wigginton's realignment of his philosophy are twofold. First, despite mounting (and well-publicized) evidence that students do not take an active part in their formal learning, school boards and school administrators remain hostile or indifferent to unconventional teaching approaches. Second, because it places such exacting demands on the teacher-advisor, cultural journalism has enjoyed only a limited appeal. In this sense it has been the proverbial mouse that roared. Doubleday has published nine Foxfire anthologies, as well as two volumes compiled by Salt, one by Bittersweet, and one by a coalition of projects in Alaska; the University of Texas Press has published a Loblolly anthology. These volumes have given the Foxfire concept a level of public notoriety that is disproportionate to the marginal impact thus far of Wigginton's ideas on classroom practice.

Accordingly, Wigginton has adopted a different strategy to reach teachers, without compromising his original philosophy. In his accustomed style, he has taken his arguments directly to his peers, for the most part circumventing the university community and other conventional channels of diffusion and validation. Like the previous waves of Foxfire dissemination, the goal is what Berman and McLaughlin call "mutual adaptability," a sine qua non of successful curriculum reform, described as "the process by which the project [read *innovation*] is adapted to the reality of its institutional setting, and teachers and school officials adapt their practices in response to the project. In terms of individual classrooms, the process consists of each teacher developing new methods and practices while adjusting the project design to classroom conditions: It is essentially 'learning by doing.'"[42]

Unlike "teacher-proof" curriculum packages that are difficult to adapt to individual teaching and learning styles, the revised Foxfire model, because it is not a standardized package, gives teachers latitude for implementing its features in idiosyncratically and culturally appropriate ways. Common sense dictates that teachers and administrators will be more receptive to the Foxfire concept in its revised version than previously. The original strategy, which entailed publication of a finished product and which abrogated conventional textbook-based pedagogy, proved too unwieldy and too controversial for most teachers to manage. The testimonial literature notwithstanding, cultural journalism's alleged benefits were not self-evident. Wigginton has strengthened his case with teachers by giving them an explicit model for incorporating his ideas *within* the framework of traditional subject matter.

NOTES

1. The key studies are Iris Weiss, *Report of the 1977 National Science Survey of Science, Mathematics and Social Studies Education* (Washington, D.C.: U.S. Government Printing Office, 1978); and Robert Stake and Jack Easley, Jr., *Case Studies in Science Education*, 2 vols. (Washington, D.C.: U.S. Government Printing Office, 1978). Others are cited in Appendix A (Bibliographical Notes).

2. A. A. Strassenburg, "The Status of Precollege Science Education: Report on a Survey," *Journal of Teaching* 8, no. 2 (1978): 111.

3. A. A. Strassenburg and Lester G. Paldy, "More about NSF-Supported Studies of Precollege Science Education," *Journal of College Science Teaching* 8, no. 3 (1979): 183–84; and James V. DeRose, J. David Lockard, and Lester Paldy, "The Teacher is the Key: A Report on Three NSF Studies," *Science and Children* 16, no. 7 (1979): 35–41.

4. Thomas Gibney and Edward Karns, "Mathematics Education—1955–1975: A Summary of the Findings," *Educational Leadership* 36, no. 5 (1979): 356–58.

5. James P. Shaver, O. L. Davis, Jr., and Suzanne W. Helburn, "The Status of Social Studies Education: Impressions from Three NSF Studies," *Social Education* 43 (1979): 151.

6. National Science Board Commission on Precollege Education in Mathematics, Science and Technology, *Educating Americans for the 21st Century: A Plan of Action for Improving Mathematics, Science and Technology Education for All American Elementary and Secondary Students so that Their Achievement Is the Best in the World by 1995* (Washington, D.C.: National Science Foundation, [1983]), 112–13.

7. Ibid., 34.

8. National Science Foundation, "Program Announcement: Precollege Science and Mathematics Education," Fiscal Year 1984; also NSF Directorate for Science and Engineering Education, "Program Announcement: Materials Development and Research," Fiscal Year 1985.

9. Paul Berman and Milbrey McLaughlin, *Federal Programs Supporting Educational Change*, vol. 3 of *Implementing and Sustaining Innovations*, Rand Report R-158918-HEW (Santa Monica, Calif.: Rand Corporation, 1978), v–vi.

10. Ibid.

11. Ibid., 37.

12. Seymour B. Sarason, *The Culture of the School and the Problem of Change*, 2d ed. (Boston: Allyn and Bacon, 1982), chaps. 4–6. Given the marginal success of previous federal reform initiatives, evaluators Ernest House and J. Myron Atkins recommend that the federal government adopt "a relatively passive" role in educational reform, "one of sustaining continual description of existing practice, not exclusively or even primarily in terms of test scores which tend to mask as much as they reveal, but also detailed portrayals of teaching practice and classroom events from which can be drawn information of considerable potential use to other teachers" (The Federal Role in Curricu-

lum Development, 1950-1980," *Educational Evaluation and Policy Analysis* 3, no. 5 [1981]: 34).

13. Sarason, *Culture of the School*, 59.

14. Ibid., 116.

15. Quoted in Michael W. Kirst and Gail Meister, "Turbulence in American Secondary Schools: What Reforms Last?," *Curriculum Inquiry* 15, no. 2 (1985): 183.

16. Ibid., 176–80.

17. Ibid., 180–81.

18. Ibid., 177.

19. U.S. Department of Education, cited in "Forum: How Not to Fix Schools," *Harper's*, February 1986, 43. In 1984, the 98th Congress allocated $100 million to the states for programs "to improve the skills of teachers and instruction in mathematics, science, computer learning, and foreign languages . . ." (Title II, "Education for Economic Security," PL 98-377, 11 August 1984).

20. North Carolina Commission on Education for Economic Growth, *An Action Plan for North Carolina* (Raleigh, N.C.: Office of the Governor, 1984); Commission on Education for Economic Growth, Budget Request to the General Assembly, June Session 1984.

21. Kirst and Meister, "Turbulence in American Secondary Schools," 179–80.

22. Sarason, *Culture of the School*, 294.

23. Berman and McLaughlin, *Federal Programs Supporting Educational Change*, 29.

24. Based on a count of project citations listed in *Exchange, Nameless Newsletter, Hands On,* and other Foxfire documents from 1973 to 1985. In 1980, Sherrod Reynolds issued the following caveat against identifying all cultural journalism as Foxfire descendants: "It has been pointed out many times, and rightfully so, that all projects in the cultural journalism network did not model themselves exclusively on Foxfire or IDEAS, and therefore should not be called 'Foxfire-type' projects. Even those projects that did use Foxfire as a point of departure have developed in different and unique ways. This constant use of 'Foxfire' to describe any and all cultural journalism efforts has caused some confusion and resentment. However, despite our best efforts, the term continues to be used because people know it; they recognize it; they know what it stands for, and it is easier to use than the unwieldy 'cultural journalism.' In a sense 'Foxfire' has become a generic term in much the same way that Levi's has come to mean jeans and Jell-O is used to refer to any flavored gelative [*sic*]. To many people, it stands for a particular approach to learning" ("National Cultural Journalism Workshop," *Hands On* 3, no. 2 [1980]).

25. Sitton, "Foxfire-Concept Publications," 80.

26. Ibid., 83.

27. Ibid., 92.

28. *Nameless Newsletter* 1, no. 1/2 (1977): 12; 2, no. 1 (1978): 17–20.

29. David N. Nungesser, "Thistledown: An Experimental Application of the Foxfire Learning Concept: An Analysis of That Concept" (Ph.D. diss., Ohio State University, 1977).

30. Robert D. England, "The Ideal Characteristics of Foxfire-Type Projects as Perceived by Teacher Advisors" (Ph.D. diss., University of Alabama, 1979), 64.

31. For example, see Thad Sitton, "The Fire that Lit Up Learning," *Teacher* 96, no. 7 (1979): 65–67. The title described Sitton's conclusions, which were drawn in the absence of any evaluative data.

32. Previous case studies have been testimonials—neither critical analyses nor evaluations. For example, see Gail Parks, "Foxfire: Experiential Education in America," in *Rural Education in Urbanized Nations*, ed. Sher; Thomas Gjelton, "Gary, Texas: The Rise of Loblolly," in *Rural Education: In Search of a Better Way*, ed. Paul Nachtigal (Boulder, Colo.: Westview Press, 1982).

33. Charles L. Perdue, Jr., "What's Wrong with Foxfire?," *Nameless Newsletter* 2, no. 2 (1979): 30.

34. Thad Sitton, "What's Wrong with 'What's Wrong with Foxfire,'" *Hands On* 2, no. 3 (1979): 23–24.

35. Duane Pitts, "More on Sitton and Perdue, or the Parched Earth People," *Hands On* 2, no. 4 (1979): 12.

36. Sitton, "Foxfire-Concept Publications," 89–91; cf. Sitton, "Cultural Journalism and Progressive Education," *Hands On* 5, no. 4 (1982).

37. Sitton, "Foxfire-Concept Publications," 79.

38. England, "Ideal Characteristics of Foxfire-Type Projects," 113.

39. Sitton, "Foxfire-Concept Publications," 95.

40. Ibid., 95–96. For further examples of the difficulties cultural journalism teachers have had with administrators, see Ellen Massey (Bittersweet) and Duane Pitts (Cracklings), *Hands On* 2, no. 4 (1979); Judith Rubenstein (Southern Lives), *Hands On* 3, no. 1 (1979).

41. Barb Reynolds (Louisiana Lagniappe), *Hands On* 2, no. 3 (1979), 13; *Hands On* 5, no. 3 (1982).

42. Berman and McLaughlin, *Federal Programs Supporting Educational Change*, 28.

TWELVE

Conclusion

A year's worth of field research, coupled with an exhaustive survey of the relevant literature, reveals that Foxfire has fallen short of the ideal envisioned by Eliot Wigginton and engendered by a cadre of "testimonial" writers (journalists and academicians alike). Measured solely by the criterion of its own mythos, the reality of Foxfire is a bit of a disappointment. For example, as previously argued, *Foxfire* magazine production has not proved to be an effective or efficient vehicle for teaching the elements of writing style; educational process has been subordinated to such exigencies as publication deadlines; students have been increasingly distanced from the locus of organizational power and responsibility; staff members have failed to apply critical elements of Wigginton's philosophy in courses purported to be applications of the Foxfire concept; and Foxfire's abortive community development thrust was an example of good intentions gone awry.

Yet throughout history, noble ideals have rarely translated into unblemished realities. In this respect, Foxfire is much like the rest of real life. Under careful scrutiny it turns out to be neither as good as one might have hoped, nor as bad as one might have feared. Moreover, when compared to conventional schooling practice (described by Goodlad, Boyer, Sizer, and other analysts as "dull and uninspired"), Foxfire fares remarkably well and merits a great deal of genuine praise. From this perspective, its weaknesses appear far less salient, particularly if one considers how virtually any teacher or educational program might have fared had either been subjected to the same kind of rigorous examination given Foxfire for an entire year.

Indeed, in an era when the foundations of public education have been shaken by a storm of criticism, Foxfire can properly be seen as a welcome example of how much dedicated teachers, motivated students, and a supportive community *can* accomplish. Its strengths and accomplishments both within and beyond Rabun County are extraordinary by any measure. The testimonial literature about Foxfire exaggerated its virtues, but the fact remains that it *has* many virtues to exaggerate. It is hardly surprising that a nation hungry for success stories would latch onto this program with such fervor.

It is intriguing (and significant) that the development of Foxfire has followed a pattern similar to what human beings experience as they progress through stages of the life cycle. On its twentieth anniversary, Foxfire was similar to other twenty-year-olds traversing what Erikson calls the crisis of identity.

By this analogy, Foxfire's genesis and early growth at Rabun Gap School can be likened to childhood. Its negative features notwithstanding, the tiny boarding/community school nurtured the fledgling project and provided a secure, family-like home for its progression to maturity. Apropos of childhood, Foxfire experienced its happiest, most energetic years during its Rabun Gap era. These were the years of the organization's rise to national prominence and its transfiguration from a community magazine project into a national publishing and educational phenomenon, the grassroots spread of Wigginton's ideas, the deployment of his students as consultants to Foxfire-like projects in far-flung corners of the nation, and the prominent role of students in organizational decision making.

Foxfire's adolescence has been spent at Rabun County High School. The crystallization of new divisions within the organization occurred in Foxfire's eleventh year (1977–78) and may be likened to the formative physical changes attending human puberty. Characteristic of normal human development, this stage of Foxfire's life cycle has been predominately quiescent and uneventful. It has also been narcissistic.

From 1977 to 1983, despite Wigginton's vigorous planning for community development, the organization itself grew increasingly insular. The majority of Wigginton's staff did not take an active role in community development planning (some even opposed Wigginton's ideas). Foxfire teachers also became increasingly isolated from the network of Foxfire-descendant projects and concentrated their energies on their own programs at the high school. Ironically, for all their good intentions, these programs became distortions of the philosophy Wigginton had originated at Rabun Gap School.

Erikson has defined identity as a personal sense of sameness and continuity from one stage of an individual's life cycle to the next. It is a sine qua non of healthy mental functioning. The so-called crisis of identity in late adolescence is precipitated by the individual's final break with familial object ties (individuation). The crisis itself is the realization that what has worked for the individual as a child and adolescent will no longer work as an adult. It is a malaise born of the self-acknowledgment that henceforth one must accept full responsibility for one's life. Liberated from previous dependencies, the individual must begin the search for a defining niche in society. For the sake of psychic well-being, this niche must be compatible with preferences and expectations (cultural, sexual, moral, and ideological) that have been shaped by previous experience and integrated into the overall personality.

In its late adolescence Foxfire experienced an identity crisis. In a curious way the organization behaved according to the pattern suggested by Erikson. In the fall of 1983, Foxfire's legal board declared that in the face of dwindling *Foxfire* book royalties, the organization would halt its community development initiatives and devote its energies to national curriculum dissemination. Wigginton and the board acknowledged that the success of this new initiative would be determined by the response of educators to his new book, *Sometimes a Shining Moment* (1985). Precipitating this shift toward the national educational arena was the acknowledgment by Wigginton and his advisors that an old dependency (Doubleday's *Foxfire* series) would no longer sustain the growth of the organization. New strategies consistent with Wigginton's educational philosophy were demanded. Foxfire's individuation from the key financial (and psychological) dependency of its childhood and adolescence occasioned the struggle for self-definition that made 1984 such a decisive year for the organization.

At the threshold of adulthood, Foxfire can justifiably take great pride in its cumulative achievements. It has been highly influential in the service of cultural preservation and has upgraded the image of Appalachia both within and beyond the region. It has projected a positive, benign view of young people, whose personal growth it has stimulated and enhanced. Moreover, it has harnessed the unique capacities of community elders for constructive social service and demonstrated the depth and variety of the contributions that the elderly have to make to the educational process. As it moves out of adolescence, Foxfire must decide if it is going to repeat the points it has already proven or take on new issues and concerns.

Looking toward the future, Foxfire faces three fundamental alternatives. First, it can keep on with "business as usual"—i.e., teaching the same courses in the same ways and continuing to focus on publishing the magazine. Wigginton has explicitly rejected this alternative on the grounds that such a course is likely to lead to Foxfire's stagnation (educationally and economically) and eventual collapse as a vibrant, pioneering initiative. Yet if he fails to assert himself forcefully to ensure his staff's compliance with the new goal of shoring up the academic side of their programs, stagnation and decline could well become Foxfire's future.

Propitious signs of Foxfire's organizational maturity can be found in the measures being taken in late 1984 to align these programs with the academic competency objectives mandated by the state. The success of the remaining two alternatives hinges on the academic integrity of Foxfire courses.

The second option for Foxfire is to mature into new spheres of activity quite distinct from its previous activities. In its first twenty years, Foxfire has projected and celebrated what might be called an innocent view of Appalachia. Critics such as Charles Perdue have charged that its brand of cultural preservation is romanticized, even mythic. Yet from a developmental perspective, these criticisms appear a bit harsh. For example, is it reasonable to expect that an organization's social consciousness (like that of a young person) would be as developed or mature in its incipiency and early years as at a later time in its life cycle?

During these formative years Foxfire only nodded in the direction of a direct engagement of students in community issues. Efforts such as the "Betty's Creek Issue" remained the exception rather than the rule. Students were conspicuously absent from the planning and decision making that surrounded Wigginton's Mountain City Project, an idea that never engendered the wholehearted support of either his staff or legal board.

If Foxfire is to realize its full potential as a "mature" adult, it must deal with its community and region on an adult's level. Optimally, Foxfire (with the full engagement of its students) would renew its community development efforts to make Rabun County a reasonable and productive place in which native Appalachians might continue to live. As a beginning, students should be involved in research (and publishing) on economic, social, and political issues affecting Rabun County and its surrounding communities. The Rabun County Land-ownership Study is a start in this direction, but it (and projects like it) must become an organizational priority if Foxfire's community growth is to continue.

The third, and final, alternative is for Foxfire to essentially stop its maturation at this point and spend its time proselytizing and assisting other schools and communities to emulate the accomplishments it has already attained. In pursuing this option, the organization would be committed to correcting its internal weaknesses—so that it would become the strongest possible model it can be of experiential education at the high school level.

None of these alternatives is preordained. The first path is the easiest, yet least palatable, option for Wigginton. Of the three paths, it is also the least consistent with his educational philosophy and personal temperament. The second path is the most conflict-ridden and most difficult. Devoting his organization and students to the sphere of community social action would risk its status of being "above the fray" of local problems and politics. While it might engender major community benefits, it also might ultimately undermine Foxfire's broad base of community support. The third path represents a middle road for Foxfire between standing still and moving far ahead in its maturation. National curriculum dissemination is a reasonable, respectable strategy and the path most consistent with Wigginton's conservative temperament.

As stated previously, if Wigginton continues with his present staff and they do not keep pace with him, path one is guaranteed. Full commitment to the social reform agenda of path two will necessitate hiring new staff with business expertise and social action commitments. Path three (enhancing the replicability of Foxfire and providing teacher training) will require either new staff or a more academic version of the present staff.

As Foxfire approached its twentieth anniversary, its emphasis and direction lay along path three. In 1984 Wigginton presented a two-year plan to his boards that entailed the development of Foxfire curriculum guides and the rejuvenation of the cultural journalism newsletter *Hands On*. The initial catalyst for the dissemination of Wigginton's educational ideas would be *Sometimes a Shining Moment* (1985). Wigginton envisioned that this volume would stimulate a national dialogue about Foxfire pedagogy. The curriculum guides would be available for teachers interested in tailoring the Foxfire concept to many courses in a variety of disciplines. *Hands On* would serve primarily as a forum for discussion of the issues and concerns raised in Wigginton's book.

Path three is not an easy alternative for Wigginton. Foxfire is a reflection of both his genius as an innovator and his willingness to give teaching his life's priority. Yet, as every national study of teaching has indicated, these traits are not abundant commodities within the profession. The success of path three hinges on Wigginton's ability to make his ideas *accessible* to, and *achievable* by, teachers who are neither extraordinarily gifted nor obsessive about their vocation.

The cornerstone of Foxfire's curriculum dissemination plan is Foxfire I, the details of which are specified in *Sometimes a Shining Moment*. Specifically designed for students with marginal writing skills (yet thoroughly appropriate for higher-level students), this unique course integrates both intellectual and personal growth skills in a fashion consistent with Deweyan pedagogy. *In theory*, its key elements are highly replicable.

However, the ideal of replicability and the fact of replication are entirely separate issues. The history of American educational reform is not sanguine in this regard. In Rabun County, Foxfire I has been like a hothouse plant, nurtured and coddled by Wigginton. The challenge now is to find ways to make this good idea work for teachers in places where Wigginton is not there to continuously assist and encourage them.

Two obstacles, common to all educational reforms, threaten the widespread replication of the latest version of the Foxfire concept. First, the idea may not ever reach substantial numbers of educators. After all, how many teachers and teacher trainers will actually read *Sometimes a Shining Moment*? And how many of these readers will choose to alter their familiar patterns in order to take up the opportunity Wigginton has placed before them? Second, there is the danger that today's educators, like Dewey's disciples in years past, will bastardize or trivialize Wigginton's concept. Unlike the other alternatives, the eventual success of path three is largely *out* of Wigginton's hands—and *in* the hands of the nation's teachers, education professors, and policymakers.

Thus Foxfire's future remains an open question: Will it find its place in American educational history as a "shining moment" or will it be the start of a "shining movement"? Properly replicated, Foxfire *has* the potential to be the catalyst for a new wave of school improvement combining academic integrity, social consciousness, and the sheer pleasure of experiential education in the service of America's youth. Therefore, Foxfire's fate is of interest and importance not only to Foxfire itself, but also to everyone concerned about enhancing the quality of America's public schools.

Epilogue

Since completing the manuscript for *Foxfire Reconsidered* in 1986, I have returned to Rabun County on several occasions and have observed fundamental changes in the organization, the most notable of which have been measures taken to strengthen Foxfire's academic agenda and significant progress made toward creating a "teacher outreach" program. These changes are embodiments of the decision to make Foxfire the strongest possible model it can be of experiential education at the high school level.

Along Foxfire's academic front, Wigginton has added a research course for Rabun County High School seniors to complement College English, his advanced composition course. Students in the new course examine topics that have relevancy for Rabun County or southern Appalachia, and they write semester term papers according to the format prescribed by the Modern Language Association. An "A" paper for Wigginton requires four interviews, two of which may be conducted by telephone; ten copyrighted sources; and one primary source, preferably statistical data. (For a paper on the Ku Klux Klan in north Georgia, one student interviewed a Klan Imperial Wizard who brought along his white sheets and other regalia.) In his classroom Wigginton has compiled a small library of books, periodicals, and statistical data on southern Appalachia for students' research. Each student contributes to this repository by submitting a file of the information gathered on his or her topic during the semester; this "data file" is available for future use by students interested in updating the topic.

Wigginton's decision to use the new course as a source of magazine and book articles appears to have resolved his quandary about how to move students beyond the publication formulas that were routine at Foxfire in the mid-1980s. The course also incorporates the study of local and regional issues in a fashion consistent with the social philosophy Wigginton has espoused for over fifteen years but has been reluctant to implement in the magazine class. In short, the research paper provides the *opportunity* for students to move to higher order skills and issues while giving them experiences and attitudes intended to help with college paper-writing—the "next step" in the Deweyan/Foxfire curriculum spiral beyond basic cultural journalism.

The Foxfire English curriculum provides Rabun County High School students with the option to earn five of the eight English credits now required for graduation. In Wigginton's view, the optimal sequence of spiraling language arts skills is Foxfire I and Appalachian literature in the ninth or tenth grade, Foxfire II in the eleventh grade (one or two semesters), and College English and the research paper course in the twelfth grade. Wigginton has noted a "dramatic difference" between the performance of seniors in the research course who have taken Foxfire II and those who bypassed it: "The Foxfire kids are far ahead in terms of their ability to deal with all the research variables involved."

Other Foxfire programs, in varying degrees, have expressly incorporated academic skills, especially in the language arts. For example, Cook now teaches a radio production class for which students submit written scripts, many of which are broadcast on a thirty-minute Foxfire radio program aired weekly by a local station. In 1987–88 Cook, Reynolds, and Wigginton began to "team-teach" Foxfire I, which they revised for the eighteen-week semester to introduce "all of Foxfire" to students in the service of composition skills—but not as a prerequisite for other Foxfire courses. The debate at Foxfire surrounding Reynolds's music program has largely subsided; Wigginton has discerned that the music performance classes and Foxfire string bands render too valuable and too popular a school and community service to alter. Now Reynolds also teaches a six-week segment on the folk art of storytelling to seventh-graders, who revolve through a sequence of "mini-courses" intended to help them choose a general direction for their secondary studies. Hilton Smith, who joined Foxfire in 1984–85, teaches a government/economics course, now a regular Foxfire offering, which stresses a functioning knowledge of the American political system and current issues, and applications thereof in "real world" projects, e.g., school and community opinion surveys. The Rabun County High School administration has agreed to set aside the last period of the school day as a planning/coordination time for all Foxfire teachers.

In December of 1987, the time of my last visit to Foxfire, the first videotape and *Foxfire* magazine article from the Rabun County Landownership Study, inaugurated three years earlier, neared completion. These materials emphasize the changing pattern of landownership in the county and its implications for the local economy and political structure. While this particular study has never had an organizational priority (the three-year production time suggests as much), Wigginton has acted on his commitment to get Rabun County High School students involved in county and regional issues by expressly designing his research course as a vehicle for this kind of activity.

In the spring of 1986, Foxfire received a five-year, $1.5 million grant from Mr. Bingham's Trust for Charity, a private foundation, to support the dissemination of Foxfire's approach to classroom instruction. To direct the "teacher outreach" program, Wigginton appointed Hilton Smith, who, in addition to over twenty years of teaching experience in conventional and alternative high schools, has a Ph.D. in educational administration and three years of experience as a researcher for the Southern Association of Colleges and Schools. Smith has coordinated a twofold strategy for curriculum dissemination: first, affiliations with colleges and universities; and second, the development of curriculum guides of transferable Foxfire courses, case studies, filmstrip/video illustrations of Foxfire courses, and a teacher "handbook" to complement Wigginton's pedagogical treatises, *Moments* and *Sometimes a Shining Moment*.

The first part of this strategy has entailed attracting elementary, middle school, and secondary teachers to participate in summer workshops and academic-year graduate courses taught by Wigginton and Smith on four college campuses. The thematic content of these programs has been Deweyan/Foxfire pedagogy, with Wigginton's *Sometimes a Shining Moment* as a text. As the major course requirement, participants design and implement, with an eye to the specific courses they teach, "a cluster of instructional activities which are both academically sound and consistent with an experiential, community-based philosophy." In keeping with the Foxfire pedagogy, the teachers *and* their students are expected to refine and revise (and perhaps alter entirely) these instructional units. The teachers are eligible to apply for Foxfire "mini-grants" to defray the costs of materials and equipment needed to implement the activities; receipt of these awards, as much as $1,000, obligates teachers to submit written case studies of their experiences for possible future publication and distribution by Foxfire. Foxfire sponsors periodic follow-up, "renewal" sessions throughout the year to give teachers the opportunity to share their experiences and to troubleshoot any problems.

With the advice and assistance of nationally prominent educators, Wigginton and Smith have designed a set of questionnaires to help assess the impact of these courses on teacher attitudes and performance. A member of Foxfire's national advisory board conducts taped interviews with all participants prior to and following each course or workshop. The results of this phase of the evaluation, coupled with the case studies and other participant reports, will provide a partial data base for validating Foxfire's teacher outreach strategy as a model for disseminating innovative pedagogy.

Foxfire has established two campus sites in Appalachia as regional bases for its dissemination efforts: Berea College, Kentucky, home of a Foxfire summer workshop; and North Georgia College, where Foxfire conducts a summer graduate course. Foxfire has a third affiliate at Cornell University, site of a summer workshop for Cornell area teachers. The fourth campus-based program—a graduate course for metro-Atlanta teachers offered by Georgia State University—adds what Smith calls a "critical new ingredient" to the teacher outreach project: "Foxfire's first attempt to work with a large group of urban public school teachers." Foxfire also has formal ties with Breadloaf in Vermont, where Wigginton teaches a one-week session in a summer writing project; and the University of Idaho, which offers an academic-year course in Foxfire pedagogy taught by university faculty, with occasional visits by Wigginton or a staff member (for "quality control").

Wigginton and Smith's goal is to encourage and facilitate self-sustaining networks of Foxfire teachers around the four campus-based programs; these teachers will recruit others for the Foxfire programs and serve as mentors for less experienced colleagues. The Eastern Kentucky Foxfire Network, founded in 1986, now has a full-time regional coordinator (supported by several foundation grants independently of Foxfire funding) who advises Network teachers on implementing instructional units and writing case studies, coordinates resource development, recruits teachers for the summer workshop, and teaches the workshop with Wigginton. Teachers in the Georgia State University and Cornell programs began organizing their networks in the summer of 1987. In the fall of 1987, Wigginton and Smith instituted a teacher fellowship program that brings teachers to Foxfire for a full year's immersion in the program's philosophy and practice; these teacher fellows will return to their home school districts to create instructional models and, ideally, to initiate new Foxfire networks.

The second prong of Foxfire's dissemination strategy—desktop publishing of curriculum materials—has two primary components, both of which are currently in progress: curriculum guides of Foxfire courses and case studies of the projects implemented by participants in Foxfire courses and workshops. Initially, the curriculum guides will be mailed free of charge to teachers anywhere who want to implement them, with the stipulation that they provide Foxfire with a written review and critique of the materials; staff members will subsequently revise the guides to incorporate this feedback and provide case examples "from the field." These materials will be available, at cost, for teachers anywhere.

Beyond Foxfire's invigorated academic emphasis, which dovetails with the teacher outreach program, the organization has instituted other changes to remedy problems that were salient at the time I completed my fieldwork with the organization. For example, Foxfire appears to have resolved its dilemma of maintaining the Foxfire Center by finally hiring a full-time conservator, Robert Murray, a former construction teacher at the high school. This appointment, expressing the organization's commitment to maintain the land, buildings, and ecology of the property, provides a balance to Foxfire's new educational priorities, which extend far beyond the Rabun County community.

Throughout 1986–87, in an attempt to involve students directly in organizational decision making, the Foxfire staff invited them to attend the weekly staff meetings, segments of which were devoted to eliciting student opinion and discussion on selected topics. The student volunteers who attended the meetings (which were open to all Foxfire students) carried organizational information back to the Foxfire classes for further discussion and an occasional vote. Despite an auspicious beginning—an average of eight students per meeting during the first year—attendance in 1987–88 had dwindled to an average of only one student per meeting. In addition to other factors complicating the strategy—students' extracurricular activities, after-school jobs, and transportation limitations—it appears that the issues students have been asked to consider have not been engaging enough to sustain continuing interest.

Along Foxfire's financial front, two factors have mitigated, at least in the short term, pressures on the endowment, which by 1988 had increased to over $2.1 million. First, for the next few years foundation largess will cover Smith's salary and administrative expenses, and half of the salaries for Wigginton, Cook, Reynolds, and Margie Bennett. Thus far, however, Wigginton's efforts to secure direct support for the endowment have been largely desultory. Second, *Foxfire 9*, the last of the Doubleday series, sold an unexpected 60,000 copies in its first eight weeks; as anticipated, it sparked a renewed demand for the previous volumes, which Doubleday reprinted by the thousands.

Added responsibilities associated with the expansion of Foxfire's English curriculum at Rabun County High School and the organization's teacher outreach program do not appear to have diminished Wigginton's energy or enthusiasm for working with young people. In a spring report to Foxfire's boards in 1987, he made the following note:

> Talk about wearing kids out: two weeks ago a student and I did a Thursday afternoon teacher workshop in Athens, drove to Atlanta that night, presented a proposal to a foundation officer the next morning, spoke to four hundred people at a books-and-author luncheon at the Georgia IRA Conference at noon, drove to Macon to do a four p.m. teacher workshop there, and then drove back to the Professional Association of Georgia Educators Conference at 7:30 that night. . . . That was almost too much for one day, but I'll tell you something: the student I had with me was a tenth grader who had never before spoken in public. By the time we finished, he had spoken to well over a thousand people, total, in four different locations— and the two big conference speeches both resulted in standing ovations— and suddenly I had a very professional, accomplished student with me instead of a scared kid. His mother was present for the final speech, and we all went out together afterwards, and that was the proudest woman I've ever seen. Period.

In closing the letter, Wigginton indicated that he was not about to slow down: "Ah hell. It's still fun. It's really still fun. I thought I'd be bored by now, but it just gets more and more interesting."

APPENDIX A

Bibliographical Notes

The major repository of Foxfire documents is the Foxfire Center in Mountain City, Georgia. Housed in the Center's cabin archives are all the audio tapes and transcriptions of Foxfire contact interviews since 1967, as well as the manuscripts of numerous *Foxfire* articles. All *Foxfire* publications and most organizational reports, legal and financial documents, funding proposals, and letters are located here. Documents concerning IDEAS and the dissemination of the Foxfire concept are located in the Georgia Department of Archives and History (Atlanta), which also houses Wigginton's correspondence with college associates, Mary Hambidge, and Doubleday, Inc. The state archive requires written permission from Wigginton before granting access to his private correspondence.

Foxfire History and General Information

The single best source of information on the history of Foxfire's Rabun Gap School tenure (1966–77) is Wigginton's semiautobiographical *Sometimes a Shining Moment* (Garden City, N.Y.: Anchor Press/Doubleday, 1985). The author punctuates his narrative of the rise of Foxfire with numerous anecdotes, letters, memoranda, and journal entries. Regarding Foxfire's years at Rabun County High School, however, this volume provides only sparse information. Wigginton's pedagogical treatise *Moments* (Washington, D.C.: IDEAS, 1975) also includes rich anecdotal material from Foxfire's Rabun Gap era, e.g., the Harvey Miller episode and the JFG coffee commercials. Wigginton's periodic reports to the various Foxfire boards (1971–85) provide an indispensable, detailed chronicle of organizational history at both high schools. Other useful sources include Foxfire's legal board minutes, investment portfolios, annual budget statements, publishing contracts, Wigginton's personal correspondence with former students, and the organization's voluminous correspondence with Doubleday, Inc., IDEAS, Foxfire legal board members, national advisory board members, and numerous other individuals, e.g., Jimmy Carter, Alex Haley, Herbert Kohl, and Richard Dorson. The correspondence with the National Endowment for the Humanities (1978–84), Kresge Foundation (1979), Charles Stewart Mott Foundation (1978–84), and Public Welfare Foundation (1982–84) provides indispensable information on Foxfire's community development initiatives.

My history of Foxfire would hardly have been complete without information drawn from the numerous *Foxfire* publications, which in addition to folkloric and instructional materials, feature descriptions of Foxfire programs and activities over the past twenty years. These volumes include *Foxfire* magazine (1967–86); Wigginton, ed., *The Foxfire Book* (Garden City, N.Y.: Anchor Press/Doubleday, 1972); Wigginton, ed., *Foxfire 2* (Garden City, N.Y.: Anchor Press/Doubleday, 1973); Wigginton, ed., *Foxfire 3* (Garden City, N.Y.: Anchor Press/Doubleday, 1975); Kaye Carver and Myra Queen, eds., *Memories of a Mountain Shortline* (Rabun Gap, Ga.: Foxfire Press, 1976); Wigginton, ed., *Foxfire 4* (Garden City, N.Y.: Anchor Press/Doubleday, 1977); Wigginton, ed., *Foxfire 5* (Garden City, N.Y.: Anchor Press/Doubleday, 1979); Wigginton, ed., *Foxfire 6* (Garden City, N.Y.: Anchor Press/Doubleday, 1980); Paul Gillespie, ed., *Foxfire 7* (Garden City, N.Y.: Anchor Press/Doubleday, 1982); Linda Page and Wigginton, eds., *Aunt Arie: A Foxfire Portrait* (New York: F. P. Dutton/Foxfire Press, 1983); Wigginton and Margie Bennett, eds., *Foxfire 8* (Garden City, N.Y.: Anchor Press/Doubleday, 1984). Organizational activities are also chronicled in the *Clayton Tribune* and Foxfire's new community newsletter, *Foxfire Reflections*.

Statements of Foxfire philosophy may be found in Wigginton's introductions to seven *Foxfire* books, in *Moments* (cited above) and, most recently, in *Sometimes a Shining Moment* (cited above). Wigginton has also discussed his pedagogy in the following articles: "Doing Real English," *Media & Methods* 5, no. 5 (1969): 38–39; "The Foxfire Concept Can Work for You," *Media & Methods* 14, no. 3 (1977): 49–52; "Is Your School Doing Its Job? Lessons from the Foxfire Experience," *Southern Exposure* 10, no. 1 (1982): 53–59; "Beyond Foxfire," *Journal of Experiential Education* 1, no. 2 (1978); "The Foxfire Concept," in *Teaching Mountain Children*, ed. David Mielke (Boone, 1978), 208–21.

Wigginton has discussed his friendship with Mary Crovatt Hambidge in "Mary Hambidge," *Foxfire*, Fall 1973, 209–24, 254–55. Karin

Schaller has described Mary Hambidge's career in Rabun County in "Mary Crovatt Hambidge," *Fiber Arts,* September/October 1984, 24–25. A gossipy account of internecine strife at the Hambidge Center after Mary Hambidge's death and Wigginton's departure is Nathan James, "What Did Mary Say?," *Brown's Guide to Georgia,* October 1982, 50–55, 82–88.

Journalistic and testimonial accounts of Foxfire include the following: David Shapiro, "Discovering a Sense of Past & Place," *Saturday Review,* 29 April 1972, 36–38; David Johnson, "They Learned & Loved It," *New York Times,* 5 April 1972; Peggy Thompson, "Old-Timers Tell All to *Foxfire,*" *Smithsonian,* December 1971, 46–51; David W. Hacker, "The Joy of Learning," *National Observer,* 4 March 1972; John Pennington, "A Mountain Success Story," *Atlanta Journal & Constitution Magazine,* 9 April 1972, 8–9, 23–38; Arthur Gordon, "The Magic Glow of Foxfire," *Reader's Digest,* November 1973, 67–72; Patricia Peterson, "The Foxfire Concept," *Media & Methods* 10, no. 3 (1973): 16-18; Peggy Thompson, "In the Footsteps of 'Foxfire,'" *American Education* 8 (1972): 4-10; "Foxfire," *Senior Scholastic,* September 1972, 16-17; Thad Sitton, "Bridging the School-Community Gap: The Lessons of Foxfire," *Educational Leadership* 38 (1980): 248–50; "Spreading Foxfire," *Time,* 14 August 1972, 43; "50 Faces for America's Future," *Time,* 6 August 1979, 48; Gail Parks, "Foxfire: Experiential Education in America," in *Rural Education in Urbanized Nations,* ed. Jonathan P. Sher (Boulder, Colo.: Westview Press, 1981), 277–300; Thad Sitton, "Foxfire: The Fire That Lit Up Learning," *Teacher* 96 (1979): 65–67; WNBC Television, "The Foxfire Glow" (New York, 1982); Daniel Mack, "The Foxfire Experience Reviewed," *Harvard Educational Review* 46 (1976): 477–80; B. Drummond Hayes, Jr., "Publishing a Journal Ignites Student Interest in Learning," *New York Times,* 24 October 1975; Neil Maxwell, "High School Journal Spawns Small Empire and Host of Imitators," *Wall Street Journal,* 2 July 1975. Useful accounts of the *Foxfire* play are Susan Cooper, "The Making of the Play," *Guthrie Theater Program Magazine,* 1981; and D. C. Denison, "How 'Foxfire' Journeyed to Broadway," *New York Times,* 7 November 1982.

Criticisms of Foxfire by academic folklorists have appeared in the following: Richard Dorson, "The Lesson of 'Foxfire,'" *North Carolina Folklore Journal* 21, no. 4 (1973): 157–59; Richard Dorson, "Professor Dorson's Response," *North Carolina Folklore Journal* 22, no. 2 (1974): 39–40; Henry Glassie, review of *The Foxfire Book,* in *Natural History,* January 1973, 97–98; Lynwood Montell in *Oral History Association Newsletter* 7, no. 4 (1973): 4; Charles Perdue, "What's Wrong with

Foxfire?," *Nameless Newsletter* 21 (Winter 1979): 30–31; and Charles Perdue, "The Americanization of John Egerton and Aunt Arie, *Appalachian Journal* 11, no. 4 (1984): 437–41. Favorable critiques are Guy Owen in *Tennessee Folklore Society Bulletin* 38, no. 3 (1972): 84–85; William M. Clemments, *Folklore Forum* 5, no. 4 (1972): 151–53; and Austin E. Fife in *Journal of American Folklore* 86 (1973): 196–97. Wigginton's side of the folklore/fakelore controversy may be found in "A Reply to the Lesson of Foxfire," *North Carolina Folklore Journal* 22, no 2. (1974): 35–36; and "Mr. Wigginton's Reply to Professor Dorson's Response": 40–41. Dorson and Wigginton finally reached a rapprochement of sorts in Dorson and Inta Carpenter, "Can Folklorists Work Together?," *North Carolina Folklore Journal* 26, no. 1 (1978): 3–13; and Wigginton, "Comment": 14–17. Carlos C. Drake provides an excellent discussion of the heated debate in his skillful review of *Foxfire* books in *Western Folklore* 35 (1976): 281–87. While Drake is mildly critical of Foxfire, he recommends that professional folklorists emulate its example by showing greater respect for the feelings of their informants: "Some of us would admit that the sacred precincts of academe, including folklore's rather thorny rose garden, protect from outside scrutiny the sad sterility of many self-serving efforts at 'basic research.'"

Documents published by IDEAS and Foxfire related to the Foxfire dissemination include *Exchange* (1973–76), *Nameless Newsletter* (1977–79), and *Hands On* (1979–82, 1985–86). These newsletters contain descriptions of cultural journalism projects and workshops, technical information, and letters from teacher advisors and professional folklorists. A brief history of IDEAS's role in the Foxfire dissemination is IDEAS, "Final Report, The Foxfire Program, Grant No. 730-0084, 1 October 1972–30 September 1974," submitted to Ford Foundation, 25 February 1975. Thad Sitton's dissertation, "The Foxfire-Concept Publications: A First Appraisal" (University of Texas, 1978), remains the only substantive treatment of the grassroots spread of the Foxfire concept, although the author's findings are limited to thirty-five cultural journalism projects. A follow-up survey to determine why some projects have endured and others have failed is sorely needed. Two other dissertations related to the Foxfire dissemination are thinly researched and shed no light on how the learning concept works in practice. David Nungesser's "Thistledown: An Experimental Application of the Foxfire Learning Concept" (Ohio State University, 1977) is an uncritical description of the author's own Foxfire-type project, lacking pedagogical and sociological analysis. Robert England's "The Ideal Characteristics of Foxfire-Type Projects as Perceived by Teacher-

Advisors" (University of Alabama, 1979), a trivial report of what twenty-seven users of the Foxfire concept think should be happening in their projects, is equally devoid of critical analysis.

Rabun County

The only existing volume of Rabun County history is Andrew Ritchie's outdated *Sketches of Rabun County History* (By the author, 1948), which includes a narrative history of the Rabun Gap School. A more recent description of Rabun Gap School is Peggy Wilson's uncritical treatise, *A Time to Sow, A Time for Planting* (Clayton, Ga.: n.p., 1978).

The *Clayton Tribune* remains the best source for Rabun County political and educational issues. Sandy S. Cook's M.A. thesis, "The Structure of a Successful Community Development Corporation in a Rural Area: A Recommendation to the Foxfire Fund, Inc." (Baylor University, 1983), is a thorough and convenient source of economic and demographic data on Rabun County in the 1980s. Other relevant publications are *Georgia Today: Rabun County Facts at a Glance*, Georgia Department of Community Affairs, 1985; and Thomas Hodler and Howard Schretter, *The Atlas of Georgia* (Athens, Ga.: University of Georgia, Institute of Community and Area Development, 1986).

Rabun County High School officials were generous enough to grant me access to student records for the class of 1984, as well as to school curriculum guides, daily announcement sheets, class rankings, SAT scores, and school rules and regulations. An official at the Rabun County Tax Assessor's Office in Clayton directed me to the county tax digest for information on total acreage held by the National Forest Service, Georgia Power Company, and other private industries.

Educational Contexts

The term "progressivism" has divergent meanings in the context of American educational reform history. In *The One Best System* (Cambridge, Mass.: Harvard University Press, 1974), David Tyack has ably demonstrated that progressive education had an administrative wing—a powerful alliance of career educators and leaders in business, the professions, and municipal government who, in the name of science and democracy, imposed centralized governance, management by experts, and standardized testing/sorting mechanisms on urban and rural schools alike between 1890 and 1940. Tyack labeled these structural reformers "administrative progressives." The consequences of their reforms for schooling, especially the perpetuation of

racism and maintenance of the existing social hierarchy, are delineated in works by Michael Katz, Clarence Karier, Samuel Bowles and
Herbert Gintes, and other writers of the revisionist school of American educational historiography. For the Foxfire study I limited my
investigation of progressive education to the classroom reform wing
of the movement—the "pedagogical progressives," whose major intellectual leader and the focus of much subsequent controversy was John
Dewey. This wing has included child-centered advocates, social reconstructionists, "life adjustment" educators, and "radical romanticists."
Lawrence Cremin's immensely readable *The Transformation of the School*
(New York: Viking, 1962) remains the definitive study of the pedagogical progressives, revisionist challenges to some of his interpretations notwithstanding. Particularly useful is the author's eloquent
statement of Deweyan pedagogy and its subsequent distortions by
child-centered progressives and proponents of the "activity curriculum" in the 1920s and 1930s. Cremin identified progressive education
exclusively as a curriculum reform movement—an error later corrected by Tyack's work. An excellent overview of pedagogical progressivism from the 1920s to the 1970s may be found in Daniel and
Laurel Tanner, *Curriculum Development*, 2d ed. (New York: Macmillan,
1980). Building on Cremin's analysis and numerous works by Dewey,
the Tanners effectively dissociate Dewey from the progressives who
bastardized his pedagogy. In a useful recent history, *The Troubled
Crusade* (New York: Basic Books, 1982), Diane Ravitch examines the
"life adjustment" movement of the 1940s and 1950s, the dominant
vision of progressive education in those decades, which, at the expense of intellectual development, emphasized emotional adjustment,
correct social behavior, and career planning. In frequently cited essays
in *Anti-Intellectualism in American Life* (New York: Knopf, 1963), Richard Hofstadter associates the "de-intellectualized curricula" of life
adjustment education with Dewey's disciples. Sidney Hook's *Education
and the Taming of Power* (LaSalle, Ill.: Open Court, 1973) contains a
thoughtful critique of the romantic naturalists of the 1960s, "who
either profess themselves inspired to some degree by the thought of
John Dewey or are commonly regarded by the educational lay public
as continuing his influence." Hook's attack on romantic naturalism is
strikingly similar to Dewey's criticism of the romantic progressives of
his era. The point at issue for both theorists is the naturalists' assumption that the self-initiated activity of children is inherently educative.
"Doing is a part of learning only when it is directed by ideas, which the
doing tests," Hook noted. "Doing in Dewey's sense is the experiment-
ing that is guided by an hypothesis, not the blind action that never

reaches the level of an experiment. In other words, we learn by doing, but it is a simple fallacy of conversion to infer that all doing is a form of learning." Of interest also is Herbert Kliebard's *The Struggle for the American Curriculum, 1893–1958* (Boston: Routledge and Kegan Paul, 1986), in which the author analyzes four dominant—and competing— themes of curriculum history in the twentieth century: humanism, social efficiency, developmentalism, and social meliorism. Kliebard writes that Dewey remained above the fray: "While competing interest groups eagerly looked to him for support and leadership, Dewey's own position in critical matters of theory and doctrine actually represented a considerable departure from the mainline of any of the established movements."

Dewey's major pedagogical works are essential reading for determining points of convergence and divergence between his educational theory and Foxfire practice. In *Experience and Education* (New York: Macmillan, 1938), Dewey upbraided progressive educators for slighting academic content and indulging the whims and impulses of children. This tiny, readable volume also contains an eloquent paean for bridging formal learning with the child's out-of-school experience. (It appeared at the same time as Boyd Bode's *Progressive Education at the Crossroads* [New York: Newson, 1938], which bears a striking resemblance to Dewey's critique.) Interestingly, Dewey had warned his colleagues of the potential pitfalls of progressive education a decade earlier in a speech published as "Progressive Education and the Science of Education," *Progressive Education* 5, no. 3 (1928): 197–204. Several years later, in *The Way Out of Educational Confusion* (Cambridge, Mass.: Harvard University Press, 1931), he had voiced concerns about the project method, popularized by his most famous disciple, William Heard Kilpatrick, on the grounds that "many so-called projects . . . are entered upon for such casual reasons that extension of acquaintance with facts and figures is at a minimum. In short, they are too trivial to be educative." Formulations of Dewey's model of reflective thinking appear in *Democracy and Education* (New York: Macmillan, 1916) and *How We Think* (Boston: Heath, 1910; rev. 1933). *The Child and Curriculum* (1902), in *John Dewey: The Middle Works: 1899–1924*, vol. 2, ed. Jo Ann Boydston (Carbondale: Southern Illinois University Press, 1976) contains a cogent rationale for incorporating reflective activity in the classroom. Dewey's idea of the spiral curriculum is explicitly stated in *Experience and Education*. Dewey's views on the role of the school in fostering dispositions for social service are included in *The School and Society* (1899), in *John Dewey: The Middle Works: 1899–1924*, vol. 1, ed. Boydston; and *Democracy and Education*. The following

Depression-era essays by Dewey called for infusing the curriculum with the reflective study of social problems, the goal being to create a citizenry accustomed to the application of the experimental method in personal and social problem-solving: "Education and Social Change," *Social Frontier,* May 1937, 235–38; "Education for a Changing Social Order," National Education Association *Proceedings* (1934): 744–52; "Schools in the Social Order," from Dewey, "Education and the Social Order," League for Industrial Democracy, in *Intelligence in the Modern World: John Dewey's Philosophy,* ed. Joseph Ratner (New York: Random House, 1939), 683–90; and "The Social-Economic Situation and Education," in *The Educational Frontier,* ed. William H. Kilpatrick (New York: Appleton-Century, 1933), 32–72.

Useful interpretations and criticisms of Dewey's philosophy appear in Ernest Bayles, *Pragmatism in Education* (New York: Harper and Row, 1966); John Childs, *American Pragmatism in Education* (New York: Henry Holt, 1956); J. S. Brubacher, *Modern Philosophies of Education* (New York: McGraw-Hill, 1950); Merle Curti, *The Social Ideas of American Educators* (Patterson, N.J.: Pageant, 1959); Jo Ann Boydston, ed., *Guide to the Works of John Dewey* (Carbondale: Southern Illinois University Press, 1970); and Robert E. Mason, *Contemporary Educational Theory* (New York: David McKay, 1972), the most readable introduction to the subject. An excellent history which examines the evolution of Dewey's social philosophy, and his role and influence in the social reconstructionist movement of the 1930s is C. A. Bowers, *The Progressive Educator and the Depression* (New York: Random House, 1969).

Child and Youth Services 4, no. 3/4 (1982) devotes the major part of its issue to journalistic accounts of the disparate programs nationwide currently claiming the mantle of experiential education. Among the many "action learning" programs described are a student consumer service in St. Paul, Minn.; a student-published community newspaper in Pulaski, Wis.; and a student-operated community health screening service in New York City. Studies of the learning effects of experiential education programs are reported in the following sources: Daniel Conrad and Diane Hedin, *Executive Summary of the Final Report of the Experiential Education Evaluation Project* (St. Paul: University of Minnesota, Center for Youth Development, n.d.); John P. Hill, "Participatory Education and Youth Development in Secondary Schools," (paper prepared for Better Schools, Inc., 1983); Diane Hedin, *The Impact of Experience on Academic Learning: A Summary of Theories and Review of Recent Research,* Report No. 9. (Boston: Institute for Responsive Research, n.d.); Stephen Hamilton, "Experiential Learning Programs for Youth," *American Journal of Education* 88, no. 2 (1980): 179–215;

Stephen Hamilton and R. F. Zeldin, "Learning Civics in the Community," *Curriculum Inquiry* 17, no. 4 (1987): 407–20; Andrew McKenzie and Robert White, "Fieldwork in Geography and Long-Term Memory Structures," *American Educational Research Journal* 19, no. 4 (1982): 623–32; and Ronald Bucknam and Sheara Brand, "EBCE [Experience Based Career Education] Really Works," *Educational Leadership* 40, no. 6 (1983): 66–71. These writers concur that guided reflection is a sine qua non of successful experiential education programs. The existing research, however, has focused only marginally on the relationship of experiential education and the development of cognitive/intellectual skills, leaving a conspicuous gap in the literature. Moreover, studies such as McKenzie and White's which purport to measure the effects of "experiential learning" on cognitive achievement are limited to "one shot" out-of-classroom activities, in their case, a single field trip.

The leading teacher-reformers of the 1960s and early 1970s whose careers warrant comparison with Eliot Wigginton's are Herbert Kohl, *36 Children* (New York: New American Library, 1967) and *Growing Minds: On Becoming a Teacher* (New York: Harper and Row, 1984); Jonathan Kozol, *Death at an Early Age* (Boston: Houghton Mifflin, 1967); James Herndon, *The Way It Spozed to Be* (New York: Simon and Schuster, 1965); and Pat Conroy, *The Water Is Wide* (Boston: Houghton Mifflin, 1972). Collectively, these volumes suggest that schools will not tolerate the attacks of zealous reformers on the status quo within either classrooms or the community. Reformers who desire to remain in the public schools must adopt conservative strategies.

Over the past decade there has been a voluminous literature on the deficiencies of America's public schools. The assumptions underlying the heated debate over school reform provide a useful and appropriate context for analyzing Foxfire, both as a philosophy of education and as a style of educational reform. National research studies have documented the domination of classroom practice by traditional pedagogy, despite two decades' worth of federally funded curriculum reform. The National Science Foundation's seven-volume report includes the following studies published by the U.S. Government Printing Office, Washington, D.C.: Iris Weiss, *Report of the 1977 National Survey of Science, Mathematics and Social Studies Education* (1978); Robert Stake and Jack Easley, Jr., *Case Studies in Science Education*, 2 vols. (1978); Stanley Helgeson, Patricia Blosser, and Robert W. Howe, *The Status of Pre-College Science, Mathematics, and Social Studies Education: 1955-1975*, vol. 1, *Science Education* (1977); M. Suydam and A. Osborne, *The Status of Pre-College Science, Mathematics, and Social Studies*

Education: 1955–1975, vol. 2, *Mathematics Education* (1977); K. B. Wiley and J. Race, *The Status of Pre-College Science, Mathematics, and Social Science Education: 1955–1975*, vol. 3, *Social Science Education* (1977); *The Status of Pre-College Science, An Overview and Summaries of Three Studies* (1978). Useful interpretations of these studies may be found in James DeRose, J. David Lockard, and Lester Paldy: "The Teacher Is the Key: A Report on Three NSF Studies," *Science and Children* 16, no. 2 (1979): 35–41; A. A. Strassenburg and Lester Paldy, "The Status of Precollege Science Education: Report on a Survey" and "More about NSF-Supported Studies of Precollege Science Education," *Journal of College Science Teaching* 8 (1978): 110-13, 152–85; Thomas Gibney and Edward Karns, "Mathematics Education—1955–1975: A Summary of the Findings," *Educational Leadership* 36 (1979): 356–59; James Shaver, O. L. Davis, Jr., and Suzanne W. Helburn, "The Status of Social Studies Education: Impressions from Three NSF Studies," *Social Education* 43 (1979): 150–53.

A frequently cited study of the marginal success of federal curriculum reforms in the 1960s and 1970s is Paul Berman and Milbrey McLaughlin, *Federal Programs Supporting Educational Change*, vol. 3, *Implementing and Sustaining Innovations*, Rand Corporation Report R-158918-HEW, 1978. In his excellent analysis of school reform, *The Culture of the School and the Problem of Change*, 2d ed. (Boston: Allyn and Bacon, 1982), Seymour B. Sarason builds upon the Berman-McLaughlin report in stating his case that the underlying flaw of previous curriculum reform initiatives has been their failure to alter behavioral regularities inside classrooms. Thoughtful critiques that prescribe a more passive federal role in curriculum reform are Ernest House and J. Myron Atkins, "The Federal Role in Curriculum Development, 1950–1980," *Educational Evaluation and Policy Analysis* 3, no. 5 (1981): 5–36; and Michael Kirst and Gail Meister, "Turbulence in American Secondary Schools: What Reforms Last?," *Curriculum Inquiry* 15 (1985): 169–84.

The current dialogue of educational reform is dominated by three studies, the findings of which corroborate the National Science Foundation studies and the Rand Corporation reports: John Goodlad, *A Place Called School* (New York: McGraw-Hill, 1984); Ernest Boyer, *High School* (New York: Harper and Row, 1983); and Theodore Sizer, *Horace's Compromise* (Boston: Houghton Mifflin, 1984). Beatrice and Ronald Gross have succeeded in bringing a modicum of order to the burgeoning school reform literature in their timely anthology, *The Great School Debate* (New York: Simon and Schuster, 1985). Three of the most influential national-level reform proposals—each of which calls for tighter academic standards in the service of national economic security—are: National Commission on Educational Excellence, *A Nation at Risk* (Washington, D.C.: U.S. Department of Education, 1983); Task Force on Education for Economic Growth, *Action for Excellence* (Washington, D.C.: Education Commission of the States, 1983); and National Science Board Commission on Precollege Education in Mathematics, Science and Technology, *Educating Americans for the 21st Century* (Washington, D.C.: National Science Foundation, [1983]). An example of a state-level document that makes similar assumptions about the relationship of education and economic security is North Carolina Commission on Education for Economic Growth, *An Action Plan for North Carolina* (Raleigh, N.C.: Office of the Governor, 1984). Conspicuously absent in all of these reports is any discussion of the lessons of previous educational reform movements. The documents also err to the extreme of excluding any consideration of the school's role in promoting students' affective and social growth.

Adolescence

The paradigm of adolescence as a pathology has its origins early in the historiography of adolescent psychology. In *Adolescence,* 2 vols. (New York: Appleton, 1904), G. Stanley Hall described the ages fourteen to twenty-two as a period of "storm and stress." Hall's portrait, elaborated by psychoanalytic theorists, gained popular acceptance and became the conventional wisdom about adolescence. An excellent biography and analysis of Hall's theory is Dorothy Ross, *G. Stanley Hall: The Psychologist as Prophet* (University of Chicago Press, 1972). Joseph Kett examines the Victorian social milieu that influenced Hall's quasi-scientific study of adolescence in "Adolescence and Youth in Nineteenth-Century America," *Journal of Interdisciplinary History* 2 (1971): 283–98. Kett's scholarly *Rites of Passage* (New York: Basic Books, 1977) examines the sociocultural forces that have shaped and defined adolescence from 1790 to the present. An excellent short analysis of these factors is David Bakan, "Adolescence in America: From Idea to Social Fact," *Daedalus* 100 (1971): 979–96. Other useful sources are Jerold Starr's essays, "Adolescence and Resistance to Schooling: A Dialectic," *Youth and Society* 13, no. 2 (1981): 189–227; and "American Youth in the 1980s," *Youth and Society* 17, no. 4 (1986): 323–45. Starr argues cogently that the social problems historically associated with adolescence are more properly viewed as "forms of resistance" against the "institutionalized subordination" of young people, the primary instrument of which has been the American secondary school.

The language of orthodox psychoanalytic theory presents a formidable obstacle to the novice reader. A good beginning for interpreting this recondite terminology is the frequently referenced Calvin S. Hall, *A Primer of Freudian Psychology* (Cleveland: World, 1954). Rolf Muus has provided a sorely needed compendium in *Theories of Adolescence,* 4th ed. (New York: Random House, 1982), which includes sections on Sigmund Freud, Anna Freud, Peter Blos, and Erik Erikson. Useful critiques of the psychoanalytic study of adolescence are Joseph Adelson and Margery Doehrman, "The Psychodynamic Approach to Adolescence," in *Handbook of Adolescent Psychology,* ed. Joseph Adelson (New York: John Wiley, 1980), 99–116; and Anne C. Peterson and Taylor Brandon, "The Biological Approach to Adolescence: Biological Change and Psychological Adaptation," in *Handbook of Adolescent Psychology,* 117–55.

The major works in the psychoanalytic tradition of adolescent studies are Anna Freud, *The Ego and Mechanisms of Defense* (New York: International Universities Press, 1936; rev. 1966); A. Freud, "Adolescence," *Psychoanalytic Study of the Child* 13 (1958): 255–78; and Peter Blos, *On Adolescence: A Psychoanalytic Interpretation* (New York: Free Press of Glencoe, 1962). Erik Erikson's link to these theorists is his use of psychoanalytic constructs and his portrait of adolescence as "storm and stress," the latter explicitly drawn in *Identity and the Life Cycle* (New York: Norton, 1959; rev. 1980) and *Identity: Youth and Crisis* (New York: Norton, 1968). Erikson's heavy reliance on clinical studies of disturbed adolescents weakens his conclusions about the extent of adolescent turmoil. Nevertheless, he has contributed immensely useful constructs for interpreting the adolescent experience, e.g., identity formation and psychosocial moratorium. Of particular utility to my research is Erikson's discussion in *Identity: Youth and Crisis* of the role a cultural stereotype can play in stymieing individual identity formation.

The paradigm of adolescence as benign growth originated in the 1960s and is today the most widely espoused view in the clinical and theoretical literature on adolescence. The major studies and reports in this genre include Albert Bandura, "The Stormy Decade: Fact or Fiction?," *Psychology in the Schools* 1 (1964): 224–31; F. Musgrove, *Youth and the Social Order* (Bloomington: Indiana University Press, 1964); James Masterson, Jr., "The Symptomatic Adolescent Five Years Later: He Didn't Grow Out of It," *American Journal of Psychiatry* 123 (1967): 1338–45; James Masterson, Jr., "The Psychiatric Significance of Adolescent Turmoil," *American Journal of Psychiatry* 124 (1968): 1549–53; Daniel and Judith Offer, *From Teenage to Young Manhood* (New York:

Basic Books, 1975); Daniel Offer, *The Psychological World of the Teenager* (New York: Basic Books, 1969); Daniel Offer, Eric Ostrov, and Kenneth I. Howard, *The Adolescent: A Psychological Self-Portrait* (New York: Basic Books, 1981); Denise B. Kandel and Gerald S. Lesser, *Youth in Two Worlds* (San Francisco: Jossey-Bass, 1972); David Elkind, "Egocentricism in Adolescence," *Child Development* 38 (1967): 1025–34, and "Strategic Interactions in Adolescence," in *Handbook of Adolescent Psychology*, 432–44; Martin L. Hoffman, "Moral Development in Adolescence," in *Handbook of Adolescent Psychology*, 295–343; Stanley Coopersmith, Mary Regan, and Lois Dick, *The Myth of the Generation Gap* (San Francisco: Albion, 1975); Martin Gold and Richard Petrono, "Delinquent Behavior in Adolescence," in *Handbook of Adolescent Psychology*, 495–535; John P. Hill and Franz J. Monks, "Some Perspectives on Adolescence in Modern Societies," in *Adolescence and Youth in Prospect*, ed. John P. Hill and Franz J. Monks (Atlantic Highlands, N.J.: Humanities Press, 1977); John P. Hill, "Participatory Education and Youth Development in Secondary Schools," Better Schools, Inc., 1983; Ruthellen Josselson, "Ego Development in Adolescence," in *Handbook of Adolescent Psychology*, 188–210; National Commission on the Reform of Secondary Education, *The Reform of Secondary Education* (New York: McGraw-Hill, 1973); Panel on Youth of the President's Science Advisory Committee, *Youth: Transition to Adulthood* (University of Chicago Press, 1974); Kettering Commission on Youth, *The Transition of Youth to Adulthood: A Bridge Too Long* (Boulder, Colo.: Westview Press, 1980); Carnegie Council on Policy Studies in Higher Education, *Giving Youth a Chance* (San Francisco: Jossey-Bass, 1980); Daniel Yankelovich, "Drug Users vs. Drug Abusers: How Students Control Their Drug Crisis," *Psychology Today*, October 1975, 35–42; Richard Jessor and Shirley Jessor, "Adolescent Development and the Onset of Drinking," *Journal of Studies on Adolescence* 36 (1975): 25–51; Jere Cohen, "Adolescent Independence and Adolescent Change," *Youth and Society* 12 (1980): 107–24; Colin Turnbull, *The Human Cycle* (New York: Simon and Schuster, 1983); and Richard Danzig and Peter Szanton, *National Service: What Would It Mean?* (Lexington, Mass.: Heath, 1986). A recent controversial study, the findings of which have been variously interpreted, is Lloyd Johnson et al., *Drugs and American High School Students, 1975–1983* (Rockville, Md.: National Institute of Drug Abuse/U.S. Department of Health and Human Services, 1984). While these researchers report unequivocally that drug use among teenagers declined over the period of study, they view the resulting lower levels of usage as still alarmingly high. Yet this conclusion submerges the "good news" that is both explicit and implicit in their data, most notably the implication that levels of drug use are a function of particular adolescent cohorts rather than the age group itself; in other words, a function of time and place, not biology.

Appalachian Studies

Excellent sources of general information on Appalachian history, culture, and values are the following: John C. Campbell, *The Southern Highlander and His Home* (New York: Russell Sage Foundation, 1921), still a highly regarded portrait of mountain life, based largely on Campbell's survey of the region, 1908–12; Cratis Williams, "Who are the Southern Mountaineers?," *Appalachian Journal* 1, no. 1 (1972): 48–55; Bruce Ergood, "Toward a Definition of Appalachia," in *Appalachia: Social Context Past and Present*, ed. Bruce Kuhre and Bruce Ergood (Dubuque, Iowa: Kendall/Hunt, 1983); Ronald Eller, "Land and Family: An Historical View of Preindustrial Appalachia," *Appalachian Journal* 6, no. 2 (1979): 83-109; Thomas R. Ford, "The Passing of Provincialism," in *The Southern Appalachian Region: A Survey*, ed. Ford (Lexington: University Press of Kentucky, 1962), 9–34; Loyal Jones, "Appalachian Values," in *Voices from the Hills*, ed. Robert J. Higgs and Ambrose N. Manning (Boone, N.C.: Appalachian Consortium Press, 1975); Allen Batteau, "Appalachia and the Concept of Culture: A Theory of Shared Misunderstandings," *Appalachian Journal* 7, no. 1–2 (1979–80): 9–31; Laurel Shackleford and Bill Weinberg, eds., *Our Appalachia* (New York: Hill and Wang, 1977); essays in Allen Batteau, ed., *Appalachia and America* (Lexington: University Press of Kentucky, 1983): James W. Jordan, "Frontier Culture, Government Agents, and City Folks," 239–51, and Walter Precourt, "The Image of Appalachian Poverty," 86-110; Wilma Dykeman, "Appalachia in Context," in *An Appalachian Symposium*, ed. J. W. Williamson (Boone, N.C.: Appalachian University Press, 1977; David Whisnant's *All That Is Native and Fine* (Chapel Hill: University of North Carolina Press, 1983), a thorough documentation of the settlement, folk, and craft school movements in early twentieth-century Appalachia; Charles A. Watkins, "Culture and Rumors of Culture," *Appalachian Journal* 12, no. 2 (1985), an illuminating review of Whisnant's book; and Robert Coles's highly regarded psychiatric study, *Migrants, Sharecroppers, Mountaineers*, vol. 2 of *Children of Crisis* (Boston: Little, Brown, 1971).

Traditionally Appalachian historiography has been plagued by stereotypic depictions of Southern mountaineers of which Jack Weller's *Yesterday's People* (Lexington: University Press of Kentucky, 1965) is representative. A popular early work that projected a jaundiced view of the region was *Our Southern Highlanders* (New York: Outing, 1913), an account by St. Louis librarian Horace Kephart, in which mountaineers were portrayed as "half-wild" creatures. In her embellished, often condescending work, *The Carolina Mountains* (Boston: Houghton Mifflin, 1913), Margaret Morley, like Kephart a sojourner in the highlands, ridiculed native Appalachians as lazy and inept. ("The mountaineer's method of gathering chestnuts is characteristic. Going into the woods with an axe, he selects a tree loaded with ripe nuts and chops it down."). Yet the most damaging, and most unfounded, attack on Appalachian culture came, ironically, from the preeminent British historian Arnold Toynbee, who, in *A Study of History*, vol. 2 (London: Oxford University Press, 1934), 309–13, asserted that Southern highlanders "have relapsed into barbarism under the depressing effect of a challenge which has been inordinately severe." In a letter to Toynbee, published over forty years after the fact as "An Appalachian Footnote to Toynbee's *A Study of History*," *Appalachian Journal* 6, no. 1 (1978): 29–32, sociologist James S. Brown challenged the account as "exaggerated and misleading"; in his response to Brown, Toynbee stipulated that his description had been "a composite picture formed over the last twenty-five years, as a result of a number of visits to a friend of mine living, not within the mountains, but within reach of them. . . ." In an annotation to the letters, Brown averred that he would have failed any student, "who with such limited knowledge of a people made such a bold, searing, virtually unsubstantiated denunciation." A literary descendant of Toynbee's polemic, at least on the face of it, is James Dickey's popular novel *Deliverance* (Boston, 1970). Discussions of the overt stereotypes in this piece may be found in Eliot Wigginton, *Foxfire*, Winter 1973, 158–59; and James S. Otto, "Reconsidering the Southern 'Hillbilly,'" *Appalachian Journal* 12, no. 4 (1985): 324–31. A literary treatment of the "deeper themes" of Dickey's novel, written by a native Appalachian, is Rodger Cunningham, "Crimes against Nature: The Image of the Mountaineer in *Deliverance*," Appalachian Studies Conference Proceedings, 1987. The definitive treatment of Appalachian stereotypes is Henry D. Shapiro, *Appalachia on Our Mind* (Chapel Hill: University of North Carolina Press, 1978), in which the author examines the conventional perception of Appalachia as "a strange land inhabited by a peculiar people, a discrete region, in but not of America." With scrupulous documentation, Shapiro traces the origins and consequences of Appalachian stereotypes in local-color fiction, 1880s–1890s; the settlement school movement, 1900–20; and the Southern textile industry, 1905–15. Shapiro concludes that "Appalachia possessed no reality independent of its conceptualization." An excellent abridgement of this extensive volume is Shapiro, "Appalachia and the Idea of America: The Problem of the Persisting Frontier," in *An Appalachian Symposium*, ed. Williamson.

The historiography of Appalachia is now dominated by a model of the region as a colonial appendage of the American metropolis. The most significant contribution of the colonialism school has been to illuminate the historical processes that have impoverished and disfranchised native Appalachians. This analytic model has discredited the view of Appalachia as a subculture of poverty ("deficit theory"), popularized by Jack Weller in *Yesterday's People* (cited above) and championed by a cadre of influential writers, for example, Richard Ball, who described Appalachia as an "analgesic subculture" in his culture-defaming essay, "The Southern Appalachian Folk Subculture as a Tension-Reducing Way of Life," in *Change in Rural Appalachia: Implications for Action Programs*, ed. John D. Photiadis and Harry K. Schwarzeller (Philadelphia: University of Pennsylvania Press, 1970). An early formulation of the internal colonialism model is Harry Caudill, *Night Comes to the Cumberlands* (Boston: Little, Brown, 1962), a persuasive, albeit unscholarly, account of unbridled corporate exploitation and abuse in the coal-mining counties of eastern Kentucky. Ronald Eller's *Miners, Millhands, and Mountaineers* (Knoxville: University of Tennessee Press, 1982), the best history of industrialization in Appalachia, provides the scholarly documentation Caudill's work lacked. Essays in *Colonialism in Modern America*, ed. Helen Lewis et al. (Boone, N.C.: Appalachian Consortium Press, 1978), provide further documentation for the Caudill-Eller model, specifically Helen Lewis and Edward Knipe, "The Colonialism Model: The Appalachian Case," 9–31; Helen Lewis, Sue E. Kobak, and Linda Johnson, "Family, Religion and Colonialism in Central Appalachia or Bury My Rifle at Big Stone Gap," 113–39; John Gaventa, "Property, Coal and Theft," 141–57; Warren Wright, "The Big Steal," 161–75; Anita Parlow, "The Land Development Rag," 177–98; James Branscome, "The Federal Government in Appalachia: TVA," 283–93; Ronald Eller, "Industrialization and Social Change in Appalachia, 1880–1930," 35–46; Si Kahn, "The Forest Service and Appalachia," 85-109. John Gaventa's primary contribution to this literature is his excellent case study and analysis of corporate dominance in the Clear Fork Valley, *Power and Powerlessness* (Urbana: University of Illinois Press, 1980), the most forceful example in support of the colonialism model. Other useful works in this analytic genre are Helen Lewis, "Fatalism or the Coal Industry," in *Appala-*

chia: Social Context Past and Present, ed., Kuhre and Ergood, 180–89; Gordon McKinney, "Industrialization and Violence in Appalachia in the 1890s," in *An Appalachian Symposium,* ed. Williamson, 131–34.

The only serious criticism of the internal colonialism model comes from a small group of radical scholars who argue that Appalachia is an "internal periphery" of an advanced capitalist state rather than an internal colony. Periphery theory assumes that the subjugation and exploitation of resource-wealthy peripheral regions such as Appalachia by dominant capitalist interests is a structural necessity for the growth of advanced capitalism. While colonialism theory implies banishment of the colonizers as a remedy, periphery theory implies the overthrow of capitalism. The most succinct explication of the theory is David S. Walls, "Internal Colony or Internal Periphery?," in *Colonialism in Modern America,* ed. Lewis et al., 319–49. Other statements are David S. Walls and Dwight B. Billings, "The Sociology of Southern Appalachia," *Appalachian Journal* 5, no. 1 (1977): 131–44; Jim Foster et al., "Class Political Consciousness, and Destructive Power: A Strategy for Change in Appalachia," *Appalachian Journal* 5, no. 3 (1979): 171–93; Steve Fisher and Jim Foster, "Models for Furthering Revolutionary Praxis in Appalachia," *Appalachian Journal* 6, no. 3 (1979): 171–93; Steve Fisher, "Power and Powerlessness in Appalachia: A Review Essay," *Appalachian Journal* 8, no. 2 (1981): 242–46. In *Apples on the Flood: The Southern Mountain Experience* (Knoxville: University of Tennessee Press, 1987), Rodger Cunningham applies the insights of periphery theory in an interesting "psychohistorical" treatise on Appalachian culture and history. Through an adroit handling of historical and literary texts, Cunningham demonstrates that the Scotch-Irish ancestry, the dominant cultural thread in Appalachia, has traditionally occupied a "peripheral" and dependent role in Western society.

In 1984, the Appalachian Alliance published a seven-volume report of its six-state study of landownership in the Southern highlands. The major findings of the study are easily accessible in the summary volume, *Who Owns Appalachia?* (Lexington: University Press of Kentucky, 1983). The task force researchers, some of whom were local citizens, documented a pattern of absentee corporate political control and tax evasion in the coal counties of the region. In the tourist counties, they found that the beneficiaries of resort and recreation development have been outside developers and speculators, the mountain elite, and the federal government. Useful descriptions of the study may be found in John Gaventa and Bill Horton, "Digging the Facts," *Southern Exposure* 10, no. 1 (1982): 34–39; and Patricia D. Beaver, "Participatory Research on Appalachia," in *Appalachia and*

America, ed. Batteau, 86-110. Gene Wunderlich has authored a tepid criticism of the sampling procedures used in the study in "Landowner-ship in Appalachia: The Limits of Public Interest Research," *Appalachian Journal* 11 (1984): 432–36.

The Appalachian Regional Commission's position in the debate over its role in regional affairs is best stated in ARC's twentieth anniversary issue, "Appalachia: Twenty Years of Progress," *Appalachia* 18, no. 3 (1985). Useful criticisms of ARC may be found in the landowner-ship literature cited above; also in essays in *Appalachia: Social Context Past and Present*, ed. Kuhre and Ergood: Howard Bray, "Appalachia: The View from Washington," 234–42; and James Branscome, "What the New Frontier and Great Society Brought," 247–56.

The best treatment of the history of the Highlander Research and Education Center is Frank Adams, *Unearthing Seeds of Fire* (Winston-Salem: John F. Blair, 1975). Adams's research, based largely on inter-views with Highlander's founder, Myles Horton, appears in abbrevi-ated form in "Highlander Folk School: Getting Information, Going Back and Teaching It," *Harvard Educational Review* 42 (1972): 497–520. "The Adventures of a Radical Hillbilly," the text of "Bill Moyer's Journal: An Interview with Myles Horton," Parts I & II, 5 & 11 June 1981, is replete with anecdotes from Highlander's history. A similar journalistic account is Roger Williams, "A New Role for Old Radicals," *World* 2, no. 16 (1973).

Works that bear on the relationship of education and rural develop-ment strategies in the region are Steve Fisher, "Economic Develop-ment Strategies for Appalachia in the 1980s," Highlander Research and Education Center, 1982; Jonathan P. Sher, "School-Based Com-munity Development Corporations," in *Education and Rural America*, ed. Sher (Boulder, Colo.: Westview Press, 1977), 291–346, 375–92; MDC Panel on Rural Economic Development, *Shadows in the Sunbelt: Developing the Rural South in an Era of Economic Change*, a report for the Ford Foundation, 1986; Jonathan P. Sher, "Back to Basics: Develop-ment Worthy of the Name," *Southern Exposure* 14, no. 5–6 (1986): 4–6.

As a field of scholarly endeavor, Appalachian education is in its incipiency. What exists is an inchoate mass of largely unrelated studies, many of which are polemical, few of which are based on substantive research. There are no longitudinal studies and no regional surveys. Moreover, the existing studies tend to focus on the coal-mining coun-ties of central Appalachia, especially southern West Virginia and east-ern Kentucky. While there is general agreement that Appalachia's schools generally provide poor quality education, aggregate regional data for the 1980s are difficult to find. The latest data on educational attainment (1970–76) are reported in the ARC publication, *Appalachia: A Reference Book,* 2d ed. (Washington, D.C.: Appalachian Regional Commission, 1979; supplemented in 1981). The most recent ARC-sponsored reports on education focus on regional dropout rates and dropout prevention programs; for example, J. Lamarr Cox and associates, *Study of High School Dropouts in Appalachia,* Report No. RTI/3182-01/01 FR, prepared for ARC, 1985; and Campbell Communications, Inc., *Dropout Prevention in Appalachia,* a report of ARC. Regionwide data on school performance as measured by standardized tests are lacking.

The best of the educational research studies is sociologist Alan DeYoung's work in eastern Kentucky, where the researcher has demonstrated links between educational quality and level of community economic development, reported in *Educational Performance in Central Appalachia: Statistical Profiles of Appalachian and Non-Appalachian School Districts* (Lexington: University of Kentucky Appalachian Center, 1982), an ARC-sponsored project co-authored with Charles Vaught, James J. O'Brien, and Jean A. Brymer; "The Status of Formal Education in Central Appalachia," *Appalachian Journal* 10, no. 4 (1983): 321–34; "Economic Development and Educational Status in Appalachian Kentucky," *Comparative Education Review* 29, no. 1 (1985): 47–67. De-Young's finding of a significant negative correlation between mining and quality of education provides empirical support for both colonialism and periphery theory. The only other significant statistically based analysis, only because it is frequently cited, is Una Mae Lange Reck and Gregory C. Reck, "Living Is More Important than Schooling: Schools and Self Concept," *Appalachian Journal* 8, no. 1 (1980): 19–25, in which the researchers report a greater prevalence of negative self-concept among rural mountain children than urban children outside the region. They argue emphatically that this finding supports the conclusion that "schools have been a major institutional arm of the colonization of Appalachia, participating in the denigration of regional lifestyles, perpetuating external control through discrimination, and helping to insure the continuing powerlessness of Appalachian rural people." Yet given the limited range of their sample (a single mountain community in North Carolina and an urban community elsewhere in the same state), the study has, at best, marginal generalizability.

Qualitative argument is the metier of most commentators in this field, and the only book to deal expressly with Appalachian education, *Teaching Mountain Children,* ed. David Mielke (Boone, N.C.: Appalachian Consortium Press, 1978) is filled with it. This anthology is largely a disappointment, partly because of faulty editing, partly because of the paucity of quality studies available at the time. A leading rhetorician of Appalachian education is Jim Wayne Miller, an advocate of the colonialism model, whose best essays are "A Mirror for Appalachia," in *Voices from the Hills,* ed. Higgs and Manning, 447–59; and "Appalachian Education: A Critique of Suggestions for Reform," *Appalachian Journal* 5, no. 1 (1977): 13–22. An impassioned analysis which charges "the sociopolitical elites" of eastern Kentucky with conspiracy to "perpetuate a state of peonage" through inferior schooling in the coal-mining counties is Edward H. Berman, "The Politics of Literacy and Educational Development in Kentucky," *Comparative Education Review* 22 (1978): 115–33. A similar indictment of eastern Kentucky schools is Harry Caudill, *Watches of the Night* (Boston: Little, Brown, 1976), which holds Appalachian educators culpable as well as outside corporate interests. Moderate critiques of Appalachian schooling, presented in *Teaching Mountain Children,* are Peter Schrag, "The School and Politics," 172–76; and Stanley O. Ikenberry, "Educational Reform in Appalachia: Problems of Relevance, Strategy, and Priority," 197–207. In "Bringing Home the Bacon: The Politics of School Reform," *Phi Delta Kappan* 65 (1983): 179–83, an undocumented yet colorful and well-argued essay, Jonathan P. Sher charges that governmental intervention thwarted a 1981 court decision in West Virginia which would have compelled taxation of absentee corporations in the interest of school improvement.

Portions of several previously cited works in Appalachian historiography are useful for understanding schooling in the region today: Campbell's assessment of denominational and private schools in the Southern mountains before World War I, in *The Southern Highlander and His Home;* Shapiro's examination of motives underlying church and settlement education/uplift at the turn of the century, in *Appalachia on Our Mind;* and Whisnant's analysis of settlement and folk school education in the early 1900s, in *All that Is Native and Fine.* A brief yet skillfully argued case study which challenges the conventional wisdom about educational reform in the region is Alan DeYoung and Tom Boyd, "Urban School Reforms for a Rural District: A Case Study of School/Community Relations in Jackson County, Kentucky, 1899–1986," *Journal of Thought* 21, no. 4 (1986): 25–42. Building on "cultural reproduction" theory, Roy Silver and Alan DeYoung, in "The Ideology of Rural/Appalachian Education, 1895–1935," *Educational Theory* 36, no. 1: 51–65, hypothesize that schooling in Appalachia has traditionally been an instrument for ingraining in the region's children the legitimacy of the existing social hierarchy. On the one hand, this work can be narrowly viewed as a poorly documented, unsubstantiated "grand sweep" of Appalachian educational history, in only fourteen pages, to boot. On the other hand, it can be broadly and more properly viewed as the outline of a bold thesis explicating the relationship between American industrial capitalism and the quality of schooling in a region traditionally exploited by this system. A meticulous study exploring this thesis is needed to illuminate colonialism/periphery theory as well as Appalachian education.

APPENDIX B

Methods

Overview

The general methodological approach governing my research on Foxfire is *ethnohistorical*. This eclectic approach combines traditional ethnographic procedures (participant observation and field interviews) with traditional historiographical methods (library and archival research).[1] As I have used it, ethnohistory is a methodological tool for identifying the issues and effects precipitated by Foxfire over the course of its twenty-year history. It is also a vehicle for ascertaining Foxfire's implications in several contexts of American education writ large.

In his ethnohistorical study of a Kentucky settlement school, Precourt made the following distinction between conventional educational ethnography and ethnohistory: "Ethnographic studies on education tend to be synchronic [time-flat] in orientation. The historical context, while implicit in many studies, is seldom dealt with systematically. Long-range historical trends are frequently ignored or treated only tangentially. Ethnographers obviously must observe specific events and discover how educational phenomena manifest in the stream of behavior. Ethnographers must not, however, lose sight of the fact that the unfolding of educationally relevant behavior is embedded in a broader historical complex of cultural problems and processes."[2]

In short, a longitudinal (or diachronic) view of an institution affords unique (and critical) perspectives for analyzing current institutional practices and behavior that are not available to the synchronic investigator. I took the "long view" of Foxfire not only because I found the subject interesting, but also because the methodology paralleled my research interests.[3] A more practical consideration was Eliot Wigginton's enthusiasm for an historical analysis and long-view evaluation of his program. A study of more limited focus would have suited neither his purposes nor mine.

The study has two overarching methodological components. The first is bibliographical and is discussed in Appendix A: Bibliographical Notes. The second is the field study component, the result of a year's worth of on-site research at Foxfire and in the Rabun County community. The remainder of this appendix focuses on the field research and methodological issues addressed—and raised—by the study.

I observed the following general time frame for conducting the field study in 1984: January-June (five months): classroom observations; June-August (two and a half months): research of Foxfire documents; August-December (four and a half months): community interviews (including former students). The research activity listed for each period was the *dominant*, but not the only, activity during that time. For example, I conducted interviews at Rabun County High School during the months I spent observing Foxfire classes. Conversely, I conducted daily observations in Wigginton's Foxfire II class in the fall, while spending the remaining research time on interviews. Wigginton granted me access to his letters from former students in the fall, and I set aside several days from the interviews to read and note them.

Prior to my arrival in Rabun County on 4 January 1984, Foxfire staff members had arranged for me to rent an apartment in the Mountain City community, approximately two miles from the Foxfire Center. The arrangement proved beneficial for several reasons. First, living in the community—rather than at the Foxfire Center—gave me sorely needed distance from the Foxfire organization and buffered me from forming close attachments with the teaching staff that might have biased the study. Second, the apartment was in the basement of the home of a delightful Rabun County native, a middle-aged widow who was well known throughout the county, and my friendship with her provided an entree to Foxfire contacts and other community people. Third, our friendship took the edge off the loneliness and abrasions I experienced doing fieldwork in the mountain culture. I spent many evenings drinking beer and watching baseball games with Kate or just listening to her ramblings about her friends and neighbors (who had done what to or with whom) and whatever else was on her lively mind.

Before entering the field I lacked a detailed plan for conducting the study. I assumed (correctly) that the research problems would emerge once I had acquainted myself with the Foxfire staff and observed bits and pieces of the organization's operation. Ethnographers Hammersley and Atkinson state that serendipity is a major factor in ethnographic research: "The development of the research problem is rarely completed before the fieldwork begins; indeed, the collection of primary data often plays a key role in the process of development."[4]

Participant Observation

After nearly two months of observations in Wigginton's classes, and having spent three days to a week in each staff member's classes, I still had not formulated a strategy for systematically observing the program over an entire academic quarter. The plan "emerged" during the 5 March staff meeting, when Wigginton announced that each staff member would be required to develop a curriculum guide for a transferable course he or she was teaching. I selected George Reynolds's folklore, Wigginton's Foxfire I, Mike Cook's video I, and Bob Bennett's environmental science/outdoor education as the courses that would likely be included in these guides. Given the salience of Foxfire II (magazine class) to the organization, I decided to visit one section of that class daily. Surprisingly, the only overlap was the first hour of Bennett's two-hour block and Cook's video I class.

Cook and Reynolds were generous enough to allow me into their classes on a daily basis over the twelve-week spring quarter. I also routinely observed Foxfire I over the twelve-week period, with the exception of some days when Wigginton was absent from the class. Because my interviews at the high school in the winter and spring precluded daily observations in the Foxfire magazine classes, I decided to continue these observations during the fall of 1984. After several months of strained negotiations, I reached an agreement with Bob Bennett to begin observations in his classes after 23 April (the end of the school's spring break). Thereafter, I observed at least one of his classes per week until the end of the spring quarter.

For the most part, the observations were unstructured; I focused primarily on the activity at hand, teaching style, and student-teacher interactions (including maintenance of discipline). My observations also included field trips, off-campus interviews, weekly Foxfire staff meetings, community and national advisory board meetings, Foxfire scholarship committee meetings and interviews, Foxfire parties and social functions (e.g., the annual "contacts picnic"), and Foxfire at the

Appalachian Studies Conference (Helen, Georgia), the Appalachian Marketing Conference (Cullowhee, North Carolina), the Highlander Youth Conference (New Market, Tennessee), and the Alliance Theater (Atlanta, Georgia).

During the five-month observation period, I returned to my apartment after school (and on Mondays, after the weekly staff meetings at the Foxfire Press) to type up, annotate, and organize the day's notes. I assigned a date and number to each protocol to facilitate later retrieval of the data and indexing. During this time span, I spent approximately seven hours in the field and three to four hours at the typewriter daily.

Sieber has described the difficulty of doing ethnographic research in classrooms: "The press of classroom and school routine allows researchers little latitude for accommodating their own agendas, which are fundamentally extraneous to institutional operations. In the classroom, for example, spontaneous interaction with participants is next to impossible."[5] While accurate for most school ethnographies, Sieber's generalization did not prove to be the case in my study. The informality of Foxfire classes, particularly Wigginton's magazine class and Cook's video I, gave me numerous opportunities to discuss with students and teachers the processes I was observing. Staff and students gracefully tolerated my intrusions, although some occasionally voiced complaints. In other settings, e.g., staff meetings, I remained a silent witness to processes and events.

As a participant observer, I was treated by most of the Foxfire staff as an "insider-outsider" or "marginal native." I was neither offered, nor did I seek, close personal relationships with the teaching staff. This is not to suggest that I was not a participant in organizational activities. I occasionally substituted as a teacher in classes taught by Wigginton, Cook, and Reynolds; transported students and hauled equipment; attended staff parties, picnics, and dinners; entertained guests of Foxfire (at Foxfire's expense); and lent a helping hand whenever it was requested. I even played in the high school student-faculty volleyball game.

Hammersley and Atkinson describe the importance of maintaining social distance from the research subjects in an ethnography: "While ethnographers may adopt a variety of roles, the aim throughout is to maintain a more or less marginal position. . . . The researcher generates 'creative insight' out of this marginal position of simultaneous insider-outsider. The ethnographer must be intellectually posed between 'stranger' and 'friend.' He or she is . . . a 'marginal native.'"[6]

I cultivated friendships with Foxfire's administrative staff members. My identification with these individuals, several of whom were disaffected from the Foxfire teaching staff, may have generated doubts about my objectivity as an investigator on the part of the teachers, but I have no reason to suspect that information was ever withheld from me on this account. Den Hollander views such personal identifications as a normal concomitant of field work: "It is impossible, in a community [or organization] of any extent and differentiation to remain 'socially free-floating.' One is soon faced with the necessity of choosing. There is a minimum of social contacts one needs and the investigator is identified with . . . the class, family, or clique with whom he associates most."[7]

Similarly, Pelto and Pelto argue that such identifications are a psychological necessity—which proved to be my case. "Usually anthropologists establish friendly relationships with one or two best informants. They may confide in them about problems of adjustment; they often spend working hours engaged in idle conversation or other recreational activities with these friends, and may need to rely on them for special help, such as a loan of money and supplies. The lone anthropologist is, of course, especially in need of companionship."[8]

An important methodological consideration that should have been addressed and negotiated with the staff prior to my arrival was the issue of when I would release evaluative information to the staff. Having an investigator in their classes and meetings for five months put tremendous pressure on the Foxfire staff. I was not fully aware, however, of their escalating resentment until the end of the spring quarter when the staff excluded me from part of a weekly staff meeting to decide whether I would be allowed to attend their annual retreat. This was the first and only meeting from which I was excluded during the entire year. Excerpts from field notes of the 4 June meeting recount what was happening from my perspective:

> Joyce and Ann say it would be a good idea if I "take a hike." The staff deliberates approximately fifty minutes, leaving me outside thinking that now the frustrations are really surfacing about this whole evaluation, thinking that I may have mistakenly taken Mike and Linda into my confidence, thinking that Bob is really on the warpath and sees this as an opportunity to get rid of me once and for all, thinking that I've been *too* picky, although I honestly feel that it couldn't have been done any other way, thinking that George and Mike are feeling the heat, worrying about what I'm going to tell the foundations. . . . I walk the parking lot. Mike finds me first at 5:30, says

something like, "Yes, you can come to the staff retreat, but you need to see Wig." . . . Inside Tanya tells me the opposition was [names a staff member], who is really under pressure. . . . I feel like I just got a reprieve from Cromwell.

At the 7–8 June staff retreat on Lake Burton, Wigginton asked me (without prior notice) to share my impressions from five months of observing Foxfire classes. Nonplussed and unprepared, I hedged the issue by arguing that I would be compromising the study by divulging my findings, which were very inconclusive, when I still had seven months of research in front of me. Nevertheless Wigginton pressed me to describe my initial perceptions of staff strengths and weaknesses. His insistence spurred a hasty, albeit judicious, decision on my part to discuss what I labeled tentative impressions of Foxfire. In retrospect, I believe it saved the study.

My brief comments about the dearth of academic substance in the classes of two staff members seemed to appease Wigginton. It also drew a sigh of relief from staff members, who were in a jocular, backslapping mood after the meeting. Evidently, they had feared worse from me. One staff member approached me and said: "Thanks for being honest. I'm getting tired of people always patting us on the back and telling us how wonderful we are."

Interviews

To cover the full spectrum of opinion on Foxfire and to include a sampling of oral history about the organization, I conducted interviews within the following collectivities: Foxfire staff (present and former); Foxfire students (present and former); other students, faculty, and administrators at Rabun County High School; administrators and teachers from Foxfire's Rabun Gap era; Foxfire interview contacts; community advisory board members (present and former); and community business and industrial leaders, realtors, and land developers. For the most part, I eschewed using a tape recorder during these interviews, relying instead on my acuity as a listener and speed as a writer. I had neither the time nor the energy to spend the average four hours needed to transcribe a single hour of taped interviews. Moreover, I anticipated that many subjects would object to having themselves recorded by an "outsider." As a rule of thumb, I checked quotations and clarified discrepancies with each subject during or at the end of the interview. Impatient with this procedure, particularly after an arduous five-hour interview in February, Wigginton demanded that henceforth I tape the interviews with him.

In the remainder of this section, I describe my sampling decisions and procedures, as well as the kinds of questions that guided the interviews within each collectivity.

Over the past ten years, anthropologists and ethnographers have reacted to criticisms that their traditional methodologies lacked scientific rigor by developing strategies for strengthening the reliability (replicability) and validity of their studies. While I have incorporated these strategies into my study of Foxfire—and acknowledge their utility—I would also argue that a stolid reliance on them may threaten the integrity of the study by causing the researcher to overlook key informants who have useful and reliable information to provide.

A case in point is the granddaughter of a Foxfire contact I interviewed one evening in the late summer of 1984. I had scheduled an interview with her grandmother, a well-known Foxfire contact who lived on the Little Tennessee River north of Dillard. Ethel, the grandmother, was one of the contacts who had appeared in my census sample of longtime friends of Foxfire. Her granddaughter, Rhonda, a former Foxfire student who happened to be visiting Ethel at the time of our interview, did not appear in my random sample of former Foxfire students. Yet Rhonda proved to be one of my best informants, providing valuable details about Foxfire's Rabun Gap era and students' relationships with community elders.

In other cases, I found that the quality of information I obtained depended on having the trust of the informant. During our first interview a former Foxfire student gave me a glowing report of his experience with the organization. During the two-hour interview, however, he failed to mention that as an adult he had become sorely disaffected from the organization. This information surfaced later in informal contexts (e.g., over a beer or a meal) as he and I became friends. This proved to be a pattern with other key informants, particularly individuals who worked for the Foxfire organization. In short, I experienced what anthropologists Molgaard and Byerly had learned in a different context: "More than anything else, what worked was the time-honored anthropological tradition of participating, observing, and, in general, being noticeable in the environment until the familiarity factor induced the most knowledgeable and articulate informants to agree to be interviewed."[9]

Again, these points in favor of traditional anthropological approaches do not mitigate the researcher's responsibility to address systematically threats to reliability and validity. What is suggested, however, is that formal *and* informal strategies be incorporated—on the one hand, to enhance the objectivity of the study; on the other hand, to ensure that valuable information is not overlooked.

At Rabun County High School, I interviewed those teachers whom I deemed to be most familiar with Foxfire's operation—English Department teachers, teachers who worked directly with Foxfire staff on projects, and teachers who had been at the school since Foxfire's arrival in 1977. At the administrative level, I interviewed the incumbent county superintendent, the superintendent-elect, the county curriculum director, incumbent school board members, the high school principal, assistant principals, and guidance officials.

Fortuitously, I had cultivated a cordial relationship with the business education teacher who was elected school superintendent in the November 1984 elections. This individual had allowed me to interview seniors in his typing classes. Although an administrator had intimated earlier that the vocational education teachers were disgruntled that they were having to compete for students with uncertified Foxfire teachers, I did not take the hint and ignored these teachers in my interviews. It was not until my last month in the field that I learned firsthand from the business education teacher/superintendent-elect of the discord between one group of teachers and Foxfire. I never learned how many vocational education teachers had expressed dissatisfaction with Foxfire or to what extent they were disaffected. The point is that my sampling procedure, as logical as it seemed to me at the time, almost caused me to miss some vital and illuminating information.

To obtain a representative sampling of student opinion about Foxfire, I first consulted the records of each member of the senior class (more than one hundred students) to determine what and how many Foxfire-sponsored classes she or he had taken since the eighth grade at the high school. The school's quarter system made this search particularly tedious, as I had to read and note fifteen sets of records for each student (three quarters per year for grades eight through twelve). Having compiled this list I assigned students among the following categories: "heavy Foxfire users," students with at least two quarters of an advanced Foxfire course, e.g., Foxfire II, video II; students with Foxfire I, but no higher level courses; students with some Foxfire courses, e.g., folklore, but no beginning entry courses, e.g., video I, music performance; students with no Foxfire courses. I drew a random sample from each of these groups and designed a separate interview schedule for each group.

As with several other groups of interview subjects, I used a "non-schedule standardized interview" or "unstructured schedule interview" format, described by Denzin as follows: "The 'nonschedule standardized interviewer works with a list of the information required from each respondent.' This form most closely approximates what has been called the *focused* interview, in which certain types of information are desired from all respondents but the particular phrasing of questions and their order are redefined to fit the characteristics of each respondent."[10]

I conducted unstructured schedule interviews with students in Wigginton's *Foxfire* magazine classes. This data, reflected in portions of the text, proved useful in my analysis of program processes. Attentive readers will note that I did not ask Foxfire "heavy users" to specify skills they had acquired in their Foxfire courses (see p. 339). I decided that *former* Foxfire students would have a better perspective on these skills and possibly be more objective in assessing Foxfire's strengths and weaknesses.

My major intent in collecting data from students who had low levels of involvement in Foxfire activities was to determine if there were any systematic biases discouraging some students from taking additional Foxfire courses. After drawing the samples, I obtained permission from the teachers to talk briefly with their students during class time. Given that most of these students were apathetic to the research, the emergent data were colorless and of marginal interest. While I found no biases working for or against any types of students vis-à-vis Foxfire, the time and energy to collect this information was poorly spent.

The richest source of data for the study proved to be the testimony of the former Foxfire students. This information was also the most difficult (and frustrating) to collect, given the wide dispersion of these students over the past twenty years. I began these interviews in August 1984, and they occupied the bulk of my research time until after Christmas. In January 1985, I conducted telephone interviews with former Rabun Gap Foxfire students living in places like St. Petersburg, Florida; Stone Mountain, Georgia; and Boulder, Colorado. I conducted my final interview on 29 October 1985, in Atlanta, at the party celebrating Doubleday's release of *Sometimes a Shining Moment*.

I conducted my first interviews with former Foxfire students at the Class of 1974 reunion at Rabun Gap School in June 1984. The school was gracious enough to describe my research in its informational packet to alumni and to convey my message that I would be interested in talking with former Foxfire students attending the reunion. Nine former students, scattered across the southeastern United States, allowed me to interview them during the two-day reunion. Unfortunately, I did not have a finalized set of interview questions at that time and had to telephone these people later to get their interviews aligned with those of other former students.

In September I compiled a list of all students who had contributed articles to the Doubleday *Foxfire* books (*The Foxfire Book, Foxfire 2–8*). My intent was to identify those contributors who had spent at least a year in the magazine class. The years 1966–69 posed the first quandary: the Foxfire magazine class did not exist until the fall of 1969; therefore, I opted to include in the subject population all students who had contributed materials during these years, acknowledging that some would have much higher levels of involvement than others. After 1969, the Foxfire journalism class carried a full year's academic credit; therefore, I included all students from that time to 1977, when Foxfire changed to the quarter system at Rabun County High School. In short, I included in my population of Foxfire Rabun Gap students *all* students who had contributed to the books, the first of which appeared in 1972.

Next I had to confront a thorny problem with Foxfire's years at Rabun County High School: how to determine which students had at least a full year's worth of experience in Foxfire. I decided that the only feasible measure to use was the appearance of the student's name in at least three issues (representing three quarters) of *Foxfire* magazine. A knowledgeable Foxfire staff member concurred that this was a relatively accurate measure; at a minimum, it ensured that the former student had a substantive base of experience from which to speak about the organization.

I stratified the sample, first by drawing 15% of the names from each volume produced while the organization was at Rabun Gap School (*The Foxfire Book, Foxfire 2–4*). Second, because the contributor lists were much smaller for the remaining volumes, produced at Rabun County High School, I drew up a composite list of the contributors to *Foxfire 5–8* (105 students), multiplied that number by .15 (16 students), and drew 16 names from the 29 whose names had appeared in at least three issues of *Foxfire* magazine (current Foxfire students were not included in the sample). This was a cumbersome sampling procedure, but it ensured that I had a relative balance between the Rabun Gap and Rabun County High School years.

In theory, random sampling is an effective strategy to mitigate bias in the selection of research subjects and to ensure generalizability of findings to a population. In practice, I found this strategy extremely difficult to implement. Because it committed me to tracking students who lived outside Rabun County and—in many cases—outside the region, it proved frustrating, costly, and time-consuming. In the end, I was able to collect interview data from forty-four former Foxfire students whose names had appeared in the stratified random sample—13% of nearly 340 names in the collective population (excluding current Foxfire students).

In compiling my study, I contaminated the statistical representativeness of my sample by including former students whose names were not drawn at random. In short, I wanted to ensure not only a broad spectrum of experience over the two decades of Foxfire's existence, but also the best (and worst) examples of that experience. I interviewed all former students who had served on Foxfire's community advisory board since its inception in 1973 (individuals who apparently had strong commitments to the organization), former students who had worked for Foxfire as adults, former Rabun Gap School boarding students (e.g., at the Class of 1974 reunion), and others who had figured prominently in the organization as students. The cumulative sampling procedure is best described as *purposeful*—assuring a reasonably adequate coverage of the Foxfire experience.[11]

The final tally was sixty-six former students. This figure represents approximately 19% of the total student contributors to the *Foxfire* books.

After I had identified the former Foxfire students, locating them was the next problem. A Rabun County native on the Foxfire staff directed me to the homes or workplaces of many former students and to people who knew where to contact others. The Rabun Gap School was generous enough to provide a short list of addresses from its computer file. When I was unable to contact a source, I dropped his or her name from the list and drew a replacement. Once I had exhausted my replacement lists (a total of thirty names), I ended the search.

The majority of the interviews took place in Rabun County. In some cases, I was able to intercept Rabun County expatriates returning to visit friends and family. Parents of the former students were particularly helpful in apprising me of their children's whereabouts. In many cases, however, I had to drive outside the county to locate a contact. My peregrinations led to such places as Spartanburg, South Carolina (two interviews); Franklin, North Carolina; Tignall, Georgia (near Washington); and towns and communities throughout north Georgia. The sites for these interviews ranged from living rooms to restaurants to a hotel in Atlanta. I even interviewed one man at "Filthy Dave's" bar in Mountain City—over the roar of a jukebox and clicking pool sticks.

The second major category of interviews was the Foxfire contacts—mountain elders who had shared their information with Foxfire students for nearly twenty years. I first decided to limit my population of contacts to individuals living in Rabun County or within a twenty-mile radius of the county, to include portions of Macon County, North Carolina, and Habersham County, Georgia. Next, having read through all *Foxfire* magazines from 1967 to 1982 (Wigginton's bound copies), I compiled a list of contacts who appeared to have been "regulars" in these publications. My primary criterion for inclusion in the census sample was impressionistic. I presented this list to three Foxfire staff members for validation, asking them to suggest other names I might have overlooked. I bolstered the list by adding the names of individuals whose information had appeared in at least three *Foxfire* books. The final list, which included such well-known old-timers as Buck Carver, "Aunt Addie" Norton, Ethel Corn, and Nora Garland, totaled thirty-five, of whom I was able to interview thirty.

Having identified the "regulars," I next obtained a list of all the known Foxfire contacts in the north Georgia/western North Carolina region. Here my interest was contacts who were not among the "regulars"—those with more limited involvement in the program. I identified a population of ninety-four "irregular" contacts still living within a twenty-mile radius of Rabun County. To round out the final sample, I interviewed a random sample of fifteen of these individuals. I also interviewed several additional contacts whom I had occasion to meet, and I included their information as well.

The Foxfire contacts were much easier to locate than the former students; most were retired or worked at home. Although Wigginton had suggested that I take along a student on these interviews to help allay any suspicions the contacts might have about my motives, I demurred on the grounds that I would be hard-pressed to locate willing students to accompany me. As events proved, the contacts welcomed me into their homes; although some were reticent, all were gracious and hospitable.

Concomitant with my interviews with former Foxfire students and mountain elders, I interviewed thirty-one past and present community advisory board members. Many of these individuals appeared in other interview collectivities, e.g., Foxfire contacts; in the interest of time *and* economy, I addressed Foxfire community relations in only seventeen interviews. Twelve of the individuals queried along this line were members of the local business community. To further measure community opinion, I interviewed seven realtor/developers (five of whom were drawn in a random sample) and several other key business figures in the community, e.g., the director of the Chamber of Commerce.

Serendipity played a small part in the study. I made it a practice to talk informally with guests of Foxfire who I deemed might provide insights into the organization or its influence in Appalachia and beyond. This group included visiting teachers, a Foxfire legal board member, an editor at *National Geographic* magazine, a noted Appalachian author, a free-lance journalist, and others.

Examples of Non-Schedule Standardized Interviews

The following are prototypes of non-schedule standardized interviews used with various groupings of informants.

Former Foxfire Students

1. What stands out as a memorable experience(s) from your Foxfire days?
2. What skills related to Foxfire have proved useful in your adult life?
3. Do you think of yourself as a mountain person? How did Foxfire influence that identity?
4. How did Foxfire influence your view of the mountain elderly? How do you think the elderly benefited from the Foxfire experience?
5. What was more meaningful in your high school experience than Foxfire? Less meaningful?*
6. Looking back on your experience, what changes would you have recommended in Foxfire?
7. Would you recommend that your children take Foxfire? Why or why not?

*This question proved to be confusing, and I eventually dropped it from the later interviews.

Rabun County High School Students: Heavy Users of Foxfire Magazine

1. What opportunities has the Foxfire magazine program offered you that are not available in your other courses at RCHS?
2. How do you think you have changed since being involved in Foxfire? How has your experience with the magazine influenced your attitude toward the traditional mountain culture? Toward old people?
3. How is Eliot Wigginton different from your other teachers at RCHS?
4. Why did you take Foxfire I, Foxfire II?

Rabun County High School Seniors: Non-Foxfire Users

1. Why did you *not* take any Foxfire courses at RCHS?
2. What would have been necessary or different about these courses for you to have wanted to take them?

3. Are there any characteristics of the students who have been heavily involved in the Foxfire programs that make them different from the students you know who have not been involved in the program? If so, what are these?

Foxfire Interview Contacts
1. What kinds of information have you contributed to Foxfire?
2. How have you benefited from your relationship with Foxfire?
3. What are your thoughts about Foxfire's efforts to preserve the culture of this region?*
4. Do you believe you should have been paid by Foxfire? How do you feel about the way the money has been spent?
5. What changes would you recommend for Foxfire?
*This question elicited vague and confusing responses.

Rabun County School Board Members*
1. What has been Foxfire's contribution to the schools of Rabun County?
2. What Foxfire programs would you recommend keeping if the organization went bankrupt?**
3. Three Foxfire teachers lack certification. How do you feel about this?
4. What changes would you recommend in Foxfire?
*Similar questions were put to other Rabun County school officials.
**In a few interviews I put the question as follows: If the school board had unlimited funds, what Foxfire programs would you recommend? If funds were limited, what programs? One subject told me bluntly that he thought I was asking a trick question (which I was), and thereafter I dropped the ambiguity.

Foxfire Community Advisory Board
1. What is Foxfire's community reputation?
2. What criticisms have you heard voiced against Foxfire? Were they justified?
3. What is the community advisory board's role?
4. What changes would you recommend in Foxfire?

Issues of Reliability and Validity

Prior to entering the field, I had estimated that the Foxfire study would warrant at least a full year's worth of on-site research. This estimate proved to be accurate. With the exception of several weeks of vacation time (periods of reduced activity at Foxfire), I spent the entire year collecting data. Peshkin views this kind of immersion as a sine qua non of a strong ethnographic study: "An ethnographer is an anthropologist who attempts . . . to record and describe the culturally significant behaviors of a particular society. Ideally, this description, an ethnography, requires a long period of intimate study and residence in a small, well-defined community, knowledge of observational techniques, including prolonged face-to-face contacts with members of the local group, direct participation in some of that group's activities and a greater emphasis on intensive work with informants than on the use of documentary or survey data."[12]

As stated at the outset, however, documents (primary and secondary) are an essential component of my study. Indeed, while anthropologists/ethnographers pay lip service to the need for documentation in ethnographic research, few (if any) provide substantive guidelines for using documents. The bulk of their "how to" manuals and articles focus on participant observation, interviewing, and qualitative analysis. In the research literature, triangulation of data—cross-validating information from multiple data sources—is honored far more in the breach than the observance.

Triangulation is a methodological buffer against threats to internal validity, a research concern stated as follows: "Does the ethnographer's description of social reality correspond to that reality?" In my case, the critical question is: "Have I captured the 'essence' of Foxfire?"

I would argue that the study has high internal validity on three counts. First, I spent a substantial amount of time at the research site, collecting and cross-checking data, and validating interpretations with a diversity of informants. Second, I conducted open-ended interviews, which provided rich data on how participants and others interpreted the Foxfire experience. Third, I analyzed relevant documents and conducted on-site observations, activities which provided not only a reality check on the testimonial literature, but which also resulted in abundant new insights about Foxfire's operation. Fourth, as both a courtesy and professional obligation, I submitted an early version of the manuscript to Wigginton and a knowledgeable staff member for their comments and criticisms. These individuals called to my attention errors of fact, e.g., errors in names, dates, and numbers. They also challenged my interpretations of several findings; at each of these points, I carefully reconsidered the existing interpretation in light of their remarks and other evidence I was able to gather. Reevaluation of the evidence resulted in only one substantive change in the manuscript.

Briefly, I had to negotiate three threats to internal validity: researcher bias, selection bias, and researcher effects.[13]

1. *Researcher bias.* A persistent concern in ethnographic research is the investigator's ability to remain objective in his or her study. While anthropologists/ethnographers argue that researchers should strive to remain neutral observers of social phenomenon,[14] they also stipulate that stolid objectivity is an ideal rarely if ever attained.[15] The best that can be hoped for is to reduce the threat of this bias.

When I undertook the Foxfire study, I was enthralled by the testimonial literature and believed that the reality of Foxfire would match the power of its superb rhetoric. Although I proposed a research methodology that, if rigorously implemented, would tease out the strengths *and* weaknesses in Foxfire practice, I harbored the prior expectation that Wigginton's program worked in a fashion thoroughly consistent with the claims made in its behalf.

My own ideal of Foxfire was diminished within two months of my arrival in Rabun County. My field notes from 2 March 1984, documented (albeit melodramatically) my realization that my preconceptions had biased my observations:

> I've almost missed what really may be going on at Foxfire: some old fashioned laziness. What's prompted this shift in my focus has been the realization that [staff members] may be sitting on their duffs. . . . After fully two months here, I've had blinders on. Wig is a superb force—but he is too trusting of the people around him. They need a push. [Staff members] are great with kids, but they're doing them a disservice by not expecting more from them. . . . I'm pissed, a bit panicked, frustrated. Pissed because I have to re-cover a lot of lost ground—but am looking forward to the upcoming twelve-week observational period, telling myself that I should have some real substantive stuff at the end.

Henceforth, I found myself struggling with ambivalent personal feelings about several staff members. By triangulating my data sources, and by viewing Foxfire from an ethnohistorical perspective, I mitigated the effects of my own immediate likes and dislikes. Observations within and beyond classrooms, interviews across several collectivities, and documentary evidence illuminated the strengths, as well as the shortcomings, of individual staff members and their programs. More important, this "immersion" methodology in the organization and its history allowed me to unearth the institutional underpinnings of individual staff behavior.

2. *Selection bias.* Sampling became an issue at two levels of analysis: classroom processes and individual experiences. With respect to classroom processes, the issue was which classes to observe. As stated previously, I selected for a twelve-week observational period (an academic quarter) the classes that would serve as the foundations of the Foxfire curriculum guides. I had also collected some data in these classes during the winter quarter. Because magazine production has been Foxfire's major activity—and the source of much of Wigginton's pedagogy—I collected data in this class throughout the year.

At the level of individual experiences, I identified the various collectivities of people who were directly influenced by or had knowledge and opinions of Foxfire. As discussed previously, I used the gamut of sampling procedures (census, random, purposeful) to ensure that I covered as broad a range of the Foxfire experience as possible.

3. *Researcher effects.* Foxfire staff viewed me as an outside evaluator. This role undoubtedly influenced the level and quality of information these respondents were willing to disclose. My presence may have also affected some of the processes being observed.

A powerful check against this threat was my longevity with the project and the habituation of staff members to my presence. As one visitor to Foxfire suggested, I seemed to be "part of the woodwork." In short, it would have been very difficult, if not impossible, for Wigginton and his staff to have "whitewashed" Foxfire and deceived me for an entire year.

In fact, Wigginton's intent appeared to be quite the opposite. My impression throughout the study was that he wanted a thorough, honest evaluation of his program's strengths and weaknesses. His willingness to grant me fully open access to Foxfire documents and to tolerate my presence within the organization for an entire year were persuasive measures of his sincerity. At the Foxfire staff retreat, when he solicited my impressions drawn from five months of classroom observations, he told me in front of the staff: "We voted to have you do an evaluation, and you would be of no use to us if you didn't tell us what we're doing wrong."

External validity, a statistical concept that refers to the generalization of findings to a larger population, did not apply to my research. While external validity may be logically inferred for statistically significant results derived from an experiment using a random sample, this same logic does not hold when random cases have not been drawn, as is the rule in field research. LeCompte and Goetz have stated: "In most ethnographic studies . . . the strictures required for statistical research may be difficult to apply."[16] Foxfire was not a random case, and my findings may not be generalized to other projects. The implications I have drawn in my report for educational theory, practice, and reform are embedded in appeals to reason, authority, and common experience.

Pelto and Pelto have stated the reliability issue in field research as follows: "If another observer *had been* at the particular event, and he *had used* the same techniques, would he have obtained the same results?"[17]

Without encumbering the reader with a surfeit of details, I have attempted to explain as concisely as possible my research procedures, with the proviso that some of my data came from key informants who trusted me and with whom I had a strong rapport. This information includes a general description of the social roles I played within the organization (beyond my ascribed status as an evaluator), a precise specification of the types of documents included in the study (Appendix A), a description of the various collectivities of informants and the diversity of social settings and conditions under which data were collected, and a delineation of the methods of data collection.[18]

To further enhance reliability, I incorporated in the final report numerous examples of what LeCompte and Goetz term "low-level descriptors." Distinguished from interpretive comments, these descriptors "include verbatim accounts of what people say as well as narratives of behavior and activity." They are the ethnographer's raw data. As LeCompte and Goetz note: "Those ethnographies rich in primary data, which provide the reader with multiple data from the field notes, generally are considered to be most reliable."[19] To enhance the readability of unedited excerpts from the field notes, I made cosmetic alterations before including them in the report.

NOTES

1. Essays that have been influential in defining the aims and methods of ethnohistory include: Wilbur E. Washburn, "Ethnohistory: 'History in the Round,'" *Ethnohistory* 8, no. 1 (1961): 31–48; Nancy O. Lurie, "Ethnohistory: An Ethnological Point of View," *Ethnohistory* 8, no. 1 (1961): 78–92; William N. Fenton, "Ethnohistory and Its Problems," *Ethnohistory* 9, no. 1 (1962): 1–23; Fenton, "Field Work, Museum Studies, and Ethnohistorical Research, *Ethnohistory* 13, nos. 1–2 (1966): 71–85; William C. Sturtevant, "Anthropology, History, and Ethnohistory," in *Introduction to Cultural Anthropology* (Boston: Houghton Mifflin, 1968), 451–74; Robert C. Fuler, "Ethnohistory in the United States," *Ethnohistory* 19, no. 3 (1972): 201–7; Robert M. Carmack,

"Ethnohistory: A Review of Its Development, Definitions, Methods, and Aims," *Annual Review of Anthropology* 1 (1972): 227–46; James Axtell, "Ethnohistory: An Historian's Viewpoint," *Ethnohistory* 26, no. 1 (1979): 1–13; Bruce G. Trigger, "Ethnohistory: Problems and Prospects," *Ethnohistory* 29, no. 1 (1982): 1–19; Trigger, "Ethnohistory: The Unfinished Edifice," *Ethnohistory* 33, no. 3 (1986): 253–67.

2. Walter Precourt, "Ethnohistorical Analysis of an Appalachian Settlement School," in *Ethnography of Schooling: Educational Anthropology in Action*, ed. George Spindler (New York: Holt, Rinehart and Winston, 1982), 442–51. See also, Spindler's introduction, ibid., 6–7.

3. Alan Peshkin discusses the role of personal taste in the researcher's choice of a methodology in "The Researcher and Subjectivity: Reflections of an Ethnography of School and Community," in *Ethnography of Schooling*, ed. Spindler, 53.

4. Martyn Hammersley and Paul Atkinson, *Ethnography: Principles in Practice* (London: Tavistock, 1983), 40.

5. Timothy R. Sieber, "Many Roles, Many Faces: Researching School-Community Relations in a Heterogeneous American Urban Community," in *Anthropologists at Home in North America: Methods and Issues in the Study of One's Own Society*, ed. Donald Messerschmidt (Cambridge: Cambridge University Press, 1981), 214.

6. Hammersley and Atkinson, *Ethnography*, 100.

7. A. N. J. den Hollander, "Social Description: The Problem of Reliability and Validity," in *Anthropologists in the Field*, ed. D. G. Jongmans and P. C. W. Gutkind (Assen, The Netherlands: Van Goreum, 1967), 131.

8. Pertii J. Pelto and Gretel Pelto, *Anthropological Research: The Structure of Inquiry*, 2d ed. (Cambridge: Cambridge University Press, 1978), 178.

9. Craig Molgaard and Elizabeth Byerly, "Applied Ethnography in Rural America: New Age Health and Healing," in *Anthropologists at Home in North America*, ed. Messerschmidt, 158.

10. Norman K. Denzin, *The Research Act: A Theoretical Introduction to Sociological Methods*, 2d ed. (New York: McGraw-Hill, 1978), 115–16. See also Raymond L. Gorden, *Interviewing: Strategy, Techniques, and Tactics* (Homewood, Ill.: Dorsey Press, 1975), 62–65, 92–96, 413–15.

11. For discussion of purposeful sampling, see Michael Quinn Patton, *Qualitative Evaluation Methods* (Beverly Hills, Calif.: Sage Publications, 1980), 100–107.

12. Peshkin, "The Researcher and Subjectivity," 54.

13. For discussion of internal validity threats, see Margaret LeCompte and Judith Goetz, "Problems of Reliability and Validity in Ethnographic Research," *Review of Educational Research* 52, no. 1 (1982): 44–50.

14. Pelto and Pelto, *Anthropological Research*, 183.

15. Den Hollander, "Social Description," 8–9. See also Mary Metz, "What Can Be Learned from Educational Ethnography?," *Urban Education* 17, no. 4 (1983): 401–8.

16. LeCompte and Goetz, "Problems of Reliability and Validity," 50.

17. Pelto and Pelto, *Anthropological Research,* 39.

18. For discussion of ethnographic reliability, see LeCompte and Goetz, "Problems of Reliability and Validity," 35–43.

19. Ibid., 41.

APPENDIX C

Herbert Kohl's Letter to Foxfire
24 September 1979

From: Herbert Kohl
  To: Board and Staff
       Foxfire Foundation

Dear Board and Staff,
   I would like to share with you certain concerns I have about the present condition and future direction of Foxfire and all its dependent projects. As an educator I came to Foxfire because it seemed a way to empower young people through helping them understand the dignity and strength of the culture they were born into and which despite poverty and oppression nurtured them. The value of Foxfire to me was not ethnographic or anthropological. It had to do with the young people and the older people it served and presumed to help. My questions about the current programs of Foxfire have to do with the basic issue of whether Foxfire serves or exploits the community. These questions are:
   1—Who actually produces the Foxfire Books? Are they the work of the students, who should then take pride of authorship, or are they reworked versions of material students collected? Does the staff of Foxfire and the editorial staff of Doubleday do the actual writing? If so is there any misrepresentation of this fact? Is permission granted by students to do the rewriting?
   2—Who gets the financial benefits from the books? It is usual to pay people to use their material, to publish their words and their writing. Given that the Foxfire Books are not scholarly works that appeal to

academic audiences but well packaged trade products, it seems that the people represented in the books should get the benefit. It is sensible for Foxfire to keep enough of the money to keep the project going, but when all the money goes into the land, staff salaries, and other development projects it seems to be a case of exploitation. Kenny Runion does not seem any richer for being known by several million people. I believe that the Foxfire Board has a moral responsibility to recommend that Foxfire give a fair and retroactive share of the royalties to people who appeared in the books and to make sure that they get a share of future work.

I anticipate the argument will be made that giving a little to each individual will not have the same impact as keeping the money and helping the community. However that should be for the community to decide and not for a few members of the Foxfire Board to decide in the name of the community.

3—Continuing with the question of money there is an important question about the investment policies of the advisors to the Board and to Wig. Where is the Foxfire money being invested? In corporations that are exploiting land and people and resources in Appalachia? or in other parts of the world? How much of the money is invested in ways that are likely to serve the poor people in the community since without them there could be no Foxfire.

4—What will the net effect of the ten-acre development in Mountain View [*sic*] be? When Wig pushed through the development of a sewer system, etc.[,] did he consult the community first or try to convince them of what he had already done? Who will be served by the development? Business or the poor? Why does Foxfire need to develop any more visibility? What has happened to Foxfire as a program that empowers people?

5—There are some educational questions I have. On my last visit to Foxfire I spent time in some of the classes. The music program seemed vital and educationally interesting. The Foxfire classes seemed automatic, to have been reduced to a formula. I felt a lack of student participation, of discussion and probing issues about the community. It seemed that the idea had been reduced to a formula—Foxfire 1a and Foxfire 1b. What are the educational ideas of Foxfire now? Have they changed at all over ten years? How much do the educational ideas influence the other policies? How much are they in turn influenced by financial decisions relating to expansion and becoming an economic factor within the community?

6—Who makes the decisions at Foxfire anyway? I have had a number of talks with Wig about that problem and he assures me that students make the decisions, that staff members make the decisions, etc. I find myself then asking him over and over again who could make a decision to give away the endowment, to redistribute the wealth as it were, and get no answer to that one.

7—What is the image of Appalachian culture presented by Foxfire as a whole and how does this image affect progressive causes within the community? Does Foxfire need poverty to survive? What would happen if the community changed so that the old culture was integrated into a newer more economically equitable form[?] [W]ould it still be fun to do Foxfire? And would the books sell?

8—Are there any community issues deliberately avoided? I bring this up because I understand that there is a union drive going on in the local Burlington plant and don't recall any talk about unions or labor struggle in Foxfire. I do know it has existed in the community. Are there any other issues that have been avoided? What does it mean educationally to avoid difficult issues? What is the effect it has on the total learning program? On one's students?

I have raised enough questions. My expectation is that few of them will be answered. The momentum set forth by the financial success of the Foxfire Books seems to make it hard to consider changing direction, getting smaller, concentrating on education, being a modest part of larger efforts. I do hope though that the Board and staff will consider some of the questions seriously. Given that I live in California and have become extremely busy I cannot devote the time and energy it would take to fight these issues within the Foxfire community. For that reason I submit this letter as my resignation letter hoping that some of the issues raised will be of use to the people involved in the program.

Index

A Note on the Author

John L. Puckett is Assistant Professor at the Graduate School of Education of the University of Pennsylvania. *Foxfire Reconsidered* is his first book.